WHAT IS POSTHUMANISM?

Cary Wolfe, Series Editor

WHAT IS
POSTHUMANISM?

Cary Wolfe

posthumanities **8**

University of Minnesota Press
Minneapolis
London

The poems "Metaphors of a Magnifico," "The Idea of Order at Key West," and "Esthétique du Mal" are reprinted from Wallace Stevens, *The Collected Poems of Wallace Stevens* (New York: Random House, 1982). "Esthétique du Mal" and "The Idea of Order at Key West" copyright 1936 by Wallace Stevens and renewed 1964 by Holly Stevens; "Metaphors of a Magnifico" copyright 1954 by Wallace Stevens and renewed 1982 by Holly Stevens. Reprinted by permission of Alfred A. Knopf, a division of Random House, Inc.

The poem "The World and I" is reprinted from Laura Riding, *Poems of Laura Riding* (New York: Persea Books, 1938). Copyright 1938, 1980; revised copyright 2001 by the Board of Literary Management of the late Laura (Riding) Jackson. Reprinted by permission of Persea Books, Inc., New York.

For more information about previously published material in this book, see pages 347–48.

Published by the University of Minnesota Press
111 Third Avenue South, Suite 290
Minneapolis, MN 55401-2520
http://www.upress.umn.edu

Library of Congress Cataloging-in-Publication Data

Wolfe, Cary.
    What is posthumanism? / Cary Wolfe.
        p.   cm. — (Posthumanities series ; v. 8)
    Includes bibliographical references (p.   ) and index.
    ISBN 978-0-8166-6614-0 (hc : alk. paper) — ISBN 978-0-8166-6615-7 (pb : alk. paper)
    1. Humanism.   2. Aesthetics—Philosophy.   3. Deconstruction.   I. Title.
    B821.W65 2010
    149—dc22

                                                            2009037657

Printed in the United States of America on acid-free paper

The University of Minnesota is an equal-opportunity educator and employer.

17 16 15 14 13 12 11   10 9 8 7 6 5 4 3

For my parents

Contents

Acknowledgments

IT WOULD BE FUTILE to try to list all the friends, colleagues, and even total strangers whose input and feedback helped inspire and shape this book along the way. I would therefore like to provide what I hope is a more reliable list—those who deserve thanks for inviting me to present this work in a variety of settings, either live or in print: Joseph Tabbi, Eduardo Kac, Dana Medoro, Alison Calder, Bruce Clarke, Trace Reddell, Manuela Rossini, Christian Hubert, Sid Dobrin, Sean Morey, Anat Pick, Wendy Wheeler, Ivan Kreilkamp, Cate Mortimer-Sandilands, Joan Landes, Paula Lee, Robert Brown, Marianne DeKoven, Mark Hansen, Saul Ostrow, Tom Tyler, Neil Badmington, Jodey Castricano, David Wood, Tim Campbell, Paola Cavalieri, Wendy Lochner, Salah el Moncef bin Khalifa, Chris Danta, Patricia Yeager, Susan McHugh, Jan Ritsema, Andrew McMurry, Bojana Cvejic, Aaron Jaffe, Simon Glendinning, Alf Siewers, Susan Pearson, Andrew Stauffer, Lauren Corman, Wolfgang Natter, Carla Freccero, Donna Haraway, Citlalli Reyes-Kipp, Maya Ratnam, Austin Sarat, Adam Sitze, Ann Waltner, Dan Philippon, Bruce Braun, Emily Clark, and Sara Guyer.

Portions of this work were presented in the following institutional settings, and I would like to acknowledge their support of both the intellectual and monetary kind: the Warhaft Foundation and the Centre for the Study of Applied Ethics at the University of Manitoba; the English department at the University of Illinois at Chicago; the Museum of Modern Art and the Van Alen Institute in New York; the Scientia program at Rice University; the Fifth Annual Summer Academy at Künstlerhaus Mousonturm in Frankfurt, Germany; the Rothermere American Institute at the University of Oxford; the Society for Literature, Science, and the Arts (U.S. and European chapters); the Twentieth-Century Literature Conference at the University of Louisville; the Harry Ransom Humanities Research Center at the University of Texas; the Forum for European Philosophy at the London

School of Economics; the Amsterdam School for Cultural Analysis at the University of Amsterdam; the Humanities Institute at Bucknell University; the Alice Kaplan Institute for the Humanities at Northwestern University; the Society for Textual Scholarship, the Animals and Society Institute, the Faculty of Environmental Studies, the Division of Humanities, and the Canadian Centre for German and European Studies at York University in Toronto; the Center for Cultural Studies and the History of Consciousness department at the University of California, Santa Cruz; the ASPECT program at Virginia Tech; the Center for the Study of Religion and Culture at Vanderbilt University; the Department of Anthropology at The Johns Hopkins University; the Institute for Advanced Study and the Quadrant program at the University of Minnesota; the Center for the Humanities at the University of Wisconsin; and the Institute for the Arts and Humanities and the Rock Ethics Institute at Penn State.

I also acknowledge the graduate students with whom I have worked in seminars at both SUNY–Albany and Rice University; our conversations helped shape my thinking about this work over the past several years. Helena Michie, chair of the English department at Rice, deserves credit for enabling an internal leave in 2007 that helped immensely in allowing me to finish this project, as does Marcia Carter for her help with the department's aid in various subventions and research costs that the book required. Bruce Clarke and Donna Haraway read the project for the University of Minnesota Press, and I benefited from ruminating over their incisive and nuanced editorial advice, based on a sure grasp of what this book is up to, and why. For this book and for the Posthumanities series, I owe a special debt of gratitude to the wonderful staff at the University of Minnesota Press (you know who you are) and, especially, to Press director Doug Armato for his boundless intellectual enthusiasm and editorial support.

Finally and most of all, I thank my lucky stars for Allison: artist and soul mate.

Introduction   What Is Posthumanism?

It is perhaps an appropriately posthumanist gesture to begin this book with the results of a Google search. As I write (in summer of 2008), if you Google "humanism," you'll be rewarded with 3,840,000 hits; "posthumanism" yields a mere 60,200. (Apparently humanism is alive and well, despite reports of its demise.) You will notice at a cursory glance that despite the discrepancy in numbers there appears to be much more unanimity about humanism than posthumanism. Most definitions of humanism look something like the following one from Wikipedia:

> *Humanism* is a broad category of ethical philosophies that affirm the dignity and worth of all people, based on the ability to determine right and wrong by appeal to universal human qualities—particularly rationality. It is a component of a variety of more specific philosophical systems and is incorporated into several religious schools of thought. Humanism entails a commitment to the search for truth and morality through human means in support of human interests. In focusing on the capacity for self-determination, humanism rejects the validity of transcendental justifications, such as a dependence on belief without reason, the supernatural, or texts of allegedly divine origin. Humanists endorse universal morality based on the commonality of the human condition, suggesting that solutions to human social and cultural problems cannot be parochial.

Posthumanism, on the other hand, generates different and even irreconcilable definitions. The Web site www.posthumanism.com provides a gloss on the term that most of the philosophers and scholars named on Wikipedia's page for "posthumanism"—Michel Foucault, Judith Butler, Bruno Latour, and Donna Haraway, among others—would not just refine but for the most part oppose. For the purposes of this book, I choose to see in this confusion not a cautionary tale but an opportunity.

The term "posthumanism" itself seems to have worked its way into contemporary critical discourse in the humanities and social sciences during the mid-1990s, though its roots go back, in one genealogy, at least to the 1960s and pronouncements of the sort made famous by Foucault in the closing paragraph of *The Order of Things: An Archaeology of the Human Sciences,* where he writes that the historical appearance of this thing called "man" was not

> the transition into luminous consciousness of an age-old concern, the entry into objectivity of something that had long remained trapped within beliefs and philosophies: it was the effect of a change in the fundamental arrangements of knowledge. As the archaeology of our thought easily shows, man is an invention of recent date. And one perhaps nearing its end.
>
> If those arrangements were to disappear as they appeared, if some event of which we can at the moment do no more than sense the possibility—without knowing either what its form will be or what it promises—were to cause them to crumble, as the ground of Classical thought did, at the end of the eighteenth century, then one can certainly wager that man would be erased, like a face drawn in sand at the edge of the sea.[1]

By way of another well-known genealogy—one also directly relevant to this book—posthumanism may be traced to the Macy conferences on cybernetics from 1946 to 1953 and the invention of systems theory involving Gregory Bateson, Warren McCulloch, Norbert Wiener, John von Neumann, and many other figures from a range of fields who converged on a new theoretical model for biological, mechanical, and communicational processes that removed the human and *Homo sapiens* from any particularly privileged position in relation to matters of meaning, information, and cognition.

More recently, the term has begun to emerge with different and sometimes competing meanings. The first time I used it (hyphenated, no less) was in an essay from 1995, called "In Search of Post-humanist Theory," on the work of Humberto Maturana and Francisco Varela in a special double issue of *Cultural Critique* called "The Politics of Systems and Environments" that I coedited with William Rasch.[2] That project included a roundtable conversation with Niklas Luhmann and Katherine Hayles; Hayles picked up the term (with a rather different valence, as we will see in a moment) in her book *How We Became Posthuman* (1999). Meanwhile, in the United Kingdom, critics such as Neil Badmington and Elaine Graham gravitated toward the term, with Badmington's edited collection *Posthumanism* (2000) being a notable attempt at consolidation.[3] That body of work in the UK (as suggested by the title of Badmington's subsequent book *Alien Chic: Posthumanism and the Other Within,* and by Graham's *Representations of the Post/Human: Monsters, Aliens, and Others in Popular Culture*) tended toward a sense of posthumanism perhaps best glossed (as Badmington rightly notes) in what is probably its locus classicus in recent critical writing: Donna Haraway's "A Cyborg Manifesto" (1985), which, as the title suggests, engages science-fictional thematics of hybridity, perversity, and irony (her terms) that are, you might say, radically ambivalent in their rejection of both utopian and dystopian visions of a cyborg future.[4]

Arguably the best-known inheritor of the "cyborg" strand of posthumanism is what is now being called "transhumanism"—a movement that is dedicated, as the journalist and writer Joel Garreau puts it, to "the enhancement of human intellectual, physical, and emotional capabilities, the elimination of disease and unnecessary suffering, and the dramatic extension of life span. What this network has in common," Garreau continues, "is a belief in the engineered evolution of 'post-humans,' defined as beings 'whose basic capacities so radically exceed those of present humans as to no longer be unambiguously human by our current standards.' "'Transhuman,'" he concludes, "is their description of those who are in the process of becoming posthuman."[5] As one of the central figures associated with transhumanism, the Oxford philosopher Nick Bostrom, makes clear, this sense of posthumanism derives directly from ideals of human perfectibility, rationality, and agency inherited from Renaissance humanism and the Enlightenment. (And in this, it has little in common with Haraway's playful, ironic, and ambivalent sensibility in "A Cyborg Manifesto," which is suspicious—to put it mildly—of the capacity of reason to steer, much less optimize, what it hath wrought.) As Bostrom puts it in "A History of Transhumanist Thought," transhumanism combines Renaissance humanism "with the influence of Isaac Newton, Thomas Hobbes, John Locke, Immanuel Kant, the Marquis de Condorcet, and others to form the basis for rational humanism, which emphasizes empirical science and critical reason—rather than revelation and religious authority—as ways of learning about the natural world and our place within it, and of providing a grounding for morality. Transhumanism has its roots in rational humanism."[6]

To help make his point, Bostrom invokes Kant's famous essay of 1784, "What Is Enlightenment?": "Enlightenment is man's leaving his self-caused immaturity. Immaturity is the incapacity to use one's own understanding without the guidance of another. . . . The motto of enlightenment is therefore *Sapere aude!* Have courage to use your own intelligence!"[7] Here, however, it is useful to recall Foucault's suggestion from his essay of 1984 by the same title: that if we commit to "a permanent critique of ourselves," then we must "avoid the always too facile confusions between humanism and Enlightenment," because "the humanistic thematic is in itself too supple, too diverse, too inconsistent to serve as an axis for reflection." Indeed, as Foucault notes, "it is a fact that, at least since the seventeenth century what is called humanism has always been obliged to lean on certain conceptions of man borrowed from religion, science, or politics. Humanism serves to color and to justify the conceptions of man to which it is, after all, obliged to take recourse."[8] What Foucault draws our attention to (aside from the sheer heterogeneity of the historical varieties of "humanism," several of which he enumerates) is that humanism is, in so many words, its *own* dogma, replete with its own prejudices and assumptions—what Étienne Balibar calls "anthropological universals," which are themselves a form of the "superstition" from which the Enlightenment sought to break free. For example, in social Darwinism (and this example has particular resonance for transhumanism, as its critics would be the first to point out), we find, as Balibar notes, "the paradoxical figure of an evolution which has to extract humanity properly so-called (that is, culture, the technological mastery of nature—including the mastery of human nature: eugenics) from animality, but to do so by means which characterized animality (the 'survival of the fittest') or, in other words, by an 'animal' competition between the different degrees of humanity."[9]

Against this background, I emphasize two crucial points regarding my sense of posthumanism in this book. The first has to do with perhaps *the* fundamental anthropological dogma associated with humanism and invoked by Balibar's reference to the humanity/animality dichotomy: namely, that "the human" is achieved by escaping or repressing not just its animal origins in nature, the biological, and the evolutionary, but more generally by transcending the bonds of materiality and embodiment altogether. In this respect, my sense of posthumanism is the *opposite* of transhumanism, and in this light, transhumanism should be seen as an *intensification* of humanism. Indeed, one well-known figure associated with transhumanism, Hans Moravec, draws Hayles's ire for precisely this reason. "When Moravec imagines 'you' choosing to download yourself into a computer, thereby obtaining through technological mastery the ultimate privilege of immortality," Hayles writes, "he is not abandoning the autonomous liberal subject but is expanding its prerogatives into the realm of the posthuman."[10] Hayles is no doubt right, and though she is quick to add that "the posthuman need not be recuperated back into liberal humanism, nor need it be construed as anti-human," the net effect and critical ground tone of her book, as many have noted, are to associate the posthuman with a kind of triumphant disembodiment.[11] Hayles's use of the term, in other words, tends to *oppose* embodiment and the posthuman, whereas the sense in which I am using the term here insists on exactly the opposite: posthumanism in my sense isn't posthuman at all—in the sense of being "after" our embodiment has been transcended—but is only posthuman*ist*, in the sense that it opposes the fantasies of disembodiment and autonomy, inherited from humanism itself, that Hayles rightly criticizes.

My sense of posthumanism is thus analogous to Jean-François Lyotard's paradoxical rendering of the postmodern: it comes both before and after humanism: before in the sense that it names the embodiment and embeddedness of the human being in not just its biological but also its technological world, the prosthetic coevolution of the human animal with the technicity of tools and external archival mechanisms (such as language and culture) of which Bernard Stiegler probably remains our most compelling and ambitious theorist—and all of which comes before that historically specific thing called "the human" that Foucault's archaeology excavates.[12] But it comes after in the sense that posthumanism names a historical moment in which the decentering of the human by its imbrication in technical, medical, informatic, and economic networks is increasingly impossible to ignore, a historical development that points toward the necessity of new theoretical paradigms (but also thrusts them on us), a new mode of thought that comes after the cultural repressions and fantasies, the philosophical protocols and evasions, of humanism as a historically specific phenomenon.

Here we would do well to recall Foucault's insistence on the difference between humanism and Enlightenment thought—namely, that humanism's "anthropological universals" underwrite a dogma for which the Enlightenment, if we are true to its spirit, should have no patience. As Foucault puts it, "In this connection I believe that this thematic which so often recurs and which always depends on humanism can be opposed by the principle of a critique and a permanent creation of ourselves in our autonomy: that is a principle that is at the heart of the historical consciousness that the Enlightenment has of itself. From this standpoint I am inclined to see Enlightenment and humanism in a state of tension rather than identity."[13] It is precisely at this juncture that I want to locate a fundamental intervention that this book attempts to make: namely, that even if we admire humanism's suspicion toward "revelation and religious authority" (whose stakes are all the more pitched at the current geopolitical moment),[14] and even if we take the additional posthumanist step of rejecting the various anthropological, political, and scientific dogmas of the human that Foucault insists are in tension with Enlightenment per se, we must take yet another step, another post-, and realize that the nature of thought itself must change if it is to be posthumanist.

What this means is that when we talk about posthumanism, we are not just talking about a thematics of the decentering of the human in relation to either evolutionary, ecological, or technological coordinates (though that is where the conversation usually begins and, all too often, ends); rather, I will insist that we are also talking about *how* thinking confronts that thematics, what thought has to become in the face of those challenges. Here the spirit of my intervention is akin to Foucault's in "What Is Enlightenment?"; the point is not to reject humanism *tout court*—indeed, there are many values and aspirations to admire in humanism—but rather to show how those aspirations are undercut by the philosophical and ethical frameworks used to conceptualize them. To take only two examples that I discuss later in this book, most of us would probably agree that cruelty toward animals is a bad thing, or that people with disabilities deserve to be treated with respect and equality. But as we will see, the philosophical and theoretical frameworks used by humanism to try to make good on those commitments reproduce the very kind of normative subjectivity—a specific concept of the human—that grounds discrimination against nonhuman animals and the disabled in the first place.

Similar limitations may be identified not just in the post- of transhumanism but also in some who rightly criticize it. As R. L. Rutsky points out with regard to Hayles's governing theoretical model, "The posthuman cannot simply be identified as a culture or age that comes 'after' the human, for the very idea of such a passage, however measured or qualified it may be, continues to rely upon a humanist narrative of historical change. . . . If, however, the posthuman truly involves a fundamental change or mutation in the concept of the human, this would seem to imply that history and culture cannot continue to be figured in reference to this concept."[15] In other words, there are humanist ways of criticizing the extension of humanism that we find in transhumanism (or "bad" posthumanism). Rutsky locates a central symptom of this fact in Hayles's use of the concept of mutation in *How We Became Posthuman,* where mutation is rendered, Rutsky writes, as "a pre-existing, external force that introduces change into a stable pattern (or code), and into the material world or body as well." But mutation, Rutsky points out, by definition "cannot be seen as external randomness that imposes itself upon the biological or material world—nor, for that matter, on the realm of culture. Rather, mutation names that randomness which is always already immanent in the processes by which both material bodies and cultural patterns replicate themselves."[16]

From this vantage, the problem is that there is nothing in Hayles's theoretical model of historical progression (which is derived from a specific set of humanist conventions and protocols of historiography whose problematic nature Foucault himself—under the influence of Canguilhem, among others[17]—sought to expose) that takes this fact into account. Moreover, her notion of mutation as an external force points, as Bruce Clarke has recently put it, toward "a radical distinction between matter and information, substance and form," one that remains "in a realm of dialectical antithesis, which observes that the concept of the human has lost its balance and/or its foundations, and that responds either with lament or delight."[18] But what is needed here, as Rutsky rightly points out, is the recognition that "any notion of the posthuman that is to be more than merely an extension of the human, that is to move beyond the dialectic of control and lack of control, superhuman and inhuman, must be premised upon a mutation that is ongoing and immanent," and this means that to become posthuman means to participate in—and find a mode of thought adequate to— "processes which can never be entirely reduced to patterns or standards, codes or information."[19]

In this light, it is worth recalling Clarke's suggestion that the dialectical antithesis of matter and information corresponds to the first-order cybernetics of midcentury,[20] while the mutational, as Rutsky rightly understands it, points toward the necessity of a different logic, one consonant, as Clarke has pointed out by quoting Gregory Bateson's suggestion three decades ago that "the whole of logic would have to be reconstructed for recursiveness": a logic that is fundamental to the second-order systems theory that will be articulated in these pages. From this perspective, I want to underscore what will be a major point of emphasis in this book: that systems theory in its second-order incarnation, far from eluding or narratologically mastering the mutational processes just discussed, rather subjects itself to them—traces or tracks them, as Derrida might say (for reasons that will become clear later)— in just the way Bateson calls for. As Dirk Baecker puts it, second-order systems theory "may well be read as an attempt to do away with any usual notion of system, the theory in a way being the deconstruction of its central term."[21] Moreover, it is also worth remembering Derrida's suggestion in his late essay "The Animal That Therefore I Am (More to Follow)" that perhaps the deepest logic of his investigation of "the question of the animal" is in fact "viral," in the specific sense of a mutational logic of the trace structure of any notational form, any semiotic system, that exceeds and encompasses the boundary not just between human and animal but also between the living or organic and the mechanical or technical—a contention I take up in some detail in chapters 1 and 2.[22] And it is precisely at this juncture that this book weaves together the two different senses of posthumanism that remained separate in my previous two books, *Critical Environments* and *Animal Rites:* posthumanism as a mode of thought in the first book (explored there on the parallel terrains of pragmatism, systems theory, and post-structuralism) and, in the second, posthumanism as engaging directly the problem of anthropocentrism and speciesism and how practices of thinking and reading must change in light of their critique.

It is worth amplifying for a moment the disciplinary, institutional, ethical, and political stakes of this mutational, viral, or parasitic form of thinking. As David Wills notes (in terms quite resonant with Rutsky's insistence on taking seriously the force of the mutational), it is deconstruction's "constitutive dehiscence, its originary rupture or self-division, that defines it as a disturbance, displacement, or disruption of the status quo." Such a mode of thought "has enormous potential for resisting the self-assurance of any hegemonic discourse or practice," because it infects and mutates through the very structures, privileged terms, and discursive nodes of power on which it is parasitical (think here of Derrida's method of reading). "With the force and effect of a virus," Wills remarks, it "has its invasive parasitic impact precisely there where the border lines are drawn between and among nations, religions, systems of thinking, disciplines, within and between the ontological pretension of an *is* and the thetic possibility of an *in*."[23]

I explore the force of this point for what we might call the ideology of a certain mode of contemporary historicism in literary and cultural studies in chapter 4, but for now I want to note that Wills's articulation of the viral activity of thought "within and between the ontological pretension of an *is* and the thetic possibility of an *in*" might well be taken as a shorthand definition of the fundamental distinction that is central to Luhmann's systems theory: the system/environment relation. That relation is not "an ontological pretension of an *is*" but a *functional* distinction, a temporally dynamic, recursive loop of systemic code and environmental complexity that is itself infected by the virus of paradoxical self-reference, a "thetic *in*" (to use Wills's terms) that will always constitute a "blind spot" and generate an "outside" for its own (or any) observation. For this reason, which I articulate in detail in chapter 1, "reality," in Luhmann's words, "is what one does not perceive when one perceives it."

It is here that we may locate the decisive turn of a thinking that is genuinely posthumanist, and it is also here that we may distinguish the work of Derrida and Luhmann from that of some illustrious fellow travelers in posthumanist thought. There is the Lacanian version articulated most recently by Slavoj Žižek, according to which the self-referential attempts of the domain of the Symbolic to give meaning to or "gentrify" the domain of the "presymbolic Real" only generate, as a precipitate or "remainder" of that process, the very "outside" of the Real (now understood paradoxically as both pre- and post-Symbolic) they attempt to master.[24] There is the nearly Zen-like assertion of Gilles Deleuze that "I am an empiricist, that is, a pluralist," his attempt (with Félix Guattari) "to arrive at the magic formula we all seek, PLURALISM = MONISM, by passing through all the dualisms which are the enemy, the altogether necessary enemy."[25] There is Bruno Latour's well-known assertion that "we have never been modern," his insistence that the fundamental mechanism of modernity "creates two entirely distinct ontological zones: that of human beings on the one hand; that of nonhumans on the other," even as it proliferates "hybrids of nature and culture."[26] And there is Foucault's archaeology of humanism to which I have already alluded.

But the first lesson of both Derrida and Luhmann (and in this they go beyond Foucault's genealogical method, and beyond dialectical and historical accounts of the sort we find in Hayles) is that Enlightenment rationality is not, as it were, rational enough, because it stops short of applying its own protocols and commitments to *itself*. This is, of course, the entire point of Derrida's deconstruction of many of the major concepts, texts, and figures in the Western philosophical tradition. And it is also the point of Luhmann's attention to the formal dynamics of meaning that arise from the unavoidably paradoxical self-reference of any observation—a problem that is, for him, a historical phenomenon created by modernity as a form of "functional differentiation" of social systems. Long before the historical onset of cyborg technologies that now so obviously inject the post- into the posthuman in ways that fascinate the transhumanists, functional differentiation itself determines the posthumanist *form* of meaning, reason, and communication by untethering it from its moorings in the individual, subjectivity, and consciousness. Meaning now becomes a specifically modern form of self-referential recursivity that is used by both psychic systems (consciousness) and social systems (communication) to handle overwhelming environmental complexity. In this sense, Luhmann takes the Kantian commitment to the autonomy of reason seriously but then submits that autonomy to the unavoidable problem of paradoxical self-reference—and in that sense he takes reason more seriously than Kant himself did, or at least takes it to require a more complex theoretical apparatus because of the increased complexity associated with modernity as functional differentiation.[27] As Luhmann puts it in *Observations on Modernity*, "The history of European rationality can be described as the history of the dissolution of a rationality continuum that had connected the observer in the world with the world."[28] To call such a shift historical is not, however, to fall back into the narrative historiographic method I (and Foucault) have just criticized, since this new logic itself virally infects (or deconstructs, if you like) any possible historical account—a fact that (paradoxically, if you like) makes such an account historically representative: that is to say (in Luhmann's terms), it makes it modern.[29]

Thus what Derrida and Luhmann insist on more than any of the thinkers just noted is a thinking that does not turn away from the complexities and paradoxes of self-referential autopoiesis; quite the contrary, it finds there precisely the means to articulate what I will call the principle of "openness from closure," which may itself be seen as the successor to the "order from noise" principle associated with first-order systems theory and inherited by successors such as complexity theory.[30] Here the emphasis falls, as it did not in these earlier theories, on the paradoxical fact theorized by both Luhmann and Derrida: the very thing that separates us from the world *connects* us to the world, and self-referential, autopoietic closure, far from indicating a kind of solipsistic neo-Kantian idealism, actually is generative of openness to the environment. As Luhmann succinctly puts it, self-referential closure "does not contradict the system's *openness to the environment*. Instead, in the self-referential mode of operation, closure is a form of broadening possible environmental contacts; closure increases, by constituting elements more capable of being determined, the complexity of the environment that is possible for the system."[31] In Derrida's terms, "The living present springs forth out of its nonidentity with itself and from the possibility of a retentional trace," which constitutes "the intimate relation of the living present to its outside, the opening to exteriority in general."[32]

It is crucial, as we shall see in the following chapters, that the dynamics described here are not, for Luhmann or for Derrida, limited to the domain of the human. It is thus also in this precise sense—the sense in which the viral logic articulated here must be extended, as Derrida insists, to the "entire field of the living, *or rather to the life/death relation*"[33]—that "the animal question" is part of the larger question of posthumanism. Indeed, for Derrida, these dynamics form the basis for deconstructing the various ways in which we have presumed to master or appropriate the finitude we share with nonhuman animals in ways presumably barred to them (as in the ability to know the world "as such" through our possession of language that is barred to animals, according to Heidegger). It is on the strength of that deconstruction that the question of our ethical relation to animals is opened anew and, as it were, *kept* open. In this connection, my use of Derrida and Luhmann here constitutes an extension and refinement of my deployment of the work of Humberto Maturana and Francisco Varela in "In the Shadow of Wittgenstein's Lion," where the emphasis falls on their contention that "every act of knowing brings forth world." On the one hand, they point out that for us as "languaging" beings, "every reflection, including one on the foundation of human knowledge, invariably takes place in language, which is our distinctive way of being human and being humanly active" in the world.[34] On the other hand, language arises—as it does in Luhmann's account of "meaning" versus language proper—from fundamentally ahuman evolutionary processes of third-order structural couplings and recursive co-ontogenies linked in complex forms of social behavior and communication among so-called higher animals, which have themselves emerged from specific forms of embodiment and neurophysiological organization.

Indeed, as we will see in chapter 1, there are at least three different levels here that must be disarticulated: first, the self-referential autopoiesis of a biological system's material substrate (its "conservation of adaptation" through autopoietic closure, on the basis of which—and only on the basis of which—it can engage in various forms of "structural coupling"); second, the self-referential formal dynamics of meaning (what Maturana and Varela will call, in the arena of living systems, the emergence of "linguistic domains") that some (but not all) autopoietic systems use to reduce environmental complexity and interface with the world; and third, the self-reference of language proper as a second-order phenomenon and a specific medium (what Luhmann calls a "symbolically generalized communications medium") that is used by some (but not all) autopoietic systems that use meaning. None of these levels is reducible to the others; each has its own dynamics, its own evolutionary history, its own constraints and protocols. But this irreducibility, far from frustrating our attempts at explanation, actually greatly enhances them by necessitating what Maturana calls a "nonreductionist relation between the phenomenon to be explained and the mechanism that generates it." As Maturana explains, "the actual result of a process, and the operations in the process that give rise to it in a generative relation, *intrinsically take place in independent and nonintersecting phenomenal domains.* This situation is the reverse of reductionism." And this "permits us to see," he continues, "particularly in the domain of biology, that there are phenomena like language, mind, or consciousness that require an interplay of bodies as a generative structure but do not take place in any of them"[35]—what we will shortly see Luhmann theorizing in chapter 1 as the *difference* between consciousness and communication, psychic systems and social systems, which may nevertheless be coupled structurally through media such as language.

This view has profound implications, of course, for how we think about the human in relation to the animal, about the body and embodiment. To begin with, it means that we can no longer talk of *the* body or even, for that matter, of *a* body in the traditional sense. We take for granted, in other words, Bruno Latour's assertion that "the human form is as unknown to us as the nonhuman. . . . It is better to speak of *(x)-morphism* instead of becoming indignant when humans are treated as nonhumans or vice versa."[36] Rather, "the body" is now seen as a kind of *virtuality,* but one that is, precisely for that reason, all the *more* real. If we believe, as I think we must, the contention that, neurophysiologically, different autopoietic life-forms "bring forth a world" in what Maturana and Varela call their "embodied enaction"— and if, in doing so, the environment is thus different, indeed sometimes *radically* different, for different life-forms—then the environment, and with it "the body," becomes unavoidably a virtual, multidimensional space produced and stabilized by the recursive enactions and structural couplings of autopoietic beings who share what Maturana and

Varela call a "consensual domain." "First" there is noise, multiplicity, complexity, and the heterogeneity of the environment, of what is (I put "first" in quotation marks to underscore the fact that such a statement could only arise, after all, as the observation of an autopoietic system: hence "first" here also means, because of the inescapable fact of the self-reference of such an observation, "last"; it is the environment *of* the system, not nature or any other given anteriority).[37] Second, there are the autopoietic systems that, if they are to continue their existence, respond to this overwhelming complexity by reducing it in terms of the selectivity of a self-referential selectivity or code; and this means, third, that the world is an ongoing, differentiated construction and creation of a shared environment, sometimes converging in a consensual domain, sometimes not, by autopoietic entities that have their own temporalities, chronicities, perceptual modalities, and so on— in short, their own forms of embodiment. Fourth, the world is thus a virtuality and a multiplicity; it is both what one does in embodied enaction and what the self-reference of that enaction excludes. Again, Luhmann: "Reality is what one does not perceive when one perceives it." Crucially, then, "virtual" does not mean "not real"; on the contrary, given the "openness from closure" principle, the *more* virtual the world is, the *more* real it is, because the buildup of internal complexity made possible by autopoietic closure actually *increases* the complexity of the environment that is possible for any system. In that sense, it increases the system's connection and sensitivity to, and dependence on, the environment.

Rethinking embodiment in this way, one might be tempted to invoke Deleuze and Guattari's well-known idea of the body without organs, along the lines usefully glossed by Brian Massumi: "Since the body is an open system, an infolding of impulses from an aleatory outside, all its potential singular states are determined by a fractal attractor. Call that strange attractor the body's plane of consistency. It is a subset of the world's plane of consistency, a segment of its infinite fractal attractor. It is the body as pure potential, pure virtuality."[38] But taking seriously the concept of autopoiesis—that systems, including bodies, are both open *and* closed as the very condition of possibility for their existence (open on the level of structure to energy flows, environmental perturbations, and the like, but closed on the level of self-referential organization, as Maturana and Varela put it); and taking seriously Maturana's assertion that a description in language and the generative phenomena to be described take place in "independent and nonintersecting phenomenal domains," there can be no talk of the body's plane of consistency being a subset of the world's plane of consistency. And there can be no talk of purity. Everything we know (scientifically, theoretically) and say (linguistically or in other forms of semiotic notation) about the body takes place within some contingent, radically nonnatural (that is, constructed and technical) schema of knowledge. The language (or meaning, more strictly speaking) that describes is of a different phenomenal order from that which is described. Paradoxically, that language is fundamental to our embodied enaction, our bringing forth a world, as humans. And yet it is dead. Rather, as Derrida puts it quite precisely, it exceeds and encompasses the life/death relation. That fact doesn't prevent in the least its effectivity, since effectivity (as Latour, among others, has shown) is not a matter of philosophical or theoretical representationalism.[39]

To return, then, to the question of posthumanism, the perspective I attempt to formulate here—far from surpassing or rejecting the human—actually enables us to describe the human and its characteristic modes of communication, interaction, meaning, social significations, and affective investments with *greater* specificity once we have removed meaning from the ontologically closed domain of consciousness, reason, reflection, and so on. It forces us to rethink our taken-for-granted modes of human experience, including the normal perceptual modes and affective states of *Homo sapiens* itself, by recontextualizing them in terms of the entire sensorium of other living beings and their own autopoietic ways of "bringing forth a world"—ways that are, since we ourselves are human *animals,* part of the evolutionary history and behavioral and psychological repertoire of the human itself. But it also insists that we attend to the specificity of the human—its ways of being in the world, its ways of knowing, observing, and describing—by (paradoxically, for humanism) acknowledging that it is fundamentally a prosthetic creature that has coevolved with various forms of technicity and materiality, forms that are radically "not-human" and yet have nevertheless made the human what it is. (For Derrida, of course, this includes the most fundamental prostheticity of all: language in the broadest sense.) As I have already noted, this prostheticity, this constitutive dependency and finitude, has profound *ethical* implications for our relations to nonhuman forms of life—a point I will discuss in some detail in the first half of the book.[40] It also changes how we think about normal human experience and how that experience gets refracted or queried in specific modes and media of artistic and cultural practice that form the focus of the book's second part.

The theoretical approaches I have been sketching here will be developed in greater detail in chapter 1, which attempts a sort of cross-articulation of the theoretical approaches of Jacques Derrida and Niklas Luhmann, not least to provide a context for a less-knee-jerk response for Luhmann's work than it has been accustomed to thus far in the United States. (Here, apropos David Wills's earlier observation about "the self-assurance of any hegemonic discourse or practice," it is worth mentioning that the situation is quite different outside the United States, especially in Europe, where systems theory is widely disseminated and influential in academic and intellectual life.) A central contention here will be that the similarities between systems theory and deconstruction have been hard to see because both converge on their central concept of *difference* from opposite directions. While Derrida's work begins by confronting a logocentric philosophical tradition in which difference must be released in its immanence through the work of deconstruction, for Luhmann, difference names an evolutionary and adaptive problem—specifically, the fact of overwhelming environmental complexity—that any system must find a way of addressing if it wants to continue its autopoiesis. Against this background, Derrida and Luhmann emerge as exemplary posthumanist theorists, I argue, because both refuse to locate meaning in the realm of either the human or, for that matter, the biological. Moreover, both insist on the crucial disarticulation of what Luhmann calls psychic systems and social systems, consciousness and communication, in ways famously insisted on in Derrida's early critique of the self-presence of speech and autoaffection of the voice. For both, the form of meaning is the true substrate of the coevolution of psychic systems and social systems, and this means that the human is, at its core and in its very constitution, radically ahuman and constitutively prosthetic.

Chapter 2 moves this question of meaning—its form, its evolution—

into two additional contexts that will be important for the book as a whole: the question of animal intelligence and communication, and the question of disciplinarity. A central argument of this chapter is that Derrida's theory of language (in the broadest sense, akin to Luhmann's "meaning") and its relationship to questions of subjectivity, intentionality, and the like help us see how philosophers of cognitive science such as Daniel Dennett remain within the very Cartesianism they are trying to escape. Because of their reliance on an essentially representationalist theory of language that many trained in the humanities would find dubious at best, "CogSci" figures such as Dennett not only reinscribe the Cartesian subject that their functionalism wants to critique, but also reinstate the ontological difference between humans and animals familiar to us from the philosophical tradition—a difference that turns out to have dire ethical consequences in Dennett's work. Just how difficult that Cartesianism is to escape is revealed in Derrida's analysis of the psychoanalyst Jacques Lacan's rendering of the human/animal divide in light of his theory of the "subject of the signifier"—a theory that shares more with the Cartesianism of Dennett's analytic approach on this question than one might have expected.

Chapter 3—the longest and most ambitious in the book—explores in much greater detail the relationship between different philosophical approaches and the ethical consequences attendant on those differences for thinking our relations with nonhuman animals discussed in the previous chapter. I begin by casting a hard look at the more familiar and institutionally powerful forms of bioethics, which emerge in this discussion as less an ethics per se than a branch of policy studies within the historical development of what Foucault calls biopower and governmentality. With regard to the specific ethical question I focus on here (the standing of nonhuman animals), bioethics takes for granted the underlying moral hierarchy of human/animal that it ought to be committed to questioning. We need to look elsewhere, I suggest, for more searching engagements with this problem, and I begin by examining briefly Martha Nussbaum's recent attempt, in *Frontiers of Justice,* to apply an Aristotelian "capabilities" approach, focused on the "flourishing" of particular species, to the question of justice and species difference. Despite its admirable focus on vulnerability, finitude, and embodiment as crucial dimensions of ethical thought, Nussbaum's work is hampered by numerous problems, not the least of which is its odd combination of analytic imprecision and programmatic insistence; so I turn to the philosopher Cora Diamond's remarkable body of work on this problem, which is interested not just in the question of ethics and animals but also in how confronting that question changes how we think about what justice is, and what philosophy itself may be.

Under the influence of Stanley Cavell's work on philosophical skepticism, Diamond asks us not to mistake "the difficulty of philosophy" (a propositional, if-P-then-Q kind of difficulty) for "the difficulty of reality" (which she finds on display in the novelist J. M. Coetzee's character Elizabeth Costello in *The Lives of Animals,* who is "wounded" and haunted by the animal "holocaust" going on around us daily in practices such as factory farming). Diamond's searching and original analysis points us toward a fact that will, I argue, require Derrida's work to fully articulate: that we share with nonhuman animals not just one form of finitude but two: not just the radical passivity and vulnerability announced in Jeremy Bentham's famous assertion that the question is not "can they talk?" or "can they reason?" but "can they *suffer?*" but also the kind of finitude articulated by Derrida in his critique of Lacan. That second form of finitude derives from the fundamental exteriority and materiality of meaning and communication itself, of any form of semiotic marking and iterability to which both humans and nonhuman animals are subject in a trace structure that, as he puts it, exceeds and encompasses the human/animal difference and indeed "the life/death relation" itself. For this reason, we cannot master and "erase," in any analytic of finitude or existential of being-toward-death (as in Heidegger), our radical passivity in a way that would once again separate us, definitively and ontologically, from nonhuman animals.

Chapter 4 attempts to intervene at a crucial moment in the development of what has recently come to be called "animal studies" by engaging with the question of disciplinarity. In doing so, it revisits and formalizes the questions of disciplinarity (namely, what is philosophy?) that animated the previous chapter, but it explores that question on the terrain of current U.S. literary and cultural studies and their ruling disciplinary norms, which are, at the current moment, historicist. They are historicist of a particular variety, as it turns out, one that takes for granted and reproduces a specific picture of the knowing subject

that undercuts the putative historicist commitment to the materiality, heterogeneity, and externality of historical forces: a subject that is
clearly (to put it in the terms of a Marxist historicism largely evacuated
or at least domesticated in current literary and cultural studies) an ideological expression of liberalism. It is on this level, I argue, that the real
force of animal studies is occluded and compromised by many of the
assumptions and practices that are mobilized by the template on which
it is modeled (namely, cultural studies). Rather, the full force of animal
studies—what makes it not just another flavor of "fill in the blank" studies on the model of media studies, film studies, women's studies, ethnic
studies, and so on—is that it fundamentally unsettles and reconfigures
the question of the knowing subject and the disciplinary paradigms and
procedures that take for granted its form and reproduce it. To put it another way, there are humanist ways and there are posthumanist ways
of engaging in this supposedly always already posthumanist pursuit
called animal studies. It is here—and not in the simple fact that various
disciplines have recently converged on an object of study called "the
animal"—that the deepest challenge to the disciplines posed by animal
studies may be felt.

Chapter 5 broadens this question of posthumanist studies to include disability studies as well and revisits the relationship between
language, subjectivity, and phenomenology explored in chapter 2. Here
I focus on the fascinating figure of Temple Grandin, perhaps the best-
known representative of an emergent area of contemporary U.S. culture
in which animal studies and disability studies converge. Both disability
studies and animal studies are interested in rethinking (from the ground
up, as it were) questions of subjectivity, bodily experience, mental life,
intersubjectivity, and the ethical and even political changes attendant
on reopening those questions in light of new knowledge about the life
experiences of nonhuman animals and those who are called (problematically, no doubt) the disabled. In Grandin's case, she insists that her
specific condition (a form of autism known as Asperger's syndrome)
enables her to understand more deeply how nonhuman animals such
as cows perceive and experience the world, and she has integrated that
understanding, she claims, into her designs for animal holding facilities
throughout North America. I am interested here in how Grandin's case
helps us radically denaturalize many of the taken-for-granted modes

of human perception and mentation of "normates"—not least, visual experience and an entire set of assumptions about the relationship between language and thought that I have examined in earlier chapters. I am also interested, as I end this chapter, in Grandin's insistence that disability becomes an important form of *abledness* in opening up transspecies modes of identification and thus helps us to disclose how we need to rethink the underlying models of subjectivity that ground the dominant discourses in disability studies, drawn as they are from the liberal democratic framework and its casting of subjectivity in terms of agency, autonomy, and the like.

The second half of the book does not by any means abandon the theoretical and ethical frames that occupy part I; rather, part II continues to develop them, but on different terrain, by engaging in detailed readings and interpretations of a range of cultural and artistic practices that exemplify a posthumanist sensibility or problematic as they emerge and are worked through in particular media and art forms. Chapter 6 continues to excavate the question of visuality in relation to the problem of humanism but does so by linking it to an overt thematics of nonhuman life and the question of its ethical standing that dominates the work of two very different and important contemporary artists, Eduardo Kac and Sue Coe. What I am interested in here, to put it schematically, is the following question: What is the relationship (if indeed there is one) between representationalism and speciesism? What is the connection between an artistic mode or medium and the ways of seeing and experiencing the world that they take for granted, and how do those index a certain kind of perceiving, experiencing subject? By using the work of Michael Fried and Derrida to read Sue Coe's enormous and compelling project *Dead Meat*—a compilation of drawings, paintings, and sketches based on her visits to slaughterhouses in the United States and abroad—I try to show how art that is dedicated to exposing the horrors of anthropocentrism and the violence toward animals that it countenances may nevertheless be, in its very strategies and despite itself, humanist and anthropocentric. On the other hand, art such as Eduardo Kac's, which is controversial in part because of its collaboration with genetic engineers (as in his most famous work, *GFP Bunny,* which produced a glow-in-the-dark rabbit named Alba), may nevertheless engage in a fundamentally posthumanist project in its deft deployment and exposure of certain habits of visuality and representationalism associated, as W. J. T. Mitchell and Luhmann argue, with the spectator-subject of humanism—habits that Kac's choice of medium and method is calculated to unsettle.

Chapter 7 continues the investigation of the relationship between visuality and (post)humanism on the terrain of photography and film but adds to it the relationship between sound and voice (specifically, in Lars von Trier's brilliant and, to some, infuriating film *Dancer in the Dark*). Drawing on work by Stanley Cavell, Catherine Clément, Kaja Silverman, Judith Butler, Slavoj Žižek, Derrida, and others, I attempt to draw out the ethical stakes of how the film stages a certain drama of prosthetic subjectivity and of what Žižek calls "the act as feminine" in the story of the main character Selma (played brilliantly by the pop phenom Björk)—a story that begins with her impending blindness and ends with her hanging for the crime of murder. In the process, I try to demonstrate how both Cavell's skepticism and Žižek's psychoanalysis, brilliant as they are in their local insights, remain fundamentally within the purview of a humanism that von Trier's film both mobilizes (as fantasy) and throws into question (in its filmic practice). As Luhmann might put it, *Dancer in the Dark*'s relationship to posthumanism is not just thematic (in the relationship between Selma's encroaching blindness and how it reconfigures the sight/sound relationship for the human) but also operational in its handling of the medium of film itself.

Luhmann's work is especially apt for framing our understanding of the architectural projects discussed in chapter 8, because many of them self-consciously mobilize the discourse of emergence, autopoiesis, and self-organizing systems that has become an increasingly central feature in landscape architecture in particular. That discourse asks us to reconceive the relationship between nature and culture as a system/environment relationship in which neither term is given as such, and both are a product of cospecification as they emerge from specific practices of articulation. Among the distinguished group of finalists for Toronto's Downsview Park competition, the winning entry, *Tree City*, by Rem Koolhaas and Bruce Mau, is remarkable for its bold refusal of "the realm officially known as architecture" (there are no built structures in the project) and its antirepresentationalist attempt to displace the compositional logic endemic to the problem of the "urban park"—a logic that is, after all, quite at odds with the conceptual thrust of self-organizing systems and autopoiesis invoked by all the entries. To accomplish its task, *Tree City* engages in a kind of dematerialization of the architectural medium, in which *time,* not space—and certainly not built space—becomes the constitutive medium. A similar logic of dematerialization is at work in Diller + Scofidio's *Blur* project—a manufactured cloud hovering over a lake—and it is one that raises fundamental questions of form and meaning in art that Luhmann's work will help us answer: namely, how (in the medium of architecture, no less) can the weakening, even the refusal, of form in the traditional sense constitute precisely a work's boldest formal statement? To answer that question, we need to understand that art as a social system has a unique relationship to the *difference* between perception and communication discussed in our opening chapter. The work of art, Luhmann argues, copresents that difference and "reenters" it in service of its own construction of meaning, "integrating what is in principle incommunicable—namely perception—into the communication network of society."[41] This is what allows art to have a privileged relationship to what has traditionally been called the "ineffable" and the "sublime."

That paradoxical observability of the unobservable, the communicability of the incommunicable—the fact that, as Luhmann puts it, "the activity of distinguishing and indicating that goes on in the world conceals the world"[42]—ought to sound familiar to students of romanticism, and in particular to students of Stanley Cavell's reading of philosophical skepticism as a framework for understanding the subject of chapter 9, Ralph Waldo Emerson. For Cavell, skepticism names the problem, deriving canonically from Kant's encounter with the *Ding an sich,* of "the evanescence and lubricity of all objects," as Emerson puts it, "which lets them slip through our fingers when we clutch hardest." To Cavell's brilliant rereading of Emerson, I want to add Luhmann's reading of romanticism as a reaction to modernity as a phenomenon of "functional differentiation," because it helps us see that Emerson, more than any other philosopher of his day (or, one might argue, of *any* day), puts particular pressure on the paradoxical dynamics of observation as theorized by Luhmann (as in Emerson's proclamation in *Nature* of 1836: "I am nothing, I see all"). Cavell's reading of Emerson in light of philosophical skepticism thus inaugurates a project that we will need Luhmann's systems theory to complete. If Cavell helps us to understand how Emerson reinvents philosophy by continuing to do philosophy after philosophy is, in a very real sense, impossible, then Luhmann helps us articulate more precisely how that task must become a posthumanist one, how it is precisely at his most paradoxical and illogical that Emerson is at his most systematic and rigorous in obeying a quite different logic, a logic inaugurated by modernity as functional differentiation and its unavoidable epistemological fallout.

Emerson's especially rigorous form of romanticism and his engagement of the problem of observation as theorized by Luhmann form an invaluable background for chapter 10, which engages the work of the twentieth-century poet perhaps most associated with the Emersonian legacy: Wallace Stevens. Here, however, I am less concerned with an authorial study than with extending Luhmann's investigations of the problems of form and meaning encountered in the previous two chapters into the realm of poetic form specifically. As with my reading of Emerson, my aim here is to show that Luhmann's theory of art in relation to the paradoxical dynamics of observation provides us with the tools to move beyond the critical impasses that have characterized vague discussions of Stevens's "romantic modernism." Like Emerson's philosophy, Stevens's poetry insists on our not turning away from paradoxical self-reference; it both calls for an encounter with "things exactly as they are" *and* proclaims that "what I saw / Or heard or felt came not but from myself."[43] It is not just in paradox but in the systematicity with which it is deployed that we may identify the rigor of Stevens's poetry. Far from a nonserious or "imaginative" engagement of the problem, Stevens's work uses form (in Luhmann's sense) to stage and, more importantly, to make *productive* the central paradox of meaning after the turn to functional differentiation: that self-reference (mind, imagination, or spirit in the thematics of romanticism) and heteroreference (reality, world, nature) are themselves *both* products of self-reference. Luhmann's work helps us to see that this is not, however, simply an updated form of philosophical idealism of the sort derived from Kant. It also helps us understand a fact we encountered in chapter 8: that form does not involve the material or perceptual substrate of the artwork (here, in the conspicuous absence in much of Stevens's poetry of the prosodic features typically associated with poetic form) but is rather a matter of the recursive self-reference of art's communication, what Luhmann calls art's overcoming of its own contingency. Form is not, that is, the externalization of a subjective interiority or a consciousness, and it is in that precise sense posthumanist.

In the final chapter, I return to questions that animate the middle part of the book—questions of sound, voice, music, and visuality. I revisit the work of Jacques Derrida to parse the relationship between analog and digital media on the site of David Byrne and Brian Eno's collaboration (both musical and artistic) around their remarkable record *My Life in the Bush of Ghosts* (1981). The uncanny effect of that record on almost everyone who hears it, in my experience, has to do in no small part with its use of found vocal materials drawn from a range of sources—evangelical preachers and exorcists recorded from AM radio on a boom box, anthropological recordings of mountain singers in Lebanon, and much else—sampled over gleaming studio tracks inflected by Afro-futurism and what one critic called "avant-funk." But it also has to do in complex ways with what that mix indexes, what Derrida calls the "non-contemporaneity with itself of the living present" (its virtuality, if you like), and how that fact is related to questions of media and archive.[44] What Derrida helps us see is that the dream of "grammaticalization" and "discretization" of movement, image, and sound associated with the apotheosis of digital media is just that—a dream. But it is a dream whose opposite is not some form of authenticity or presence typically associated with analog media; rather, it is a dream haunted by the "spectrality" produced by *any* media, any archival technology whose iterability and repeatability anticipate and in some sense forecast our eventual absence, our death. It is, however, precisely on the basis of that fact that the possibility of the future depends, a "living-on" or "to come," as Derrida puts it, that can only happen because (to quote his beloved Hamlet) "the time is out of joint." Only, that is, because "we" are not "we."

I. THEORIES, DISCIPLINES, ETHICS

1 Meaning and Event; or, Systems Theory and "The Reconstruction of Deconstruction"

As I said: humans can't communicate.
—NIKLAS LUHMANN, "How Can the Mind Participate
in Communication?"

THE RECEPTION OF SYSTEMS THEORY IN THE UNITED STATES—and in North America generally—over the past decade and more has been vexatious at best. In a professional academic landscape in which most critics and theorists pride themselves on moving easily and syncretically between theoretical approaches that, at an earlier moment, were thought of more as warring factions, systems theory remains odd man out. When it is understood at all, it is routinely greeted with reactions ranging from suspicion to outright anger. Critics who think of their work (rightly or wrongly) as a component of a broader political project—at least "in the last instance," to borrow Louis Althusser's well-known caveat—often view systems theory as just a grim technocratic functionalism or a thinly disguised apology for the status quo, a kind of barely camouflaged social Darwinism. In this view, systems theory—in either its first-order, Norbert Wiener version or its second-order, Niklas Luhmann retooling—gets assimilated to the larger context of post–World War II society's obsession with management, command-and-control apparatuses, informatic reproduction, homeostasis, and the like, rightly criticized by theorists like Donna Haraway in her important essay "The Biological Enterprise: Sex, Mind, and Profit from Human Engineering to Sociobiology."[1] Systems theory, instead of being invited to the party reserved for chaos and complexity theory and their interest in the unpredictability, creativity, and emergence of complex nonlinear dynamics, ends up dancing with Richard Dawkins's *The Selfish Gene*. Still others level more general charges familiar from the shopworn discourse of antitheory and lament systems theory's excessive abstraction, its lack of attention to social and historical texture, and its blind ambition to assimilate everything in its purview as grist for its universalizing mill.

If these charges sound familiar, they ought to, because they are an uncanny echo of the sorts of things that we all remember being said about deconstruction (and specifically about the work of Jacques Derrida) when it came ashore in North America in the 1970s (Derrida's *Speech and Phenomena* appeared in translation in 1973, followed in rapid succession by *Of Grammatology* in English in 1976 and *Writing and Difference* in 1978). Of course, we all got over it, and the irony need hardly be remarked (but I'll remark it anyway) that it is difficult to find anyone who has had much success in the profession of literary and cultural studies in North America who did not cut his or her teeth on just these texts and whose deployment of lessons learned from them in his or her own work is not more or less automatic and unconscious (though that has changed some over the past decade with the hegemony of certain modes of historicism in which the antitheory component is especially virulent—a question I will revisit in some detail in chapter 4).

The reasons for system theory's chilly reception in the United States are complicated, and I'm not going to investigate them in any detail here, but I'll at least offer a couple of brief speculations. One set of reasons (not to be underestimated) is disciplinary and institutional. First, as many of us remember, "deconstruction in America"—a time capsule phrase if ever there was one—made its way into universities mainly via comparative literature departments; and if you think *that* was a precarious foothold, consider that the major practitioner of systems theory (Luhmann) has entered the U.S. academy primarily by way of *German* departments (or their equivalent fractions in larger comparative literature and language departments), mainly under the rubric of German intellectual history. (Here the work of scholars such as David Wellbery, William Rasch, and Hans Ulrich Gumbrecht is exemplary.) But over the past decade, many American universities have downsized or eliminated their German departments, and it is hard for me to think of any more endangered place to be in the humanities in the United States over the past ten years, with the possible exception of classics.

Related to this question of institutional foothold is another, different deficit: the absence of a nationally disseminated journal that is tethered to the theoretical model. *Diacritics* (published out of the Comparative Literature Department at Cornell University) became something like the house journal for deconstruction in the 1970s and 1980s, but the *Stanford Literature Review*, which has done more than any single U.S. journal to consistently publish work in systems theory, is not *Diacritics*. A few special issues of other, well-known journals have been devoted to systems theory and Luhmann's work—*Theory, Culture, and Society* (published by Sage in Great Britain, though widely available in the United States), *MLN, New German Critique*, and one and a half issues of *Cultural Critique* titled "The Politics of Systems and Environments"—but nothing that has the kind of ongoing relationship to systems theory that *Representations* did and does for New Historicism. Moreover, systems theory has had to brook an even greater degree of disciplinary dissonance; where the establishing texts of deconstruction were quite identifiably within the purview of philosophy and often of literature, the major texts and figures of systems theory enter the humanities through the side door of *science:* either social science and sociology (with Luhmann), or the life sciences (in the case of Humberto Maturana and Francisco Varela), or the interface of first-order cybernetic computer science with neurology (in the case of Heinz von Foerster). Finally, there is the daunting difficulty of the theory itself, which—particularly in Luhmann's hands—gives even seasoned readers of theory pause with its extraordinary abstraction and rigor; its head-on engagement with problems of paradox, self-reference, and the like; its systematically counterintuitive findings; and its relative lack of creature comforts along the way for those who have signed on for the journey of what Luhmann unabashedly calls "super-theory." Of course, here again we should probably remind ourselves that it is hard to recall a major theoretical development about which something similar was *not* said, and some of our colleagues are old enough to remember similar complaints about the technical rigor and cold-bloodedness of that strange, alienating, scientistic approach to literary texts called (gasp!) "the New Criticism."

Other speculations could no doubt be offered about why systems theory in the United States has not emerged as the kind of factor in cultural studies that it is most obviously in Germany, but my main point is not to analyze those reasons further. Rather, it is to nudge the reception of systems theory in a different direction by strategically bringing out some of its more "deconstructive" characteristics.[2] Indeed, I hope to make clear to skeptics that much of what they like about deconstruction is also much of what they *should* like about systems theory, because systems theory in its contemporary articulation—far from conforming to the stereotypes prepared for it in the U.S. academy—"may well be read," to borrow Dirk Baecker's formulation, "as an attempt to do away with any usual notion of system, the theory in a way being the deconstruction of its central term."[3]

To take only one example, let us revisit the epigraph with which I began. On the one hand (the dominant hand), Luhmann's contention that "humans can't communicate" seems not just counterintuitive but flatly wrong; in fact (as a colleague mentioned to me recently at a conference), it seems "insulting." And yet, as I hope will be clear by the end of my comments here, Luhmann's remark (rhetorically calculated, no doubt, to cause just such a stir) makes essentially the same point about the difference between "consciousness" and "communication" that we have quite readily accepted for decades now as gospel from Derrida: namely, his deconstruction of the "autoaffection" of the voice-as-presence and of the valorizing of speech (as an index of the self-presence of consciousness to itself) over writing (a recursive domain of iterative communication that is, properly understood, fundamentally ahuman or even antihuman). I will return to the ethical implications around this question of the "metaphysical" voice in chapter 6. Similarly, I will explore in more detail in the next chapter Derrida's insistence that it is just this sort of radical separation of what Luhmann calls psychic and social systems that will lead him to reject the notion of the signifier (as in Lacan's formulation of "the subject of the signifier," which seems at first glance quite cognate to Luhmann's formulation) in favor of the articulation of writing as fundamentally a structured dynamics of the trace. Equally important for my purposes in this book, as we will see in the next three chapters, is that this trace structure of communication extends beyond the human to nonhuman animals and indeed exceeds, as we are about to see, the boundary between the living and the mechanical or technical.

6

My pairing of systems theory and deconstruction here should come as no surprise because Derrida himself announces the convergence in his own terms in early, formative texts such as *Of Grammatology*, whose first chapter, "The End of the Book and the Beginning of Writing," begins with a section entitled "The Program." There Derrida argues that "the entire field covered by the cybernetic *program* will be the field of writing," but writing understood in terms of "the *grammè*— or the *grapheme*," a writing that would name as its fundamental unit "an element without simplicity"—which is to say, an element of irreducible *complexity* (specifically as systems theory uses the term). And a temporalized complexity at that, for, as Derrida writes, "cybernetics is itself intelligible only in terms of a history of the possibilities of the trace as the unity of a double movement of protention and retention."[4]

Derrida's claim, put forth as it was in the late 1960s, may seem even now a radical one, but in fact it was lodged against the backdrop of an entire revolution in the sciences that had already taken such models as axiomatic. In fact, the first chapter of the 1965 Nobel Prize winner Francois Jacob's remarkably influential *The Logic of Life* is also called "The Programme." There Jacob reminds us that "heredity is described today in terms of information, messages, and code." What this means—and this is clearly related to Derrida's early work on both Husserl and Saussure—is that "the intention of a psyche has been replaced by the translation of a message. The living being does indeed represent the execution of a plan, but not one conceived in any mind."[5] Derrida would add to this, however, the point he presses in *Of Grammatology*:

> If the theory of cybernetics is by itself to oust all metaphysical concepts—including the concepts of soul, of life, of value, of choice, of memory—which until recently served to separate the machine from man, it must conserve the notion of writing, trace, grammè [written mark], or grapheme, until its own historico-metaphysical character is exposed.[6]

As an example of such "character," interestingly enough, Derrida cites in a footnote not Jacob but the first-generation systems theorist Norbert Wiener, who "while abandoning 'semantics,' and the opposition, judged by him as too crude and too general, between animate and inanimate etc., nevertheless continues to use expressions like 'organs of sense,' 'motor organs,' etc. to qualify the parts of the machine" (324n3). Part of what I will be arguing in what follows is that Luhmann's handling of systems theory accomplishes just the sort of "conservation" of the logic of the *grammè* that Derrida calls for, a conservation that is crucial to any posthumanism whatsoever—not only because the movement of the program-as-*grammè* "goes far beyond the possibilities of the 'intentional consciousness'" as the source and guarantor of meaning, but also because once the notion of the program is invoked, one no longer has "recourse to the concepts that habitually serve to distinguish man from other living beings (instinct and intelligence, absence or presence of speech, of society, of economy, etc. etc.)" (84).

As I have suggested elsewhere, this cross-talk between postwar science and what would come to be called "theory" is not limited to Derrida and Wiener. Indeed, perhaps the most profound backstory of all in contemporary thought is the ongoing, if episodic, influence of such new scientific discourses on thinkers who would emerge in the 1950s and 1960s to redefine the very landscape of the humanities and social sciences (think here of Foucault's interest in Jacob and Canguilhem, Lacan's in cybernetics, Lyotard's in chaos and catastrophe theory, and so on).[7] My aim at the moment, however, is not to make that historical argument. Nor is it just to play up the deconstructive aspects of systems theory, nor even to suggest, as I have been, that the largely knee-jerk reactions to systems theory in the United States have been misplaced (or at least, vis-à-vis the reception of deconstruction, rather ungenerously placed).

Rather, my emphasis here will on the usefulness of viewing second-order systems theory as (to use Luhmann's characterization) "the reconstruction of deconstruction."[8] That project hinges on systems theory's extraordinarily rigorous and detailed account of the fundamental dynamics and complexities of meaning that subtend the reproduction and interpenetration of psychic and social systems. And systems theory then takes the additional step of linking those dynamics to their biological, social, and historical conditions of emergence and transformation, a crucial move that, as Gunther Teubner has argued, deconstruction either cannot or will not undertake. It is certainly the case that Derrida's later work has been intensely and increasingly engaged with the question of social institutions in all their forms—the law, the university, the question of rights, the institution of property, and so on—and the logics that ground and sustain their reproduction. But though he has raised such questions—*worried* them might be a better term—with a degree of nuance and suppleness perhaps unmatched in contemporary theory and philosophy, Derrida has not been especially interested in articulating the relationship between the theoretical complexities of those dynamics and the historical and sociological conditions of their emergence—conditions that he suggests impel such thinking at this very moment.[9] (Whether this is a failure or a principled refusal on Derrida's part is an interesting question, and it is one I will return to later in this chapter.)

One could cite any number of Derrida's texts in this connection, but the recent collection of essays *Without Alibi* exemplifies quite well what I mean. There Derrida considers the question of what he calls "a politics *of the* virtual," of "a certain delocalizing virtualization of the space of communication, discussion, publication, archivization," against the backdrop of this larger question: "Will we one day be able, and in a single gesture, to join the thinking of the event to the thinking of the machine?"[10] "Today," he continues, "they appear to us to be antinomic. . . . An event worthy of the name ought not, so we think, to give in or be reduced to repetition," but rather "ought above all to *happen* to someone, some living being who is thus *affected* by it." The machine, on the contrary, is destined "to reproduce impassively, imperceptibly, without organ or organicity, received commands"; it obeys "a calculable program without affect or auto-affection" (72).

If we are to address the sorts of questions raised here, Derrida argues, now is the time for a new kind of thinking. "How," he asks, "is one to reconcile, *on the one hand,* a thinking of the event, which I propose withdrawing, despite the apparent paradox, from an ontology or a metaphysics of presence . . . and, *on the other hand,* a certain concept of machineness [*machinalité*]?" (136). This, he rightly observes, is "the place of a thinking that ought to be devoted to the virtualization of the event by the machine, to a virtuality that, in exceeding the philosophical determination of the possibility of the possible . . . exceeds by the same token the classical opposition of the possible and the impossible" (135). "If one day," he continues, "with one and the same concept, these two incompatible concepts, the event and the machine, were to be thought together, you can bet that *not only* . . . will one have produced a new logic, an unheard-of conceptual form. In truth against the background and horizon of our present possibilities, this new figure would resemble a monster" (73). It would be, in a word, posthumanist.

What I want to suggest, of course, is that systems theory in its second-order incarnation is just such a "monster," one whose cornerstone genetic mutation is the transfer of the concept of autopoiesis from organicity to the domain of not only psychic but also social systems, systems whose fundamental elements are not people or groups but communications and "events"—and events conceptualized along the lines Derrida lays out in the previous paragraph. We have already used deconstruction to help clarify a central point from systems theory—the separation of psychic and social systems—but here we can return the favor and use systems theory to clarify how the thinking of the event may be, in Derrida's words, withdrawn from "an ontology or metaphysics of presence."[11] On the one hand, events constitute the fundamental elements of psychic and social systems in Luhmann's scheme. On the other hand, "they occur only once and only in the briefest period necessary for their appearance (the 'specious present'). They are identified by this temporal appearance and cannot be repeated."[12] But "precisely this suits them to be the elementary units of processes," because "the system itself determines the length of time during which an element is treated as a unity that cannot be further dissolved; that period has a conferred, not an ontological character" (48). An element's unity "corresponds to no unity in the substrate; it is created by the system that uses them through their connectivity" (215); "accordingly," Luhmann continues, "an adequately stable system is composed of unstable elements. It owes its stability to itself, not to its elements; its constructs itself upon a foundation that is entirely not 'there,' and this is precisely the sense in which it is autopoietic" (48). And here, as much as anywhere, we get a specific sense of how systems theory thinks Derrida's event and machine all at once as a deconstructive enfolding of the difference between the system's iterative self-reference and the fleeting temporality of the event from the "outside"—a difference that not only serves as the very basis for the system's autopoiesis but also clarifies the fact, as Dietrich Schwanitz puts it, that "systems theory is anything but mechanistic."[13]

As for Derrida's part—you will have already guessed by my use of the term "iterative" a moment ago—we know what his version of this monstrosity of the event-machine looks like: it looks like *écriture,* *arché*-writing as *différance,* as *grammè* and as trace. For our purposes, it is all the more interesting, then, that in contrast to his notion of writing, Derrida has *interrogated* the concept of communication in a variety of contexts, and nowhere more forcefully, perhaps, than in his essay "Signature Event Context" and its related documents collected in *Limited Inc.* There he argues that his concept of writing can "no longer be comprehensible in terms of communication, at least in the limited sense of a transmission of meaning. Inversely, it is within the general domain of writing, defined in this way, that the effects of semantic communication can be determined as effects that are particular, secondary, inscribed, and supplementary."[14]

The full resonance of this last assertion in relation to the dynamics of "meaning" in systems theory will become clear in a moment, but for now we need to note as well that the difference between writing in Derrida's sense and communication as he defines it is marked by radically different relations to the question of the subject—and here, indeed, we encounter, from the point of view of humanism, part of its "monstrosity." As Derrida writes, "Imagine a writing whose code would be so idiomatic as to be established and known, as a secret cipher, by only two 'subjects'"—and "subjects" here is given in quotation marks:

> Could we maintain that, following the death of the receiver, or even of both partners, the mark left by one of them is still a writing? Yes, to the extent to that, organized by a code, even an unknown and non-linguistic one, it is constituted in its identity as a mark by its iterability, in the absence of such and such a person, and hence ultimately of every empirically determined "subject." . . . The possibility of repeating and thus of identifying the marks is implicit in every code, making it into a network *[une grille]* that is communicable, transmittable, decipherable, iterable for a third, and hence for every possible user in general. To be what it is, all writing must, therefore, be capable of functioning in the radical absence of every empirically determined receiver in general.[15]

Herein lies the radically posthumanist dimension of writing-as-difference: the subject—in a process nearly proverbial for contemporary thought from Derrida to Lacan—only comes to be by conforming to a strictly diacritical system of differences, "effects which do not find their cause in a subject or a substance, in a thing in general, a being that is somewhere present, thereby eluding the play of *difference*."[16] Moreover, those effects and relations are at once material, bodily, external, institutional, technological, and historical—they exist in all the specificity and heterogeneity of what Derrida calls their "iteration." Hence Derrida argues that "this pure difference, which constitutes the self-presence of the living present, introduces into self-presence from the beginning all the impurity putatively excluded from it. The living present springs forth out of its nonidentity with itself and from the possibility of a retentional trace. It is always already a trace." And what this means, in turn, is that "the trace is the intimate relation of the living present to its outside, the opening to exteriority in general."[17]

From the point of view of the philosophical tradition that Derrida is concerned to deconstruct, such will be the "corrupting" and "contaminating" work (the "monstrosity," if you will) of "iterability," which "entails the necessity of thinking *at once* both the rule and the event, concept and singularity"; as such, it "marks the essential and ideal limit of all pure idealization," *not* as "the concept of nonideality," as ideality's pure other, but as the impossibility (or at the least the provisionality) of idealization as such.[18] Like the undecidability that it unavoidably generates—and this will lead us to the final question we want to raise—iterability "remains *heterogeneous*" to, rather than simply opposed to, the order of the ideal, the calculable, the pure, and so on. As such, it names a form of ethical responsibility that entails vigilant attention to each specific, interfolded iteration of "rule and event," to "*this particular* undecidable" that "opens the field of decision or decidability" (116), one that "is always a *determinate* oscillation between possibilities" that takes place "in strictly *defined* situations (for example, discursive—syntactical or rhetorical—but also political, ethical, etc.). They are *pragmatically* determined" (148).

Exactly what the force and scope of this last assertion—"pragmatically determined" and in "strictly defined situations"—are for Derrida is a question that goes directly to Teubner's concerns already touched on earlier, and it is one to which I will return later in this chapter and the book (particularly in chapter 3). For now, however, I simply want to make the point that this picture of writing in the

Derridean sense (and the restructuring of the question of the subject that it pulls in its wake) does not mark a *difference* between Derrida's *écriture* and the concept of communication in systems theory; rather, it is precisely what illuminates their convergence. When Derrida uses the term "communication" in *Limited Inc,* what he really has in mind is the model of communication mobilized by *first*-generation systems theory. That model, like the speech act theory of Austin deconstructed in *Limited Inc,* seems, but *only* seems (as it turns out), to rightly refer the question of meaning to its external formal dynamics rather than to ontology, intentionality, and so on. Of course, it is this very baggage attached to the term "communication" that Luhmann's work, like Derrida's, is dead set on rejecting. In fact, "Communication and Action," the chapter in *Social Systems* that makes this clearest, explicitly references Derrida's critique of Husserl in protesting that "the metaphor of transmission"—the metaphor that dominates first-wave systems theory—"is unusable because it implies too much ontology" in the picture it gives of both meaning (the "message") and the subject who is part of its circuit.[19] Over and against this, as Schwanitz points out, both deconstruction and Luhmann's systems theory "make difference their basic category, both temporalize difference and reconstruct meaning as a temporally organized context of displacement and deferral. Both regard their fundamental operation (i.e., writing or communication, respectively) as an independent process that constitutes the subject rather than lets itself be constituted by it."[20]

Here, however, we find a diametrically reversed orientation or angle of approach in the two theories—one that, I believe, accounts for the "monstrosity" of deconstruction being relatively well received, while systems theory has tended to provoke all sorts of defensive and recuperative responses. To put this schematically, Derrida and Luhmann approach many of the same questions and articulate many of the same formal dynamics of meaning (as self-reference, iterability, recursivity, and so on), but they do so from diametrically opposed directions. As Schwanitz has pointed out, the starting point for systems theory is the question of what makes order possible and how highly organized complexity, which is highly improbable, comes into being at all. Deconstruction, on the other hand, begins with taken-for-granted intransigent structures of logocentrism and the metaphysics of presence that are already ensconced in textual and institutional form, and then asks how the subversion of those structures by their own elements can be revealed.[21]

For Derrida, contingency, temporality, the event, "noise," and so on constitute the eruptive and finally irrepressible difference at the heart of any logos or law, a difference whose unavoidability and un-masterability deconstruction aims to bring to light and sustain. For systems theory, however, this radical heterogeneity is handled within an adaptive and operational framework, as a fundamental evolution-ary *problem* for autopoietic systems that have to reproduce themselves in the face of this overwhelming difference.[22] Because of this reversal of orientation, the *descriptions* offered by systems theory ("autopoietic systems that can reduce environmental difference and complexity will continue to exist") have been misunderstood as *prescriptions* ("such sys-tems *should* exist, and difference and complexity are negative values"). But, of course, systems theory doesn't desire the reduction of differ-ence and complexity (indeed, Luhmann would be the first to insist that such would constitute a category mistake if ever there was one); it only describes how difference and complexity have to be handled by sys-tems that hope to continue their autopoiesis.

Systems theory, in other words, does not occlude, deny, or other-wise devalue difference but rather *begins* with difference—namely, the cornerstone postulate of the difference between system and envi-ronment, and the corollary assumption that the environment of any system is always already of overwhelmingly greater complexity than the system itself. Since it is obviously impossible for any system to es-tablish point-for-point correspondences between itself and its environ-ment, systems thus handle the problem of overwhelming environmen-tal complexity by reducing it in terms of the selectivity made available by the system's self-referential code; as Luhmann puts it, "The system's inferiority in complexity must be counter-balanced by strategies of se-lection." "Complexity, in this sense," he continues, "means being forced to select," and thus, in his winning formulation, "only complexity can reduce complexity."[23] Under pressure to adapt to a complex and chang-ing environment, systems increase their selectivity—they make their environmental filters more finely woven, if you like—by building up their own internal complexity by means of self-referential closure and the reentry of the system/environment distinction within the system itself in a process of internal differentiation.[24]

For example, the difference between the legal system and its environment is reintroduced in the legal system itself, which now serves as the environment for the various subsystems of the law, and the same could be said, within the educational system, about the various academic disciplines and subdisciplines, and so on.[25] This self-referential closure, however, does not indicate solipsism, idealism, or isolation but is instead crucial to understanding a fundamental principle I will return to throughout these pages, the principle of what I call "openness from closure." It "does not contradict the system's *openness to the environment*. Instead, in the self-referential mode of operation, closure is a form of broadening possible environmental contacts; closure increases, by constituting elements more capable of being determined, the complexity of the environment that is possible for the system." And this is why, Luhmann writes, "self-reference is in itself nothing bad, forbidden, or to be avoided"; indeed, it "points directly to system formation" because systems "can become complex only if they succeed in solving this problem and thus in de-paradoxicalizing themselves."[26]

What makes such systems paradoxical in the first place is the unity of the difference between the two sides of the distinction that anchors the system's code. For example, the first-order distinction between legal and illegal in the legal system is itself a product of the code's own self-reference—that is to say, the problem is that *both* sides of the distinction are instantiated by *one* side of the distinction (namely, the legal: hence the tautology "legal is legal"). But the tautological unity of this distinction may be disclosed only by a second-order observer, operating within another system and another code, which must remain blind to its paradoxical distinction if it is to use that distinction to process events for the system's autopoiesis, and so on and so forth. The formal notation for this dynamic that Luhmann borrows from George Spencer-Brown's *Laws of Form* will help make this clearer. As Bruce Clarke summarizes it, the form consists of four elements: (1) the "indication" or "marked state" of a distinction's "inside"; (2) the indication's "unmarked state," or the "outside" of the distinction; (3) the distinction itself as a unity of its marked and unmarked states; and (4) a second distinction between marked and unmarked spaces, made by a second-order observer, which will obey the same form.[27] Thus:

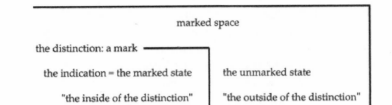

What is most interesting here, however, is that these constitutive paradoxes, far from hindering the autopoiesis of self-referential systems, in fact *force* their autopoiesis.[28] And here—in this transvaluation of the paradoxes of self-reference from paralytic to productive—the lines of relation between systems theory and deconstruction come quite clearly into view. "If we want to observe paradoxical communications as deframing and reframing, deconstructing and reconstructing operations," Luhmann writes,

> we need a concept of meaning . . . as the simultaneous presentation . . . of actuality and possibility. . . . The distinction actual/possible is a form that "re-enters" itself. On one side of the distinction, the actual, the distinction actual/possible reappears; it is copied into itself. . . . If we observe such a re-entry, we see a paradox. The re-entering distinction is the same, and it is not the same. But the paradox does not prevent the operations of the system. On the contrary, it is the condition of their possibility.[29]

This is so, Luhmann writes, because "the totality of the references presented by any meaningfully intended object offers more to hand than can in fact be actualized at any moment. Thus the form of meaning, through its referential structure, *forces* the next step, to *selection*."[30] But that selection, of course, immediately begins to deteriorate in usefulness under pressure of the temporal flow of events, the "specious present," which then forces *another* selection, and so on and so forth.

Here we encounter systems theory's version of what Derrida calls the dynamic force of *différance* as "temporization" and "spacing," as "protention" and "retention," a process that "is possible only if each so-called present element . . . is related to something other than itself, thereby keeping within itself the mark of the past element" while at the same time being "vitiated by the mark of its relation to the future element," thus "constituting what is called the present by means of this very relation to what it is not."[31] Or as Luhmann puts it, "One could say that meaning equips an actual experience or action with redundant possibilities"—namely, what *was* selected (the actual) and what could have been (the possible)—and this is crucial for any system's ability to respond to environmental complexity by building up its own complexity via the form of meaning.

This is what Luhmann means when he says that "this formal requirement refers meaning to the problem of complexity."[32] "The genesis and reproduction of meaning presupposes an infrastructure in reality that constantly changes its states," he writes. "Meaning then extracts differences (which only as differences have meaning) from this substructure to enable a difference-oriented processing of information. On all meaning, therefore, are imposed a temporalized complexity and the compulsion to a constant shifting of actuality, without meaning itself vibrating in tune with that substructure" (63). From an adaptive and evolutionary point of view, then, self-reference and the form of meaning do not indicate solipsism. Quite the contrary. As Luhmann points out, it is "unproductive for meanings to circulate as mere self-referentiality or in short-circuited tautologies. . . . One can think, 'This rose is a rose is a rose is a rose.' But this use of a recursive path is productive only if it makes itself dependent on specific conditions and does not always ensue" (61). And herein lies the difference for Luhmann between *meaning* and *information,* one that recalls Derrida's emphasis in *Limited Inc* on the specific pragmatics of iterability. Luhmann continues: "A piece of information that is repeated is no longer information. It retains its meaning in the repetition but loses its value as information. One reads in the paper that the deutsche mark has risen in value. If one reads this a second time in another paper, this activity no longer has value as information . . . although structurally it presents the same selection." Something can be meaningful, in other words, but have no informational value; or to put it another way—one that will bear directly on my discussion of form and poetry in chapter 10—form and formalism are only part of the story when it comes to meaning.

One thus "begins not with identity but with difference"—with *two* differences, in fact: the difference inherent in every experience "between what is *actually given* and what can *possibly* result from it" that is given in the internal form of meaning itself; and the difference between meaning and information that is forced on the system by environmental complexity and temporality. "Only thus can one give accidents informational value and thereby construct order, because information is nothing more than an event that brings about a connection between differences—'a difference that makes a difference.' Therefore, we encounter *the decomposition of meaning per se*," the "detautologization of meaning's self-reference" forced on the system by the adaptive pressure of the environment, of the "outside world" (75). This is why—contrary to the view of systems theory as solipsistic, imperialistic, and so on—Luhmann insists that "the difference between meaning and world is formed for this process of the continual self-determination of meaning as the difference between order and perturbation, between information and noise. Both are, and both remain, necessary. The unity of the difference is and remains the basis for operation. *This cannot be emphasized strongly enough. A preference for meaning over world, for order over perturbation, for information over noise is only a preference.* It does not enable one to dispense with the contrary" (83; italics mine).

In the form of meaning, then, we find that systems increase their contacts with their environments paradoxically by *virtualizing* them. "Meaning is the continual actualization of potentialities," Luhmann writes,

> but because meaning can be meaning only as the difference between what is actual at any given moment and a horizon of possibilities, every actualization always also leads to a virtualization of the potentialities that could be connected up with it. The instability of meaning resides in the untenability of its core of actuality; the ability to restabilize is provided by the fact that everything actual has meaning only within a horizon of possibilities . . . [that] can and must be selected as the next actuality. . . . Thus one can treat the difference between actuality and possibility in terms of temporal displacement and thereby process indications of possibility with every (new) actuality. Meaning is the unity of actualization and virtualization, of re-actualization and re-virtualization, as a self-propelling process. (65)

This "virtualization" via meaning is an extraordinarily powerful evolutionary dynamic, and it is put to good use by both psychic and social systems. Indeed, Luhmann insists, "Not all systems process complexity and self-reference in the form of meaning"—and here one could think of various biological systems[33]—"but for those that do, it is the *only* possibility. Meaning becomes for them the form of the world and consequently overlaps the difference between system and environment" (61). Or as Luhmann sometimes characterizes it—in a formulation resonant not only with Derrida's essays such as "Structure, Sign, and Play" but also with Emerson's philosophy and the core preoccupations of romanticism—"The relationship between meaning and world can also be described with the concept of decentering. As meaning, the world is accessible everywhere: in every situation, in any detail," which is to say that "the world is indicated in all meaning. To that state of affairs corresponds an a-centric world concept" (70), and hence "the closure of the self-referential order is synonymous here with the *infinite openness of the world*" (62).

This coimplication of psychic and social systems via the formal dynamics of meaning, combined with Luhmann's simultaneous insistence on the strict separation of psychic and social systems as discrete autopoietic entities, marks one of systems theory's most difficult and counterintuitive features—but also one of its most powerful innovations. In a formulation as matter-of-fact as it is beguiling, Luhmann writes: "Humans cannot communicate; not even their brains can communicate; not even their conscious minds can communicate. Only communication can communicate."[34] "What we experience as our own mind operates as an isolated autopoietic system," he points out, and in fact, that isolation is "an indispensable condition of its possibility" (170). There is "no conscious link between one mind and another," nor is there any "operational unity of more than one mind as a system"—all of which, Luhmann argues, is essentially taken for granted at this point by contemporary neurophysiology (170). Indeed, he asks, how could any psychic system maintain its own functions if it shared its unity with other minds? How could I deliver a lecture if I shared the moment-to-moment ebb and flow of psychic activity of even one other consciousness in the room? In this sense, "communication," Luhmann writes, "operates with an unspecific reference to the participating state of mind; it is especially unspecific as to perception. It cannot copy states of mind, cannot imitate them, cannot represent them. This is the basis for the possibility of communication's building up a complexity of its own" (178).

Our intuitions, of course, would seem to suggest otherwise, and this is so precisely because psychic systems and social systems have coevolved, each serving as the environment for the other, and this "has led to a common achievement, employed by psychic as well as social systems."[35] That achievement, of course, is meaning. "Meaning," Luhmann writes, "is the true 'substance' of this emergent evolutionary level. It is therefore false (or more gently, it is falsely chosen anthropocentrism) to assign the psychic . . . ontological priority over the social. It is impossible to find a 'supporting substance' for meaning. Meaning supports itself in that it enables its own self-referential reproduction. *And only the forms of this reproduction differentiate psychic and social structures*"—namely, "whether consciousness [in the case of psychic systems] or communication [social systems] is chosen as the form of operation" (98). Here, as I have already suggested, we find Luhmann's answer to Derrida's critique of the autoaffection of the voice and of consciousness as presence in *Speech and Phenomena, Of Grammatology,* and elsewhere: of the fallacy that writing or communication could be referred for its efficacy as a representation to an ontic substrate of consciousness and the psychic system, whereas in fact it is the ontologically unsupported ur-dynamic of writing (Derrida) or meaning (Luhmann) that is fundamental and allows psychic and social systems to interpenetrate. And as we will see in later chapters (8 and 10), the disarticulation and interpenetration of consciousness and communication are crucial to how art (and within that, poetry) engages in a particular form of communication that is barred to other social systems.

The difficulty in understanding this disarticulation of consciousness and communication, Luhmann points out (in a disarmingly commonsensical moment),

> lies in that every consciousness that tries to do so is itself a self-referentially closed system and therefore cannot get outside of consciousness. For consciousness, even communication can only be conducted consciously and is invested in further possible consciousness. *But for communication*

this is not so. Communication is only possible as an event that transcends the closure of consciousness: as the synthesis of more than the content of just one consciousness. (99)

The confusing of consciousness and communication, if one wants to put it that way, is precisely why "the concept of meaning must be employed on such a high theoretical level. Meaning enables psychic and social systems to interpenetrate, while protecting their autopoiesis; meaning simultaneously enables consciousness to understand itself and continue to affect itself in communication, and enables communication to be referred back to the consciousness of the participants" (219).

The all-important medium that allows this interpenetration via the form of meaning to take place is, you will have already guessed, *language.* But "this does not mean language determines consciousness," Luhmann writes; "psychic processes are not linguistic processes," he continues, "nor is thought in any way 'internal dialogue' (as has been falsely maintained). It lacks an 'internal addressee.' There is no 'second I,' no 'self' in the conscious system, no 'me' vis-à-vis an 'I,' no additional authority that examines all linguistically formed thoughts to see whether it will accept or reject them and whose decision consciousness seeks to anticipate" (272). Luhmann's point here no doubt takes for granted similar formulations throughout Derrida's early work in *Speech and Phenomena, Of Grammatology,* and elsewhere, but the emphasis in Luhmann falls rather differently, on the evolutionary aspects of this disarticulation. What is important for Luhmann is that one must do justice to the powerful role of language in the coevolution of psychic and social systems while simultaneously paying attention to their autopoiesis and self-referential closure. On the one hand, "the evolution of social communication is only possible in a constantly operative link with states of consciousness," which is provided by the medium of language; on the other hand, language "transfers social complexity into psychic complexity" (*SS* 272) in a process generically referred to in contemporary theory as "subjectification" or "subject formation."[36] "The social system places its own complexity, which has stood the test of communicative manageability, at the psychic system's disposal," but at the same time, language (and, even more, writing) ensures "for the communication system what Maturana calls the conservation of adaptation: the constant accommodation of communication to the mind. They define the free space of autopoiesis within the social communication system."[37]

For Luhmann, then, language is not constitutive of either psychic or social systems but is rather a specific, second-order phenomenon—a type of "symbolically generalized communication media"—that those systems use in the services of the *first*-order processes of meaning for maintaining their own autopoiesis while at the same time enabling them to interpenetrate and use each other's complexity to mutual benefit.[38] From Luhmann's point of view, language is "not just a means of communication, because it functions in psychic systems without communication" in the strict sense of having to take place (94); but at the same time, "communication is also possible without language" and may take place in all sorts of nonlinguistic ways, "perhaps through laughing, through questioning looks, through dress," and so on (150).

In fact, what is fundamental about communication for Luhmann is not its (dis)relation to language but that it is a "synthesis of three selections" (147): information (the content, if you like, to be communicated), utterance (the specific, pragmatic communicative event or behavior selected to communicate information), and understanding (a receiver's processing of the difference between information and utterance that completes the communicative act) (140–42, 147, 151). Again, the issue is not just difference; *all* forms of meaning, of which communication is a specific instance, operate by means of difference; the issue is whether (to remember Gregory Bateson's phrase) an utterance is a "difference that makes a difference" in terms of the system's autopoiesis. Or as Luhmann puts it, "difference *as such* begins to work if and insofar as it can be treated as information in self-referential systems" (40). To recall Luhmann's earlier example of the value of the deutsche mark, an utterance, once repeated, may retain the same form as *meaning* but lose its status as *information;* it retains the same form but has lost its capacity to "select the system's states" (40)—not because its form has changed but because the state of the system has. This fact draws our attention, in turn, to what Derrida in *Limited Inc* calls the "specific," "pragmatically determined" nature of any instance of undecidability, the emphasis on which would seem to run counter to Luhmann's assertion that "communication is realized if and to the extent that understanding comes about" (147). Here again, however, Derrida and Luhmann converge on the same point from opposite directions; while Derrida emphasizes the *final* undecidability of any signifying instance, Luhmann stresses that even so, systems *must* decide; they must selectively process the difference between information and utterance if they are to achieve adaptive "resonance" with their environments. Thus underneath this apparent divergence is a shared emphasis—against "relativism" and "anything goes" reflexivity—on the determinate specificity of the signifying or communicative instance that must be negotiated, which is precisely why in *Limited Inc* Derrida *rejects* the term "indeterminacy" because it occludes an understanding of the "*determinate* oscillation between possibilities (for example, of meaning, but also of acts)."[39]

In Luhmann as in Derrida, writing takes center stage as the paradigm of communication, but only because it exemplifies a deeper "trace" structure (the *grammè* of the program, as it were) of meaning— a paradigm whose essential logic is for Luhmann only intensified by the sorts of later technical developments, beginning with printing, in which we have already seen Derrida himself keenly interested in texts like *Without Alibi* and *Archive Fever*. In this light, the problem with "oral speech," as Luhmann describes it, is that it threatens to collapse the difference between information and utterance, performatively subordinating information to utterance and presuming their simultaneity— "leaving literally no time for doubt," as Luhmann puts it[40]—in precisely the manner analyzed in Derrida's early critique of the subordination of writing to speaking. But if the value of language is that it is "the medium that increases the understandability of communication beyond the sphere of perception" (160), then writing is its full realization. "Only writing," Luhmann observes, "enforces the clear distinction between information and utterance," and "only writing and printing suggest communicative processes that react, not to the unity of, but to the difference between utterance and information. . . . Writing and printing enforce an experience of the difference that constitutes communication: they are, in this precise sense, more communicative forms of communication" (162–63).

Language, then, may be "a medium distinguished by the use of signs"—one that is capable of "*extending* the repertoire of understandable communication *almost indefinitely in practice*," an achievement whose significance "can hardly be overestimated." But "it rests, however, on functional specification. Therefore one must also keep its boundaries in view" (160). For Luhmann—and this is something like the negative image or reverse aspect of Derrida's early reading of Saussure, specifically his drawing out the full implications of Saussure's contention that language is a diacritical system that operates "without positive terms"—to subsume the dynamics of meaning under the theory of the sign is to ignore what he calls the "basal, recursive self-reference" that "forms the context in which all signs are determined" (71). Hence "the concept of the symbolic generalization of meaning's self-reference replaces the concept of the sign that until now has dominated the theoretical tradition" (94). And it also provides an important bridge between Derrida's contention that the trace structure of writing/communication is not limited to the domain of the human and the linguistic alone—a contention that Luhmann's work allows us to situate within a coevolutionary account of the relations between meaning, communication, language, and the forms of complexity they make possible in psychic and social systems.

For Luhmann, whether or not to understand Derrida precisely in terms of the theoretical tradition of the sign has been a matter of some uncertainty—an uncertainty that mirrors, to a large extent, broader disagreements in theory and philosophy about how Derrida is to be read, and whether, moreover, the same understanding applies to his earlier versus later work.[41] At certain times, Luhmann suggests a high degree of translatability between the two theories, while at others he is concerned to keep his distance.[42] But my point here is not to rehearse these differences (much less to suggest which understanding of Derrida is "right"); nor is it to further systematize the relationship between Luhmann and Derrida along the lines already carried out quite ably by critics such as Dietrich Schwanitz, David Wellbery, Drucilla Cornell, Hans Ulrich Gumbrecht, and others. Rather, my point is to suggest that if systems theory needs deconstruction in the sense I touched on at the outset, then deconstruction also needs systems theory to help carry out work toward which it has, in comparison, only gestured.

This complementarity rests, as I have been arguing, on two fundamental disarticulations in Luhmann that are at the core of Derrida's work as well: the disarticulation of psychic and social systems and, on an even more fundamental level, the disarticulation of the formal dynamics of meaning from language per se. In my view—and I will develop this claim in detail over a range of contexts in the next three chapters—it is from this double disarticulation that the ethical and political ambitions of deconstruction derive. Those ambitions—and how they are motivated by a certain set of theoretical commitments—are aptly expressed by Derrida at moments like this one in the interview "Eating Well," to which I will have occasion to return more than once during these pages:

> If one reinscribes language in a network of possibilities that do not merely encompass it but mark it irreducibly from the inside, everything changes. I am thinking in particular of the mark in general, of the trace, of iterability, of *différance*. These possibilities or necessities, without which there would be no language, *are themselves not only human*. . . . And what I am proposing here should allow us to take into account scientific knowledge about the complexity of "animal languages," genetic coding, all forms of marking within which so-called human language, as original as it might be, does not allow us to "cut" once and for all where we would in general like to cut.[43]

At such moments, Derrida unfolds the implications of the point he first made, for U.S. audiences, in *Of Grammatology:* that the form (and force) of *différance,* the *grammè,* and the trace indicates a recursive, iterative dynamics of meaning that exceeds the rather tidy purview of human linguisticality alone. As Derrida puts it in *Of Grammatology,* "In all senses of the word, writing thus *comprehends* language" (7). And it is on the strength of that theoretical commitment that the ethical issues involved—in this particular case, issues related to what is popularly known as "animal rights"—arise.

Similarly, in a remarkable late essay on Lacan's rendering of the human/animal divide vis-à-vis the "subject of the signifier," which I explore in some detail in the next chapter, the *ethical* question of our obligations to nonhuman beings is generated by a *theoretical* articulation of the force of the trace (versus the Lacanian "signifier") that pushes Derrida's thought very much in the direction of Luhmann's work on the dynamics of meaning in autopoietic systems. As Derrida puts it there, "It is difficult to reserve, as Lacan does, the differentiality of signs for human language only, as opposed to animal coding. What he attributes to signs that, 'in a language' understood as belonging to the human order, 'take on their value from their relations to each other' and so on, and not just from the 'fixed correlation' between signs and reality, can and must be accorded to any code, animal or human."[44]

Not only do such passages make clear that Derrida is offering us not a theory of language, nor even one of writing, but a far more ambitious, and thoroughly posthumanist, account of the paradoxical and deconstructive dynamics of meaning; they also make it clear that the account of meaning in systems theory should be viewed as the "reconstruction of deconstruction," one that provides the sort of rigorously articulated analysis toward which deconstruction only gestures philosophically (but for that very reason, in a sense, more provocatively than the "science" of Luhmann's sociology). This joining of forces between deconstruction and systems theory is crucial, I would like to think, not just from systems theory's vantage but from deconstruction's as well. Derrida points toward this necessity in an important footnote in *Positions*, where he writes:

> The critique of historicism in all its forms seems to me indispensable. . . . The issue would be: can one criticize historicism in the name of something other than *truth and science* (the value of universality, omnitemporality, the infinity of value, etc.), and what happens to science when the *metaphysical* value of *truth* has been put into question, etc? How are the effects of science and of truth to be reinscribed? . . . Finally, it goes without saying that in no case is it a question of a *discourse against truth* or against science. (This is impossible and absurd, as is every heated accusation on this subject.) And when one analyzes systematically the value of truth . . . it is not in order to return naively to a relativist or sceptical empiricism.[45]

If we believe Gunther Teubner, such a perspective only draws into even sharper focus the need to supplement deconstruction with systems theory, whose explanatory force resides not only in a renovation of science that enables it to take account of self-reference and the manifold challenges of constructivism, but also in its ability to link these epistemological innovations to the historical emergence and specificity of particular social forms. Moreover, Teubner suggests, systems theory thus enables us to understand a crucial fact about social and political effectivity that in his view is lost on—or at least lost *in*—deconstruction: that the disclosure of paradox does not in itself threaten the autopoiesis of social systems, a point that in turn bears on the putative political force of deconstruction's philosophical intervention. As Teubner puts it—and this would, I think, actually amount to taking seriously Derrida's insistence on the specific, pragmatically determined character of all instances of iteration and undecidability, now writ large— "Derrida's nightmare" is that

> it is the secret of autopoiesis that social systems are no longer threatened by the paradoxes of their deconstructive reading. Autopoietic self-reproduction means that in routine operations they are constantly de-paradoxifying their foundational paradox. Thus, they are capable of deconstructing deconstruction, of course not in the sense that they can exclude it on a long-term basis but in the sense that they shift, displace, disseminate, historicize deconstruction itself, which drastically changes the conditions of its possibility.[46]

What this suggests for Teubner is that a deconstruction that took account of "the foundational paradoxes of emerging social systems, would need to become historical, especially to recognize its own transformations. While the basic structures of the paradox remain the same, social processes of their invisibilization and the threatening moments of their re-emergence depend on historical contingencies. . . . The distinctions which are used for de-paradoxification," he continues, "are dependent on historical-societal conditions of plausibility, of acceptability, are contingent on binding knowledge in particular societies."[47]

Now one might well argue that Derrida's work—particularly his later investigations of questions of justice in relation to law, rights, and so on (both in his own work and in that of his interlocutors)—is quite cognizant of this fact and indeed does what it does precisely to confront such systems of "binding knowledge" with internal paradoxes and contradictions to which they must respond. But my larger point here is that the ahistorical, asociological character of deconstruction is not at all obviously a *failure* per se on Derrida's part, as Teubner would have it; indeed, it might well be viewed, from the vantage Derrida voices above on the "effects of truth," as a resolutely philosophical *refusal.* Derrida's rejoinder to Teubner would no doubt be that systems theory—even on Luhmann's terms—cannot have its science and eat it too. This is so because, as Luhmann explains, the particular kind of operation that uses distinctions in the services of designation is called "observation." "We are caught once again, therefore, in a circle: the distinction between operation and observation appears itself as an element of observation."[48] Empiricism, in other words, must always give way to contingent (and deconstructable) self-reference, even if we acknowledge that observation takes place always in "pragmatically determined" instances of historical articulation.

From a Derridean point of view, then, the advantage that Teubner finds in Luhmann's historically oriented analysis would simply be referred back to an empiricism whose untenability Luhmann himself makes clear. Luhmann, Derrida would argue, cannot maintain that "there exists no observer-independent, given reality,"[49] and at the same time hold that "self-reference designates the unity that an element, a process, or a system is for itself. 'For itself' means independent of the cut of observation by others."[50] If it is indeed the case that "both attributions, observer attribution and object attribution, are possible," and that "the results can therefore be considered contingent,"[51] then this means from a Derridean point of view that the empiricism on which any historicism depends and tacitly trades is rendered permanently problematic. What we are really dealing with is a specific undecidability, in the domain of meaning, about what sorts of attributions are made, by whom and to whom, and with what particular effects. Thus when Luhmann holds that "the difference between self-reference in the object and self-reference in the analysis, between the observed and the observing system, comes to be reflected in the problem of complexity,"[52] what this really means, in Derridean terms, is "comes to be reflected in the deconstructibility of the very distinctions upon which such a formulation depends."

Moreover, Derrida would surely be the first to argue that even if such distinctions are tenable in "analytical" terms (to take Luhmann's procedure at its word), when they come to be expressed *in language,* then our ability to draw clear boundaries between what Luhmann calls the "empirical," "analytical," and "semantic" dimensions of observation/ description is only further eroded. There are, then, at least three orders of complexity here: the autopoietic self-reference (neither analytical, logical, nor linguistic per se) of any system that makes self-reference and heteroreference a product of its own self-referential closure; a second level of complexity in which some of those autopoietic systems use the form of *meaning* to process environmental complexity and reproduce themselves; and a third level of autopoietic systems that, in addition to using basal self-reference and meaning, also use *language*. To acknowledge as much is, from a Derridean point of view, simply to take account of what we have already discussed as the "contaminating" force of iterability—its "monstrosity," as Derrida puts it—which mitigates against the kind of conceptual ideality that would appear to be in play in Luhmann's assumption that the "empirical," "analytical," and "semantic" dimensions can be so neatly separated. Hence, as Derrida insists in *Limited Inc*, "there can be no rigorous analogy between a scientific theory . . . and a theory of language," and in fact, "it is more 'scientific' to take this limit, if it is one, into account and to treat it as a point of departure for rethinking this or that received concept of 'science' and of 'objectivity'" (118).

What is involved here, then (to return to the text of Derrida's with which we began), is a certain difference between Derrida and Luhmann in relation to thinking "the grammar of the event." As Derrida insisted for over forty years, "I don't know what a grammar of the event can be," except, as Peggy Kamuf puts it in her introduction to *Without Alibi*, as "a reduction, a cancellation of the very thing being called 'event.'"[53] Of course, Luhmann would respond that the only way any of us are even around to declare such an inability at all is precisely on the basis of a prior "reduction" of environmental complexity, one that provides the autopoietic conditions of possibility for raising such questions (or any questions) in the first place. Or in Luhmann's words: "One must be capable of generating both continuity and discontinuity, which is easier in reality than in theory."[54]

2 Language, Representation, and Species
Cognitive Science versus Deconstruction

I WANT TO BEGIN WITH A STORY—a dog story, in fact. It's a story about an experiment in canine signifying abilities that appeared on June 11, 2004, in my hometown newspaper, the *Houston Chronicle*. It was a reprint of an article that appeared that same day in the *Washington Post*, which in turn was about the lead article in the June 11, 2004, issue of *Science*. The *Post* story carried the title "Common Collie or Uberpooch: German Pet's Vocabulary Stuns Scientists." I prefer my hometown headline, "Dogs May Be as Smart as Owners Think They Are," because it unwittingly directs us toward a question that I will insist is essential to addressing these kinds of issues, a question that definitively separates cognitive science (represented here by Daniel Dennett) and deconstruction (in the person, here, of Jacques Derrida). That question is what language is and how it is related to our ideas about subjectivity, consciousness, and the like. And *that* question, in turn, cannot be addressed without investigating our assumptions about what knowledge is and the kinds of knowledge we can have of ourselves and of others—in this case (the hardest case, perhaps) nonhuman others (represented here by the taxonomy *Canis familiaris*). In the most general terms, then, the issue that separates cognitive science and deconstruction is one that goes all the way down, both epistemologically and ethically: whether or not knowledge—including knowledge of our own subjectivity and that of others—is representational and, within that, how we are to construe the relationship between epistemological and ontological questions.

In light of these concerns, the sort of intervention I am attempting here is of particular moment because Daniel Dennett's work is often regarded as a more philosophically attuned version of what is taken to be a core feature of cognitive science generally: that it is thought to be, in its functionalism, resolutely postontological and postrepresentational in precisely this way. In this light, Dennett's work presents itself as a less reductive and more nuanced version of what Terrence Deacon, in *The Symbolic Species,* characterizes as "materialistic reductionism," which offers in theories of mind and consciousness "the dominant alternative to the Cartesian perspective." It is exemplified, he writes, "by the theoretical claim that the mind is like the sort of 'computation' that takes place in electronic computers. In simpler terms, minds are software (programs) run on the hardware (neural circuits) of the brain." The "strong" version of this claim (or the weakest, depending on your point of view) is called "eliminative materialism," which holds that "notions such as mind, intention, belief, thought, representation, and so on will eventually be eliminated in discussions of cognitive processes in favor or more mechanistic synonyms that refer to chemical-electrical signaling processes of the brain. Mentalistic terms, it is suggested, are merely glosses for more complex brain processes that we at present do not understand."[1]

With those contexts in mind, let us return to the story of Rico the Uberpooch (if he is one). According to the various reports, this nine-year-old border collie living in Germany with his human companions has recently been shown in "a series of careful studies" carried out by Julia Fischer, a biologist at the Max Planck Institute for Evolutionary Anthropology in Leipzig (a good pedigree, I'd say), to have "a stunningly large vocabulary of about 200 words" that correspond to a collection of toys, balls, and the like, a range comparable to that of great apes, dolphins, and parrots that have undergone extensive training in language experiments.[2] In these experiments, Rico and his owner were placed in one room, and ten of the dog's toys were placed in another. The dog was then instructed by his owner to retrieve two randomly selected objects named by the owner while the owner remained secluded in the separate room to avoid any chance of Clever Hans activity. In forty tests, Rico was accurate thirty-seven times. Even more impressively, in the next phase of the study, the researchers put seven of his toys in the room along with one he had never seen before. The owner then called out the unfamiliar name of the new toy, and Rico was correct in seven out of ten tries. Finally, in the last phase, researchers tested Rico a month later, and he still remembered the name of the new toy three out of six times without having seen it since the first test—a rate of success equivalent to that of a human three-year-old.[3]

The key finding of the study, we are told, is that Rico is apparently capable of a process called "fast mapping"—an ability to instantly assign a meaning to a new word, a strategy human toddlers use to learn language at a prodigious rate, and a skill thought to be exclusively the province of humans. Rico apparently "can do something scientists thought only humans could do: figure out by process of elimination that a sound he has never heard before must be the name of a toy he has never seen before" (Stein). According to the authors of the study, all of this suggests "that mammals developed abilities to understand sounds before humans learned to speak" (Czuczka), and Rico's remarkable learning abilities "may indicate that some parts of speech comprehension developed separately from human speech." "You don't have to be able to talk to understand," Dr. Fischer observes. And Sue Savage-Rumbaugh—whose language acquisition work at Georgia State University with the bonobo Kanzi is well-known—goes even further in a commentary published in the same issue of *Science,* suggesting that "if Rico had a human vocal tract, one would presume that he should be able to say the names of the items as well, or at least try to do so" (Stein).

Of course, we might well add to this appendix of scientific commentary that appears alongside the publication of the study in *Science* the remarks of Daniel Dennett (the director of the Center for Cognitive Studies at Tufts University), whose books *Consciousness Explained* and *Kinds of Minds: Toward an Understanding of Consciousness* would seem to shed light not only on what we have discovered about the cognitive abilities and mental life of our Uberpooch but also on the ethical implications thereof. Indeed, from Dennett's point of view, it is hard to overstate how much it matters, in ethical terms, that we are able to be as specific as possible about the cognition and consciousness of particular beings. "What makes a mind powerful," he writes, "indeed, what makes a mind conscious—is not what it is made of, or how big it is, but what it can do. Can it concentrate? Can it be distracted? Can it recall earlier events? . . . When such questions as these are answered, we will know everything we need to know about those minds in order to answer the morally important questions."[4] As Dennett puts it, "Membership in the class of things that have minds provides an all-important guarantee: the guarantee of a certain sort of moral standing. Only mind-havers can care; only mind-havers can mind what happens" (4).

As I have already suggested, Dennett's functionalist approach to questions such as "what is a mind-haver?"—not "what *is* it?" but "what can it do?"—is perhaps what he is best known for, but what I want to argue now is that Dennett's apparent functionalism and materialism are unable to escape the spell of the very philosophical tradition (whose most extreme expression is Cartesian idealism) that he supposedly rejects. In *Kinds of Minds* and throughout his work, Dennett rightly rejects the idea that "some central Agent or Boss or Audience" (73)—what he also sometimes calls a "Cartesian puppeteer" (80)—takes in and "appreciates" the information produced by the neural networks and uses it to "steer the ship" of subjectivity (73). In what he debunks as "the myth of double transduction," the nervous system first transduces input from its environment (light, sound, temperature, etc.) into neural signals, and then, in a second moment, "in some special central place, it transduces these trains of impulses into some *other* medium, the medium of consciousness!" (72). "The idea that the network *itself* could assume the role of the inner Boss and thus harbor consciousness seems preposterous," but that is exactly what happens, he argues, in the distributed networks in both brain and body from which consciousness arises (73). To ask for something more—to assume that "what *you* are is something *else,* some Cartesian *res cogitans* in addition to all this brain-and-body activity"—is to "betray a deep confusion," because what you are "just *is* this organization of all the competitive activity between a host of competences that your body has developed" (155–56). To "ask for more" is to remain captive to what he calls "the Cartesian theater," the specter of a disembodied, free-floating "central knower" or "self" who stands aside from and above these processes, at once the product and appreciator of them.

Dennett's apparently robust, materialist account of embodied consciousness and mentation, buttressed by an impressive understanding of neural networks, evolutionary processes, perceptual mechanisms, and the like, would seem to find an apt accompaniment in an understanding of language within the context of a larger prosthetics of signifying systems in all their technicity and exteriority, one that would seem quite consonant with contemporary theorists in the humanities and social sciences from Derrida and Kittler to Bateson and Luhmann.[5] The source of our greater intelligence when compared to our mammalian relatives, he argues, is not the size of our brains but "our habit of *off-loading* as much as possible of our cognitive tasks into the environment itself—extruding our minds (that is, our mental projects and activities) into the surrounding world, where a host of peripheral devices we construct can store, process, and re-present our meanings, streamlining, enhancing, and protecting the processes of transformation that *are* our thinking"—a process that "releases us from the limitations of our animal brains." And "thanks to our prosthetically enhanced imaginations," he continues, "we can formulate otherwise imponderable, unnoticeable metaphysical possibilities."[6]

The problem is that it is not clear how such prosthetic processes and devices can be said to constitute—to "store, process, and *re-present*" (in Dennett's words)—"our" thinking. After all, if we pay attention to the material, social, technical, and cultural complexities of such devices, then in what sense can the internal psychic states Dennett calls "our thinking" be said to be "re-presented" by such devices? And this is obviously true not just for storage devices such as archives, encyclopedias, books, and the institutional and disciplinary contexts in which they are embedded, but also for that first and most fundamental prosthesis of all, language itself, which cannot be said to "re-present" "our" thinking for at least two reasons. First, as Niklas Luhmann has put it (with characteristic astringency), language, like all forms of communication, "operates with an unspecific reference to the participating state of mind; it is especially unspecific as to perception. It cannot copy states of mind, cannot imitate them, cannot represent them."[7] Second, there can be no "re-presentation" of "our" thinking in language because the meaning of an utterance is always subject to differential interpretation, an interpretation that itself takes place within multiply embedded protocols, traditions, conventions, and so on. (If this weren't the case, then it would be a private language, and we couldn't use it to communicate "our" thinking at all.) All of which—as David Wills has reminded us in multiple registers in his wonderful book *Prosthesis* (and elsewhere)— is built in to the very logic of the prosthetic itself. As Wills puts it, we are dealing here with technologies "of the exteriorization of memory of which writing is a, if not *the,* fundamental historically identifiable form." And this has serious consequences for how we think about subjectivity, because "technology, in these terms, is the extemporization, the movement out of self-presence that permits and defines memory," a "prosthetization of the animate or the human" that not only makes it difficult to rigorously "distinguish the human from its inanimate other" but also makes us "forever removed from ourselves" as the very condition of what it means to be human.[8]

But the primary problem with Dennett, as we are about to see, is not just that he overlooks how the prosthetic nature of the human permanently destabilizes the boundaries between "our" thinking and anyone—or more radically, any*thing*—else's. It is that he then—in a subsidiary move—uses a fundamentally representationalist concept of language that reinstalls the disembodied Cartesian subject at the very heart of his supposedly embodied, materialist functionalism. Indeed, it is on this basis that the ontologically unique status of the human—and all the ethical consequences that flow from it—is established in Dennett's work.

Now few would argue with Dennett's observation that "there is no step more uplifting, more explosive, more momentous in the history of mind design that the invention of language," through which *Homo sapiens* "stepped into a slingshot that has launched it far beyond all other earthly species in the power to look ahead and reflect." But we begin to glimpse the problem with Dennett's theory in passages like the following: "The free-floating rationales that explain rudimentary higher-order intentionality of birds and hares—and even chimpanzees—are honored," he writes, "in the designs of their nervous systems, but we are looking for something more: we are looking for rationales that are *represented* in those nervous systems."[9]

The problem here is not, as he argues in "Animal Consciousness: What Matters and Why," his insistence that we should be "analyzing patterns of behavior (external and internal—but not 'private'), and attempting to interpret them in the light of evolutionary hypotheses regarding their past or current functions."[10] The problem here is that this "something more" turns out to be another version of the very "user-illusion" that Dennett wants to reject—a user-illusion provided by

Dennett's misunderstanding of language as something that can "represent rationales in a nervous system," as he puts it.

I want to pause for a moment to emphasize, however briefly—in part to make it clear that I am not just picking on Dennett—that this theoretical misunderstanding and phenomenological misuse of language are common problems in work in and around the philosophical implications of cognitive science, and I find them even in work that I admire by Gerald Edelman, Humberto Maturana, and Francisco Varela, among others.[11] Indeed—to take only the last example—Maturana and Varela offer an extremely valuable account of the evolutionary emergence of language proper from "linguistic domains"—an account that reaches back to Gregory Bateson's important work on "meta-communicative frames" in mammalian communication (especially in forms of "play"), and forward to the latest work in these areas by Noam Chomsky, Marc Hauser, and others.[12] Maturana and Varela rightly conclude that, on the basis of experimental evidence, some nonhuman animals are "capable of interacting with us in rich and even recursive linguistic domains," and they even declare that, based on these facts, language remains "a permanent biologic possibility in the natural drift of living beings."[13] But though it is certainly useful (to combine their language now with Bateson's) to distinguish participation in a meta-communicative frame ("linguistic domains") from the meta-meta-communicative frame that is language proper—the ability to make "a linguistic distinction of a linguistic distinction" (210), as they put it—it is question-begging in the extreme, as we have already seen, to make the ontological category of subjectivity depend solely on this last attribute. For as we have already seen, to declare, as Maturana and Varela do, that "self-consciousness, awareness, mind—these are phenomena that take place in language" (230), is to make a statement that, if it is true, is self-refuting (since, as Luhmann would put it, only *language* takes place in language—which is to say, in a domain *external* to the "self" of "self-consciousness").

To return, then, to Dennett: he argues that "the sort of informational unification that is the most important prerequisite for *our* kind of consciousness is not anything we are born with, not part of our innate 'hard-wiring,' but in surprisingly large measure is an artifact of our immersion in human culture." So far, so good. But then Dennett's formulation takes a bizarre turn indeed:

What that early education produces in us is a sort of benign "user-illusion"—I call it the Cartesian Theater: the illusion that there is a place in our brains where the show goes on, towards which all perceptual "input" streams, whence flow all "conscious intentions" to act and speak. I claim that other species—and human beings when they are newborn—simply *are not beset* by the illusion of the Cartesian Theater. Until the organization is formed, there is simply no user in there to be fooled.[14]

But how, one might ask, is this really any different from the Cartesianism that Dennett rejects, particularly when we remember his insistence on the difference between "the free-floating rationales that explain rudimentary higher-order intentionality of birds and hares" that are merely a product of "the designs of their nervous systems" and the "something more" of human intentionality and consciousness, "rationales that are *represented* in those nervous systems"?

Take, for example, the tortured trajectory of the following argument: "Many animals hide but don't think they are hiding. Many animals flock but don't think they are flocking," Dennett argues in *Kinds of Minds;*[15] they have "know-how," as he puts it, but not "represented knowledge" (154). Eventually, some creatures began

off-loading problems into the world, and just into other parts of their brains. They began making and using representations, but they didn't know they were doing so. They didn't need to know. Should we call this sort of unwitting use of representations "thinking"? If so, then we would have to say that these creatures were thinking, but didn't know they were thinking! Unconscious thinking—those with a taste for "paradoxical" formulations might favor this way of speaking, but we could less misleadingly say that this was *intelligent but unthinking* behavior, because it was not just not reflective but also not reflectable-upon. (154)

The problem here is that "reflectable-upon" behavior and "represented knowledge" in Dennett's scheme depend on the assumption that language can provide, by means of a grammatical fiction, the very user-illusion that Dennett has just disavowed. Doubly problematic is that this conceptual and phenomenological restabilization of the subject by means of language—putting Humpty Dumpty back together again, as it were—not only constitutes an illusion but also forms the very ontological specificity of the human itself, an ontological specificity that is no different in principle from the Cartesianism Dennett rejects. Only here language is doing the work previously carried out by the Cartesian *cogito*.

As an example of such "intelligent but unthinking" behavior, Dennett offers the "distraction display" among some species of low-nesting birds, who, when predators approach their nest, put on an ostentatious show of feigned injury, captivating the predator's attention and promising an easy kill that the predator, now drawn away from the vulnerable eggs, is never quite able to make (121–22). Such behaviors among nonhuman animals are quite abundant and well-known, but none of them, Dennett argues, manifests what he calls the workings of a "third-order intentional system":

> An important step toward becoming a person was the step up from a *first-order* intentional system to a *second-order* intentional system. A first-order intentional system has beliefs and desires about many things, but *not* about beliefs and desires. A second-order intentional system has beliefs and desires about beliefs and desires, its own or those of others. A third-order intentional system would be capable of such feats as *wanting* you to believe that it *wanted* something. (120)

If this has a familiar ring to it, it should, because it is exactly the strategy that Jacques Lacan famously uses—in his essay of 1960, "The Subversion of the Subject and the Dialectic of Desire in the Freudian Unconscious"[16]—to juridically separate the human from the animal as that being, alone among the living, who can *lie by telling the truth*. The animal, in Lacan's terms, can pretend, but not *pretend to pretend*— only the human, as "subject of the signifier," can do that. As Jacques Derrida summarizes Lacan's position in a recent essay—and here the distance between Dennett's discourse and Lacan's will become absolutely minimal:

> There is, according to Lacan, a clear distinction between what the animal is capable of, namely, strategic pretense . . . and what it is incapable of and incapable of witnessing to, namely, the deception of speech [*la tromperie de la parole*] within the order of the signifier and of Truth. The deception of speech . . . involves lying to the extent that, in promising what is true, it includes the supplementary possibility of telling the truth in order to lead the other astray, on order to have him believe something

other than what is true (we know the Jewish story recounted by Freud and so often quoted by Lacan: "Why do you tell me that you are going to X in order to have me believe you are going to Y whereas you are indeed going to X?"). According to Lacan, the animal would be incapable of this type of lie, of this deceit, of this pretense in the second degree, whereas the "subject of the signifier," within the human order, would possess such a power and, better still, would emerge as subject, instituting itself and coming to itself as subject *by virtue of this power,* a second-degree reflexive power, a power that is *conscious* of being able to deceive by pretending to pretend.[17]

As I have already suggested, one of the ironies of Dennett's discourse is that even as it promises a rigorous, clear-headed view of these complexities—"Don't confuse ontological questions (about what exists) with epistemological questions (about how we know about it)!" he admonishes in the opening pages of *Kinds of Minds*—it reproduces *in detail* the Cartesian position it claims to move beyond, and does so, moreover, precisely because it is unwilling or unable to pursue the full implications of the "'paradoxical' formulations" (such as "intelligent but unthinking behavior") that it leads itself into but refuses to think through.

As Derrida's later work makes clear, that Cartesianism rests on two fundamental points: (1) the assertion that animals, however sophisticated they may be, can only "react" but not "respond" to what goes on around them. And this is so because (2) the capacity to respond depends on the ability to wield concepts or representations, which is in turn possible only on the basis of language—and precisely in the sense voiced by Dennett when he writes, "No matter how close a dog's 'concept' of cat is to yours extensionally (you and the dog discriminate the same sets of entities as cats and noncats), it differs radically in one way: the dog cannot consider its concept. . . . No languageless mammal can have a concept of snow in the way we can, because a languageless mammal has no way of considering snow 'in general' or 'in itself.'"[18]

Two points need to be registered here—one experimental or scientific, as it were, and one philosophical. First, as Donna Haraway has recently pointed out, the entire picture of language and nonhuman mental life has become considerably more complicated during the past several years. Indeed, even Noam Chomsky has recently argued, in a paper coauthored with two Harvard researchers, that "the available data suggests a much stronger continuity between animals and humans with respect to speech than previously believed. We argue that the continuity hypothesis thus deserves the status of a null hypothesis, which must be rejected by comparative work before any claims of uniqueness can be validated. For now, this null hypothesis of no truly novel traits in the speech domain appears to stand." This conclusion is based in no small part on the authors' contention that even if we distinguish between language in the broad sense—"composed of many interacting subsystems (sensori-motor and computational-intentional) that do not necessarily evolve as a unit," as Haraway puts it—and language in a more narrow sense (the recursive ability to "generate an infinite range of expressions from a finite set of elements," as they write), linguistic uniqueness in this second sense "must be a testable hypothesis, not an assumption rooted in premises of human exceptionalism" (in Haraway's words).[19] Most of the recent experimental data, as it happens, does not tend in the direction of an unquestioned exceptionalism. In fact, Chomsky and his colleagues argue that the "powerful capacities" such as those that manifest themselves in the capability of "discrete infinity" that characterizes language in the narrow sense "might well have evolved," in Haraway's words, "in domains other than communication (such as territory mapping, spatial navigation, and foraging) and then been hijacked for communication in ways uncoupled from tight constraints of function" (373n44). And this, of course, has profound implications for the ontological—and eventually, ethical—status of nonhuman beings, for it would lead us to disarticulate these questions from language ability in the limited sense, rather than assimilate and collapse them, as Dennett has done. As Marc Hauser— one of Chomsky's coauthors—argues in a separate study (and again I quote Haraway), this means that "organisms possess heterogeneous sets of mental tools, complexly and dynamically put together from genetic, developmental, and learning interactions throughout their lives, not unitary interiors that one either has or does not have."[20]

This, in turn, leads me to my second point, the philosophical one: that Dennett's supposedly hard-nosed, materialist account of embodied consciousness falls in line not just with the philosophical idealism of Descartes but also that of Heidegger, whose characterization of the animal as that which "has a world in the mode of not-having" depends, as Derrida argues in *Of Spirit,* on the inability of the animal to "have access to entities *as such* and in their Being" because of a lack of language that is "not primarily or simply linguistic" but rather, as Derrida puts it, "derives from the properly *phenomenological* impossibility of speaking the phenomenon."[21] In light of Derrida's critique, then, Dennett's discourse takes its place in a long line of philosophers from Aristotle to Lacan, Kant, Heidegger, and Levinas, all of whom, as Derrida puts it, "say the same thing: the animal is without language. Or more precisely unable to respond, to respond with a response that could be precisely and rigorously distinguished from a reaction."[22] "Even those who, from Descartes to Lacan, have conceded to the said animal some aptitude for signs and for communication," Derrida continues, "have always denied it the power to *respond*—to *pretend,* to *lie,* to *cover its tracks* or *erase* its own traces"—hence the fallback position we find here in Dennett and Lacan, when more explicitly metaphysical versions of humanism are no longer available: the difference between communication and metacommunication, signifying and signifying *about* signifying, thinking and *knowing* you're thinking, and so on.

But the problem with this position, as Derrida points out, is that "it seems difficult in the first place to identify or determine a limit, that is to say an indivisible threshold between pretense and pretense of pretense." "How could one distinguish," he continues,

> for example in the most elementary sexual parade or mating game, between a feint and a feint of a feint? If it is impossible to provide the criterion for such a distinction, one can conclude that every pretense of pretense remains a simple pretense (animal or imaginary, in Lacan's terms), or else, on the contrary, and just as likely, the every pretense, however simple it may be, gets repeated and reposited undecidably, in its possibility, as pretense of pretense (human or symbolic in Lacan's terms). . . . Pretense presupposes taking the other into account; it therefore supposes, simultaneously, the pretense of pretense—a simple supplementary move by the other within the strategy of the game. That supplementarity is at work from the moment of the first pretense.[23]

The distinction between the inscription of the trace and its erasure as the means by which to juridically separate the human from animal fares no better. As Derrida argues in that same essay—"and this is why so long ago I substituted the concept of trace for that of signifier," he begins by saying—"the structure of the trace presupposes that *to trace* amounts to *erasing a trace* as much as to imprinting it. . . . How can it be denied that the simple substitution of one trace for another, the marking of their diacritical difference in the most elementary inscription—which capacity Lacan concedes to the animal—involves erasure as much as it involves the imprint? It is as difficult to assign a frontier between pretense and pretense of pretense, to have an indivisible line pass through the middle of a feigned feint, as it is to assign one between inscription and erasure of the trace" (137; first italics mine). The point here, as Derrida argues, is "less a matter of asking whether one has the right to refuse the animal such and such a power . . . than of asking whether what calls itself human has the right to rigorously attribute to man . . . what he refuses the animal, and whether he can ever possess the *pure, rigorous, indivisible* concept, as such, of that attribution. Thus, were we even to suppose—something I am not ready to concede—that the 'animal' were incapable of covering its tracks, by what right could one concede that power to the human, to the 'subject of the signifier'?" (138).

What Derrida helps us to see—and we can only see it if we have the "taste for 'paradoxical' formulations" that Dennett suggests we ignore—is that just because a particular discourse operates within parameters and conventions that we think of as "scientific," or presents itself as a materialist rendering of the problem of consciousness in relation to embodiment, does not mean that the discourse is not metaphysical. As a *methodological* consideration for such a discourse, language appears as a rather unimportant, second-order phenomenon whose job is to be as transparent as possible to the concepts (and beyond that, the objects) it represents (which is why the eventual goal for "materialistic reductionism" can be to eliminate language altogether). At the same time, paradoxically, this apparently insubstantial thing called language constitutes the phenomenological and indeed ontological and ethical divide between human and nonhuman subjectivity; paradoxically, it constitutes the phenomenological specificity of the very being who then, in an idealist abstraction if ever there was one, rises above it to deploy it literally at will—or, in Dennett's terms, by "intention."

Indeed, what Derrida writes about Austin and speech act theory in "Signature Event Context" applies even more pointedly to the recovery and maintenance of the humanist subject in Dennett, as what Derrida there calls "a free consciousness present to the totality of the operation, and of absolutely meaningful speech *[vouloir-dire]* master of itself: the teleological jurisdiction of an entire field whose organizing center remains *intention*"—an intention that expresses itself, for instance, in the difference between pretending and pretending to pretend, thinking and knowing you're thinking, and so on.[24] And this, as we will see in multiple contexts throughout the next two chapters, has far-reaching consequences for the rigor and objectivity of the knowledge that we think we can have of ourselves and of other, nonhuman beings, a rigor and objectivity that analytical philosophy and cognitive science have typically reserved for themselves over and against the "merely epistemological" quandaries of poststructuralist philosophy. For as Derrida points out, "it is not certain that what we call language or speech acts can ever be exhaustively determined by an objective science or theory"; indeed, "it is more 'scientific' to take this limit . . . into account and to treat it as a point of departure for rethinking this or that received concept of 'science' and of 'objectivity.'"[25]

All of this might be viewed as "merely theoretical," if you like, were it not for the fact that Dennett himself insists that the ethical stakes of determining which creatures have minds—a determination that depends, in turn, on a specific relation to language—are dire indeed. On the one hand, Dennett argues that "the ethical course is to err on the side of overattribution, just to be safe," when considering the possibility of nonhuman minds, because the ethical consequences of being niggardly and then later being found wrong could be grave.[26] At the same time, however, he writes: "'It may not be able to talk, but surely it thinks!'—one of the main aims of this book has been to shake your confidence in this familiar reaction" (159). But because a deeply flawed theory of talking is central to a representationalist notion of thinking in Dennett's work, and because only things that think (that is to say, both think *and know* they are thinking) have minds, and because only things that have minds (and, we might add, *know* they have minds!) merit ethical consideration, Dennett is forced to embrace ethical implications that, despite his generous gestures to the contrary, would seem to run counter to the supposed point of his entire project, which is to take seriously the status—epistemologically and ethically—of different kinds of minds.

Take, for example, Dennett's rendering of the difference between pain and suffering, which unwittingly reproduces the very Cartesianism that Dennett has time and again declared the enemy. Dennett writes that "we might well think that the capacity for suffering counts for more, in any moral calculations, than the capacity for abstruse and sophisticated reasoning" (162).[27] But on this point, Dennett follows Descartes almost to the letter. Descartes—who is often misunderstood on this point—insisted not that animals do not feel those sensations we call pain but only that they do not *experience* them as suffering because there is "no one home," no subject of the *cogito* to do the experiencing; and thus the pain is not morally relevant.[28] Similarly, Dennett argues that "for such states to matter—whether or not we call them pains, or conscious states, or experiences—there must be an enduring subject *to whom* they matter because they are a source of suffering" (161).

My point here, of course, is not that human and nonhuman animals all experience the same kinds or levels of suffering; even the most ardent animal rights philosophers, such as Peter Singer, agree that they do not.[29] My point is that the difference between "pain" and "suffering" in Dennett turns out to be not just a difference in degree but a difference in *kind,* an *ontological* difference, one that simply reproduces on another level the difference between thinking and knowing you're thinking, having thoughts and having represented thoughts, and so on.[30] The problem, in other words, is with the unwitting Cartesianism of Dennett's "enduring subject," which in turn leads him (not surprisingly) to embrace some ethical conclusions that should, I think, give us pause. For example, when Dennett attempts to draw out the ethical consequences of his contention that "human consciousness . . . is a necessary condition for serious suffering" (165), he ends up suggesting that "a dissociated child does not suffer as much as a non-dissociated child" (164). And just as different forms of being human in the world are rewritten, as they are here, in terms of a homogeneous Cartesian ideal, so nonhuman beings, in all their diversity, are now rendered not as fully complete forms of life that are radically irreducible to such a thin, idealized account of what counts as subjectivity but rather as diminished or crippled versions of that fantasy figure called the human—the Cartesian *cogito* now rewritten as the user-illusion qua enduring subject. Nonhuman animals are now seen as "creatures that are *naturally* dissociated—that never achieve, or even attempt to achieve, the sort of complex internal organization that is standard in a normal child and disrupted in a dissociated child" (164).

The problem here is not the ethical foregrounding of pain and suffering. The problem is that Dennett's ontological distinction between pain and suffering is based on a set of phantom abilities, anchored by but not limited to language and its imagined representational capacities in relation to the world of things, that no subject, either nonhuman or human, possesses in fact. I will return to these issues in much greater detail in the next chapter, but for the moment we can get an even sharper sense of this by reference to Derrida's very different approach to the question of nonhuman suffering, which takes place, ironically enough, by way of the utilitarian philosopher Jeremy Bentham, who anchors the animal rights philosophy of Peter Singer. The relevant question here, Bentham asserts, is not "can they talk?" or "can they reason?" but "can they *suffer*?" For Derrida, putting the question in this way "changes everything," because "from Aristotle to Descartes, from Descartes, especially, to Heidegger, Levinas and Lacan,"—and, we might add, to Dennett—posing the question of the animal in terms of the capacity for either thought or language "determines so many others concerning *power* or *capability [pouvoirs]*, and *attributes [avoirs]*: being able, having the power to give, to die, to bury one's dead, to dress, to work, to invent a technique."³¹ What makes Bentham's reframing of the problem so powerful is that now "the question is disturbed by a certain *passivity* . . . a not-being-able." "What of the vulnerability felt on the basis of this inability?" Derrida continues; "what is this non-power at the heart of power? . . . What right should be accorded it? To what extent does it concern us?" It concerns us directly, in fact, for "mortality resides there, as the most radical means of thinking the finitude that we share with animals, the mortality that belongs to the very finitude of life, to the experience of compassion."³²

From this vantage—to return now to the story with which we began—we can derive from the exploits of Rico the Uberpooch an unexpected lesson whose ethical as well as epistemological resonance we are now in a position to appreciate: that even though thinking about the consciousness, intelligence, and emotional and mental lives of nonhuman animals in terms of their linguistic abilities has historically been a crucial means for getting such questions on the table *at all*,[33] it may not be the best way, and it is certainly not the only way, of approaching these questions. Indeed—and I will explore this point on a much broader canvas in my discussion of Temple Grandin in chapter 5— Rico's prodigious signifying abilities may be only one sign among many others (and only the one most readily legible to us, as language-dependent creatures) of a thinking (if that's what we want to call it) that we ought to be interested in not because it is a diminished or dim approximation of ours but because it is part of a very different way of being in the world that calls on us to rethink, ever anew and vigilantly so, what we mean by "person," "mind," "consciousness"—that entire cluster of terms and the ethical implications that flow from them. In this light, as Derrida suggests, "It would not be a matter of 'giving speech back' to animals, but perhaps of acceding to a thinking, however fabulous and chimerical it might be, that thinks the absence of the name and of the word otherwise, as something other than a privation."[34]

What I am suggesting here is that your theory of language matters, and it matters not just epistemologically (as we'll see in chapter 3) or methodologically (chapter 4) because all sorts of consequences, both ontological and ethical, follow in its wake—consequences that I have here tried to draw out on the terrain of the question of species difference and the question of subjectivity. But I am also suggesting that there is an interdisciplinary imperative we need to undertake when addressing such complex questions. If it is true that cognitive science has an enormous amount to contribute to the area of philosophy that we used to call phenomenology—if it has even, in a way, taken it over— then it is also true that the textually oriented humanities have much to teach cognitive science about what language is (and isn't) and how that, in turn, bears on any possible philosophy of the subject (human or animal). This is simply to say that it will take all hands on deck, I think, to fully comprehend what amounts to a new reality: that the human occupies a new place in the universe, a universe now populated by what I am prepared to call nonhuman subjects. And this is why, to me, post-humanism means not the triumphal surpassing or unmasking of something but an increase in the vigilance, responsibility, and humility that accompany living in a world so newly, and differently, inhabited.

3   Flesh and Finitude

Bioethics and the Philosophy of the Living

But who, me?

—JACQUES DERRIDA, *Limited Inc*

Bioethics, Inc.

What is bioethics now? With what questions is it properly concerned? And how is its ability to address those questions predisposed or foreclosed by a certain set of theoretical and philosophical commitments? To ask the question "What can bioethics be thinking?" is to raise the question of not just its institutional norms, which are powerfully vested indeed, but also its philosophical norms. In that light, I will make the case that bioethics in its dominant mode of practice needs to undertake what one recent philosopher calls (following Wittgenstein) a "grammatical redescription"[1] of its chosen domain if it is to more fully and responsibly address the "bio-" of "bioethics"—the question of what Derrida calls simply (but not so simply) "the living in general."[2] At stake here is not just a style of doing philosophy, but more important who and what can count as a subject of ethical address. And from this vantage, one of the central ironies of bioethics in its dominant institutionalized form is that it is subtended by a certain notion of the human that remains—despite wave after wave of changes in our understanding of the "bio-" of bioethics—not only uninterrogated but indeed retrenched, and nowhere more clearly (or more predictably) than in the confidence with which the boundary between human and nonhuman animals is taken for granted as an ethical (non)issue—the very difference, ironically enough, that would seem thrown completely open to question by the very biotechnical and scientific developments with which contemporary bioethics is so concerned.

I make no pretense at giving anything like a complete picture of contemporary bioethics, but I can at least provide a snapshot with reference to one or two of its best-known practitioners. A glance at the table of contents of one of the leading textbooks in the field, the collection *Contemporary Issues in Bioethics,* edited by Tom Beauchamp and LeRoy Walters, will give at least some sense of the sorts of issues that occupy the field: (1) "patient-professional relationships," with particular focus on "patients' rights" and "specific patient populations" (this last including essays on involuntary hospitalization of the mentally ill, medicine in an aging society, and "caring for 'socially undesirable' patients," among others); (2) "management of medical information," with essays focusing on issues of confidentiality and the law, "patient self-determination," informed consent, and the truthful disclosure of "bad news" to patients and families; (3) abortion and "maternal-fetal relations," with essays debating the moral and legal aspects of abortion and the rights of mothers to pursue or decline various types of treatment; (4) euthanasia and assisted suicide, including legal aspects of the patient's refusal of treatment, "voluntary active euthanasia" as well as physician-assisted suicide, and a concluding pair of essays about "the right to die"; (5) "justice in the distribution of health care," which leads off a section on access to health care (here the reader will find essays on managed care and universal access and health-care "rationing"); (6) biomedical research and technology, with essays predominantly on ethical issues and past abuses in human research subjects, and a smaller section on ethical issues in animal research; (7) eugenics and human genetics, including essays on eugenics programs in the twentieth century (including Nazi Germany and population control in China), a suite on the Human Genome Project, and another on human gene therapy and genetic enhancement; (8) a section on reproductive technologies and surrogate parenting arrangements, including infertility, in vitro fertilization, cloning, and "regulating assisted reproduction"; and (9) public health and the global AIDS epidemic, with sections on "the duty to warn and not to harm," testing and screening programs, and issues in clinical research on HIV/AIDS.[3]

Of particular interest here too are the particular sorts of documents and authors included. To be sure, one finds the usual academic essay in abundance, but roughly 25 to 30 percent of the contributions are from legal, corporate, governmental, or professional organizations or bodies. We find, for example, the American Medical Association's Council on Ethical and Judicial Affairs contributing a document titled "Fundamental Elements of the Patient-Physician Relationship" (v), the American Hospital Association providing "A Patient's Bill of Rights" (vi), contributions by the President's Advisory Commission on Consumer Protection and Quality in the Health Care Industry, the Council of Europe, the World Medical Association and similar bodies, and a large number of legal documents and rulings by the Court of Appeals of both the United States and the District of Columbia, Supreme Courts of both the United States and California, and various branches of state and federal government. All of which raises a question that goes to the very heart of contemporary bioethics: the question of "codification," which involves, as Derrida notes, the complex interrelations between those who theorize the rules and norms and those who legislate and *enforce* them.[4] In that light, the first point I'd like to make about what this snapshot suggests—and this is the first sense in which I intend the "Inc." of my heading to resonate—is that contemporary bioethics in its most institutionally powerful form is largely if not exclusively within the purview of *policy studies* and, within that, policies in health care and medicine, with all the strings attached that one might expect. From this vantage, the very title "bioethics" is itself misleading insofar as the word means an "ethics" of *the living* and not, say, "biomedical research and health care decision-making procedures."

Indeed, contemporary bioethics is best understood, perhaps, not as an ethics at all, in the sense that someone like Derrida will use the word, but rather as a textbook example of what Michel Foucault has analyzed as the rise of "biopower" during the modern period. According to Foucault, power before the eighteenth century consisted chiefly in the right to decide life and death, the right "to *take* life or *let* live"; more broadly—and derivative of this—it was "a subtraction mechanism, a right to a portion of the wealth, a tax of products, goods and services . . . essentially a right of seizure: of things, time, bodies, and ultimately life itself." But the eighteenth century saw the emergence and consolidation of a different kind of power, one that Foucault characterizes as not "juridical" but rather "strategic," "a power bent on generating forces, making them grow, and ordering them, rather than one dedicated to impeding them, making them submit, or destroying them. There has been a parallel shift in the right of death, or at least a tendency to align itself with the exigencies of a life-administering power and to define itself accordingly. This death that was based on the right of the sovereign is now manifested as simply the reverse of the right of the social body to ensure, maintain, or develop its life" by means of "a power that exerts a positive influence on life, that endeavors to administer, optimize, and multiply it, subjecting it to precise controls and comprehensive regulations."[5]

As Foucault puts it in one of the more important passages in all of his later work, one worth quoting at length:

> This was nothing less than the entry of life into history, that is, the entry of phenomena peculiar to the life of the human species into the order of knowledge and power, into the sphere of political techniques. It is not a question of claiming that this was the moment when the first contact between life and history was brought about. On the contrary, the pressure exerted by the biological on the historical had remained very strong for thousands of years; epidemics and famine were the two great dramatic forms of this relationship that was always dominated by the menace of death. But through a circular process, the economic— and primarily agricultural—development of the eighteenth century, and an increase in productivity and resources . . . allowed a measure of relief from these profound threats: despite some renewed outbreaks, the period of great ravages from starvation and plague had come to a close before the French Revolution; death was ceasing to torment life so directly . . . Western man was gradually learning what it meant to be a living species in a living world, to have a body, conditions of existence, probabilities of life, an individual and collective welfare, forces that could be modified, and a space in which they could be distributed in an optimal manner. For the first time in history, no doubt, biological existence was reflected in political existence. (264)

Within this general historical shift and mutation in the forms of power comprising modern society, the areas of health and what will come to be called the biomedical take on new, politically central roles directly linked to the reproduction of both the state and capitalist relations (263). "Such a power," Foucault continues, "has to qualify, measure, appraise, and hierarchize, rather than display itself in its murderous splendor. . . . The judicial institution is increasingly incorporated into a continuum of apparatuses (medical, administrative, and so on) whose functions are for the most part regulatory" (266). In this context, he argues, "the emergence of the health and physical well-being of the population in general" becomes "one of the essential objectives of political power," which focuses on "how to raise the level of health of the social body as a whole. Different power apparatuses are called upon to take charge of 'bodies,' not simply to exact blood service from them or levy dues, but to help and, if necessary, constrain them to ensure their own good health. The imperative of health: at once the duty of each and the objective of all."[6] Not surprisingly, then:

> Medicine, as a general technique of health even more than as a service to the sick or an art of cures, assumes an increasingly important place in the administrative system and the machinery of power—a role which is constantly widened and strengthened throughout the eighteenth century. The doctor wins a footing within the different instances of social power. The administration acts as a point of support and sometimes a point of departure for the great medical inquiries into the health of populations, and conversely doctors devote an increasing amount of their activity to tasks, both general and administrative, assigned to them by power. A "medico-administrative" knowledge begins to develop concerning society, its health and sickness, its conditions of life, housing, and habits, which serves as the basic core for the "social economy" and sociology of the nineteenth century. And there is likewise constituted a politico-medical hold on a population hedged in by a whole series of prescriptions relating not only to disease but to general forms of existence and behavior.[7]

As even a cursory glance at the table of contents of *Contemporary Issues in Bioethics* suggests, bioethics as it is currently institutionalized represents something like the apotheosis of this medico-administrative edifice and its dense imbrication in contemporary apparatuses and institutions of state and economic power, serving, as it were, as its self-designated conscience. The obvious problem with this is that the functions of conscience and those of establishing policies palatable to both state and economic power do not always or even often go hand in hand, and while there may be precious few compulsions on the side of conscience for the field of bioethics, there is no shortage of them on the side of policy. Indeed, professional bioethicists routinely cultivate relations with the biomedical research industry and its university liaisons that would seem to mitigate against the kind of skepticism and autonomy that the role of self-designated conscience would demand.[8]

Of course, practicing bioethicists would be the first to say that they *must* do this if they are not to be cut out of the decision-making process about biomedical research policy altogether—but that simply proves the point that in contemporary bioethics, the tail does indeed wag the dog in an arrangement that one critic calls *Real Ethik:* "To simply declare certain procedures [such as human cloning] immoral and call for an immediate and permanent ban is to ignore brazenly the history of technology, one lesson of which might fairly be summarized as 'If it can be done, it will be done.'" This dictates what one bioethicist calls a "pragmatic approach" to bioethics, in which, for example, we are wasting our time "huffing and puffing about an international ban on human cloning." "Get over it," he asserts, "it's not going to happen."[9]

Of course, such a position—which might be characterized as dropping the pretense that the fox is not guarding the chicken coop—might well be a cause for concern, and some of it has come from within the community of bioethicists themselves. Carl Elliott, who is concerned to make the field more philosophically nuanced and responsive to the real complexities it faces, puts it this way: "If the occupational hazard of philosophy is uselessness, that of medicine is an unthinking pragmatism. When bioethics is driven solely by clinical concerns, usually those of the hospital, it runs the danger of getting stuck in a permanent feedback loop in which the same issues are discussed again and again. . . . Constrained by the demand for immediately useful answers, clinical ethics (at its worst, at any rate) comes dangerously close to being a purely technical enterprise carried out in isolation from any kind of deep reflection about the examined life." It will come as no surprise, then, as Elliott puts it, that "the law is the *lingua franca* of bioethics. The language in which bioethics is discussed revolves around largely quasi-legal notions such as consent, competence, rights to refuse treatment, to have an abortion and so on. Many writers have targeted the language of rights and autonomy for special criticism. . . . But I also think that the law's influence on bioethics has been much deeper and more subtle. It has given us a picture of morality as somehow like the law in *structure*."[10]

One last glance at *Contemporary Issues in Bioethics* will help make the point. The collection is fronted by an opening section on ethical theory, at whose core lies a section titled "Ethical Principles," of which in the authors' view there are three primary ones: "respect for autonomy," "beneficence," and "justice."[11] The first, emerging from an essentially Kantian view of the person as end and not means, is defined as "freedom from external constraint and the presence of critical mental capacities such as understanding, intending, and voluntary decision-making capacity" (a picture of the subject, drawn from the liberal philosophical tradition, that we will have ample opportunity to scrutinize later). In this view, if autonomy is to be limited, it is only because it conflicts with one or both of the other two principles: beneficence, which is defined as the "active promotion of good, kindness, and charity," including the core directive *primum non nocere* (above all, do no harm) (20); and the principle of justice, which the authors define in the following way: "Common to all theories of justice is a minimal, beginning principle. Like cases should be treated alike, or, to use the language of equality, equals ought to be treated equally and unequals unequally." In bioethics, this principle tends to take the form of a focus on "distributive justice," the "fair, equitable, and appropriate distribution . . . of primary social goods, such as economic goods and fundamental political rights" (22), including access to various kinds of health care, the ability to pay for such access, and so on.[12]

As Elliott points out, "these kinds of discussions take a fairly predictable form," in which bioethicists "conventionally take concepts like 'person' and define (or redefine) them so that they can be strictly and consistently applied. Once language is thus refined, we will know how words should be used and thus how we should act."[13] Elliott continues, "This way of reasoning says: we can figure out what to do in this case if we can just get straight about what a person is. That is, we know how to treat a person, so if we decide that this marginal being is a person—a fetus, an anencephalic or a neurologically damaged adult"—or, say, a primate used in biomedical research—"then a conclusion about how we should morally treat that marginal being will logically follow" (159).

But the problem here, from Elliott's point of view, is "the notion that we can somehow define what a person is apart from our *moral attitudes* towards persons, and that once we get the definition right, this will tell us what our moral attitudes should be" (159). "But this is not the way our moral grammar works," he argues; "in fact, just the opposite. Our moral attitudes are not *grounded* by a theory of persons; they are *built into our language*. Part of what we mean by the word 'person' entails a certain moral attitude" (160). And when Elliott says "moral grammar" here, he means it in a specifically Wittgensteinian sense, as in Wittgenstein's well-known statement that "to imagine a language is to imagine a form of life."[14] And equally Wittgensteinian is Elliott's contention that "bioethics generally, if implicitly, assumes its subject matter to be questions of conduct and (sometimes) character. . . . It does not conventionally consider questions about the sense or meaning of life, and it considers only in very awkward constructions (such as 'quality of life') those questions about what makes life worth living. These are ultimate questions about the framework against which our judgments of value get their sense, but they are for the most part absent, or at least hidden, in mainstream bioethics."[15]

To put it another way, it may be that the pragmatism of *Real Ethik* in bioethics dictates shifting "from policies of stark authorization/prohibition to a web of regulation and incentives, from ultimatums to real diplomacy, from grandstanding to nuance and compromise"[16]—but in the name of *what,* exactly, against what "background," to use the Wittgensteinian term? The answer typically given by bioethics is "to maximize the general social welfare and to minimize harm,"[17] but as we shall see, and as Elliott has already suggested, this reply begs all sorts of questions, not the least of which is how it can be distinguished from a simple appeal to social norms and, more pointedly, the prejudices and pragmatic expediencies on which such consensus is based. Of these prejudices, none is more symptomatic of the current state of bioethics than prejudice based on species difference, and an incapacity to address the ethical issues raised by dramatic changes over the past thirty years in our knowledge about the lives, communication, emotions, and consciousness of a number of nonhuman species—a prejudice that bioethics shares with the very core of a centuries-old humanism that contemporary bioethics and its sci-fi scenarios appear (but only appear) to have always already left behind.[18] This is entirely to the point for the field of contemporary bioethics, of course, simply because millions of animals are "used" in the area of biomedical research each year.[19]

Elliott's observation about moral attitudes not being "grounded by a theory of persons" but rather "built into our language" is perfectly exemplified by the bioethicist Arthur Caplan's attempt to confront (or evade) the question of our obligations to nonhuman animals, especially those used in biomedical research, in a recent essay on the ethical complexities of xenotransplantation (using animal organs for transplantation into humans). I choose Caplan not because he is an easy mark, a retrograde voice in the field; quite the contrary, he is in many ways one of its more progressive voices. And he is certainly one of its most visible; in addition to running the University of Pennsylvania Center for Bioethics, he is a regular columnist for MSNBC and appears regularly in the major media as the designated expert in contemporary bioethics.

Caplan's essay "Is the Use of Animal Organs for Transplants Immoral?" puts on display exactly the kind of confusion that Elliott objects to, and on every page evinces the kind of contamination of ethics by pragmatic expediency and ethnocentrism that is the hallmark of the *Real Ethik* of contemporary bioethics.[20] At the core of the essay, Caplan argues that it is acceptable to use some animals, even primates, to "demonstrate the feasibility of xenografting in human beings," and that this is so for a familiar set of reasons. First, he argues that the differences "in the capacities and abilities" of humans and primates (he lists the familiar litany: language, tool use, rationality, intentionality, and so on) justify a different moral status. He concedes that all of these are found in nonhuman species, but he asserts that "humans are capable of a much broader range of behavior and intellectual functioning than is any other primate species," and that therefore humans and nonhuman animals are not "moral equivalents."[21]

One might well begin by observing that there is a fundamental slippage here that needs to be clarified before we can make any real headway on this question. As even the most famous animal rights philosopher on the planet, Peter Singer, has argued, the question is not and has never been whether humans and nonhuman animals are "the same" morally. As Singer puts it, the issue "is *not* saying that all lives are of equal worth or that all interests of humans and other animals are to be given equal weight, no matter what those interests may be. It *is* saying that where animals and humans have similar interests—we might take the interest in avoiding physical pain as an example, for it is an interest that humans clearly share with other animals—those interests are to be counted equally, with no automatic discount just because one of the beings is not human."[22]

A further problem with Caplan's position is that it is open to the objection by means of what is often called "the argument from marginal cases." As the philosopher Paola Cavalieri puts it, "Concretely it is not true that all human beings possess the attributes that allegedly mark the difference between us and the other animals. It is undeniable that there exist within our species individuals who, on account of structural problems due to genetic or developmental anomalies, or of contingent problems due to diseases or accidents, will never acquire, or have forever lost, the characteristics—autonomy, rationality, self-consciousness, and the like—that we consider as typically human."[23] This objection also undermines Caplan's second point: "Human beings can be ethical," he writes. "They may act this way only rarely and some may never do so, but we are creatures capable of moral activity and moral responsibility. Humans can be moral agents, while animals, even other primates, are moral subjects."[24] As we have just seen, however, even if this assertion is true of nonhuman animals, it is certainly not true of all human beings—namely, those "marginal cases" just referenced. And yet we refrain from using them to harvest organs, while we do so with other animals who are demonstrably superior in relevant moral characteristics.

Moreover, as Cavalieri points out, a position such as Caplan's rests on a fundamental slippage between the question of "moral agents" and "moral patients." "This view may appear plausible," she writes, "but is in fact ambiguous. It can indeed mean two different things: (a) that only rational and autonomous beings can be morally responsible, or (b) that only what is done to rational and autonomous beings has moral weight." As Cavalieri puts it, "If the moral agent is a being whose *behavior* may be subject to moral evaluation, the moral patient is a being whose *treatment* may be subject to moral evaluation."[25] From this vantage, it is irrelevant, as Caplan puts it, that "animals are incapable of being held to account for what they do," since the fundamental issue here is not *their* behavior but rather *our* treatment of them. (One might say the same, after all, of a human being suffering from severe schizophrenia, or a small child, or an elderly person suffering from Alzheimer's disease, and so on.)

Caplan's final line of defense in response to the marginal-cases problem is perhaps the most telling and disturbing of all. The reason that even the severely retarded or permanently comatose person should not be used in the same research in which we use a more fully endowed great ape

> has nothing to do with the properties, capacities, and abilities of children or infants who lack and have always lacked significant degrees of intellectual and cognitive function. The reason they should not be used is because of the impact using them would have upon other human beings. . . . The assessment of the morals of how we treat each other and animals does not hinge simply on the properties that each possess[es]. Relationships must enter into the equation as well, and when they do the balance begins to tip toward human rather than animal interests when there is a conflict.[26]

The problem with this position, of course, is twofold (at least). Ethically speaking, it is a not even thinly disguised appeal to ethnocentrism and prejudice under the cover term "relations"—in this case, prejudice on the basis of species membership; and logically speaking, it is utterly circular.

As for the first, this appeal to "relational" rather than individual characteristics, though it seems commonsensical and clearheaded enough, is in fact ethically pernicious, and just how pernicious is revealed by a little experiment that Cavalieri conducts with it in her book *The Animal Question*. First she quotes the same relational position held by Caplan—this time from the work of Robert Nozick. "Perhaps it will turn out," Nozick contends,

> that the bare species characteristic of simply being human . . . will command special respect only from other humans—this is an instance of the general principle that the members of any species may legitimately give their fellows more weight than they give members of other species (or at least more weight than a neutral view would grant them). Lions, too, if they were moral agents, could not then be criticized for putting other lions first.[27]

But what is revealed about this position, Cavalieri asks, if we plug in other terms instead?

Perhaps it will turn out that the bare racial characteristic of simply being white . . . will command special respect only from other whites—this is an instance of the general principle that the members of any race may legitimately give their fellows more weight than they give members of other races (or at least more weight than a neutral view would grant them). Blacks, too . . . could not then be criticized for putting other blacks first. (80)

Caplan may want to fall back on the view that says "that we are powerful and the primates are less so; therefore they must yield to human purposes." "This line of response," he contends, "is far removed from the kinds of arguments that should be mustered in the name of morality."[28] But the point here is that in reality that *is* the kind of argument Caplan is making. As Tom Regan puts it, "Might, according to this theory, does make right. Let those who are the victims of injustice suffer as they will. It matters not so long as no one else . . . cares about it. . . . As if, for example, there would be nothing wrong with apartheid in South Africa if few white South Africans were upset by it."[29]

In more strictly philosophical terms, at the core of this position is a fundamental, self-defeating confusion familiar to us since Hume's Law, which insists on "the distinction between facts and values," that "what ought to be" cannot be derived from "what is."[30] Caplan doesn't just confuse the question "what *ought* we to do?" with the question "what are people *likely* to do?"; he in fact subordinates the former to the latter. In doing so, bioethics becomes little more than the status quo with apologies.

Moreover—to return to my second point—it is not just that the position is ethnocentric; it is also circular, to wit: "we care about being X because we think of them as 'persons,'" and "we think of them as 'persons' because we care about them." But what is needed here, of course, is a *disarticulation* of the question of "persons" from the question of membership in the species *Homo sapiens*. And from this vantage, the Wittgensteinian point about moral attitudes being "built into our language" is not some sort of positivism (though it is sometimes understood that way) that holds that we should simply take for granted what "we" mean by "persons." On the contrary, it suggests that we should be extraordinarily—indeed, philosophically—attuned to how "forms of language" (what we say, what we write, how we ask philosophical questions) open up certain lines of thought—indeed, the imagining of whole worlds—and foreclose others.

From this point of view, it is precisely the *ungroundedness* of what is meant by "persons," to take the example at hand, that requires our diligence about how philosophical questions are formulated. In this light, what becomes clear is that the philosophical impoverishment of bio-ethics overdetermines—or perhaps we should say, leaves undisturbed—its ethical parochialism. So when Caplan asks if it is ethical to use animals in research to study the feasibility of cross-species xenografting, and responds that "in part, the answer to this question pivots on whether or not there are plausible alternative models to the use of animals,"[31] it is obvious that the question ostensibly being asked has already been decided, since the question is really not "can we consider using them?" but simply "under what pragmatic circumstances?"

Beyond "Rights"

So far, I have been responding to the shortcomings of bioethics in its own terms—that is to say, the terms of analytical philosophy and what is sometimes called its "justice tradition." As I hope I have shown (far too hastily, I'm afraid), even in its own terms it is woefully inadequate—both ethically and philosophically—for confronting the complex questions of life, death, and our relations to other living beings that far exceed what bioethics currently constitutes as its unified field. At this juncture, we might move in one of two directions. Along one tack, we might remain within the purview of the analytical tradition and work more diligently to apply it consistently and dispassionately to the questions just raised—which is essentially what we find in the work of Cavalieri, Regan, and Singer. Conversely, we might shift to another way of doing philosophy altogether, one that has a very different notion of the relationship between the practice of philosophy and the kinds of questions that animate, or ought to animate, bioethics. I want to explore both options here, with the eventual aim of showing how the limitations of the analytic tradition for confronting these questions pivot on a certain understanding of the relationship between language, philosophical concepts, and subjectivity that short-circuits our ability to think questions of ethics in relation to the living with the kind of subtlety and rigor they demand.

Before moving to that part of my argument, however, I want to look briefly at one of the more recent attempts within the analytic tradition to redress some of the problems we have already discussed: Martha Nussbaum's use of an Aristotelian framework in *Frontiers of Justice: Disability, Nationality, Species Membership* (2006). My concern here will be to show the limits of philosophical humanism for thinking about the status of nonhuman beings and our relations and duties to them, which stems in part from its inability to *locate* the question properly. More specifically, if philosophical work that takes the moral status of nonhuman animals seriously is, in some obvious sense, post-humanist (in the sense that its want to challenge the ontological and ethical divide between humans and nonhumans is itself a linchpin of philosophical humanism), such work may still be quite humanist on an internal theoretical and methodological level that recontains and even undermines an otherwise admirable philosophical project (a point I'll return to in the next chapter). So what I will try to do here is map a kind of philosophical or theoretical spectrum that moves from humanist approaches to posthumanism (or anti-anthropocentrism) to *posthumanist* approaches to posthumanism. And my point here will be not to pursue a kind of "more-posthumanist-than-thou" sweepstakes but to bring out in a detailed way how the admirable impulses behind *any* variety of philosophy that challenges anthropocentrism and speciesism—impulses that I respect wherever they may be found—demand a certain reconfiguration of what philosophy (or "theory") is and how it can (and cannot) respond to the challenge that all the philosophers discussed here want to engage: the challenge of sharing the planet with nonhuman subjects and treating them justly.

Such differences should not obscure a remarkable fact with which I'd like to begin: that figures as diverse as Nussbaum, Cora Diamond, and Jacques Derrida all set out from the same starting point that anchors our ethical response to nonhuman animals: namely, how our shared embodiment, mortality, and finitude make us, as Diamond puts it, "fellow creatures" in ways that subsume the more traditional markers of ethical consideration such as the capacity for reason, the ability to enter into contractual agreements or reciprocal behaviors, and so on—markers that have traditionally created an ethical divide between *Homo sapiens* and everything (or every*one*) else. Peter Singer might be added to the list as well, for Singer, more than thirty years ago in *Animal Liberation,* drew attention to a passage buried (as Paola Cavalieri has reminded us) in a footnote in Jeremy Bentham's *Introduction to the Principles of Morals and Legislation* that also serves, remarkably enough, as a crucial locus for Derrida's later work on "the question of the animal."[32] "What else is it that should trace the insuperable line?" Bentham asks. "Is it the faculty of reason, or, perhaps, the faculty of discourse? But a full-grown horse or dog is beyond comparison a more rational, as well as a more conversable animal, than an infant of a day, or a week, or even a month, old. But suppose the case were otherwise, what would it avail? The question is not, Can they *reason?* nor, Can they *talk?,* but Can they *suffer?*"[33] For Singer as well as for Derrida, Bentham's passage—with its rejection of the relevance of "talk" and "the faculty of discourse" as an ethically decisive difference between humans and nonhumans—marks a signal advance beyond the well-known "political animal" passage in Aristotle, which, as Derrida has noted, inaugurates an entire philosophical tradition of thinking the difference between human and nonhuman animals in terms of the human's ability to properly "respond" to its world rather than merely "react" to it, an ability made possible (so the story goes) by language.

We will return to this point in some detail later, but for the moment it is worth quoting Aristotle by way of contrast. "Now, that man is more of a political animal than bees or any other gregarious animals is evident," Aristotle writes.

> Nature, as we often say, makes nothing in vain, and man is the only animal whom she has endowed with the gift of speech. And whereas mere voice is but an indication of pleasure or pain, and is therefore found in other animals (for their nature attains to the perception of pleasure and pain and the intimation of them to one another, and no further), the power of speech is intended to set forth the expedient and inexpedient, and therefore likewise the just and the unjust.[34]

Bentham shifts the focus, however, to the fact that the capacity for suffering, as Singer puts it, "is not just another characteristic like the capacity for language or higher mathematics. . . . The capacity for suffering and enjoyment," he continues, "is *a prerequisite for having interests at all,* a condition that must be satisfied before we can speak of interests in a meaningful way."[35] Now one might think that the question of suffering, and more broadly of finitude and mortality that links us with nonhuman animals, would be a rather philosophically straightforward matter, but, as we shall see, exactly the opposite is the case. In fact, this question will be handled in different and even opposed ways by Singer, Nussbaum, Diamond, and finally Derrida—differences that will be definitive for understanding the difference between what I am calling humanist and posthumanist approaches to the question of nonhuman (and human) animal life.

Nussbaum, for example, asserts that "utilitarianism has contributed more than any other ethical theory to the recognition of animal suffering as evil," but she rejects Singer's utilitarian view for many of the same reasons outlined by (among others) Tom Regan in *The Case for Animal Rights* (1983). For her, not only is its "sum-ranking" of "interests" problematic, but it is also, in a fundamental way, beside the point of justice per se. As for the first charge, because the core utilitarian principle is "the greatest good for the greatest number" of interest-holding beings (of whatever species, in Singer's scheme), utilitarianism "seems to have no way to rule out, on grounds of basic justice, the great pain and cruel treatment of at least some animals" whose treatment (in a circus, say) might be justified on the grounds that the suffering of ten or twenty animals brings greater pleasure, on balance, to hundreds of thousands of human beings. (As Regan summarizes the problem succinctly, "The victim's pleasures and pains carry no more moral weight than the equal pleasures and pains of anyone else. To count his pleasures or pains more heavily is ruled out by the egalitarianism claimed as one of the virtues of classical utilitarianism.")[36] The problem, in other words—and this is Nussbaum's second point—is that utilitarianism provides no way for animals to be *direct* subjects of justice: "It seems that the best reason to be against slavery, torture, and lifelong subordination," she writes, "is a reason of justice, not an empirical calculation of total or average well-being" that might or might not entail the maltreatment of a particular sentient being.[37] Moreover (and again the point is articulated in great detail by Regan),[38] the derivation of fundamental "interests" from the principle of suffering is itself problematic, for as Nussbaum notes, "It is natural to ask . . . whether pleasure [and] pain are the only things we ought to be looking at when we consider the entitlements of animals. It seems plausible to think that there may be goods they pursue that are not felt as pain and frustration when they are absent." And the reverse is true as well: for example, in "the pain involved in the effort required to master a difficult activity" (345).

As an alternative, Nussbaum argues not for the contractarian (or "social contract") view promoted by John Rawls (whose limitations in this case ought to be obvious enough)[39] but for the "capabilities" approach that she derives from Aristotle. Now it may seem odd that Aristotle would be chosen as a guide in this realm, given his decisive separation of humans from nonhuman animals on the basis of speech and rationality. As Gary Steiner argues, however, there is a tension in Aristotle's writings between the zoological texts (such as *History of Animals* and *Parts of Animals*) and the psychological, metaphysical, and ethical works (such as *On the Soul* and the *Nicomachean Ethics*).[40] In the zoological texts, Aristotle "attributes to animals capacities that he treats in the psychological and ethical writings as applying only to human beings—capacities such as character, intelligence, ingenuity, and emotion"; and he "provides a hint of the interpretation of such attributions when he says that 'we call the lower animals neither temperate nor self-indulgent except by a metaphor' because 'these have no choice or calculation'" (71). Steiner's position is that for Aristotle, clearly "there is a cosmic scheme of things, and human beings are superior to animals in that scheme because only humans possess the contemplative ability that likens us to the gods" (60)—an ability, as we have seen, decisively linked with reason and with speech. "Ultimately," Steiner writes, "he is unable to do justice to both sides of the dichotomy between the human and animal realms. But he may come closer to doing so than any other Western advocate of the superiority of human beings over animals," chiefly on the strength of the broader (but also specifically nonethical) context provided by the zoological writings (72).

It is this ambiguity in Aristotle's position that Nussbaum seizes upon. We might say, then, that Nussbaum tries to do for Aristotle what Regan did for Kant: retrofit their theories by rejecting the central role of rationality as an ontological and ethical dividing line between humans and nonhuman animals. Hence the rather one-sided reading (if we believe Steiner) of Aristotle that we find in Nussbaum:

> The capabilities approach, by contrast, sees rationality and animality as thoroughly unified. Takings its cue from Aristotle's notion of the human being as a political animal . . . it sees the rational as simply one aspect of the animal, and, at that, not the only one that is pertinent to a notion of a truly human functioning. More generally, the capabilities approach sees the world as containing many different types of animal dignity, all of which deserve respect and even awe. The specifically human kind is indeed characterized, usually, by a kind of rationality, but rationality is not idealized and set in opposition to animality; it is just garden-variety practical reasoning, which is one way animals have of functioning. (159)

Moreover, she writes, the Aristotelian idea of the human as the political animal must receive the proper accent—the political *animal*—so that we properly understand the human being as "not just a moral and political being, but one who has an animal body, and whose human dignity, rather than being opposed to this animal nature, inheres in it, and in its temporal trajectory" from cradle to grave, which involves long periods and sometimes unexpected modes of dependency and vulnerability as embodied beings (87–88).

Thus, while the capabilities view "includes an idea related to the contractarian idea of 'freedom'" (88), it by definition rejects the grounding of that freedom in a conception of the person as "free, equal, and independent" (87). What is fundamental to the ethical standing of both humans and nonhumans—and this is readily brought into focus in animal rights philosophy by the analogy between the situation of nonhuman "higher" animals and severely disabled human beings—is not the contractarian idea "that only those who can join a contract as rough equals can be primary, nonderivative subjects of a theory of justice" (327), but rather the embodiment and finitude of creatures of whatever species who may be deemed, to use Tom Regan's term, the "subject of a life."[41] As we have already seen, this criterion is not reducible to sentience and suffering per se, nor is the rightness or wrongness of how such beings are treated subject to the "sum-ranking" of "interests" that we find in Singer's utilitarianism. Instead the rightness or wrongness of our treatment of such subjects—human or nonhuman— is in Nussbaum's view determined by the extent to which it enables or impedes their "flourishing," a flourishing that is based on a more or less empirical assessment of the capabilities, needs, characteristic behaviors, and so on of the particular being in question. "The general aim of the capabilities approach in charting political principles to shape the human-animal relationship," she writes, "would be that no sentient animal should be cut off from the chance for a flourishing life, a life with the type of dignity relevant to that species, and that all sentient animals should enjoy certain positive opportunities to flourish."[42]

At this juncture, it would be possible—indeed, were I an analytic philosopher, it might be imperative—to point out some of the many problems with Nussbaum's approach even within the purview of its own terms. For example, it is not clear that it marks any advance over Regan's rights position as articulated nearly twenty-five years ago, with which it shares several core features (the rejection of utilitarian sum-ranking and of its abstraction of "interests" from the beings who hold them as mere "receptacles"; the rejection of contractarian theories; the assertion that nonhuman animals may be *direct* subjects of justice and not just indirect or derivative ones; and, most important, the nearly complete overlap of Nussbaum's account of beings capable of "flourishing" with Regan's "subject-of-a-life").[43] In fact, Regan's view would seem to avoid two fundamental problems that plague the latter two-thirds of Nussbaum's treatment of the animal question, where she attempts to draw out the conclusions of her view: first, the problem of determining what counts as *human* "flourishing" (does it include hunting? the exercise of evolutionary predatory instincts? the right to procreate to the point of overpopulation? and so on);[44] and second, the unavoidability (given her position) of falling into precisely what she criticizes in the utilitarians, namely, the problem of "balancing" competing rights to "flourishing" (human and nonhuman) just as the utilitarians must rank competing "interests."

Indeed, what we might characterize as the methodological minimalism of both Singer's account of interests and Regan's of the subject-of-a-life is calculated to avoid what Geoffrey Harpham calls the "human essentialism" that plagues Nussbaum's later work, where Aristotle is called on as "the first thinker to try and pick out those features of human life most distinctive of humanity and therefore most worth cultivating." But "missing from the inventory of acceptable human passions," Harpham notes, "are aggression and anger. . . . Only those passions that are, in a sense, dispassionate and responsive to the patient work of philosophy are to be considered part of the human essence; the rest are merely 'constructed by social evaluations.'"[45] Most problematic of all here, of course, is the notorious "List of Central Human Functional Capabilities" that shows up regularly in Nussbaum's later work.[46] It includes capabilities such as "being able to move freely from place to place; having one's bodily boundaries treated as sovereign . . . having opportunities for sexual satisfaction . . . Being able to use the senses, to imagine, think, and reason—and to do these things in a 'truly human' way . . . Being able to search for the ultimate meaning of life in one's own way. Being able to have pleasurable experiences, and to avoid non-necessary pain . . . [Being able to] experience longing, gratitude, and justified anger," and so forth. As Harpham notes, in the eyes of her critics, Nussbaum has hereby "reduced the world's needs to a refrigerator list of to-dos; she has unwittingly suggested that Steven Hawking and Stevie Wonder are less than human; she has begged the question by using phrases as 'non-necessary pain' (in an earlier version, 'non-beneficial pain') and 'justified anger,'" and "she has altogether ignored the problems associated with the fact that subjective interpretation and judgment must be involved in measuring particular cases against general principles." Indeed, as Harpham notes, it is the "List" that fellow philosopher Mary Beard declared, in the *Times Literary Supplement,* "a frightful muddle which verges on the ludicrous."[47]

My aim here, however, is not so much to take Nussbaum's work on its own terms but to respect and rearticulate more successfully the impulse behind her Aristotelian conception that "situates human morality and rationality firmly within human animality, and insists that human animality itself has dignity. There is dignity in human neediness, in the human temporal history of birth, growth, and decline, and in relations of interdependency and asymmetrical dependency."[48] We can begin to glimpse the limitations of Nussbaum's philosophical humanism for doing justice to such an impulse by turning to a very different kind of philosopher (though one still within the analytic tradition): Cora Diamond. In her recent essay "The Difficulty of Reality and the Difficulty of Philosophy," Diamond focuses on a literary text that appears more than once in Nussbaum's *Frontiers of Justice:* J. M. Coetzee's *The Lives of Animals.* In that book, the main character, the novelist

Elizabeth Costello, is haunted—"wounded," to use a figure that Cora Diamond highlights—by how we treat nonhuman animals in practices such as factory farming, a systemized and mechanized killing that she compares (to the consternation of some) in its scale and its violence to the Holocaust of the Jews during World War II. At a dinner after one of her invited public lectures, she is asked by the president of the university whether her vegetarianism "comes out of moral conviction," and she responds, against the expectations of her hosts, "No, I don't think so. . . . It comes out of a desire to save my soul." And when the university administrator politely replies, "Well, I have a great respect for it," she retorts impatiently, "I'm wearing leather shoes. I'm carrying a leather purse. I wouldn't have overmuch respect if I were you."[49]

What haunts Costello here also torments another of Coetzee's characters, David Lurie in the novel *Disgrace*. Lurie, a literature professor in South Africa whose career ends abruptly after he has an affair with a female undergraduate and is charged with sexual harassment, moves to the country, where his daughter Lucy has a small farm, and begins volunteering at the local animal shelter, where he assists in euthanizing the scores of animals, mainly dogs, for whom no homes can be found. Lurie has never thought of himself as "a sentimentalist," as he puts it, and he takes to the work reluctantly. But then, gradually, he becomes absorbed in it. "He had thought he would get used to it," Coetzee writes. "But that is not what happens. The more killings he assists in, the more jittery he gets." Then, one Sunday night as he is driving back from the clinic, it hits him; "He actually has to stop at the roadside to recover himself. Tears flow down his face that he cannot stop; his hands shake. He does not understand what is happening to him." For reasons he doesn't understand, "his whole being is gripped by what happens in the [surgical] theatre."[50]

Both characters experience head-on the unnerving weight and gravity of our moral responsibilities toward nonhuman animals. But both moments insist on something else, too, something that also, in a different way, unsettles the very foundations of what we call "the human." Both moments acknowledge a *second* kind of "unspeakability": not only the unspeakability of how we treat animals in practices like factory farming but also the unspeakability of the limits of our own thinking in confronting such a reality—the trauma, as Diamond puts it, of "experiences in which we take something in reality to be resistant to our thinking it, or possibly to be painful in its inexplicability."[51]

Writ large, in the terms of the (post)Enlightenment philosophical tradition, this is often referred to as the problem of philosophical skepticism, and part of what Diamond is interested in pressuring is the extent to which these two questions are (or are not) the same. On this point, Diamond draws on the work of Stanley Cavell, who has explored the problem of skepticism with remarkable nuance and range over the past forty and more years (a body of thought I will revisit in some detail in chapter 7). Working through figures as diverse as Kant, Descartes, Emerson, Wittgenstein, Austin, and Heidegger (among others), Cavell has plumbed the consequences of what it means to do philosophy in the wake of what he calls the Kantian "settlement" with skepticism. As Cavell characterizes it in *In Quest of the Ordinary,* "To settle with skepticism . . . to assure us that we do know the existence of the world, or rather, that what we understand as knowledge is *of* the world, the price Kant asks us to pay is to cede any claim to know the thing in itself, to grant human knowledge is not of things as they are in themselves. You don't—do you?—have to be a romantic to feel sometimes about that settlement: Thanks for nothing."[52] But if, in Cavell's reading of Kant, "reason proves its power to itself, over itself" (30) by logically deriving the difference between the world of mere appearances (phenomena) that we can know and the world of the *Ding an sich* (noumena) that our knowledge never touches, then we find ourselves in a position that is not just odd but in fact profoundly unsettling, for philosophy in a fundamental sense then fails precisely insofar as it succeeds. We gain knowledge, but only to lose the world.

The question in the wake of skepticism thus becomes what it can mean to (continue to) do philosophy after philosophy has become, in a certain sense, impossible. One thing it does *not* mean, if we believe Diamond, is to think that such "resistance" of the world ("the difficulty of reality," to use the phrase Diamond borrows from John Updike) could be dissolved or overcome by ever more ingenious or accomplished propositional arguments, ever more refined philosophical concepts (or, for that matter, by the making of lists). Indeed, to think that it can, to mistake "the difficulty of philosophy" for the "difficulty of reality" (as do the philosophical "Reflections" published at the end of *The Lives of Animals,* Diamond suggests), is to indulge in a "deflection" of a reality that impinges on us—"befalls" us, as Wittgenstein once put it—in ways not masterable by the crafting of analytical arguments. (That is why, for Diamond, Elizabeth Costello doesn't offer one in defense of her vegetarianism; and it is also why Costello is quick to point to the inconsistency of her own practices with regard to animal products.) It is that impingement, that "pressure" of reality, that overtakes David Lurie on the drive back from the clinic. He literally does not know what is happening to him; he has no reasons for it, and he can't explain it. And yet it is the most real thing in the world.

These fundamental challenges for philosophy are sounded out by Cavell in his reading of the philosopher most important to him, Ralph Waldo Emerson, and I will revisit that relationship in some detail in chapter 9. Emerson writes in his most important essay, "Experience": "I take this evanescence and lubricity of all objects, which lets them slip through our fingers then when we clutch hardest, to be the most unhandsome part of our condition." For Cavell, this moment registers the confrontation with skepticism, certainly, but it also voices an understanding of how philosophy must change in the wake of that confrontation. For the "unhandsome" here names not just the Kantian *Ding an sich,* but also, Cavell writes, "what happens when we seek to deny the stand-offishness of objects by clutching at them; which is to say, when we conceive thinking, say the application of concepts in judgments, as grasping something."[53] When we engage in that sort of deflection, we only deepen the abyss—"when we clutch hardest"—between our thinking and the world that we want to understand. The opposite of clutching, on the other hand—what Cavell calls "the most handsome part of our condition"—is facing the fact that "the demand for unity in our judgments, that our deployment of concepts, is not the expression of the conditionedness or limitations of our humanness but of the human effort to escape our humanness."[54] Philosophy can hence no longer be seen as mastery, as a kind of clutching or grasping via analytical categories and concepts that seemed, for Heidegger, "a kind of sublimized violence"—the kind of violence that Nussbaum's critics find on display most egregiously, of course, in the "List."[55] Rather, the duty of thinking is not to deflect but to suffer (remember Costello's woundedness) what Cavell calls our "exposure" to the world.

Diamond is much attracted to this term in the sense that she tries to bring out with reference to a poem by Ted Hughes, "Six Young Men," whose last stanza she quotes to open "The Difficulty of Reality." The poem concerns the uncanny sense of confronting a photograph of young, carefree men taken not long before they are all killed in World War I:

> That man's not more alive whom you confront
> And shake by the hand, see hale, hear speak loud,
> Than any of these six celluloid smiles are,
> Nor prehistoric or fabulous beast more dead;
> No thought so vivid as their smoking blood:
> To regard this photograph might well dement,
> Such contradictory permanent horrors here
> Smile from the single exposure and shoulder out
> One's own body from its instant and heat.

What the poem helps to underscore is not just "the experience of the mind's not being able to encompass something which it encounters"[56] but also the unnerving proximity of life and death—and thus the important connection she will develop between the exposure of our concepts to the confrontation with skepticism and the *physical* exposure to vulnerability and mortality that we suffer because we, like animals, are embodied beings. As Diamond puts it in a key moment in her essay, unpacking her sense of Costello's startling assertion that "I know what it is like to be a corpse":

> The awareness we each have of being a living body, being "alive to the world," carries with it exposure to the bodily sense of vulnerability to death, sheer animal vulnerability, the vulnerability we share with them. This vulnerability is capable of panicking us. To be able to acknowledge it at all, let alone as shared, is wounding; but acknowledging it as shared with other animals, in the presence of what we do to them, is capable not only of panicking one but also of isolating one, as Elizabeth Costello is isolated. Is there any difficulty in seeing why we should not prefer to return to moral debate, in which the livingness and death of animals enter as facts that we treat as relevant in this or that way, not as presences that may unseat our reason? (74)

But there is yet a third type of exposure or finitude that is crucial here as well, as practiced readers of Heidegger (or, for that matter, of Cavell or Derrida) will already have guessed: our exposure—in a radical sense, our *subjection*—to language and writing in ways that bear directly on what it means to do philosophy, what philosophy *can* do in the face of these existential and ethical challenges. One further consequence of everything we have been saying thus far is that the relationship between philosophical thinking ("concepts") and philosophy as a *writing* practice now takes on unprecedented importance (which is why Heidegger, and Derrida, and Cavell write the way they do—which is to say, "unphilosophically," even "literarily"). Against the backdrop of what is often referred to as the "linguistic turn" in twentieth-century philosophy, we find a direct line of connection between the problem of philosophical skepticism and the work of Wittgenstein on language that will prove so important to Diamond and, in a different way, to Cavell. But it is also on this point, as I will try to bring out later, that crucial differences emerge between this sort of work, emerging as it does out of an especially adventurous wing of the analytical tradition, and the work of Derrida, who construes the consequences of the relation between philosophy and language, of our finitude in relation to both, in ways that bear directly on how we may and may not think of our relations to ourselves and to nonhuman animals.

Diamond's earlier work is worth revisiting here in some detail. As she insists in an essay from 2001 called "Injustice and Animals," our "grammatical redescription" of a philosophical problem is crucial and in some sense determinative of our ability to do justice to the ethical challenges it entails.[57] For Diamond, the fundamental question of *justice* issues from an essentially different conceptual realm from the question of "rights." As she argues (elaborating on some ideas of Simone Weil), "when genuine issues of justice and injustice are framed in terms of rights, they are thereby distorted and trivialized," because the language of rights still bears the imprint of the context in which it was shaped: Roman law and its codification of *property* rights—not least, of course, property rights over slaves (120). But the question of justice cannot be reduced to the question of the fairness or unfairness of a share. "The attempt to give voice to real injustice in the language of rights," Diamond argues, "falters because of the underlying tie between rights and a system of entitlement that is concerned, not with evil done to a person, but with how much he or she gets compared to other participants in the system" (121). In rights discourse, she argues, "the *character* of our conflicts is made obscure" by what Wittgenstein would call a poor grammatical description of the problem of justice (124).

Instead, what generates our moral response to animals and their treatment is our sense of the mortality and vulnerability that we share with them, of which the brute subjection of the body—in the treatment of animals as mere research tools, say, or in the torture of political prisoners in war—is perhaps the most poignant testament. For Diamond, the "horror at the conceptualizing of animals as putting nothing in the way of their use as mere stuff" depends on "a comparable horror at human relentlessness and pitilessness in the exercise of power" toward other humans (136). What the rights tradition misses, in her view, is that the "capacity to respond to injustice as injustice" depends not on working out (from a safe ontological distance, as it were) who should have a fair share of this or that abstract "good" but on "a recognition of *our own* vulnerability"—a recognition not demanded and in some sense actively avoided by rights-oriented thinking (121).

We can get a sense of the implications of this view for the grain of Diamond's thinking by following her discussion of a highly publicized case several years ago. In a videotape smuggled out of the University of Pennsylvania's Head Injury Laboratory, researchers and lab workers were shown making fun of a baboon who had been subjected to massive head injury in their experiments and was now serving as a mere prop for their jokes, as one of the lab workers posed with one animal who had large cranial sutures, and the rest of the staff—including the director of the lab—laughed at the animal and made fun of his "punk look" (148n41). Viewers almost without exception find this tape shocking and deeply disturbing—but not, Diamond argues, in a way accountable (or defensible) by either side of the animal rights debate. For Diamond, the nub of the issue here is that "the animal's body, which is all it has, as a poor man's body may be all he has, is turned into the mere butt of your jokes"; the animal "lacks the power to get away, or to resist," and what is morally repugnant is to make this disempowerment, this absolute subjection, the occasion for jokes. But the moral repugnance of such a thing is not easily accounted for by the rights framework, fixated as it is on the dependence of rights on interests, and interests in turn on a more or less naturalistic conception of the good of the animal. "Not being a butt of humor is not taken to be part of its good," Diamond writes. "It may seem to a defender of animal rights that, although we should not ridicule animals, it will be hard to make out that we owe it *to the animals* not to ridicule them. In the background here is the idea that we cannot owe it to animals . . . unless they would *suffer* from such treatment; and the idea would be that an animal cannot suffer from being ridiculed if it is not even aware that it is being ridiculed" (137–38).

What such an insight points toward is that "there is something wrong with the contrast, taken to be exhaustive, between demanding one's rights and begging for kindness—begging for what is *merely* kindness. The idea that *those* are the only possibilities is . . . one of the main props of the idea that doing injustice *is* failing to respect rights" (129). Contemporary moral theory thus "pushes apart justice, on the one hand, and compassion, love, pity, tenderness, on the other" (131), but Diamond's understanding of the question "has at its center the idea that a kind of loving attention to another being, a possible victim of injustice, is essential to any understanding of the evil of injustice" (131–32). In this light, one might well agree with Weil's suggestion, as Diamond does, that in fact "rights can work for justice or for injustice," and as such the concept of rights possesses "a kind of moral noncommitment to the good" (128). In an important sense, in other words, rights are beside the point of justice per se, and "the language of rights is, one might say, meant to be useful in contexts in which we cannot count on the kind of understanding of evil that depends on loving attention to the victim" (139).

There are, in other words, two different and in fact incommensurable kinds of value here (121)—a point missed by both sides of what Diamond calls "that great arena of dissociated thought, contemporary debate about animals' rights."[58] The problem with *both* sides of the debate—represented by, say, Peter Singer on one side and, on the other, the philosopher Michael Leahy and his avatar Thomas O'Hearne in *The Lives of Animals*—is that they are locked into a model of justice in which a being does or does not have rights on the basis of its possession (or lack) of morally significant characteristics that can be empirically derived. Both sides argue "that what is involved in moral thought is

knowledge of empirical similarities and differences, and the testing and application of general principles of evaluation."[59] And so, as
Diamond puts it in "The Difficulty of Reality," "the opposite sides in
the debate may have more in common than they realize. In the voices
we hear in the debate about animal rights, those of people like Singer
on the one hand and those of Leahy and the fictional O'Hearne on the
other, there is shared a desire for a 'because': because animals are this
kind of being, or because they are that kind of being, thus-and-such is
their standing for our moral thought" (71). But what Diamond hears in
both sets of voices is an evasion of our "exposure" to an arena of moral
complexity in which (to quote Cavell) "the other can present me with
no mark or feature on the basis of which I can *settle* my attitude" (71).

Part of the reason for that, of course, is that such attitudes are
far from the thin, if-P-then-Q abstractions that a certain kind of philosophy takes them to be. They are thick with psychological vexation
and rife with contradictory impulses and attachments. So Diamond is
concerned to show not just that such a picture of ethics confuses the
question of justice with the "mediocre" level of mere rights but also
that it bears no resemblance to what she suggests is our moral *life*.[60] For
her, proponents of animal rights in the analytical tradition are wrong
when they insist that the distinction between human and animal is not
ethically fundamental. At the same time, however, those who *oppose*
animal rights within that same analytical tradition are wrong about
how the difference between humans and animals *is* relevant. "The notion 'human being' is of the greatest significance in moral thought,"
she argues, but not because it is a "biological notion" (264). Rather, the
concept of "human being" "is a main source of that moral sensibility
which we may *then* be able to extend to nonhuman animals." "We can
come to think of killing an animal as in some circumstances at least
similar to homicide," she continues, "but the significance of doing so
depends on our already having an idea of what it is to kill a man; and
for us (as opposed to abstract Moral Agents) the idea of what it is to kill
a man does depend on the sense of human life as special, as something
set apart from what else happens on the planet."[61]

For Diamond, then, it is crucial to take account of "what human
beings have *made of* the difference between human beings and animals."[62] As she puts it elsewhere:

If we appeal to people to prevent suffering, and we, in our appeal, try to obliterate the distinction between human beings and animals and just get people to speak or think of "different species of animals," there is no footing left from which to tell us what we ought to do. . . . The moral expectations of other human beings demand something of me as other than an animal; and we do something like imaginatively read into animals something like such expectations when we think of vegetarianism as enabling us to meet a cow's eyes. There is nothing wrong with that; there *is* something wrong with trying to keep that response and destroy its foundation.[63]

So for Diamond, it is not by denying the special status of human being but by intensifying it that we can come to think of nonhuman animals not as bearers of interests or as rights holders but rather as something much more compelling: fellow creatures. That phrase "does not mean, biologically, an animal, something with *biological* life," but rather refers to our "response to animals as our fellows in mortality, in life on this earth."[64] Hence the difference between human and nonhuman animals "may indeed start out as a biological difference, but it becomes something for human thought through being taken up and made something *of*—by generations of human beings, in their practices, their art, their literature, their religion,"[65] practices that enable us to "imaginatively read into animals" expectations that originate in the human, the "other than an animal."

Given her critique of the rights framework and her emphasis on compassion, not standing, as fundamental to justice, it may come as a surprise that Diamond finds in the contemporary animal *rights* movement a commitment to justice not available in the concept of mere animal *welfare*. "The welfarist view," she writes, "is essentially that we should ease the burdens we impose on animals without getting off their backs, without ceasing to impose burdens on them, burdens that we impose because we *can,* because they are in general helpless" to resist us. But "the force of the animal rights movement comes from the sense of the profound injustice of this"—a sense, however, that its dominant language of *rights* is not equipped to articulate. But if we reject the opposition, all too dominant in contemporary moral theory, of justice and compassion, rights and pity, what is revealed is "a kind of pitilessness at the heart of welfarism, a willingness to go ahead

with what we do to the vulnerable, a willingness to go on subjecting them to our power because we can," that is different not in structure but only in degree from what goes on in the animal research labs.
"'Willingness' is indeed too weak a word," she writes; "we *will* not
give up a form of life resting on the oppression of others; and the will
to continue exercising power in such ways . . . is inseparable from the
'compassion' we express in welfarism"—one that has nothing to do
with the grounds of justice in embodiment, vulnerability, and finitude
as Diamond conceives it.[66]

Double Finitude, or Taking Bioethics off Autopilot

The originality and subtlety of Diamond's position lie in no small part,
then, in her separation of the question of justice from the discourse of
rights—and beyond that in her insistence that vulnerability and compassion are very much to the point of justice, and in a profound sense
lie at its very heart. Diamond's nuanced thinking of these questions
helps us to bring out more precisely the oddly disjunctive and muddled
character of Nussbaum's work that is created by how her chosen philosophical approach forecloses and frustrates her altogether admirable
attempt to move beyond the reduction of the problem of justice for
nonhuman animals to "interests" that we find in utilitarianism and
replace it with a broader view of "capabilities" and "flourishing" that
"takes an interest not just in pleasure and pain, but in complex forms
of life and functioning."[67] Both agree, as Nussbaum puts it, that "the
best reason to be against slavery, torture, and lifelong subordination is
a reason of justice, not an empirical calculation of total or average well-
being" (343). Similarly, Nussbaum, like Diamond, insists that the power
of "sympathetic imagining" of the lives of nonhuman animals of the
sort made available by literature (but not only there) is important and
relevant to questions of moral judgment. As she puts it, "imagining the
lives of animals makes them real to us in a primary way, as potential
subjects of justice" (355). It is entirely symptomatic in this regard, however, that while the force of literature for Diamond is its *difference* from
philosophy, its ability to confront propositional, analytic thought with
its own limitations (even unnervingly so, as in Hughes's "Six Young
Men"), for Nussbaum literature serves as a kind of kinder, gentler sup-

plement to analytic philosophy's project of "sentimental education," stirring in us identifications, empathetic responses, and projections that may then be readily formalized in analytical propositions (411). As Harpham succinctly puts it, "In Nussbaum, the specificity of literature as a discourse, an object of professional study, is almost altogether erased and replaced by a conception that treats it bluntly as moral philosophy. The aesthetic is made to serve the aims of culture and morality in a dedifferentiated unity rarely seen in the modern world." And philosophical reading is thus calculated to "extract maxims that could guide contemporary policy makers, economists, or jurists."[68]

Similarly, the change in philosophical approach that would seem to be required by Nussbaum's attempt to honor the importance of "sympathetic imagining" in questions of justice—the very impulses that drive her away from the thin accounts of utilitarianism and contractarianism—is immediately foreclosed by her insistence that "justice is the sphere of basic entitlements" and that what is lacking in the contract theory of a Rawls is "the sense of the animal itself as an agent . . . a creature to whom something is due."[69] As Diamond's work suggests, however, such a philosophical approach only reinstates the reduction of questions of justice to questions of entitlement that the capabilities approach was meant to resist in the first place, thus "pushing apart" the questions of justice and compassion in precisely the way that Nussbaum had resisted in both utilitarian and contractarian approaches—a separation made all the more acute by Nussbaum's characteristically fuzzy insistence that on the one hand, "compassion overlaps with the sense of justice, and a full allegiance to justice requires compassion for beings who suffer wrongfully," but on the other, "compassion itself is too indeterminate to capture our sense of what is wrong with the treatment of animals" (337)—a wrong that must presumably be directed at their entitlements as rights-holding agents. As Diamond would be the first to point out, however, what is "indeterminate" is not our compassion for the suffering of nonhuman animals but the idea that "rights" and "entitlement" bear anything other than a completely contingent relationship (derived from the historically and ideologically specific character of our juridical and political institutions and the picture of the subject of rights that they provide) to the question of justice for nonhuman animals. Or to put it slightly otherwise, the idea that animals deserve justice because they are moral agents and not just moral patients, while perhaps problematic in its own right,[70] undercuts Nussbaum's earlier assertion that the key link between humans and nonhuman animals as subjects of justice is not their agency but exactly the opposite: their shared finitude as embodied, vulnerable beings.

I would like to turn now to Jacques Derrida's later work to provide an example of how the admirable impulses behind Nussbaum's attempt to think the questions of justice and moral standing for nonhumans might motivate a very different view of what philosophy is, eventuating in theoretical and methodological commitments that avoid not just the sort of problems we have just been discussing in Nussbaum but also limitations in Diamond's remarkable set of essays on these questions. At first glance, Derrida's work seems quite consonant with Diamond's, beginning with three main features. First, Derrida emphasizes, like Diamond (and like Nussbaum), that the fundamental ethical bond we have with nonhuman animals resides in our shared finitude, our vulnerability and mortality as "fellow creatures" (a phrase he too invokes at key moments in his argument). Second, Derrida shares with Diamond (against Nussbaum) a certain understanding of what ethics is: not propositionally deriving a set of rules for conduct that apply generically in all cases but confronting our "exposure" to a permanent condition in which (to use Cavell's phrase) "there is no way to settle our attitude." Third, Derrida also insists that crucial to both of these is "to show," as Diamond puts it in an earlier essay, "how philosophical misconceptions about language are connected with blindness to what our conceptual life is like"[71]—a blindness that is everywhere on display, as I have been suggesting, in Nussbaum's attempt to think "the animal question."

It is here, I think, that Diamond's approach, as illuminating and searching as it is, runs aground. She is certainly right to suggest that our ability to think questions of bioethics depends fundamentally on the understanding—indeed, the theory—of language that we bring to it. But what we find in her work, I believe, is an understanding of how language operates in a philosophical context—an understanding directly linked to her notion of "human being"—that undermines her attempt to open the question of justice beyond the human sphere alone. I choose to focus on Derrida in this connection not just because of his well-known theory of language as *écriture,* dissemination, trace, and so on but also because we find in his recent work a gathering of terms around questions of justice and the living that is strikingly similar to what we have seen in Diamond. It will come as a surprise to any reader, I think, that in his recent work on ethics and the question of nonhuman others, Derrida returns to what serves in Singer's work as the benchmark for the ethical consideration of animals: namely, the utilitarian philosopher Jeremy Bentham's contention that the relevant question here is not "can they talk," or "can they reason," but "can they suffer?" For Derrida, putting the question in this way "changes everything," because "from Aristotle to Descartes, from Descartes, especially, to Heidegger, Levinas and Lacan," posing the question of the animal in terms of either the capacity for thought or language "determines so many others concerning *power* or *capability [pouvoirs],* and *attributes [avoirs]:* being able, having the power to give, to die, to bury one's dead, to dress, to work, to invent a technique."[72] What makes Bentham's reframing of the problem so powerful is that now "the question is disturbed by a certain *passivity.* It bears witness, manifesting already, as question, the response that testifies to sufferance, a passion, a not-being-able." "What of the vulnerability felt on the basis of this inability?" he continues; "what is this non-power at the heart of power? . . . What right should be accorded it? To what extent does it concern us?" It concerns us directly, in fact, for "mortality resides there, as the most radical means of thinking the finitude that we share with animals, the mortality that belongs to the very finitude of life, to the experience of compassion."[73]

In Derrida as in Diamond, the vulnerability and, ultimately, mortality that we share with nonhuman animals, and the compassion that they elicit—what Diamond characterizes as the capacity to be harmed, but also to be "brought up short" of inflicting harm on another by recognition of that capacity[74]—lie at the core of the question of ethics: not just mere kindness but *justice.* For Derrida too, "what is still presented in such a problematic way as *animal rights*" has a force quite independent of the philosophical framework that usually accompanies it, a force that "involves a new experience of this compassion," one that has opened anew "the immense question of pathos," of "suffering, pity and compassion; and the place that has to be accorded to the interpretation of this compassion, to the sharing of this suffering among the living, to the law, ethics, and politics that must be brought to bear upon this experience of compassion." For Derrida, then, the point of the animal rights movement, however flawed its articulation, is "to awaken us to our responsibilities and our obligations with respect to the living in general, and precisely to this fundamental compassion that, were we to take it seriously, would have to change even the very basis . . . of the philosophical problematic of the animal."[75]

For Derrida too, the force of the animal rights movement outstrips its own ability to articulate the questions it addresses, questions that require an alternative conception of ethics to the rights tradition of analytical philosophy as it manifests itself in Singer and others. For Singer, as we have seen, ethics means the application of what Derrida will elsewhere characterize as a "calculable process"—in this case quite literally—of the utilitarian calculus that would tally up the interests of the particular beings in question in a given situation, regardless of their species, and would determine what counts as a just act by calculating which action maximizes the greatest good for the greatest number.[76] In doing so, however, Singer would reduce ethics to the very antithesis of ethics in Derrida's sense because it would overleap what Derrida calls "the ordeal of the undecidable," which "must be gone through by any decision worthy of the name."

> A decision that didn't go through the ordeal of the undecidable would not be a free decision, it would only be the programmable application or unfolding of a calculable process. It might be legal; it would not be just. . . . And once the ordeal of the undecidable is past (if that is possible), the decision has again followed a rule or given itself a rule, invented it or reinvented, reaffirmed it, it is no longer *presently* just, fully just.[77]

"Ordeal" is indeed the word we want here, which is one reason Diamond rivets our attention more than once on Elizabeth Costello's "rawness" of nerves, her sufferance of a responsibility that is both undeniable and unappeasable. But what the rights view of ethics gives us instead—in either the Singer or Nussbaum version—is a deflection of this fully ethical ordeal, one in which, as Diamond puts it, "We would be *given* the presence or absence of moral community (or thus-and-such degree or kind of moral community) with animals."[78] Aside from thus being the antithesis of the ethical in Derrida's sense, such a calculation, in its derivation of the shared interests of human and nonhuman animals, would confuse what Diamond calls "biological concepts" with the concepts proper to *ethical* thought. This is what Derrida has in mind (and more, as we are about to see) in his criticism of a "biological continuism, whose sinister connotations we are well aware of," one that ignores "the abyssal rupture" between human and nonhuman forms of life, but also *within* and *between* different forms of nonhuman animal life.[79] I have "thus never believed," he writes, "in some homogeneous continuity between what calls *itself* man and what *he* calls the animal."[80]

At this juncture, however—and it is marked quite precisely by Derrida's emphasis on "what calls *itself* man and what *he* calls the animal"—some fundamental differences between Derrida and Diamond begin to come into view, not least in the articulation of this peculiar thing called "the human." We can get a sense of this difference by returning to the crucial role that vulnerability, passivity, and, ultimately, mortality play here for both Diamond and Derrida. Let us recall Diamond's contention that "we can come to think of killing an animal as in some circumstances at least similar to homicide, but the significance of doing so depends on our already having an idea of what it is to kill a man."[81] Such an idea depends, however, on a relation to our own mortality that is rejected in Derrida's work; for Derrida, contra Diamond, we *never* have an idea of what death is *for us*—indeed, death is precisely that which can never be *for us*—and if we did, then the ethical relation to the other would be immediately foreclosed.

This is clearest, perhaps, in Derrida's reading of Heidegger and his concept of "being-toward-death," a concept that appears—but only appears—to do justice to the passivity and finitude in which the ethical resides. As Richard Beardsworth characterizes it, for Derrida, Heidegger *appropriates* the limit of death "rather than returning it to *the other* of time. The existential of 'being-towards-death' is consequently a 'being-able' *(pouvoir-etre)*, not the impossibility of all power" whose passivity and vulnerability tie the self to the other in an ethical relation. For Derrida, on the other hand,

> the "impossibility" of death for the ego confirms that the experience of finitude is one of radical passivity. That the "I" cannot experience its "own" death means, firstly, that death is an immanence *without* horizon, and secondly, that time is that which exceeds my death, that time is the

generation which precedes and follows me. . . . Death is not a limit or horizon which, re-cognized, allows the ego to assume the "there" [as in Heidegger's being-toward-death]; it is something that never arrives in the ego's time, a "not-yet" which confirms the priority of time over the ego, marking, accordingly, the precedence of the other over the ego.[82]

For Derrida, then, "no relation to death can appear as such," and "if there is no 'as' to death," then the "relation to death is always mediated through an other. The 'as' of death always appears *through* an other's death, *for* another" (118). Beardsworth quotes Derrida: "The death of the other thus becomes . . . 'first,' always first." Hence, Beardsworth argues, "The recognition of the limit of death is always through another and is, therefore, at the same time the recognition of the other" (118). And since the same is true *of* the other in relation to its *own* death, what this means is that "death *impossibilizes* existence," and does so both for me *and* for the other—since death is no more "for" the other than it is for me (132). But it is, paradoxically, in just this impossibility that the possibility of justice resides, the permanent call of the other in the face of which the subject always arrives "too late." Or to put this in somewhat different terms, when Diamond affirms Costello's assertion that "I know what it is like to be a corpse," Derrida's response would be "No, you don't. Only the other does, and for that you are held hostage (to use Levinas's term) in unappeasable ethical debt to the other"—hence the otherwise odd idea of the "gift" of death (to borrow from Derrida's book by the same title). To put it another way, there is the suggestion in Diamond, I think, that imaginative and literary projection can somehow achieve in this instance what propositional, syllogistic philosophy cannot achieve (the nonconceptual, nonlogical force of "I know what it's like to be a corpse"), but Derrida would see this, too, as a "deflection" of "exposure": exposure not just to mortality but also to a certain estranging operation of language, to a second kind of finitude whose implications are enormous (a point I'll return to in just a moment).

Such is the full resonance, I think, of Derrida's recent contention with regard to Bentham that "the word *can [pouvoir]* changes sense and sign here once one asks 'can they suffer?' The word wavers henceforth. As soon as such a question is posed what counts is not only the idea of a transitivity or activity (being able to speak, to reason, and so on); *the important thing is rather what impels it towards self-contradiction, something we will later relate back to auto-biography."*[83] What Derrida has in mind by the "auto-" of "autobiography" is exemplified in Diamond's picture of the human in relation to ethics, a picture in which, as in Heidegger, vulnerability, passivity, and finitude are recuperated as a "being-able" and a "transitivity," thus ontologizing and hypostatizing the split between the human and the other—*all* its others—across which the human then reaches in an act of benevolence toward an other we imagine is enough like us to warrant ethical treatment. This only reinforces our suspicion that this human being is an essentially homogeneous and undifferentiated creature that is capable of a more or less transparent relationship to its own nature, a relationship that it *then* expresses in and through language and may *then* extend benevolently—or not—to the nonhuman other.

This seems clear enough, for example, in Diamond's contention that the "basis for justice" lies in the human being's "unreasoned expectation of good," one that "can, if we are willing to attend to it, stop us from inflicting harm" (not "that it generally or even frequently happens," she admits, "that people *are* thus inhibited").[84] We should recall here too her contention that "the moral expectations of other human beings demand something of me as other than an animal; and we do something like imaginatively read into animals something like such expectations when we think of vegetarianism as enabling us to meet a cow's eyes."[85] In both these examples, what the language of "unreasoned good," "moral expectations," and "imaginatively read into" unsuccessfully attempts to paper over is just how undifferentiated in relation to itself the "human" is in this account, and how hypostatized its relations to the nonhuman other have become. And matters are not helped any by her contention that "our *hearing* the moral appeal of an animal is our hearing it speak—as it were—the language of our fellow human beings."[86]

There are two distinct issues here that we need to treat in turn. The first, of course, is who, exactly, these "fellow human beings" are, particularly if we have ruled out recourse to "a biological concept," as Diamond insists we should. The second—and I will return to this in a moment—is that even if we know who those "fellows" are, what does it mean to say that there is "a language" proper to them, and that the animal must speak it if it is to be heard morally? As for the first issue, perhaps the most succinct way to make my point is simply to note the question of ethnocentrism that it begs, a problem made all the more acute by Diamond's rejection of reference to biological or scientific co-ordinates (which might be viewed as independent of cultural determi-nations). For example, she writes in "Experimenting on Animals" that if we want to know whether it is a good thing "to treat dogs differently from other animals, or cows differently from other animals,"

> it is absurd to think these are questions you should try to answer in some sort of totally general terms, quite independently of seeing what particular human sense people have *actually* made out of the differ-ences or similarities you are concerned with. And this is not predict-able. If the Nuer, for example, had not actually made something hu-manly remarkable out of giving cows a treatment quite different from that accorded other animals, one could not know that "singling cows out for special treatment" could come to that. . . . The modes of life and thought of our ancestors, including their moral thinking, have *made* the differences and similarities which are now available for us to use in our thinking and our emotions and decisions. (351)

Diamond may be right, of course, that "we are never confronted with the existence of 'beings' with discoverable empirical similarities and differences, toward which we must act, with the aid of general principles," in such and such a way (351). But the problem is that there is nothing in Diamond's position to prevent us from carrying out ex-actly the same sort of thought experiment here that we saw Cavalieri carry out earlier with Nozick's relational view of ethics. (To wit: "If the Germans, for example, had not actually made something humanly re-markable out of giving Aryans a treatment quite different," and so on.) Rather, the only thing that *does* stop us is the extraordinarily hedged and finally empty contention that we may readily distinguish between attitudes toward racial difference, species difference, sexual difference, and so on that are "humanly valuable" and those that aren't (351). Of course, one community's "humanly valuable" is another's "humanly deplorable," which is exactly the question with which the whole dis-cussion began.

We seem, then, to be faced with a double bind: How can we agree with Diamond's rejection of basing ethical questions on empirical data and "biological concepts" and at the same time distance her view from the pernicious ethnocentrism harbored by a relational or completely culturally referenced view of ethics? Derrida captures the problem when he asks the same question about historicism, which is structured by precisely the same dilemma: can one criticize it "in the name of something other than *truth and science* (the value of universality, omni-temporality, the infinity of value, etc.), and what happens to science when the *metaphysical* value of *truth* has been put into question. . . . How are the effects of science and truth to be reinscribed?"[87] The problem here, in other words, is that the ethnocentric "we" might have been forcibly opened to take account of what lies beyond its comfort zone by appeal to the "universality" and "omnitemporality" of "truth and science" that exceeds any ethnocentric determination (which is essentially how the appeal to empirical interests functions in animal rights philosophy); but that seems no longer possible in any straight-forward sense, even if, as Derrida remarks in the same note, the point of raising this difficulty "is not in order to return naively to a relativist or sceptical empiricism."

At this juncture, then, we suspect that a different way of thinking these problems may be necessary, a way suggested (but only suggested, I think) by Diamond's remarkable essay "The Difficulty of Reality." In her earlier work, as I have been arguing, we find something like the problem we see in Richard Rorty's concept of "belief": that there is nothing *in the relation of the ethnos to itself* ("what we have made of" the human/animal difference) that installs alterity not *outside* the self-enclosed subject of the *ethnos* (who may then benevolently recognize— or not—such difference from a safe and secure ontological distance, as it were) but rather at its very core, as the truth of the subject itself.[88] In this light, part of the strength and attraction of Diamond's "The Difficulty of Reality" is precisely its "weakness." Where the emphasis in earlier essays was on our *ability* (Derrida's *pouvoirs*) to *extend* imagi-natively an apparently secure sense of "the human" to animals (hearing them "speak our language," seeing in them expectations of us as "other than animal"), here, when we try to put into words the experience of "the difficulty of reality" that we find bodied forth in Ted Hughes's "Six Young Men" or Coetzee's *The Lives of Animals,* "the words fail us, the words don't do what we are trying to get them to do. The words make it look as if I am simply unable to see over a wall which happens to separate me from something I very much want to see. But the fact that the words are apparently too weak to do what I am demanding from them does not mean that the experience here of *powerlessness* has been shown to involve a kind of grammatical error" (8).

The force of this turn in Diamond's thought, and its consequences for ethics, can be extended and elaborated by means of Derrida's work, which would help us to articulate more fully the implications of the fact that there are *two* kinds of finitude here, two kinds of passivity and vulnerability. The first type (physical vulnerability, embodiment, and eventually mortality) is paradoxically made unavailable, *inappropriable,* to us by the very thing that makes it available—namely, a second type of "passivity" or "not being able," which is the finitude we experience in our subjection to a radically ahuman technicity or mechanicity of language, a technicity that has profound consequences, of course, for what we too hastily think of as "our" concepts, which are therefore in an important sense not "ours" at all.

And here, then, we arrive at the third point of contact—but also finally of difference—between Diamond and Derrida that I noted earlier: "how philosophical misconceptions about language are connected with blindness to what our conceptual life is like," to use Diamond's phrase. Derrida's point would be not only that we don't have a concept of the human but also that it's a good thing too, because it is only on the strength of that weakness that we are able to avoid both horns of the dilemma brought to light in Diamond's work: on the one hand, the constant threat of ethnocentrism that a certain understanding of Wittgenstein flirts with (we do what we do because of "what we have made of the difference between humans and animals," which keeps us from lapsing into "biological continuism"); and, on the other hand, the mining for ethical universals that, for philosophers such as Singer, Regan, and Nussbaum, would attempt to counter this very threat by uncovering first principles of ethics via the anti-ethnocentric autonomy of reason. Derrida, I am suggesting, makes available a "third way," whose response would be that, yes, it is true that what we think of as the principles of personhood, morality, and so on are inseparable from who we are, from our discourse as a "mode of life" (to put it in Wittgenstein's terms). But at the same time, "we" are not "we"; we are not that "auto-"

of "autobiography" (as in Derrida's "The Autobiographical Animal") that humanism "gives to itself." Rather, "we" are always radically other, already in- or ahuman in our very being—not just in the evolutionary, biological, and zoological fact of our physical vulnerability and mortality, our mammalian existence but also in our subjection to and constitution in the materiality and technicity of a language that is always on the scene before we are, as a precondition of our subjectivity. And this means that "what *he* calls 'man,'" what "we" call "we," always covers over a more radical "not being able" that makes our very conceptual life possible.

Even more important, perhaps—at least for the topic at hand—is that this passivity and subjection are shared by humans and nonhumans the moment they begin to interact and communicate by means of any semiotic system. As Derrida puts it in a well-known passage from the interview "Eating Well":

> If one reinscribes language in a network of possibilities that do not merely encompass it but mark it irreducibly from the inside, everything changes. I am thinking in particular of the mark in general, of the trace, of iterability, of *différance*. These possibilities or necessities, without which there would be no language, *are themselves not only human*. . . . And what I am proposing here should allow us to take into account scientific knowledge about the complexity of "animal languages," genetic coding, all forms of marking within which so-called human language, as original as it might be, does not allow us to "cut" once and for all where we would in general like to cut.[89]

At this juncture, we can feel the full force of the difference between Derrida's posthumanist position and how Diamond's humanism formulates the relation between language, ethics, and the human/animal divide. In "Injustice and Animals," she suggests that applying the concept of justice to nonhuman animals is "a response to communicative pressure," which she defines thus: "In our various activities, including our attempts to think about our lives and to make sense of what we experience and what we do, we can use words well or badly. The ways of speaking we find in response to activities and experiences may accommodate a merely superficial kind of 'meaning it'; or we may be able to find words that more fully render experiences or activities, *words that can be meant more fully*."[90] But I think it is clear by now that the distinction between superficially "meaning it" and *really* "meaning it" is bound to fare no better than Lacan's distinction between *really* pretending and just pretending to pretend that I discussed in the previous chapter. In both cases, what is at stake is the recovery and maintenance of the humanist subject as "auto-," as "a free consciousness present to the totality of the operation, and of absolutely meaningful speech *[vouloir-dire]* master of itself: the teleological jurisdiction of an entire field whose organizing center remains *intention*"—an intention that expresses itself in the difference between pretending and pretending to pretend, meaning something superficially and *really* meaning it.[91]

It is over and against this recovery of humanism by what one might think of as the analytic-with-apologies tradition that Derrida counterpoises what he characterizes as the "corrupting" and "contaminating" work of "iterability," the trace, and so on.[92] As we saw in the opening chapter, iterability "does not signify simply . . . repeatability of the same, but rather alterability of this same idealized in the singularity of the event. . . . It entails the necessity of thinking *at once* both the rule and the event, concept and singularity"; as such, it "marks the essential and ideal limit of all pure idealization," but *not* as "the concept of nonideality," as ideality's pure other (119). Like the undecidability that it generates, iterability "remains *heterogeneous*" to, rather than opposed to, the order of the ideal, the calculable, and the pure. Hence the *form* of ethical responsibility it entails is of another order altogether: tending to each specific concatenation and iteration of "rule and event," to "*this particular* undecidable" (116) that "is always a *determinate* oscillation between possibilities," one that takes place "in strictly *defined* situations (for example, discursive—syntactical or rhetorical—but also political, ethical, etc.)." And as Derrida emphasizes, such instances are "*pragmatically* determined" (148).

Equally important for Derrida—and this is crucial to situating the question of "the animal" in the broader context of posthumanism that we have been developing—is that this second form of finitude, this second kind of "not being able," renders uncertain and unstable— "unsettled," in Cavell's terms—the relationship of the human to itself because it renders unstable not just the boundary between human and animal but also between the organic and the mechanical or technological. And here, perhaps more clearly than anywhere else, we can locate the most radical sense of Derrida's posthumanism, which finds the generative force of the *nonliving* at the origins of any living being, human *or* animal, who communicates (and this in the broadest sense) with another. For these reasons—because of the estrangement of the "the human" from the "auto-" that "we" give to ourselves—the relation between the human and nonhuman animals is constantly opened anew and, as it were, permanently. It is a wound, if you will, that can never be healed and is only further excavated and deepened by the very iterative technologies (thinking, writing, speech) that we use to try and suture it. As Derrida summarizes it in a recent interview:

> Beginning with *Of Grammatology,* the elaboration of a new concept of the *trace* had to be extended to the entire field of the living, *or rather to the life/death relation,* beyond the anthropological limits of "spoken" language. . . . At the time I stressed that the "concepts of writing, trace, gramma, or grapheme" exceeded the opposition "human/nonhuman." All the deconstructive gestures I have attempted to perform on philosophical texts . . . consist in questioning the self-interested misrecognition of what is called the Animal in general, and the way in which these interpret the border between Man and Animal.[93]

I stress this intercalation of the boundary between the biological/organic and the mechanical/technical in relation to the infra- and transhuman in no small part because Diamond herself is extremely interested in it—most conspicuously, of course, in her reading of the "exposure" of the photograph in Ted Hughes's "Six Young Men": a technological, archival artifact that confronts us with "a shuddering awareness of death and life together."[94] Here, however, Diamond and Derrida pull us in different and perhaps even opposite directions, for Diamond then glosses that exposure in terms of Costello's contention that "I know what it is like to be a corpse"—a contention whose significance she unpacks along the following lines in the final paragraph of her essay, as a kind of rejoinder to pragmatism: "A language, a form of thought, cannot (we may be told) get things right or wrong, fit or fail to fit reality; it can only be more or less useful. What I want to end with is not exactly a response to that: it is to note how much that coming apart of thought and reality belongs to flesh and blood" (12). Derrida's point, however, is that this "coming apart" is not *just* of flesh and blood but is also born of the fact that our *relation* to flesh and blood is fatefully constituted by a technicity with which it is prosthetically entwined, a diacritical, semiotic machine of language in the broadest sense that exceeds any and all presence, including our own.[95]

That it *is* "in the broadest sense" can be brought out by looking briefly at Derrida's own confrontation with an exposure of the sort Diamond is interested in (in this case, an exposure of a piece of film)—a confrontation that will have considerable resonance for my discussion of the relationship between technology, ethics, and archive in the final chapter. In a set of conversations with Bernard Stiegler published in English as *Echographies of Television*, Derrida is concerned to differ with Roland Barthes's suggestion in *Camera Lucida* that "the photo is literally an emanation of the referent. From a real body which was there proceed radiations that come to touch me, I who am here. . . . A kind of umbilical cord ties the body of the photographic thing to my gaze."[96] Instead Derrida insists that "the modern possibility of the photograph joins, in a single system, death and the referent."[97] What he means by this rather enigmatic formulation is that a kind of spectrality inheres in the technology of the image because of its fundamental iterability:

> Because we know that, once it has been taken, captured, this image will be reproducible in our absence, because we know this *already,* we are already haunted by this future, which brings our death. Our disappearance is already here. . . . And this is what makes our experience so strange. We are spectralized by the shot, captured or possessed by spectrality in advance.
>
> What has, dare I say, constantly haunted me in this logic of the specter is that it regularly exceeds all the oppositions between visible and invisible, sensible and insensible. A specter is both visible and invisible, both phenomenal and nonphenomenal: a trace that marks the present with its absence in advance. (117)

Derrida then tells a story that is haunting in its own right about his participation in Ken McMullen's film *Ghostdance,* where he improvised a scene with the French actress Pascale Ogier, in which he asks her, "And what about you, do you believe in ghosts?" and she replies, "Yes, now I do, yes." "But imagine the experience I had," Derrida says,

> when, two or three years later, after Pascale Ogier had died, I watched the film again in the United States, at the request of students who wanted

to discuss it with me. Suddenly I saw Pascal's face, which I knew was a dead woman's face, come onto the screen. She answered my questions: "Do you believe in ghosts?" Practically looking me in the eye, she said to me again, on the big screen: "Yes, now I do, yes." Which now? . . . I had the unnerving sense of the return of her specter, the specter of her specter coming back to say to me—to me here, now: "Now . . . now . . . now, that is to say, in this dark room on another continent, in another world, here, now, yes, believe me, I believe in ghosts."

But at the same time, I know that the first time Pascale said this, already, when she repeated this in my office, already, this spectrality was at work. It was already there, she was already saying this, and she knew, just as we know, that even if she hadn't died in the interval, one day, it would be a dead woman who said, "I am dead," or "I am dead, I know what I'm talking about from where I am, and I'm watching you," and this gaze remained dissymmetrical, exchanged beyond all possible exchange . . . the other gaze met, in an infinite night. (120)

So here is Elizabeth Costello again, in a different light: "What I know is what a corpse cannot know: that it is extinct, that it knows nothing and will never know anything anymore. For an instant, before my whole structure of knowledge collapses in panic, I am alive inside that contradiction, dead and alive at the same time."[98] And here is Hughes again, by the light of day that is also, if we believe Derrida, the light of night:

> That man's not more alive whom you confront
> And shake by the hand, see hale, hear speak loud,
> Than any of these six celluloid smiles are,
> Nor prehistoric or fabulous beast more dead;
> No thought so vivid as their smoking blood:
> To regard this photograph might well dement,
> Such contradictory permanent horrors here
> Smile from the single exposure and shoulder out
> One's own body from its instant and heat.

In the end, however—and this is the final difference I want to mark between the Cavell/Diamond line and Derrida—Derrida derives from this "dementing" force, which bleeds together organism and machine, living and dead, "prehistoric beast" and one's own human "instant and heat," a kind of law or general economy, the fundaments of which reach all the way back to his earliest work. As he puts it in *Echographies of Television* (and this descends directly from my earlier discussion of the nonappropriability of death that constitutes my indebtedness to the other), this relationship constitutes an "inheritance," a "genealogy of the law";[99] before the specter of the dead we are "'before the law,' without any possible symmetry, without reciprocity" (120):

> The wholly other—and the dead person is the wholly other—watches me, concerns me, and concerns or watches me while addressing to me, without however answering me, a prayer or an injunction, an infinite demand, which becomes the law for me: it concerns me, it regards me, it addresses itself only to me at the same time that it exceeds me infinitely and universally, without my being able to exchange a glance with him or with her. (120–21)

This is most obvious, perhaps, in the best-known example of the spectral phenomenon that Derrida discusses—Shakespeare's *Hamlet,* where the relationship between inheritance, law, responsibility, and spectrality is particularly (even Oedipally) pronounced. But it would also seem to be the case with Hughes's six young men in the photograph, to whom we, as the living, feel a strange kind of responsibility and debt that is unsettling because unanswerable, a point powerfully put in motion early in Diamond's essay. In Derrida's words, "the other comes *before* me" (122).

But we know, from Derrida's vantage, that this responsibility cannot be met—it is "an infinite demand"—because of the law of iterability itself. He writes, "If the law of iterability . . . exceeds the intentional structure that it renders possible and whose teleo-archaeology it limits, if it is the law not merely of intentionality (nor for that matter merely of the language or the writing of man), then the question of the specificity of intentionality in this field without limits remains open."[100] In the face of the pragmatic and determinate forms of treatment visited by humans upon nonhuman others, in the face of the injustices noted by all the thinkers I have been discussing, the question is: how can I "intend" otherwise in actions that, even if groundless and without purity or ideality of origin in a (speaking or thinking) subject, nonetheless find their mark, we might say, in material effects on other living beings?

The issue here, in other words, is that if we do take seriously the pragmatic specificity of the relationship of iterability and intention, then the first thing we are bound to notice is this: human and (at least some) nonhuman animals may be, in a phenomenological or ontological sense, more or less equally subjected to the exteriority and materiality of the trace in a way that only "the living" can be; that is what it means to be "mortal," to be "fellow creatures," to be *subjected*. But what is not at all shared equally, even if this is the case, is the material disposition of that fact in practices and institutions whose effects bear very differently on human and nonhuman animals—effects Derrida himself is, of course, well aware of.[101] To put it another way, humans and animals may share a fundamental "non-power at the heart of power," may share a vulnerability and passivity without limit as fellow living beings, but what they do *not* share equally is the power to materialize their misrecognition of their situation and to reproduce that materialization in institutions of exploitation and oppression whose effects are far from symmetrical in species terms. From this vantage, the issue is not only "what *should* we do?—the question of justice that Derrida would have us confront anew in each iteration, without recourse to "calculation" and ethical formulae—but also "what *will* we do?" in the face of such challenges.

As David Wood puts it in his searching discussion of Derrida's interview "Eating Well," "there is a place for argument, proof, and demonstration in philosophy," but "what this critical function opens onto are more or less motivated *possibilities of response*"—and, with regard to deconstruction specifically, the ability "to respond to what has not been adequately schematized, formulated, etc."[102] In Wood's view, those possibilities are evacuated—eviscerated, we might say—by Derrida in two ways in "Eating Well," where he explicitly rejects vegetarianism as a more ethically responsible answer to the question "How should one eat?" First, Derrida frames the question in such a way "as to incorporate and interiorize the actual eating of animals inside the symbolic eating of anything by anyone" (30), so that the specific practice of eating animals becomes simply one more version of the larger symbolic structure by which "Man" in the Western philosophical tradition secures its transcendence through mastery of nature, repression of the body—everything that Derrida associates with the term "carnophallogocentrism" (30). In so doing, Derrida evacuates the difference—the material alterity—between different sacrificial structures and practices. And the result of this "assimilation," as Wood puts it, is "to the extent that in this culture sacrifice in the broad (symbolic) sense seems unavoidable, there would seem to be little motivation for practical transformations of our engagement in sacrificial behavior" (31).

Second, what he calls "Derrida's ambivalence toward vegetarianism" seems to be consonant with deconstruction's idea of ethics as "a practice of eternal vigilance," one that cannot "become some sort of alternative ethical seal of approval" for vegetarianism or anything else. But the problem here is that "the avoidance of that widening path of resistance to violence that is vegetarianism could end up preserving— against the temptations of progressive practical engagement—the kind of good conscience that too closely resembles a 'beautiful soul'" (32). In other words, the "eternal vigilance" of deconstructive ethics, which depends on always attending, without the aid of predetermined judgments and formulae, to the specific iteration of event and rule, here threatens to flip-flop into the opposite of vigilance, one whose "good conscience" resides in the security of its knowledge that there is no such thing as a good conscience.

To put it slightly otherwise, Wood would force on Derrida the same distinction drawn earlier by Diamond: "Is Derrida (merely) an animal welfarist?" In the end, do we find in Derrida's work on ethics and the animal a reproduction—to quote Diamond once again—of "a kind of pitilessness at the heart of welfarism, a willingness to go ahead with what we do to the vulnerable, a willingness to go on subjecting them to our power because we can, because it suits us to do so," a willingness that "is inseparable from the 'compassion' we express in welfarism."[103] What such a vantage point discloses is an essential tension in Derrida's work on ethics between his insistence that we pay vigilant attention to the particular instance of decision, of justice, in all its thickness and heterogeneity, without letting formulae and maxims do the work for us, and a general law or economy of iterability that would render such decisions nonuniversalizable, decisions whose foundations are local only (while what is *not* local is the unavailability of such foundations from which to universalize).

This is not to say that Derrida's position is without ethical force— quite the contrary. Regarding items six and seven in *Contemporary Issues in Bioethics* with which I began this chapter (biomedical research and eugenics), Derrida forcefully rivets our attention—as no one else in poststructuralist philosophy has done—on the "infernal" and "monstrous" conditions created for animals in product testing and factory farming by "more and more audacious manipulations of the genome" and other "genetic *forms of knowledge*" and the "*techniques* of intervention" related to them that have reduced the animal to a mere vehicle for products and commodities.[104] Moreover (as I noted in the opening pages), he would call our attention to the process of "codification" in bioethics, whereby the overdetermining material, political, and economic relations between those in bioethics who formulate the rules and norms and those who legislate and enforce them are laid bare.[105]

But Derrida's position bears on the pragmatics of contemporary bioethics with which I began this chapter only at the extremes (the "pragmatic" instance of judging particular cases, on the one hand, and the "ordeal of the undecidable" that attends such judgment and in principle makes universalization impossible), while current bioethics as a brand of policy studies and the edifice of law it takes for granted operate precisely in the middle zone abandoned by Derrida (the maintenance or modification of generic, universalizable norms in and through particular cases, *and* the legal model of "personhood," with all its philosophical underpinnings, that underwrites the process). Derrida would have us pay attention to the specific instance of decision in a way foreclosed by the generality and logic of the law itself, since the force of such specific instances for Derrida is, in principle, their ability to revolutionize or exceed the law itself, their call for us to realize that what is legal may not be just (and vice versa). (Here one might readily think not just of issues regarding our treatment of animals such as xenotransplantation but also of issues such as assisted suicide, the case of Terri Schiavo, and the like—all of which would seem to depend on pragmatic particulars that obtain, as it were, "beneath" the level of the law and often create a jarring contradiction between what is legal and our sense of what is just.)

At the other extreme, Derrida's general economy of iterability would prevent the generalization of such decisions, taken in aggregate, into a larger edifice or structure—a new legal doctrine, if you like—and would highlight the differences and even the abyss between the intentionality that would attempt unilaterally to deploy such structures and the material and archival force of such structures themselves. What this means for bioethics in the pragmatic sense is that Derrida is of little use in enabling us to formulate new guidelines about particular surgical or experimental procedures that we could then generalize on behalf of more progressive policies. But he is of immense use in forcing us to live with the fact that no matter how such policies are drawn, the distinction between human and animal should be of no use in drawing them.

4 "Animal Studies," Disciplinarity, and the (Post)Humanities

What began in the early to mid-1990s as a smattering of work in various fields on human-animal relations and their representation in various endeavors—literary, artistic, scientific—has, as we reach the end of the new millennium's first decade, galvanized into a vibrant emergent field of interdisciplinary inquiry called animal studies or sometimes human-animal studies. In what follows, I want to suggest that *both* rubrics are problematic in light of the broader context in which they must be confronted—the context of posthumanism. More specifically, I hope to make it clear that the questions that occupy (human-) animal studies can be addressed adequately only if we confront them on not just one level but two: not just the level of content, thematics, and the object of knowledge (the "animal" studied by animal studies) but also the level of theoretical and methodological approach (*how* animal studies studies "the animal"). Just because we direct our attention to the study of nonhuman animals, and even if we do so with the aim of exposing how they have been misunderstood and exploited, that does not mean that we are not continuing to be humanist—and therefore, by definition, anthropocentric. Indeed, one of the hallmarks of humanism—and even more specifically that kind of humanism called liberalism—is its penchant for that kind of pluralism, in which the sphere of attention and consideration (intellectual or ethical) is broadened and extended to previously marginalized groups, but without in the least destabilizing or throwing into radical question the schema of the human who undertakes such pluralization. In that event, pluralism becomes *incorporation,* and the projects of humanism (intellectually) and liberalism (politically) are extended, and indeed extended in a rather classic sort of way.

To put it this way—in terms of the ideological stakes of disciplinarity—is to signal that there are multiple contexts within which the question of animal studies, disciplinarity, and the humanities might be discussed had we world enough and time—contexts toward which I can only rapidly gesture here. One of these would be the changing status of the humanities themselves—a change sometimes described in the language of crisis—in relation to what used to be called "the public sphere" and the more general questions of the humanities' social, cultural, and political role in a world that appears to need and value humanistic knowledge less and less.[1] One might also—moving outward to larger contexts—situate this question in the context of the changing role and function of the university as an institution, especially as that role has been reshaped by forces associated with the corporatization of social institutions generally.[2] And one might, moreover, explore both those issues—disciplinary change and institutional change—along the lines cultivated by Alan Liu's discussion of the humanities in terms of the broader context of knowledge work in *The Laws of Cool* (2004). Still farther afield, one might ask after the role and status of animal studies in the context of growing attention to the biopolitical and to questions of biopower that derive at least from the work of the Frankfurt school (and beyond that, Marx's famous discussion of "species being" in the Economic and Philosophical Manuscripts of 1844), wend their way through Michel Foucault's later work, and receive contemporary attention from thinkers ranging from Giorgio Agamben and Roberto Esposito to Jacques Derrida and Judith Butler, among others. For surely the question of biopower radically changes our view of the "animality" of the human in ways marked, for example, by Agamben's distinction between *bios* (which marks "the form or way of life proper to an individual or group") and *zoé* (which expresses "the simple fact of living common to all living beings").[3] For biopolitical theory, the animality of the human becomes a central problem—perhaps *the* central problem—to be produced, controlled, or regulated for politics in its distinctly modern form.

Literary and Cultural Studies in the United States: Historicism, Theory, and Disciplinarity

I want to begin, however, with a more modest focus on the discipline in which I am housed, literary and cultural studies, where the relations between animal studies, the humanities and its mission or missions, and the problem of disciplinarity are being conjugated in an especially energetic and wide-ranging way. In that context, it is all the more important to note that the discipline itself has in recent years reached what feels to many like a crisis of coherence, a disciplinary threshold of some sort.[4] The sharpest symptom, perhaps, is the schism that has been brewing for some time now (to put it schematically) between scholars committed primarily to matters of history and scholars committed primarily to matters of theory (and, in a different register, the relation of form and meaning) in the study of literature and culture. And while historicism, broadly speaking, has no doubt ruled the day for some time now on the strength of the early momentum garnered by innovative works in New Historicism in fields such as early modern and romantic studies, there are signs that this is changing, in part because the dominant modes of historicism being practiced now seem to many a regression to the kind of *old* historicism that New Historicism itself sought to move beyond.

Critiques of the situation from across the intellectual and political spectrum are not hard to find. The romanticist Thomas Pfau, for example, is among the more strident critics, though he might best be characterized as an intellectual historian. Pfau observes that this more recent mode of historicism, though it "disavows the strong penchant for 'grand narrative' . . . in favor of so many specialized micro-analyses," cannot achieve "its recurrent quest for 'local transcendence'" (to borrow Alan Liu's famous formulation) "without underlying and largely unexamined ideological commitments of its own"—an "implicit framework" that Pfau pares down the following tacit assumptions:

> 1. *The Axiom of the Archive:* that specialized research, understood at the recovery of previously "overlooked" materials and sources, amounts to a mode of knowledge-production whose significance is taken to be self-certifying.
> 2. *The Axiom of Contextualism:* that the "new" materials so recovered largely imply their own causal and argumentative force simply by being (materially, biographically, or idiomatically) associated with a contextual "field" whose outline is either being presupposed outright or inferred from the interpretive community (re)currently husbanding it.
> 3. *The Axiom of Pluralism* (or "indifferentism"): that the power and

significance of contemporary critique arises from the primitive accumulation of so many disaggregated voices and archival projects, with the further assumption that critical knowledge will spontaneously arise from the open-market interaction of (presumptively) equivalent/ indifferent perspectives.

4. *The Axiom of Retroactive Liberation* (or "secularization"): that an institutional, professional, and transactional mode of critique will eventually liberate historical meanings from their alleged past entrapment in religious or ideological norms and values and, in doing so, will restore for us their temporarily "missed" yet always "intended" authentic (secular) core.

5. *The Axiom of Critique as a Guarantor of Historical Progress:* that the transactionalism of modern, institutional knowledge effects a teleological progression towards a hypostatized Liberal community envisioned as a wholly transparent, inclusive, tolerant, and exhaustively informed. Crucially, though, this telos can only be articulated in a language of permanent deferral and (in what constitutes a diametrical reversal of Aristotelian thought) is being defined by the *absence* of any specific norms or contents rather than by the practical acknowledgment of their supra-personal authority.[5]

Pfau's quarrel with this mode of historicism, as you will have already gathered, is not just methodological—not just, for example, with "the self-imposed restriction of recent models of inquiry to tightly localized and circumscribed chronotypes (biographically conceived time spans, the *punctum* of this or that local "event," dates of publication, etc.)" (7). It is also ideological, insofar as such an approach "ultimately reproduces a decisive—albeit unexamined and doubtful— axiom that underwrites . . . the political and economic projects of classical Liberalism and their subsidiary rhetoric of emancipation, progress, growth, and political 'rights'" (7). Given the extensive discussion in the last chapter, it hardly needs saying that this linkage between methodology and ideology has particular resonance in the context of animal studies, where the same concept of rights—namely, in the form of "animal rights"—has been crucial to the emergence and consolidation of the very field that now is eager to move beyond that paradigm.

What also drops out in many manifestations of contemporary literary historicism, if we believe Ellen Rooney, Susan Wolfson, and others who contributed to the special *MLQ* issue of 2000 on "The

New Formalism," is the question—one might even say the very disciplinarity—of reading (and not just in the narrow sense of reading *literary* forms such as the sonnet or the novel). As Rooney puts it:

> The effects of the attenuation of the category of form include the reduction of every text to its ideological or historical context, or to an exemplar of a prior theory (content) . . . and the generalization of reading-as-paraphrase, which robs cultural *and* literary studies of the power to make any essential contribution to critical work already moving confidently ahead in history, sociology, anthropology, and communications. These are all disciplines that have long since mastered the art of reading-as-summary, reading sans form.[6]

Admittedly, we would do well here to keep in mind Marjorie Levinson's reminder that it is useful in such cases to distinguish between "*new* historicism" and "new *historicism*"[7]—between many of the founding, first-generation texts of New Historicism by Stephen Greenblatt, Jerome McGann, and others (which were, she argues, quite demonstrably concerned not just with the articulation of form and historical content but also with questions of the aesthetic and of pleasure [560–61]) and the work of "those hapless 'followers' and mere practitioners" (560), as one critic puts it, which treats the text—*any* text, be it poem, novel, Supreme Court ruling, political speech, or advertisement—as merely a site for mining content, an alibi "sufficient to get the machinery of 'archaeology' and archive-churning" up and running (561).

Surely Rooney is right that the real issue here is "not to transcend the New Historicism, poststructuralism, cultural materialism," or "any of the other critical interventions marking literary studies in the late twentieth century" (18)—it's not about picking your favorite brand name and taking sides, in other words—but to engage the question of *disciplinarity* in literary and cultural studies: what they can contribute, specifically, that could not be handled just as well (or better) by other fields such as history or sociology or philosophy. As she puts it, "for a critical reader bereft of the category of form, the subject matter of literary and cultural analysis loses all standing as a *theoretical* object, an object situated and at work in a critical or disciplinary field" (18–19).

To raise the question of cultural studies in this context, though, only brings the problem into sharper focus, for as Rooney points out, that field is "perhaps even more intractably caught than literary criticism in the dilemma of defining its own proper form"; it is "a welter of competing (and even incompatible) methods, and a (quasi-) disciplinary form increasingly difficult to defend, intellectually or politically" (21). Indeed, if we believe Tilottama Rajan, cultural studies isn't part of the solution, it's part of the problem, and (like the historicism criticized by Pfau) it is one with identifiable ideological contours. In Rajan's view, in fact, cultural studies in the United States and North America (the United Kingdom and Australia would require somewhat different analyses, as she rightly notes) has evolved from a site of "decentering innovation" into "a symbiosis with globalization" and the New World Order, in which "its dereferentialization is what makes it dangerous to some of its original components"[8]—an ambivalent situation discussed in similar terms recently by Gayatri Spivak in *Death of a Discipline*. In Rajan's view, the "inclusive vagueness" (69) that for Rooney plagues cultural studies is precisely what has enabled it early on to garner new territory, but this inclusiveness masks the fact that it is also subtly, and predictably, selective; it includes postcolonialism (but not Homi Bhabha), gender studies (but not Hélène Cixous or French feminism); it rewrites the entire field of psychoanalysis as "essentialist," and privileges "Benjaminian storytelling, autobiography, and subjective experience, ostensibly to insist on local knowledge, but really to reinstate self-expression and identity politics" (71).

As "a soft sell for, and a personalization of, the social sciences" (74), the effect of academically mainstreamed cultural studies is, Rajan suggests, "to simulate the preservation of civil society after the permutation of the classical public sphere" into an essentially market and consumerist logic of "representation" (69–70). It meets the demand that "all sectors be economically represented in the curriculum, which is most efficiently managed by reducing texts to cultural soundbites" (75). For such an ideological project, she notes, it should come as no surprise that "the social is now the unquestioned ground of the humanities. Nor do the humanities even want to claim a way of thinking the social from the outside" (74)—an observation that echoes Pfau's insistence on the need to retain a critical dimension for the humanities in the face of the historicist principle of "immanence." Drawing on the work of the Italian philosopher Gianni Vattimo, she amplifies Rooney's observations on historicism's text-as-paraphrase by observing that the teleology of the new cultural studies, under the guise of "pluralism," is "'of absolute self-transparency' based on total communicability."[9] Cultural studies thus involves a repurposing of reading and thinking; it is "a pragmatic use of the humanities within a modular structure that appears to promote dissidence" by its pluralism of content and identities but instead "interpellates minority identities and localisms into a disciplinary complex" (77). Thus, for example, Bhabha's concepts of "alterity" and "migrancy," rather than exerting a critical force that is radically heterogeneous to—radically other than—the liberal *socius* and its ruling protocols, instead become recontained as pluralism by cultural studies' normalizing ideological function for civil society: "Though civil society contains diverse subgroups, it mediates their antagonisms, holding together different classes and interests by providing their members with recognition" (76). And hence, Rajan argues, disciplines of "slow thought" committed to the nontransparency of these relationships become relegated to the margins of cultural studies ("symptomatically reflected in the turn away from poetry" in literary and cultural studies, as she shrewdly notes); they are therefore seen as an active, even pernicious, impediment to the liberal project of incorporation and "recognition" that is an expression of, not a critique of, globalization. As she notes, reflecting on the special 2001 issue of *PMLA* titled "Globalizing Literary Studies," the idea of "heterogeneous global audiences" that is so taken for granted in contemporary cultural studies "is an oxymoron that conceals a deep contradiction in claiming the synchronicity of the unique and the universal, and the global reach of Western notions of 'heterogeneity'" (75).

All these critics, as you might guess, see a crucial role for theoretical reflection in addressing the intellectual miasma that is contemporary literary and cultural studies—not because theory is a specialized obsession, but precisely because it isn't. As Rooney notes, the issue is "not nostalgia for theory as a master discourse but anxiety over the status of theoretical *debate* as a moving force that articulates disciplinary forms. . . . Neither literary nor cultural studies can proceed in the absence of such an arena: it is a necessary disciplinary effect, even as it fosters the transformation and *denaturalization of disciplinary practices*."[10] And in the absence of such theoretical reflection—to put an even finer point on it—the disciplinary hegemony of historicism becomes nothing more (or less) than an exercise in the very presentism that historicists routinely lay at the doorstep of theory. Indeed, as Rooney observes, one result of this lack of theoretical reflection by the dominant modes of historicism is that, ironically enough, they become an unwitting "echo of the earliest epoch of literary studies," in that "thematic analysis has become virtually the sole mode of 'formal' analysis effectively at work in literary and cultural studies" (28).

Does this mean that there is no such thing as "good" historicism? Of course not, as Levinson's careful distinction between "*new* historicism" and "new *historicism*" ought to make clear. But it does mean that any historicism needs to confront the difference between historicity and historicism—that is to say, the difference between the material, institutional forces it is interested in and the modes and protocols of knowledge by which those materials are *disciplined*, by which they are given *form*: protocols that are, by definition, always already reductive, not just in the strict epistemological sense of being selective but also in the *empirical* terms favored by historicism itself. Indeed, as none other than Franco Moretti has pointed out with regard to the project of literary history, "the majority of books disappear forever—and 'majority' actually misses the point: if we set today's canon of nineteenth-century British novels at two hundred titles (which is a very high figure), they would still be only about *0.5 percent* of all published novels."[11] As Moretti notes, to take account of this fact—99.5 percent, "the others, nothing. Gone"—is to change our very idea of what literary history is, and to change it in ways that, say, the Annales school and Fernand Braudel were keenly interested in, ways that only further sharpen the question of whether the dominant *forms* of current historicisms in literary and cultural studies— namely, narrative, paraphrase, and the linear, biographical, and generational chronotopes noted by Pfau—are, in fact, historicism *at all,* rather than simply a domestication of the very problem and force of historicity itself.[12] In short, historicism has to be aware of the historicity of its *own* modes of disciplinary practice, its own forms. And it can't do that without theory.

In this context, it is telling that both Rooney and Wolfson (on behalf of formalism, no less) note that a major lacuna in current modes of historicism in U.S. literary and cultural studies is Marxist aesthetics. Marxism grappled as no other contemporary body of thought has with precisely the questions that occupy literary and cultural historicists today, particularly those who think of themselves as politically progressive: namely, the ideological and political function of culture in relation to economic infrastructures, civil society, and the relations of national and international contexts, both geopolitical and economic, as they bear on those questions.[13] This is not to say, of course, that figures such as Lukács, Brecht, Adorno, Macherey, Althusser, Bloch, Mannheim, and others agreed at all on these issues. Rather, it is to remind us that the dubious practices of paraphrase, reading for theme, privileging the biographical and the generational chronotope, the local context, and so on—and, most importantly, the instrumentalization of cultural forms as a mere vehicle for sociological or historical content— that plague contemporary literary and cultural studies received intensive scrutiny for decades in Marxist theory's debates over socialist realism, the ideological and political character of modernism and its formal experimentation (as in the so-called Brecht/Lukács debate), and much else besides. And yet this remarkable body of work does not inform the landscape of current historicist practice in literary and cultural studies in the United States in any fundamental way.

Rajan sees the role of theory in the current context in rather different terms but likewise finds its signal value in "denaturalizing" disciplinary formations, its ability to exercise a destabilizing, antisystemic force in relation to disciplinarity in general—a kind of "asystasy," to use a term she borrows from Schelling,[14] "that unworks the Idealism (and imperialism)" of any practice, including "theory" itself (80). She finds this project of "an asystatic deployment of fields of knowledge to unsettle one another" inherited and sustained by Michel Foucault in his early work, but in a historically specific articulation, one that prevents the gesture toward theory from becoming a master discourse. As she reminds us, *The Order of Things* denaturalizes and decenters disciplines not only in response to the crisis of the university as a culture and institution in late 1960s France (one whose disciplinary forms hamstrung its ability to respond to the social crisis at hand); it also "culminates in a criticism of the 'human sciences': the modern academy's bridging of the humanities and social sciences under the form of a corporate merger" (81). Foucault's analysis of the emergence of the disciplines is, in a word, anti-ideological.

What Are Disciplines?

I want to supplement Rajan's account of Foucault's work on disciplinarity with John Rajchman's to make a slightly different point, one whose stakes will only gradually come into focus in the remainder of the chapter. A crucial emphasis of Foucault's early work is this: If we take the question of disciplinarity seriously, we have to first of all admit that disciplines do not derive their constitutive protocols from their objects of attention. Quite the contrary, disciplines constitute their objects through their practices, theoretical commitments, and methodological procedures—and they do so quite selectively. This is a seemingly simple point, but it is one, as we shall see, with far-reaching consequences.

From the early 1960s to the late 1970s, in *The Order of Things, The Archaeology of Knowledge,* and *Discipline and Punish,* Foucault undertakes what Rajchman calls "nominalist histories"—not "histories of things, but of the terms, categories, and techniques through which certain things become at certain times the focus of a whole configuration of discussion and procedure."[15] He thus seeks "to challenge the universal, objective, and progressive image of unified science inherited from the Enlightenment" and instead embarks on an "attempt to discover an irreducible plurality of 'territories' and 'objects' of knowledge, characterized by anonymous tacit procedures," an account that emphasizes "the relative autonomy of discourses" (53). Two further and very important consequences flow from this commitment. First, this means that there is no such thing as "society as a whole" (55), since the idea of "a whole and universal society" has now been "dispersed" into a range of different practices, discourses, and disciplines (59). Second—since one of Foucault's great objects of analysis is "the group of techniques, terms, and categories that concern the subject"— this means that Foucault's work continues and indeed intensifies twentieth-century challenges, such as Heidegger's or Wittgenstein's, to "the post-Cartesian philosophy of the subject" (52). In scrutinizing the "various kinds of systems through which people have come to identify themselves as subjects," Foucault, in short, undertakes a trenchant posthumanism on the terrain of the subject to match his anti-universalism in the domain of the object.[16]

We can extend and sharpen Foucault's account of disciplinary formations with Niklas Luhmann's more recent work on social systems. In doing so, I hope to make some headway on what James Chandler has recently characterized as the "need to rearticulate the disciplinary system after three decades of 'add on' fields and programs." To do so, Chandler suggests, we must "work toward a better understanding of how the scheme of the disciplines might be said to compose a system"—a project that he likewise finds powerfully initiated in Foucault's work.[17] Like Foucault, Luhmann does not make individuals the fundamental, constitutive elements of society; like Foucault, he is therefore "suspicious of the universalist vocation of the intellectual"[18]—not because (as in Foucault) such an understanding would mitigate against "our capacity to find alternatives to the particular forms of discourse that define us" by "uncovering the particularity and contingency of our knowledge and our practices" (60), but because, for Luhmann, such universalism (desirable though it may be) is actually impossible under modernity, now understood as a process of "functional differentiation." For Luhmann as for Foucault, then, "society as a whole" cannot be said to exist—nor can, by extension, the public sphere in anything like the classical sense—but what Luhmann is able to articulate more clearly and at the same time more radically is how these twin claims (no social holism, no universal intellectual) do not amount to "rejecting science as such or criticizing *all* rational discourse" (59). Rather, it means for Luhmann that the *form* of rationality itself under modernity is paradoxical—and paradoxical in ways that produce precisely what Rajan calls the "asystasy" in and through which disciplines destabilize and expose each other.

Now it may seem odd to invoke systems theory in this context, given that both Pfau and Rajan, despite their vast intellectual differences, think of the idea of system (and its companion idea, information) as the apotheosis of everything their accounts of disciplinarity aim to critique.[19] This is so, I think, because both are operating with a concept of "system" (and of adjacent terms such as "information") that is markedly out of date, one that would apply to the first-order systems theory of the 1950s (Norbert Wiener, for example), but not to the work in second-order systems theory of Maturana and Varela, Heinz von Foerster, Luhmann, and others. Indeed, for these thinkers, the concept of system might best be described (to use a concept from Adorno to which both Pfau and Rajan would be amenable) as an effort to think "detotalized totality." In fact, as Dirk Baecker puts it in a passage I invoked in the opening chapter, systems theory after the second-order turn may best be understood "as an attempt to do away with any usual notion of system, the theory in a way being the deconstruction of its central term."[20] To put it this way—and I will amplify the point in chapters 8 through 10—is simply to remember why Luhmann's work is particularly interested in the core problematic of romanticism formulated by Kant and Hegel that occupies both Pfau and Rajan[21]—a problematic it attempts to redescribe in a context well articulated by Derrida's observation that

> the critique of historicism in all its forms seems to me indispensable. . . . The issue would be: can one criticize historicism in the name of something other than *truth and science* (the value of universality, omnitemporality, the infinity of value, etc.), and what happens to science when the *metaphysical* value of *truth* has been put into question, etc.? How are the effects of science and of truth to be reinscribed?[22]

This is precisely the project, I would argue, that Luhmann undertakes in his later work, which becomes more and more "philosophical," if you like, in *both* of the senses invoked by Pfau and Rajan: as a universalizing discourse (Pfau) that retotalizes differentiation, seriality, specialization, and so on in terms of a kind of normativity and systematicity produced by modernity as fundamentally a form of functional differentiation; and as a theory of the contingency and constructedness of knowledge that detotalizes philosophy's idealism and imperialism in the terms described by Rajan. Hans Georg Moeller summarizes this quite well:

> Luhmann's relation to philosophy can . . . be compared to Hegel's relation to religion (as expressed in the *Phenomenology of Spirit*). For Hegel, religion was, with respect to its highest purpose, a thing of the past. . . . Neither its semantics nor its general structure could be fully accepted any longer. . . . Its "essence" had to be expressed in a more self-reflective way, in a language and in a form that represented a higher understanding.[23]

Similarly, for Luhmann, "*philosophy* had become with respect to its highest purpose, a thing of the past," and so what Luhmann unabashedly calls a "supertheory" of society, a theory of "universal relevance," can no longer be housed in philosophy, given philosophy's disciplinary norms and protocols.[24] Hegel's *Aufhebung* from religion to philosophy now becomes Luhmann's from philosophy to theory—and this movement is driven, as Luhmann repeatedly insists, by historical forces. Like Hegel's scheme, Moeller writes, Luhmann's "claims to be thoroughly conceptualized and to return to its beginning—in other words, a coherent whole instead of a linear argument."[25] Unlike Hegel's, however, Luhmann's theory acknowledges its own contingency—that is, it acknowledges its modernity, that it is itself a product of functional differentiation. Or as Moeller observes, "What a supertheory says has to make general sense to it. But this sense itself is not general, it is contingent on the theory that is constructing this horizon of sense in the first place."[26]

With this background in mind, we can now move to investigate in more detail Luhmann's radicalization of the analysis of disciplinarity carried out in Foucault's early work—one made possible by Luhmann's crucial turn, in his middle and late work, to the theory of autopoiesis as key to understanding social systems. As we saw in the opening chapter, Luhmann appropriates the concept from the work in biology of Humberto Maturana and Francisco Varela to make sense of the seemingly paradoxical fact that systems are both open *and* closed; to exist and reproduce themselves, they must maintain their boundaries and integrity through a process of self-referential closure; and it is only on the basis of this closure that they can then engage in "structural coupling" with their environment.[27] Like neurophysiological autopoietic systems, their fundamental logic is "recursive"; they use their own outputs as inputs in an ongoing process of "self-making" or "self-production," and they constantly (re)produce the elements that in turn produce *them*.

In Luhmann's scheme, disciplinary formations would, strictly speaking, be viewed as elements of the social system called "education," but I believe they may be profitably thought of as subsystems that follow the same systemic logic, which both produce and depend on their own elements for their autopoiesis (journals, conferences, research groups, protocols of advancement and recognition, etc.). From this vantage, disciplines would deploy the distinction that is fundamental to all systems—the distinction "system/environment"—but would articulate it in their own specific form, thus (and this is a basic postulate of systems theory) using it to reduce and process the overwhelming complexity of an environment that is by definition always already exponentially more complex than any particular system itself. As we saw earlier, this selectivity does not, however, indicate solipsism. Quite the contrary, for as Luhmann puts it in *Social Systems,* self-referential closure "does not contradict the system's *openness to the environment.* Instead, in the self-referential mode of operation, closure is a form of broadening possible environmental contacts; closure increases, by constituting elements more capable of being determined, the complexity of the environment that is possible for the system" (37).

As we saw in chapter 1, the adaptive pressure to develop a highly selective code—a pressure generated by the system's inferiority in complexity in comparison with the environment—leads, in turn, to an increasing *internal* differentiation within the system itself. The system/environment distinction is then repeated *internally* in the system, so that, for example, the entire legal system now becomes the environment for the various legal subsystems, which must themselves respond to (or achieve "resonance" with) the broader changes in the legal system itself. In building up their own internal complexity through increased internal differentiation, systems are able to enhance their ability to respond to a rapidly changing environment by, in a sense, slowing it down. Increased selectivity buys time. But in doing so—in increasing their environmental resonance by building up their own internal complexity, by simply "doing what they do"—social systems create more complexity in the environment of other systems even as they try to reduce it for themselves (177), hence the nearly paradigmatic situation associated with "postmodernity": hypercomplexity.[28]

For Luhmann, then, as we know from our earlier discussions, *all* observations, whether by the legal system, the economic system, or any other, are contingent and selective constructions and reductions of an environment that cannot be grasped holistically or in any totalizing fashion. This means that there is no "given" environment "out there" that can be cognitively approached or "represented" in its totality. What this means is not only that all systems and all observations are self-referential; it also means that, paradoxically, the difference between self-reference and external reference (or "hetero-reference") is itself a *product* of self-reference, in the same way that the "outside" of the environment is always the outside *of* a specific "inside." This fact, however, cannot be observed by the system that, at the same time, wants to use that distinction to carry out its operations. *That* observation can only be made by a *second-order* observer, using a *different* code (in this case, education), which likewise must remain "blind" to the paradoxical nature of *its* constitutive distinction, which can only be disclosed by *another* observer, and so on and so forth. As Luhmann points out, "The designations that usually register this state of affairs are relativism, conventionalism, constructivism. One can summarize the meaning of these concepts in the thesis of a loss of reference." But if this is to be taken as a (again paradigmatic) "critique" of postmodernity, such a critique assumes a position of totalization that is by definition no longer available in the context of modernity understood as functional differentiation. "This thesis marks their negative content," Luhmann continues. "Its negativity, however, only arises in a historical comparison with the premises of ontological metaphysics, with its religious safeguards, its cosmos of essences, and its normative concept of nature."[29]

Several important consequences may now be drawn from Luhmann's analysis. First, as was already clear in Foucault's work, disciplines take their specificity not from the objects of their attention but from the specific protocols of their discourses (Foucault), their communications and observations (Luhmann). Or as Luhmann puts it in somewhat different terms, "a first step toward the comprehension of modernity therefore consists in the distinction between problems of reference and problems of truth."[30] The disarticulation of reference and truth thus helps us understand, in turn, a crucial second point: how the object of disciplinary knowledge is not therefore "lost" under modernity's "loss of reference" but is rather, in a very real sense, greatly enhanced. As Luhmann puts it in the introductory chapter to *Social Systems:*

> One can now distinguish the system/environment difference as seen from the perspective of an observer (e.g., that of a scientist) from the system/environment difference as it is used within the system itself,

the observer, in turn, being conceivable himself only as a self-referential system. Reflexive relationships of this type don't just revolutionize the classical subject-object epistemology . . . they also produce a very much more complex understanding of their objects via a very much more complex theory design. (9)

In a process that Luhmann calls "semantic overburdening," "the system being observed is covered over with a procedure of reproducing and increasing its complexity that is impossible for it. In its analysis science uses conceptual abstractions that do not do justice to the observed system's concrete knowledge of its milieu or to its ongoing self-experience. On the basis of such reductions—and this is what justifies them—more complexity becomes visible than is accessible to the observed system itself. . . . In this sense it overburdens its object's self-referential order. . . . This overburdening is immanent in every observation" (56). To put it another way, it is not just unavoidable, but crucial and immensely productive, to keep open the difference between first- and second-order observation, to insist on a nonreductive relation of problems of reference and problems of truth: to remember, with Maturana, that the internal mechanisms of an observed phenomenon and a second-order observation of them *"intrinsically take place in independent and non-intersecting phenomenal domains."*[31] All observations, then, may be carried out only on the basis of self-referential closure, but that closure, because it produces both environmental complexity and semantic overburdening, produces more possibilities for connection, more *openness*.

This analysis helps us understand, in turn, a third crucial point: that disciplinary differentiation (or "specialization") is not something to be lamented, avoided, or overcome; rather *"universalization* can be achieved only through *specification."*[32] This is the tenor in which I would like to hear Immanuel Wallerstein and his coauthors in the recent report *Open the Social Sciences* when they write:

> The claim to universality, however qualified . . . is inherent in the justification of all academic disciplines. That is part of the requirement for their institutionalization. The justification may be made on moral, practical, aesthetic, or political grounds, or some combination thereof, but all institutionalized knowledge proceeds on the presumption that the lessons of the case at hand have significant bearing on the next case, and that the list of potential cases is, for all practical purposes, endless.[33]

When Wallerstein and his coauthors say "universalizing," the reading I want to suggest is not "totalizing" (which is likely Wallerstein's own) but the sense voiced in Rajchman's reading of Foucault when he suggests that "history doesn't exist" for Foucault—not because it's not *real,* but because "there is no one thing all our histories are about, even though there may seem nothing about which we cannot write a history."[34]

Fourth and finally, given everything we have just said, it is clear that just as disciplinary formations are not constituted by objects but by communications (Foucault's "discourses"), neither are they constituted by *persons.* For Luhmann—and this seems less counterintuitive after revisiting Foucault—the fundamental elements of social systems are not people but communications. In fact, as Dietrich Schwanitz suggests, "The individual human being belongs to each of these functionally differentiated subsystems for only short periods of time with only limited aspects of his person depending on his respective role as a voter, pupil, reader, patient, or litigant. It is his fundamental exclusion from society that allows the occasional re-entry of the individual under particular circumstances. . . . Modern society develops a semantics of individuality that regards the individual as alien, unfamiliar, unpredictable, and free."[35] This means we can say that people can participate in interdisciplinarity even if disciplines can't, *only* if we are willing to give up the traditional notion of "person." Only, that is, if we become posthumanist.

Locating the Animal of Animal Studies, or Posthumanism

So how does all of this affect our view of animal studies in relation to the question of disciplinarity, especially the disciplinarity of literary and cultural studies? In my view, it means that we should *not* try to imagine some super-interdiscipline called "animal studies" (an understandable desire, of course, for all who work on cultural studies of nonhuman animals), but rather recognize that it is only in and through our disciplinary specificity that we have something specific and irreplaceable to contribute to this "question of the animal" that has recently captured the attention of so many different disciplines: not something *accurate* to contribute but something *specific* (and there is a world of difference between those two claims). What we need, then, is not interdisciplinarity but *multidisciplinarity* or perhaps *transdisciplinarity*—but a transdisciplinarity understood not (to take one recent formulation) as "a critical evaluation of terms, concepts, and methods that transgresses disciplinary boundaries" as a means to a "higher level of reflexivity," one that "accepts the task of making itself transparent by thematizing the conditions of its own speech." Rather, we need to understand transdisciplinarity as a kind of distributed reflexivity necessitated, as we have just seen, by the fact that (by definition) *no* discourse, no discipline, can make transparent the conditions of its own observations.[36]

In this sense, transdisciplinarity means a distributed network of first- and second-order observers (disciplines) that, precisely by "doing what they do," call into question—and are called into question by—other disciplinary formations. Such is the case, as we saw in the last chapter, in Cora Diamond's suggestion that literature confronts philosophy with the degree to which philosophy's characteristic modes of thinking about our moral responsibilities to animals are in fact evasions or deflections of a traumatic question that in some profound sense defies thought—a trauma that philosophy attempts to mitigate by turning it into a problem of propositional argumentation. Or to take another example, as I argued in chapter 2, literary studies has an important role to play in showing how the theory of language typically relied on in cognitive science—and how that theory is typically related to questions of consciousness and cognition—smuggles back into the category of subjectivity the very Cartesianism that cognitive science says it wants to overcome by means of its resolutely functional mode of analysis.[37]

To say that an object of study will actually be enriched by the ongoing differentiation of disciplines is not, however, to invoke a tepid pluralism—far from it. As Luhmann points out—and here he defines in a nutshell the incoherent epistemological and ideological core of much work in contemporary cultural studies—"the laziest of all compromises, is to agree on 'pluralism.' This both begins and avoids the deconstruction of the distinction between subject and object. We concede to each subject its own way of seeing, its own worldview, its own interpretation, as with the reader of Wolfgang Iser, but only in a framework that at the same time allows for the 'objective' world, text, and so forth."[38] Instead, a better way to imagine some ever more complete or thorough representation of nonhuman animals via interdisciplinary practice is to recognize, as I have been suggesting, that the enrichment of the object of study via "semantic overburdening" can only happen *by means of* disciplinarity and its differences. This may be what is (falsely) called "relativism," but it is also what, under the conditions of modernity, is called "knowledge."

Crucial to a posthumanist understanding of disciplinarity, then— and to posthumanism in general, I would argue—is the fundamental principle of "openness from closure" that Luhmann's work helps us theorize: that taking seriously the phenomena of self-reference and autopoietic closure in disciplinary systems leads not to solipsism but, quite the contrary, to the ability for the system to increase environmental contacts and, in the process, produce more environmental complexity for other systems, which in turn challenges other disciplines to change and evolve if they want to remain resonant with their changing environment. This marks an entirely different—because *post*humanist— valence from a fundamental assumption endemic to many contemporary discussions of (inter)disciplinarity: that even if disciplines can't transcend disciplinary closure, *people* can. As one critic writes on behalf of interdisciplinarity and a fairly standard set of desires associated with it, disciplinary practice "becomes a productive rather than a reproductive environment" when, "in the spirit of critical reflection meanings and values of traditional pedagogy can be scrutinized. . . . The intersubjectivity of meaning can be exposed," he continues, "and educational institutions, the classroom, the discipline, and the university can be seen to construct and condition knowledge. In this way literary study, as the study of textuality . . . reveals the epistemological structures that organize how we know, how our knowledge gets transmitted and accepted, and why and how students receive it."[39]

But as Foucault would surely be the first to point out—and here he would follow in the footsteps of his teacher Louis Althusser's critique of Antonio Gramsci's humanism—such a picture, appealing as it may be, relies on the fantasy of a subject who escapes the constitutive blindness (that is, the contingency and selectivity) that in fact makes knowledge possible. "Critical reflection," in other words, names the ability to pick up and put down disciplinary discourses at will without being bound by them, to master without being mastered by the finitude of knowledge—all, ironically enough, in the services of ostensibly *identifying* various forms of finitude that overdetermine disciplinary practice. In reinscribing the familiar figure of the human as the subject-of-reflection, such a view reproduces an entire set of assumptions and protocols that are not just intellectually but also ideologically specific, as both Pfau and Rajan (among many others) have pointed out. In so doing, it constitutes the reverse of what I have been trying to derive from the Foucault/Luhmann account of disciplinarity: not the "openness from closure" that results from taking the self-reference and autopoiesis of disciplinarity seriously, but rather *closure from openness* (or rather, *apparent* openness) in the reproduction of a liberal humanist subject who then, on the basis of "reflection," undertakes various forms of pluralism.

More important for the topic at hand, such a picture of critical consciousness and its ability to rise above disciplinary and discursive finitude actually closes off the human from the nonhuman and thus reinstates the human/animal divide in a far less visible but far more fundamental way, while ostensibly gesturing (but only gesturing) beyond humanism itself.[40] And it is the status, structure, and tacitly governing set of assumptions of that form of subjectivity—and not just the range of its content and its interests, however putatively progressive, multicultural, or anti-anthropocentric—that must be fully examined. To use Derrida's terms, it is a question, as we saw in the last chapter, of the precise nature of the "auto-" of the "autobiographical animal," the concept of "the human" that the human falsely "gives to itself" to then enable its recognition—from a safe ontological distance, as it were—of the nonhuman other in a gesture of self-flattering "benevolence" wholly characteristic of liberal humanism.

As I argued in detail there, equally important for understanding the relationship of disciplinarity to subjectivity that I have been discussing—and this is the point usually overlooked in Derrida's later work on "the question of the animal"—is that there are *two* kinds of finitude here under which the "man" of the *humanities* labors; and, moreover, that the first type (physical vulnerability, embodiment, and eventually mortality) is paradoxically made unavailable, *inappropriable,* to us by the very thing that makes it available: namely, a second type of "not being able," a second type of finitude that we experience in our subjection to the radically ahuman technicity of language (understood in the broadest sense of any semiotic system). This last fact, as we have seen, has profound consequences for what we too hastily think of as "our" concepts, our readings, our histories, which are therefore in an important sense not ours at all. If literary and cultural studies are interested in sign systems of all kinds in their formal, material, and semantic aspects (as one would presume them to be), then they must, I am arguing, confront the enormous implications of this fact for their disciplinarity.

What Derrida enables us to formulate—but so does Luhmann, in a different register—is that yes, it is true that what we think of as personhood, knowledge, and so on is inseparable from who "we" are, from our culture, discourses, and disciplines; but at the same time, we are not we; we are not that "auto-" of autobiography that humanism "gives to itself." As we saw in the previous chapter, equally important for the topic of animal studies is Derrida's insistence that this second type of finitude—the estranging prostheticity and exteriority of communication—is shared by humans and nonhumans the moment they begin to respond to each other by means of any semiotic system in the most rudimentary sense—an assertion also clearly shared by Luhmann's unequivocal postulate that problems of autopoietic self-reference do not apply to humans, or to consciousness, or even to biological or organic systems, alone.[41]

In different registers and with different objectives, then, Derrida, Luhmann, and Foucault help us clarify the point—and the ethical stakes of the point, if we believe Derrida—that many of the confusions surrounding the question of interdisciplinarity stem from the fact that we continue to think the question in terms of persons and "a subject-centered semantics," that is, precisely, in terms of humanism. The virtue of paying attention to the thinkers I have been discussing is not only do they make it clear that disciplines aren't persons; they also make it clear that *persons aren't persons,* in the sense of the definition of "person" that humanism "gives to itself." And it is here, at this precise juncture, that animal studies becomes a subset of the larger problematic of *post*humanism.

All the foregoing helps to clarify, I hope, two crucial and often misunderstood aspects of posthumanism as I use the term: first, that it is not antihistorical but only antihistoric*ist* in the sense I have outlined; and second, that it is not posthuman or antihuman but rather simply post*humanist*. As for the first (as I have already suggested on the heels of Marjorie Levinson's useful distinction between "*new* historicism" and "new *historicism*"), the distinction humanism/posthumanism is completely asymmetrical, in fact, to the distinction historicism/formalism. To insist that the difference between historicity and historicism be recognized (as we saw Franco Moretti suggesting earlier) is simply to insist that if the past is far more heterogeneous and complex—far more *ahuman* and strange, as the Annales school held—than the accounts of it we have inherited, it is also true that the present from which those accounts issue as products of specific practices and protocols is heterogeneous *to itself* in ways actively repressed by the recasting of a vast historical, cultural, and anthropological field within the protocols of humanism and the subject of knowledge it reproduces in and through those protocols.

As for the second point—that posthumanism is anti- or post-human—my sense of posthumanism does not partake of the fantasy of the posthuman described by N. Katherine Hayles, which imagines a triumphant transcendence of embodiment and "privileges informational pattern over material instantiation, so that embodiment in a biological substrate is seen as an accident of history rather than an inevitability of life."[42] On the contrary, as Derrida's point earlier suggests, it requires us to attend to that thing called "the human" with *greater* specificity, *greater* attention to its embodiment, embeddedness, and materiality, and how these in turn shape and are shaped by consciousness, mind, and so on. It allows us to pay proper attention, with Maturana and Varela, to the material, embodied, and evolutionary nature of intelligence and cognition, in which language, for example, is no longer seen (as it is in philosophical humanism) as a well-nigh-magical property that ontologically separates *Homo sapiens* from every other living creature. Rather, it may now be viewed as an essentially non- or ahuman emergence from an evolutionary process—what Maturana and Varela call the emergence of "linguistic domains" from larger processes of social interaction and communication among animals including but not limited to *Homo sapiens*. That radically ahuman evolutionary emergence in turn makes possible language proper and the characteristic modes of consciousness and mentation associated with it, but remains tied (as in body language, kinesics, and more general forms of symbolic semiology) to an evolutionary substrate that continues to express itself in human interaction.[43]

And yet everything I have just said would not be possible—would be literally unthinkable—without readily identifiable models, concepts, terms, and so on (disciplinary developments in information theory, cognitive ethology, semiology, to name just a few) that are distinctly *modern* disciplinary products with their own particular histories and developments of the sort described by Foucault in *The Order of Things*. Thus we find ourselves in a strange but inescapable loop, in which our ability to understand—more fully and more thickly than humanism—"the human" depends on "posthumanist" theoretical and methodological innovations that end up revealing, to paraphrase Lyotard, that the posthuman comes both after (chronologically) and *before* (as its robust material, embodied, and evolutionary condition of possibility) the human of humanism.[44] What we find "after" humanism as it were, is what we might call, turning Adorno's famous phrase upside down, not the "preponderance of the object" but the "preponderance of the *subject*." What I want to locate here, then, is a second crucial and indeed determinative dimension in which the question of posthumanism is central. It is not just, as Neil Badmington and others have rightly observed, that "the 'post-' of posthumanism does not (and, moreover, cannot) mark or make an absolute break from the legacy of humanism."[45] It also means that while we may share Hayles's view that various visions and versions of the triumphantly disembodied posthuman, such as Hans Moravec's, continue to rely on (indeed imperialize) "a liberal humanist view of the self,"[46] we must also recognize that there are liberal humanist ways of engaging in this very critique.

Does this mean, then, that "posthumanism" as I am using the term is simply a thinly veiled synonym for "systems theory" or "deconstruction?" Not at all, as the signal impact of that discipline called science in the context of animal studies ought to make clear. But it does mean (as the quotation from Derrida's "Eating Well" on "scientific knowledge" earlier suggests) that science, though it appears to eschew a subject-centered semantics, can avoid its *own* form of idealism only if it confronts the fact, as Luhmann puts it, that "science can no longer comprehend itself as a representation of the world as it is, and must therefore retract its claim of instructing others about the world. It achieves an exploration of possible constructions that can be inscribed in the world and, in so doing, function as forms."[47] This does not mean, of course, that the knowledge thereby produced is worthless or cannot have operational value; on the contrary—as Bruno Latour, for instance, would be the first to suggest—it can have operational value and effectivity only *because* it is such a reduction of complexity. This means, in turn, that "the break between transcendental idealism and radical constructivism" (67) recognizes the fact of "polycontexturality," to use Gotthard Gunther's term: that is, that the distinctions "true/untrue" and "self-reference/external reference" are not only to be distinguished but also, as Luhmann puts it, "are located at right angles to each other. They have no mutually unbalancing effects" (65).[48]

From this vantage, then, posthumanism can be defined quite specifically as the necessity for any discourse or critical procedure to take account of the constitutive (*and* constitutively paradoxical) nature of its own distinctions, forms, and procedures—and take account of them in ways that may be distinguished from the reflection and introspection associated with the critical subject of humanism. The "post-" of posthumanism thus marks the space in which the one using those distinctions and forms is not the one who can reflect on their latencies and blind spots while at the same time deploying them. That can only be done, as we have already seen, by another observer, using a different set of distinctions—and that observer, within the general economy of autopoiesis and iterability, need not be human (indeed, from this vantage, never was "human"). It is only on this basis (which is not, strictly speaking, a "basis" at all, but a nonplace, a *form of difference*) that a first-order observer (the "subject" in humanist parlance) is opened, and unavoidably so, to the alterity of the other: not by "taking thought" or by benevolent reflection but by the very conditions of cognition and communication, conditions that, in their constitutive "blindness," generate the *necessity* of the other.

This is why even though animal studies may be viewed as in one sense "just another" field, it is, in the sense I have just described, *not* just another field. On the one hand, it could certainly be seen as what James Chandler calls the latest incarnation of a "subdisciplinary field," one of "a whole array of academic fields and practices" that since the 1970s "have come to be called *studies:* gender studies, race studies, and cultural studies, of course, but also film studies, media studies, jazz studies"; the list is virtually endless.[49] But for the reasons I have been outlining, I think we must also see animal studies as not just another in the long list of "fill-in-the-blank studies" itemized by Chandler. It's not just that I want to resist the homogenizing force of such a designation, which suggests that what are radically different problems, constituencies, and formations are somehow equivalent; nor is it only because of all the reservations (some of which I noted earlier) that the designation "studies" invites. Rather, the point I want to emphasize—and it is one obscured by the generic moniker of "studies," which occludes the crucial link between the two forms of finitude we examined a moment ago that reside at the heart of animal studies in a uniquely determining way—is that one can engage in a *humanist* or a *posthumanist* practice of a discipline, and that fact is crucial to what a discipline can contribute to the field of animal studies.

For example, just because a historian devotes attention to the topic of nonhuman animals—let's say, the awful plight of horses used in combat operations during World War I—doesn't mean that humanism and anthropocentrism aren't being maintained and reproduced in his or her disciplinary practice insofar as the disciplinary subject doing the history remains isolated from the "viral" effects of the second form of finitude, and all its implications, that I discussed earlier. And insofar as that is the case, that disciplinary practice undermines on a second level what looks like an anti-anthropocentric endeavor, because its form of disciplinary subjectivity is founded on a constitutive repression of a less visible—but for that very reason all the more fundamental—bond between human and nonhuman animals as beings who not only live and die as embodied beings, but also communicate with each other in and through a second form of finitude that encompasses the human/animal difference, forming a bond that is all the more powerful because it is "unthinking" and in a fundamental sense unthinkable. So even though—to return to our historian example—your concept of the discipline's *external* relations to its larger environment is posthumanist in taking seriously the existence of nonhuman subjects and the consequent compulsion to make the discipline respond to the question of nonhuman animals foisted on it by changes in the discipline's environment, your *internal* disciplinarity may remain humanist through and through.

We may now, then—to move toward a conclusion—suggest a more overarching schema in which such a procedure might be called "humanist posthumanism," locating itself at one corner of a plane, in which the Y axis denotes external relations (–/+ humanism/anthropocentrism) and the X axis denotes internal disciplinarity (–/+ humanism/anthropocentrism). Such a schema is not meant to be exhaustive, of course, merely indicative; nor does it preclude recognizing that the desirability of a given position in such a schema must be contextualized. (I suggest, for example, that if you are interviewing with the local newspaper about animal overpopulation in your community and you want to win over readers to your point of view, you would do well to gravitate toward the internal disciplinary discourse that characterizes the humanist end of the spectrum.) In this view, the designation "humanist posthumanism" would apply as well, as I have argued elsewhere, to the Kantian animal rights philosophy of Tom Regan, the utilitarian animal liberation position of Peter Singer, or the capabilities approach of Martha Nussbaum in *Frontiers of Justice*.[50] Meanwhile, at the diagonally opposed corner of this schema, "posthumanist humanism" would consist of being posthumanist in internal disciplinarity, but humanist in the continued external insistence on the ethical and, broadly speaking, ontological efficacy of the human/animal divide. Here—to stay for the moment only with figures about whom I have written—one might think of the work of a Richard Rorty or a Slavoj Žižek. For example, Rorty's strident antifoundationalism, his critique of both philosophical realism and idealism as shared forms of "representationalism," his rejection of the view of philosophy as "the mirror of nature," surely kicks the props out from under the humanist subject of knowledge in its disciplinary practice. Yet Rorty's liberalism finds in such a deconstruction of philosophical representationalism no charge to rethink the hierarchy of human/animal, as animals remain excluded (as anything but, presumably, derivative or "indirect" subjects of justice) from the liberal "conversation" about political ends to which philosophy for Rorty is clearly subordinated.[51]

As for Žižek, his well-known attacks on liberal multiculturalism in general and on neopragmatism in particular (which are surely right

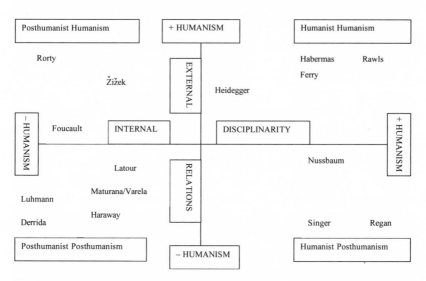

Fourfold disciplinarity: humanist versus posthumanist, internal versus external.

as far as they go) would seem to separate him decisively from a figure such as Rorty.[52] Žižek's disciplinary antihumanism would be located not in his antifoundationalism but rather precisely in his *attack* on anti-foundationalism's evasion of the more fundamental fact, identified by Lacan, of "Truth *as contingent*"—not as "constructed" or "relative" in the sense associated with neopragmatism but as the radical senseless-ness of the Lacanian Real, which (as Lacan famously put it) "resists sym-bolization absolutely."[53] And yet to realize, as I have argued elsewhere, that in Žižek "the animal" is always already simply a metonymy either for the Lacanian Real or, in the case of pets, for the Symbolic, is to real-ize that although Žižek maintains a resolutely antihumanist account of the relationship between thought, psychic formations, and language or the Symbolic, he is nevertheless humanist and anthropocentric in his inability to rethink what I have called the "distribution" of subjectiv-ity across species lines.[54] As for Foucault, his account of disciplinarity, and his own disciplinary practice, would appear to be posthumanist for reasons I have already discussed at some length. Yet Foucault's external relations to humanism are difficult to assess at this point—not only be-cause of some striking differences between his earlier work (my focus here) and his later investigations of "the care of the self" (in which a certain humanism returns to the fore, if we believe Žižek),[55] but also because we are just beginning to be able to understand the full implications of Foucault's concepts of biopower and biopolitics for trans-species relations.

As for the category of humanist humanism, that perhaps needs little elaboration, because nearly all our social and political institutions and most of our public intellectuals take such a formation for granted (I might cite here—again among those I have written about—Habermas, Rawls, and Luc Ferry). And that leaves posthumanist posthumanism, which has to do with understanding—and understanding the consequences of—the very redefinition of what humanistic knowledge is after the disciplinary subjectivity at its core, the notion of the human that it "gives to itself," has been rewritten along the lines I have been exploring here in the work of Derrida and Luhmann (and elsewhere in the work of Deleuze and Guattari, Bruno Latour, Donna Haraway, and Maturana and Varela). In short, the external or ahuman forces that historicists and formalists alike in literary and cultural studies presume to constitute the always already post- of their posthumanism (political institutions, economic infrastructures, geopolitical and strategic configurations and events, but also social institutions and conventions such as art forms and their genres and media, modes of domesticity and intersubjectivity, and the like) must always be conjugated within a *second* kind of externality and ahumanity—a second kind of finitude that, as Derrida helps us see, fatefully binds us to nonhuman being in general, and within that to nonhuman animals, as the very condition of possibility for what we know and for sharing it with another. It is, in other words, a question of *locating* the "animality" of animal studies— in this case, I would wager, where one might least expect it.

5 Learning from Temple Grandin
Animal Studies, Disability Studies, and Who Comes after the Subject

OF THE VARIOUS CONTEMPORARY FIELDS of interdisciplinary cultural studies that emerged over the past decade, two of the most philosophically ambitious and ethically challenging are animal studies and disability studies. Both are often taken to be the latest chapters in the academic assimilation of the so-called new social movements (civil rights, feminism, environmentalism, gay and lesbian activism, and so on) that have fundamentally reshaped the study of society and culture over the past thirty years or more. As we saw in some detail in chapter 3, part of what makes animal studies significant (and disability studies is no different in this respect) is that it poses fundamental challenges, as these earlier movements have, to a model of subjectivity and experience drawn from the liberal justice tradition and its central concept of rights, in which ethical standing and civic inclusion are predicated on rationality, autonomy, and agency. That agency, in turn, is taken to be expressive of the intentionality of one who is a member of what Kant called "the community of reasonable beings"—an intentionality that is taken to be more or less transparent to the subject itself.

Part of my aim in this chapter is to extend the argument of chapter 3 to the question of disability, with an eye toward gleaning what animal studies and disability studies have to teach each other about who or what comes "after" the subject as it is modeled in liberal humanism.[1] Both animal studies and disability studies show us something about the limitations of this model and in doing so call on us to rethink questions of ethical and political responsibility within what I have been characterizing as a fundamentally posthumanist set of coordinates.[2] In the wake of this "after," new lines of empathy, affinity, and respect between different forms of life, both human and nonhuman, may be realized in ways not accountable, either philosophically or ethically, by the basic coordinates of liberal humanism.

Both animal studies and disability studies have intersected in what has recently emerged as a small subfield of its own: authors who claim that their condition has enabled for them a unique understanding of nonhuman animals and how they experience the world. The most famous of these is probably Monty Roberts, the famed "horse whisperer," who was born with a severe form of color blindness called achromatopia that allows him to see only blacks, whites, and a remarkably subtle scale of grays.[3] For that very reason, however, he developed early in life a keen perception of movement that has allowed him to read the body language of horses with amazing subtlety and precision.[4] Then there is the case of Dawn Prince-Hughes, who claims that her experience with Asperger's syndrome enabled her to have an unusually keen understanding of the nuances of the social interactions and communications of a group of zoo gorillas. As with Monty Roberts, this was crucial for the evolution of her own self-understanding, enabling her to move from being "a wild thing out of context," living on the margins of society, to completing a Ph.D. in anthropology and eventually to becoming an author and editor. Gorillas, she says, "taught me how to be civilized."[5]

And then there is the case I will be discussing here, Temple Grandin, who reflects on her life with autism in three books published over the past nineteen years. Grandin—an animal science Ph.D. who has designed one-third of all the livestock-handling facilities in the United States—insists that her experience with autism and its specific characteristics (the intensely visual rather than verbal quality of her mental life, the acute sensitivity to tactile stimulation, and so on) has given her a special understanding of how nonhuman animals experience the world, one that has enabled her to design animal holding and processing facilities that are far more humane for the animals involved. I am less concerned with evaluating Grandin's assessment of her own case and its broader implications—an assessment that is often problematic, in my view—than with mobilizing her observations about her experience toward my own critical ends.

Grandin's story was first brought to national attention by Oliver Sacks in an article published in the *New Yorker* in 1994.[6] The opening lines of Sacks's foreword to Grandin's second book, *Thinking in Pictures*, gesture toward what makes her case so instructive for my purposes. Sacks calls Grandin's first book, *Emergence: Labeled Autistic*, "unprecedented and, in a way, unthinkable" "because there had never before been an 'inside narrative' of autism; unthinkable because it had been medical dogma for forty years or more that there *was* no 'inside,' no inner life, in the autistic, or that if there was it would be forever denied access or expression."[7]

As we saw in chapter 2, that dogma is founded in no small part on the too-rapid assimilation of the questions of subjectivity, consciousness, and cognition to the question of language ability—a dogma that is perhaps even more entrenched in the humanities and social sciences than in areas such as medicine. Indeed, as many scholars have argued, the shibboleth "where there is reason, there is a subject" morphs, in the twentieth century, into "where there is *language,* there is a subject."[8] In this light, the title of Grandin's second book—*Thinking in Pictures*— would constitute an oxymoron even for some fairly sophisticated contemporary philosophers of consciousness and cognition, such as our example in chapter 2, Daniel Dennett; as she herself notes bluntly, "I would be denied the ability to think by scientists who maintain that language is essential for thinking."

Grandin's work is written squarely in the face of this dogma, and it is filled with examples of her ability to cross-reference her own experience and those of the animals who are handled in facilities she has designed. She points out, for example, that because her mental life is intensely visual, not verbal, she is acutely aware of how different a cow's visual experience is from our own. Because cattle derive from prey species (and because their eyes are mounted on the side of the head), their visual system is geared toward detecting novel movement in an extraordinarily wide field of vision. But the price they pay for this nearly 360-degree panorama is a very narrow frontal field in which they have good depth perception. This contrasts pointedly, of course, with the visual systems of predatory species—including the cats and dogs with whom many of us are most accustomed to interacting— whose eyes are mounted in front, enabling acute depth perception and the ability to gauge distance quite accurately.

One result of this visual specificity for cattle is that they "are frightened by high contrasts of light and dark as well as by people and objects that move suddenly." Grandin observes, "I've seen cattle that were handled in two identical facilities easily walk through one and balk in the other. The only difference between the two facilities was their orientation to the sun" (22). And not surprisingly, cattle respond sharply to small visual stimuli that humans don't even register—a length of chain dangling from a feedlot fence, a reflection in a puddle of water on the runway to a dip vat, a crumpled white plastic bottle rocking in the wind (143).

Grandin insists in her most recent book, *Animals in Translation,* that "being a visual thinker was the start of my career with animals . . . because animals are visual creatures, too. Animals are controlled by what they see. When I say I'm a visual thinker," she continues, "I don't mean just that I'm good at making architectural drawings and designs. . . . I actually think in pictures. During my *thinking* process I have no words in my head at all" (17). In fact, she often characterizes her mental processes in terms of a videotape library or CD-ROM that she scans for specific images, which then get "languaged" and narrativized in a second-order process. "My mind is like a web browser," she writes in one article. "When I lecture, the language is mostly 'downloaded' out of memory from files that are like tape recordings. I use slides or notes to trigger the opening of different files. . . . I look at visual images on the 'computer monitor' of my imagination, then the language part of me describes those images."[9]

Grandin's books are full of such examples, and what is most interesting about them is that here, visual prowess—instead of being stereotypically expressive of the humanist *ability* to survey, organize, and master space that finds canonical expression (as many scholars have noted) in tropes ranging from the Renaissance theory of perspective, to Freud's parsing of the evolutionary sensorium in *Civilization and Its Discontents,* through Sartre's discussion of the Gaze, to Foucault's panopticon, and finally to the various contemporary modes of electronic surveillance culture—is instead offered here as an index of *disability.* Even more interesting, Grandin's visuality is implicated in what are, for humanism, two ontologically opposed registers, both of them radically inhuman or at least ahuman: on the one hand, the general animal sensorium, within which sight is only one of the senses (and for many animals not the dominant one); and, on the other hand, the opposed register of the technical and mechanical: Temple Grandin as recording, storage, and playback device, as she describes it. I will explore in greater detail in chapter 7 this essentially prosthetic nature of the visual and its implications, but for now I want simply to note that in Grandin's story, in other words, visuality may be animal, it may be technical, but it is *anything but* "human"—all the more so, paradoxically enough, for being so "accurate" and acute.

A corollary of this—and I will return to this question in some detail in the next two chapters as well—is that what we think of as "normal" human visuality does *not* see—and it does not see that it does not see. Here, we should remember, especially from chapter 1, how the theory of observation and its necessary "blind spot" as developed by Niklas Luhmann and others serves as a posthumanist rejoinder to humanism's trope of visuality-as-mastery that I referenced a moment ago. But we could also be more down to earth and simply note that this "not seeing" is crucial to the human being's (and to *any* being's) organization of an overwhelming flood of visual input into a field of *meaning.*

We might recall in this connection Grandin's discussion of a well-known set of experiments exploring what is called "inattentional blindness" in humans. Daniel Simons, the head of the Visual Cognition Lab at the University of Illinois, showed test subjects a videotape of a group of students in a hallway, moving about and passing two basketballs to and fro, and asked the test subjects to count the number of passes made. After the tape has been rolling for a while, a person (a woman) in a gorilla suit walks onto the screen, faces the camera, beats her chest with her fists, and then leaves. What is remarkable is that 50 percent of those watching the tape do not even register the person in the gorilla suit; even when prompted later specifically about it. It's not that they don't remember seeing it, exactly; it's that they apparently never registered seeing it in the first place. But the point I want to stress is that this blindness takes place because of an entire framework of socially conditioned expectations about meaning and the visual field.[10] As Grandin summarizes it, "It's not that normal people don't see the lady dressed in a gorilla suit at all; it's that their brains screen her out before she reaches consciousness" (65). Moreover, research suggests, as Grandin puts it, that "inattentional blindness works at a *high level of mental processing,* meaning that your brain does a lot of processing be-fore it allows something into consciousness" (66).

What we have here, then, are two different kinds of "not-seeing." The first is the transformation, by "normal" subjects, of an unstruc-tured flood of sensory input into a semiotically organized visual field of meaning, which itself depends not only on biological constraints particular the organism but also on an entire set of social-symbolic conventions, forms, and expectations." The second, by contrast, is Grandin's "abnormal," hyperacute, almost photographic visuality that does *not* organize and harmonize objects in the visual field in terms of reason (literally, their *ratio*) but instead gets mired, visually hiccup-ping, if you will, in a heterogeneous flotsam of particulars—puddles shocked with glare, bright lengths of dangling chain—none of which becomes furniture for the eye as agent of *ratio* or *logos*.

We will examine in some detail in chapter 7 the nature of such a visual field in relation to questions of prostheticity and the filmic me-dium, but here I want to index it to what Jacques Derrida, in *Memoirs of the Blind,* calls "the ruin" of vision.[11] In Derrida's terms, it is the blind, the *dis*abled, who "see" the truth of vision. It is the blind who most readily understand that the core fantasy of humanism's trope of vision is to think that perceptual space is organized around and for the look-ing subject; that the pure point of the eye (as agent of *ratio* and *logos*) exhausts the field of the visible; that the "invisible" is only—indeed, merely—that which has not yet been seen by a subject who is, in prin-ciple, capable of seeing all.

Over and against this—as one might already guess by my discus-sion of the spectral in relation to photography and film in chapter 3—Derrida argues that the invisible is "not simply the opposite of vision," not simply its negative image, the visible in waiting, already there but simply as yet unseen. Rather—and this should retain considerable resonance for my critique in chapter 7 of a certain representationalist notion of vision in contemporary art—space is not "essentially mas-tered by [*livré a*] the look," as Derrida puts it.[12] He elaborates the point in a difficult passage from *Memoirs of the Blind,* the opening gestures of which have particular resonance for Grandin's hypervisuality, a visual registration of objects that is so detailed and acute that the viewed ob-ject itself becomes strangely opaque:

In order to be absolutely foreign to the visible and even to . . . the possibility of the visible, this invisibility would still inhabit the visible, or rather, it would come to haunt it to the point of being confused with it. . . . The visible *as such* would be invisible, not as visi*bility*, the *phenomenality or essence* of the visible, but as the singular body of the visible itself, *right on* the visible—so that, by emanation, and as if it were secreting its own *medium,* the visible would produce blindness. . . . To be the other of the visible, *absolute* invisibility must neither take place elsewhere nor constitute another visible, that is, something that does not yet appear or has already disappeared. . . . This nonvisible does not describe a phenomenon that is present elsewhere, that is latent, imaginary, unconscious, hidden, or past; it is a "phenomenon" whose inappearance is of another kind.[13]

The invisible, then, remains *heterogeneous* to the visible, a "spatialization" of the visual, as Derrida calls it, that is quite obviously at work, for example, not only in the autistic's "blinding" visuality but also in the radical asymmetries and heterogeneities among all the different life-forms who see—and for that very reason do *not* see—in specific ways because of their neurophysiological constraints. After all, does it make sense to say that a ring-tailed lemur "does not see" the object of the bat's echolocation? That a starfish "does not see" the image in an insect's compound eye? Moreover, as Derrida observes, in the context of philosophy and ethics, "from its first words on, Metaphysics associates sight with knowledge," but he insists that "we must also know how to hear, and to listen. I might suggest somewhat playfully that we have to know how to shut our eyes in order to be better listeners."[14] This decentering of sight is all the more important because, as he reminds us—in a passage that has considerable resonance with his critique of the humanist subject as a creature of "abilities" and "capabilities" that we examined in the previous two chapters—"the modern dominance of the principle of reason had to go hand in hand with the interpretation of the essence of beings as *objects,* an object present as representation *(Vorstellung),* an object placed and positioned *before* a subject. This latter, a man who says 'I,' an *ego* certain of itself, thus ensures his own technical mastery over the totality of what is."[15]

To reframe the question of the visual in this way—to cut it loose from its indexical relation to the human, to reason, and to the representational mastery of space itself, and set it adrift within the generalized animal sensorium as "merely" the equal of the dog's sense of smell or the horse's sense of touch (and in some contexts, inferior to those)—is to appreciate more fully Derrida's observation that "a dehierarchization of the senses displaces what we call the real, that which resists all appropriation."[16] And it provides a useful context for "hearing" the philosophical as well as zoological resonance of Grandin's attention to the specificity and intensity of other forms of sensory experience. (For example, she notes that cattle have "supersensitive" hearing and are especially sensitive to high-pitched noises such as the hissing of pneumatic brakes on a truck or a bus. In fact, she suggests that "the sounds that upset cattle are the same kinds of sounds that are unbearable to many autistic children.")[17]

Even more interesting, given her claim that autistics, "normal" functioning humans, and nonhuman animals exist on what she calls "the great continuum," is Grandin's discussion of spatial and tactile experience in animals and autistics. She notes, for example, that just as cattle have a "flight zone" that varies from zero to over one hundred feet (depending on how tame the cattle are and how agitated they are at the moment), so autistic children "often lash out when they stand close to other children while waiting in a line. . . . Having another child accidentally brush up against them can cause them to withdraw with fear like a frightened animal." For many autistics, however, though "a light unexpected touch triggers flight, . . . a firm touch . . . is calming" (147).

This phenomenon is at the center of one of the more remarkable discussions in the book: the "squeeze machine" that Grandin invented when she was a teenager. She notes that it had long been observed, but not really understood, that autistic children often like to wedge themselves under mattresses or in tight spaces or roll up tightly in blankets or rugs (62). She reports that as a child she often daydreamed "about constructing a device that would apply pressure to my body. I visualized a box with an inflatable liner that I could lie in," like "being totally encased in inflatable splints" (63). One day, while watching cattle on her aunt's ranch being held in the "squeeze chute" for vaccinations, she noticed that some of the cattle suddenly relaxed when pressed between the large panels on each side. A few days later, after experiencing a severe panic attack, she actually got inside the chute and asked her aunt to close the head restraint bars around her neck and slowly squeeze the sides of the chute against her. "At first," she writes, "there were a few moments of sheer panic as I stiffened up and tried to pull away from the pressure. . . . Five seconds later I felt a wave of relaxation, and about thirty minutes later I asked Aunt Ann to release me. For about an hour afterward I felt very calm and serene" (63). The magnitude of the experience for Grandin is hard to exaggerate: "This was the first time," she writes, "I ever felt really comfortable in my own skin" (63).

This extraordinary sensitivity to touch and pressure is a quite common phenomenon with autistics, Grandin reports, and "even though the sense of touch is often compromised by excessive sensitivity, it can sometimes provide the most reliable information about the environment" (65). In extreme cases, autistics actually have severe problems locating the boundaries of their own bodies. One patient, in a book about her own famous case, reports that she could only perceive one part of her body at a time and had no sense of it as forming a whole unit, and she "tapped rhythmically and sometimes slapped herself to determine where her body boundaries were" (66). In fact, Grandin suggests that the well-known behavior of some nonverbal autistics of constantly tapping and touching things may be an effort "to figure out where the boundaries are in their environment, like a blind person tapping with a cane" (66).

The autistic's body boundary problem is at the core of another remarkable moment in *Thinking in Pictures*, which dramatizes in an especially powerful way many of the themes I have been discussing thus far. Grandin was hired to redesign an extremely cruel system used for the kosher slaughter of cattle, replacing it with a chute that would gently hold the animal in a standing position while the rabbi performed the final deed. "It worked best when I operated the hydraulic levers unconsciously, like using my legs for walking," she writes.

> I had to force myself to relax and just allow the restrainer to become part of my body. . . . Through the machine, I reached out and held the animal. When I held his head in the yoke, I imagined placing my hands on his forehead and under his chin and gently easing him into position. Body boundaries seemed to disappear. . . . The parts of the apparatus that held the animal felt as if they were an extension of my own body, similar to the phantom limb effect. . . . During this intense period of

> concentration I no longer heard noise from the plant machinery. . . .
> Everything seemed quiet and serene. It was almost a religious experi-
> ence. . . . I was able to look at each animal, to hold him gently and make
> him as comfortable as possible during the last moments of his life. . . . A
> new door had been opened. It felt like walking on water. (41–42)

Now, many things could be said about this passage,[18] but for the moment I would simply like to draw our attention to how here, disability
becomes the *positive,* indeed *enabling,* condition for a powerful experience by Grandin that crosses the lines not only of species difference
but also of the organic and inorganic, the biological and mechanical.
In a kind of dramatization of the category meltdowns identified canonically in Donna Haraway's "Cyborg Manifesto," disability here
positively makes a mess of the conceptual and ontological coordinates
that Grandin's rendering of the passage surely reinstates rhetorically
on another level.

This realization—that what we traditionally think of as disability
can be a powerful and unique form of abledness—is a fundamental assumption for recent work in disability studies.[19] Here, however, I want
to interpret the significance of this moment in Grandin's work, and
her case in general, in a way that diverges from some of the dominant
paradigms of recent disability studies. At first blush, the most obvious
way for animal studies and disability studies to make common cause
might seem to be within a shared liberal "democratic framework,"
which, as philosopher Luc Ferry puts it, "counts on the progress of
'the equality of conditions'" to gradually increase the sphere of legal
rights and ethical recognition. In this view—and this is essentially the
procedure of Martha Nussbaum's *Frontiers of Justice,* discussed in chapter 3—nonhuman animals and the disabled would be seen as simply
the latest traditionally marginalized groups to have ethical and legal
enfranchisement wholly or partially extended to them in an expanding democratic context that entails what Nancy Fraser has called the
"politics of recognition."[20]

But a fundamental problem with the liberal humanist model is
not so much what it wants as the price it pays for what it wants: that in
its attempt to recognize the uniqueness of the other, it reinstates the
normative model of subjectivity that it insists is the problem in the first
place. I am not suggesting that working to liberalize the interpreta-

tion by the courts of the Americans with Disabilities Act is a waste of time, or that lobbying to upgrade animal cruelty prosecutions from misdemeanor to felony status is a bad thing. What I am suggesting is that these pragmatic pursuits are forced to work within the purview of a liberal humanism in philosophy, politics, and law that is bound by a historically and ideologically specific set of coordinates that, because of that very boundedness, allow one to achieve certain pragmatic gains in the short run, but at the price of a radical foreshortening of a more ambitious and more profound ethical project: a new and more inclusive form of ethical pluralism that it is our charge, now, to frame. That project would think the ethical force of disability and nonhuman subjectivity as something other than merely an expansion of the liberal humanist ethnos to ever newer populations, as merely the next room added onto the (increasingly opulent and globalizing) house of what Richard Rorty has called "the rich North Atlantic bourgeois democracies."[21]

Derrida is especially forceful on this point in a recent interview on what he has called "the question of THE (so-called) animal," which we explored in chapter 3. "For the moment," he suggests, "we ought to limit ourselves to working out the rules of law [droit] such as they exist. But it will eventually be necessary to reconsider the history of this law and to understand that although animals cannot be placed under concepts like citizen, consciousness linked with speech . . . etc., they are not for all that without a 'right.' It's the very concept of right that will have to be 'rethought.'" Derrida's point here is not just the obvious one that we "cannot expect 'animals' to be able to enter into an expressly juridical contract in which they would have duties, in an exchange of recognized rights," but rather—and more pointedly—that "it is within this philosophico-juridical space that the modern violence against animals is practiced, a violence that is at once contemporary with and indissociable from the discourse of human rights." And from this vantage, it makes perfect sense to conclude, as Derrida does, that "however much sympathy I may have for a declaration of animals rights that would protect them from human violence," it is nevertheless "preferable not to introduce this problematic concerning the relations between humans and animals into the *existing* juridical framework."[22]

In disability studies, the accent falls within a somewhat different vector of the liberal humanist framework. To borrow the distinction used by Paola Cavalieri (which she borrows in turn from G. J. Warnock), if animal rights discourse typically focuses on the status of the "moral *patient*," disability discourse tends to focus equally on the question of the "moral *agent*." As Cavalieri puts it, "If the moral agent is a being whose *behavior* may be subject to moral evaluation, the moral patient is a being whose *treatment* may be subject to moral evaluation."[23] In disability discourse, in other words, the emphasis falls on the right of the disabled to subjectivity of a particular and circumscribed type: subjectivity as *agency*.

Against this background, we can more fully appreciate Cora Kaplan's observation, in a recent collection on feminism and disability, that "human anomaly . . . continues to trouble the rhetoric of liberal individualism, testing both its ethics of tolerance and its fetishization of autonomy and agency as conditions of human status and civic participation." "Viewed from a long term perspective," she continues,

> the continuing debate about the rights of citizens, and the price of increased agency for them, is itself a legacy of liberalism's historically mixed messages about autonomy and social justice, an ongoing paradox that remains as radically unresolved in the liberalisms that characterize late-twentieth-century social democracies as it did in the "classic" liberalism of the nineteenth century.[24]

What Kaplan calls the "fetishization of agency" endemic to the liberal concept of subjectivity is everywhere on display in a recently published collection of papers in *PMLA* from a high-profile conference at Emory University in March 2004, "Disability Studies and the University." In the introduction to the collection, for example, the authors trumpet the fact that "we have the right to leave the hospital and travel the earth," that "people with disabilities are on the move"; "after years of being probed and studied, disabled people have begun themselves to probe and study" and now emerge "not as objects of study but as knowledge producers."[25] Here, obviously enough, the valences of the "normal" liberal subject (active not passive, subject not object of knowledge, producer not product, and so on) are called on to validate and legitimize the subjectivity of the disabled, and the rallying cries are taken from the playbook of liberal citizenship: "access," "rights," "privileges," "participation."

This "fetishization of agency" in disability studies is understandable, of course, for all sorts of historical, institutional, and strategic reasons. As participants in the Emory conference regularly note, the trajectory of disability studies in the academy has been closely linked to the legal struggles of the disabled for basic needs such as access to public spaces, human services, and the like. At the same time, however, it is interesting to see that some of the participants call for disability studies to move beyond the familiar theoretical models and orthodoxies of its past. The activist and author Simi Linton, for example, argues that "we need to grapple with the absence of an overarching term that subsumes everyone—the vector on which disability falls." She suggests—after the divisive strategies of the past, which sought to stake out and hold on to the specificity of disability as a category (which would resist seeing obesity, for example, as a disability)—that we now "need to find a new way of talking about the place of disabled people in the universe and to find the place of disability in some universal."[26] Similarly, Lennard Davis—one of the founding figures of disability studies in the academic humanities in the United States—argues from a somewhat different vantage that the template of identity politics that characterized much early work in disability studies must be abandoned. "If disability studies is to remain viable," he argues, "it will have to incorporate into its collective vision the kind of complexities with which post-identity theory is grappling."[27]

What I have been suggesting, of course, is that Grandin's example of the relationship between disability and trans-species affinity directs us toward the possibility of taking up just this sort of project in a more profound and, I think, ultimately broad-based way: a way that we can begin to understand in light of Derrida's insistence that "there is not *one* opposition between man and non-man; there are, between different organizational structures of the living being, many fractures, heterogeneities."[28] But underneath them all, as we have seen in earlier chapters, is a shared finitude, a shared "passivity," to use Derrida's term, that runs directly counter to the liberal model of the subject as above all a creature of volition, autonomy, and agency, of "*power or capability [pouvoir]*, and *attributes [avoirs]*: being able, having the power to give, to die, to bury one's dead, to dress, to work, to invent a technique."[29]

But the blockage in disability studies on this point—to return now to the papers from the Emory conference—is remarkable, to say the least, and that blockage short circuits the sort of project that both Linton and Davis, in their different ways, call for. In fact, in all the essays collected in the special *PMLA* issue—they make up 143 double-column pages—not once does the relationship between disability and trans-species affinity in this broader ethical project come up, though Grandin herself is mentioned at least once. The most pointed irony of all, perhaps, occurs in Rosemarie Garland-Thomson's essay, where she observes that "although we value biodiversity in our environment, we devalue physical and mental variety."[30] Here Garland-Thomson would seem to echo Derrida's contention that the problem with the phrase *"the* Animal" is that "within the strict enclosure of this definite article . . . are *all the living things* that man does not recognize as his fellows, his neighbors, or his brothers. And that is so in spite of the infinite space that separates the lizard from the dog, the protozoon from the dolphin, the shark from the lamb, the parrot from the chimpanzee."[31] Similarly—or at least apparently so—Garland-Thomson argues "for applying the vibrant logic of biodiversity to humans." But even as she echoes Derrida's reading of the significance of Bentham's question "can they *suffer?*" in her recognition that "our bodies need care; we all need assistance to live," that "our society emphatically denies vulnerability, contingency, and mortality,"[32] she is unable to recognize that these ethical imperatives extend *across* species lines and bind us, in our shared vulnerability, to other living beings who think and feel, live and die, have needs and desires, and require care just as we do.

Most ironic of all, in this light, is one example she offers of recent, positive changes in images of disability in mass culture: a magazine cover of a stereotypical tall, slender, female model, dressed in evening gown for a night on the town, but accompanied by a German Shepherd service dog. She writes, "The juxtaposition of the elite body of a visually normative fashion model with the mark of disability forces the viewer to reconfigure assumptions about what constitutes the attractive, the desirable, and the livable life" (526). Yes, but only at the expense of doing to nonhuman "differents" what "normates" have traditionally done to the disabled. Now I want to stress that my point here is not to play the oldest and most predictable trump card in the identity politics deck—"my constituents are more marginalized and unrecognized than yours"—but rather to suggest that, instead of seeing the nonhuman animal as merely a prop or tool for allowing the disabled to be mainstreamed into liberal society and its values, wouldn't we do better to imagine this example as an irreducibly different and unique form of subjectivity— neither *Homo sapiens* nor *Canis familiaris,* neither "disabled" nor "normal," but something else altogether, a shared trans-species being-in-the-world constituted by complex relations of trust, respect, dependence, and communication (as anyone who has ever trained—or relied on—a service dog would be the first to tell you)?[33]

What I have in mind, then, is a different sort of project, one that is consonant with the suggestion made by the editors of a recent collection on disability and postmodernism that work associated with poststructuralism "can contribute an enormous amount to *the development of inclusive societies,* which is surely as important as the challenge to the hegemony of normativism" that is more typical of mainstream work in disability studies.[34] As they rightly argue, "existing theories of disability—both radical and mainstream—are no longer adequate . . . considering the range of impairments under the disability umbrella; considering the different ways in which they impact on individuals and groups over their lifetime," and—particularly to the point for my purposes here—"considering the intersection of disability with other axes of inequality" (15).

Such a project points us toward the necessity of an ethics based not on ability, activity, agency, and empowerment but on a *compassion* that is rooted in our vulnerability and passivity—"this non-power at the heart of power," as Derrida puts it. In this light, the ethical force of our relation to the disabled and to nonhuman others is precisely that it foregrounds the necessity of thinking ethics *outside* a model of reciprocity between "moral agents"; indeed (as thinkers from Levinas and Lyotard to, more recently, Zygmunt Bauman have argued), the ethical act might instead be construed as one that is freely extended without hope of reciprocation by the other. As Bauman puts it, the problem with an ethics based on reciprocity is that it implies *"calculability of action."* "What more than anything else sets the contractually defined behavior apart from a moral one," he continues, "is the fact that the 'duty to fulfill the duty' is for each side dependent on the other side's record. . . . It is, so to speak, in the power of my partner to set me (by design or by default) 'free,' to 'unbind' me from my duties." But those duties, he argues, are *"heteronomic"; "*my relation to the Other is *programmatically* non-symmetrical, that is, not dependent on the Other's past, present, anticipated or hoped-for *reciprocation."* Hence all ethical models based on reciprocity and contractualism ignore the fact that "'we' becomes a plural of 'I' only at the cost of glossing over the I's multidimensionality"—a multidimensionality that cannot be calculated, that is a radically embodied form of finitude not only of the disabled and of nonhuman subjects but also of the "normate" subject itself, now returned to itself as *other* with a new sense of its own nonnormative contingency.[35]

I will end then, on a very different note from what one typically finds in calls for animal rights and disability access, one that returns us to the transvaluation of the trope of vision as an index of humanism with which the chapter began. It looks forward, as we will see, to the next two chapters and will recall, I hope, my discussions in chapter 3 of J. M. Coetzee's riveting fiction as read by Cora Diamond. At the end of *Memoirs of the Blind,* Derrida writes:

> We all know about the episode in Turin . . . where [Nietzsche's] compassion for a horse led him to take its head into his hands, sobbing. . . . Now if tears *come to the eyes,* if they *well up in them,* and if they can also veil sight, perhaps they reveal, in the very course of this experience . . . an essence of the eye. . . . The eye would be destined not to see but to weep. For at the very moment they veil sight, tears would unveil what is proper to the eye. And what they cause to surge up out of forgetfulness . . . would be nothing less than . . . the *truth* of the eyes, whose ultimate destination they would thereby reveal: to have imploration rather than vision in sight, to address prayer, love, joy, or sadness rather than a look or a gaze. . . .
>
> The blindness that opens the eye is not the one that darkens vision. The revelatory or apocalyptic blindness, the blindness that reveals the very truth of the eyes, would be the gaze veiled by tears. (126–27)

II. MEDIA, CULTURE, PRACTICES

6 From Dead Meat to Glow-in-the-Dark Bunnies

The Animal Question in Contemporary Art

THIS CHAPTER BEGINS AT THE INTERSECTION of two questions: one, apparently quite complicated; the other, apparently quite simple. The first question—explored in some detail in the first half of the book—concerns the ethical standing of (at least some) nonhuman animals. It is a question with which we are confronted every day in the mass media (indeed, entire cable television networks are now built around the presumption of its possibility), and it has increasingly captivated not just scientific fields like cognitive ethology, ecology, and cognitive science but also areas in the humanities such as philosophy, psychoanalysis, theory, and cultural studies generally. For the purposes of this chapter, I will assume that the ethical standing of at least some nonhuman animals is not just a live issue but one increasingly taken for granted (even if how to formulate that ethical standing remains a complex question). I allow myself this luxury in no small part because the two artists whose work I will be addressing take that standing for granted, as they have affirmed in a variety of contexts.

The second question seems, by comparison, much more straightforward and perhaps almost trivial in comparison to the weight of the first, but that is part of the reason I want to take it up here. When contemporary artists take nonhuman animals as their subject—our treatment of them, how we relate to them, and so on—what difference does it make that those artists choose a particular representational strategy (and—a question I can't fully explore here—a particular medium or art form such as painting, sculpture, installation, or performance, to name just a few). To put this more directly: there clearly has been in contemporary art an explosion of interest in what Derrida calls "the question of the animal" as theme and subject matter.[1] When addressing this topic, however, it is all too easy to fall into what Slavoj Žižek, with characteristic astringency, has in another context called "an un-dialectical obsession with content."[2] What I am interested in, on the other hand, is how particular artistic strategies themselves depend on or resist a certain humanism that is quite independent of the manifest content of the artwork: the fact that it may be "about" nonhuman animals in some obvious way.

In the contexts of the visual and visuality that I developed in the previous chapter and will continue to excavate in the chapter that follows, we can bring the question I have in mind into even sharper focus along the following lines: If, as many of the most important contemporary thinkers have suggested, certain representational strategies (say, the Renaissance theory of perspective, or Bentham's panoptical rendering of architectural space, or the production of the gaze and spectatorship in film as critiqued by feminist film theory in the 1980s, and so on) can be indexed to certain normative modes of humanist subjectivity that they reproduce *by the very nature of their strategies*, then we are well within our rights to ask—to put it succinctly, for the moment—what the relationship is between philosophical and artistic representationalism.

These are precisely the sorts of questions that practicing artists routinely engage in connection with the specific demands of particular representational media. They bear very directly on not just the artistic challenge but also the larger philosophical and ethical challenge of speaking *for* nonhuman animals, speaking *to* our relations with them, and how taking those relations seriously unavoidably raises the question of who "we" are, of the notion of the "human" that, as we saw in chapter 3, the "autobiographical animal" (to use Derrida's phrase) gives to itself—a question that may be answered quite indirectly not in the manifest content of the artwork or its "message" but in its formal strategies.

The Ethics of (Dis)figuration: Sue Coe's *Dead Meat*

We find many faces in the paintings and drawings collected in Sue Coe's book *Dead Meat*, a collection of sketches, paintings, and drawings that Coe compiled over a six-year period while traveling to slaughterhouses and feedlots around North America.[3] Hundreds of faces, even thousands, perhaps. And we don't have to find them. They find us. As in "Cow 13" or "Pigs in a Circle," they stare out at us on nearly every page, by turns fearful, afflicted, or innocent. What is remarkable here, though, is that the faces belong mainly to the animals— "livestock," so called. In fact, it is hard to find a human being with a face at all, and when we do find them, as in "Electrocution" or "There Is No Escape," they are usually misshapen or contorted. How are we to understand this?

One way that suggests itself immediately is by means of the theorization of the ethics of "the face" in contemporary philosophy and theory—a debate that has conspicuously involved Emmanuel Levinas, Jacques Derrida, and Gilles Deleuze and Félix Guattari, among others. Levinas theorizes the ethical call of the face as the site of an unanswerable obligation to which I am held "hostage," to use his term, in an infinite responsibility to the other. As Derrida has observed, however, though the subject is held hostage to the other by the first imperative of the intersubjective relation—"thou shalt not kill"—in Levinas (as in the Judeo-Christian tradition generally), this is not understood as a "thou shalt not put to death the living in general." For Levinas, the subject is "man" whose ethical standing is secured by his access to both *logos* and the Word, and so, as Derrida puts it, in Levinas the subject resides in "a world where sacrifice is possible and where it is not forbidden to make an attempt on life in general, but only on the life of man."[4] As we have seen earlier, however, for Derrida the animal "has its point of view regarding me. The point of view of the absolute other, and nothing will have ever done more to make me think through this absolute alterity of the neighbor than these moments when I see myself naked under the gaze of a cat."[5] And from the vantage of Deleuze and Guattari, Derrida's critique of Levinas here might be viewed as leaving intact a certain humanist schema of the scopic and the visual, which their critique of "faciality" in *A Thousand Plateaus* is calculated to dismantle in its insistence that the face is not a location, still less a body part, but rather a kind of "grid" or "diagram" that configures the space of intersubjective relations and desire itself, making them available only at the expense of "fixity" and "identity."[6] To put it schematically, Deleuze and Guattari might well ask of Derrida how the moment of being looked at by his cat—not just "naked" but *"seeing myself naked under the gaze*

of a cat"—can be divorced from the face. How can the looking-back of
the animal—and the ethical call harbored by that look—be disengaged
from the humanism for which the face (and faciality generally) is perhaps the fundamental figure?

The art historian and critic Michael Fried gives a rather different account of the face from the Levinasian one in his book *Realism,
Writing, Disfiguration: On Thomas Eakins and Stephen Crane,* where he
offers an analysis of figuration and representation that will help to shed
light on the particularity of Sue Coe's strategies and how we might
assess their ethical force.[7] The key point of contact with the motifs
we have sounded out thus far, however briefly, is readily voiced in the
title of the essay on Crane that makes up the second half of Fried's
book, "Stephen Crane's Upturned Faces," where the intense visuality
of Crane's prose is also indexed to *the face*—and to the blank page as
its double or stand-in—and its ethical call on us. Pertinent here too
is the fact that in Crane, in Eakins, and in Coe, we will be dealing
with—immersed in, really—scenes of violence and responsibility: primarily war (as in Crane's *The Red Badge of Courage*), the surgical theater
of Eakins' great painting *The Gross Clinic,* and, of course, the killing
floors of Coe's *Dead Meat.*

What Fried finds in Crane is "a mode of literary representation
that involves a major emphasis on acts of *seeing,* both literal and metaphorical."[8] But what is usually called Crane's "impressionistic" style
should instead be understood, Fried argues, as a remarkable plumb-
ing of the relationship of "a primitive ontological difference between
the allegedly upright or 'erect' space of reality and the horizontal
'space' of writing," which manifests itself in Crane as "an implicit contrast between the respective 'spaces' of reality and literary representation" (99). This difference is related to the extraordinary (and extraordinarily haunting and even uncanny) network of faces in Crane's
fiction—primarily, faces of the dead that stare back at us with unseeing
eyes—by virtue of the requirement "that a human character, ordinarily
upright and so to speak forward-looking, be rendered horizontal and
upward-facing so as to match the horizontality and upward-facingness
of the blank page" (99). On the one hand (and here the connection to
Coe's animal faces is quite clear) the faces of the dead—like the blank
page—stare back at us and ask for our conferral of meaning, through

representation, on their abjection or suffering (this is rendered in an especially powerful way in Crane's war fiction). But at the same time, as figures for the "'unnatural' process" of writing itself—when "the upward-facingness of the corpse, hence of the page," is considered "not so much as a brute given [but] as a kind of artifact"—they are *products* of that very process of representation itself (100).

In trying to bring the reader/viewer face to face with the world through writing, however, the writer only succeeds in *de*facing the world or, to use Fried's term, disfiguring it. The dilemma in Crane is that the more he succeeds in this enterprise, the more he, in another sense, fails. This is so, Fried argues, because insofar as those "desemanticizing" aspects of Crane's writing (visuality, sonority, dialect, and manipulation of perceptual scale, just to name a few) do their job, they interpose themselves, in their own materiality, between the reader and the world that that "realist" project was supposedly intended to represent, so that the world (though he doesn't put it this way) almost becomes a "host," if you will, for an essentially "vampiristic" relationship to the writerly or representational project. As Fried asks: "Wouldn't such a development threaten to abort the realization of the 'impressionist' project as classically conceived? In fact would it not call into question the very basis of writing as communication—the tendency of the written word partly to 'efface' itself in favor of its meaning in the acts of writing and reading?" (119–20).

For Fried, this uncanny or vampiristic quality of Crane's style is symptomatic of Crane's need to performatively confront "the scene of writing" through "a mechanism of displacement" and "to do so in a manner that positively obscured the meaning of those representations from both writer and reader." "And this suggests," he continues,

> that the passages that describe the faces and recount responses to them are where Crane's unconscious fixation on the scene of writing not only comes closest to surfacing in a *sustained* and deliberate manner but also, precisely owing to the 'manifestly' dreadful nature of the faces and of the vicissitudes that befall them, is most emphatically *repressed*. In other words, the thematization of writing as violent disfigurement and its association with effects of horror and repugnance but also of intense fascination allowed the writer, and *a fortiori* the reader, to remain unconscious of the very possibility of such a thematization. (120–21)

We are now in a position to glimpse how different things are in Coe's handling of what we could call, after Fried, the scene of representation or figuration, whose index in both cases is a certain rendering— and in Crane's case, *rending*—of the face. We remember Fried's observation "that a human character, ordinarily upright and so to speak forward-looking, be rendered horizontal and upward-facing so as to match the horizontality and upward-facingness of the blank page" (99). In Coe, however, we find a double reversal of this dynamic. First, the violence that in Crane renders the human corpse horizontal and facing upward is in *Dead Meat* associated with a force that takes the "naturally" occurring horizontality of the animals portrayed (living, as they do, on all fours) and renders it strongly vertical—namely, in the endless rows and rows of hoisted, hanging animal corpses in the slaughterhouse and the packing plant that we find in images such as "Horse Slaughterhouse" or "Poultry Plant Fire." It is as if the animals cannot be allowed to assume the vertical, upright posture reserved (as even Freud tells us in *Civilization and Its Discontents*) for the human, without at the same stroke being *defaced*—in many cases, quite literally (i.e., beheaded).

At the same time—a strict corollary by this logic—the slaughterhouse workers remain mired in a strongly horizontal plane, and, not surprisingly, their faces are often "beastly" or "animalistic" in the traditional, speciesist sense of the word, as in "Electrocution" or "Scalding Vat and Scraping Machine." The logic that systematically works its way through most of these pieces, then, is that the concrete, individual animal body (an individuality emphasized in pieces such as "Cow 13" and "Goat outside Slaughterhouse") is, through a process of corporately organized Taylorization, mechanistically born, bred, killed, and dismembered in a process through which it comes to have meaning for the "carnophallogocentric" *socius* (to use Derrida's well-known term) only by being reconstituted as "meat" or "pork"—a semantic transformation and mystification that is itself paralleled by the material manifestation of identical, shrink-wrapped packages of brightly colored meat in the grocery store counter now thoroughly dissociated from the reality of its material production.[9] And this systematic violence against the animals is itself doubled by a less brutal, though no less systematic, violence that attends the workers who are forced by the na-

Sue Coe, *Goat outside Slaughterhouse P.A.,* 1990. Copyright 1990 Sue Coe. Courtesy of Galerie St. Etienne, New York.

ture of capitalism itself to do such work—a point graphically captured in Coe's rendering of the meatpacking workers in painting after painting and explicitly thematized in works such as "Capital/Labor."

Second, however—and this is the point I would like to emphasize—what we find here is not the "excruciated" relationship to representation that Fried emphasizes in Crane and Eakins but rather its apparent displacement onto forces external to the work of representation itself—forces whose effects the artwork registers and then intensifies. The violence we find here is not "artifactual" (associated with the inescapable violence and disfiguration of representation itself) but is instead associated with the external (that is to say, extrarepresentational) forces of capitalism and factory farming. We could say, in other words, that (in contrast to Fried's Crane) Coe's painting aspires to the condition of writing, but writing understood not as representation divided against itself—not as *différance* or iterability, to borrow Derrida's terms, which are invoked by Fried[10]—but as the direct communication of a semantic and as it were external content, of which the artwork is a faithful (or perhaps "dramatic") enough representation to didactically incite ethical action and change on the part of the viewer.

Yet precisely here an interesting problem manifests itself. While Coe is certainly within her rights to see the ethical function of (her) art, at least in one sense, as drawing our attention, as powerfully as possible, to the untold horrors of the slaughterhouse, on another level—and it is this level that will be handled with considerable sophistication, I think, in Eduardo Kac's work—that ethical function and the representationalism it depends on rely on a certain disavowal of the violence (what Fried calls the "disfiguration") of representation itself, which immediately leads to an obvious question we might ask of Coe: If the ethical function of art is what Coe thinks it is, why not just show people photographs of stockyards, slaughterhouses, and the killing floor to achieve this end? To put it another way, what does art *add*? And what does it mean that her art has to be *more* than real to be real? Isn't the "melodrama of visibility" (to use Fried's phrase) that we find in *Dead Meat,* which is calculated to "give the animal a face," also, in another sense, an *effacement* of the very reality it aims to represent, one that quite conspicuously manifests itself in the hyperbole, disfiguration, and melodrama of Coe's work? The paradoxical result for Coe's work, then, is that it appeals to us to read it as directly (indeed, melodramatically) legible of the content it represents, but the only way it achieves that end is *through* its figural excess, which is precisely *not* of the slaughterhouse but of the interposing materiality of representation itself.

We can unpack the implications of this point by remembering Fried's discussion of "what might be called a drama, some would even say a melodrama, of visibility" in Eakins's *The Gross Clinic,* which may be brought into sharp contrast with the very different "melodrama" we find in Coe's *Dead Meat* project.[11] My point here in calling Coe's work "melodramatic" is not that it exaggerates what really goes on in a slaughterhouse but that in Coe's work, *nothing is hidden* from us. On the contrary, the paintings seem to form a kind of theater calculated to produce a "surefire effect" (to use Fried's characterization of "theatricality") by "playing to the audience," as the figures in the paintings—human and animal—repeatedly look out at us, imploringly, fearfully, or sadistically, as if the entire affair inside the space of the painting is

Thomas Eakins,
The Gross Clinic,
1875. Philadelphia
Museum of Art.
Gift of the Alumni
Association to
Jefferson Medical
College in 1878
and purchased by
the Pennsylvania
Academy of the
Fine Arts and
the Philadelphia
Museum of Art
in 2007 with the
generous sup-
port of more than
3,500 donors.

staged *only* for us.[12] Unlike the experience of the viewer in what Fried calls the "absorptive" tradition in painting that culminates in modern-ist abstraction, the viewer in Coe's work isn't "denied," as Fried puts it, but rather addressed and held responsible, even culpable, for what is being shown inside the frame.

Here—to return to *The Gross Clinic*—two conspicuous features of Eakins's painting noted by Fried are very much to the point: the rendering of the surgical patient's body, and the cringing figure of an older woman, usually taken to be the patient's mother. As for the first, Fried notes that "the portions of the body that can be seen are not read-ily identifiable, so that our initial and persisting though not quite final impression is of a few scarcely differentiated body parts rather than of a coherent if momentarily indecipherable ensemble."[13] In fact, Fried likens this presentation to something like a dismembering, an act of "deliberate aggression" and even "sadism" that ultimately is an index of "the attitude toward the viewer that that rendering implies"—an especially intense version of the attitude typical of what Fried elsewhere famously calls the "absorptive" tradition in painting (59). Similarly, the cringing figure dramatizes "the pain of seeing," in both "the emphatic *emptiness* of her clawlike left hand," the "violent contortion" of which is "apprehended by the viewer as a threat—at a minimum, an offense—to vision as such," and "the *sightlessness* that . . . she so feelingly embodies" (62). In these "aggressions," as Fried calls them, these gestures of "disfiguration," Fried finds in the painting "an implied affront to seeing," a "stunning or, worse, a wounding of seeing—that leads me to imagine that the definitive realist painting would be one that the viewer literally could not bear to look at" (64–65).

Here we get a precise sense of the differences between the force of "disfiguration" at work in Eakins's representationalism and in Coe's. In Coe, although there is disfiguration aplenty, it is never a disfiguration that resists vision or interpretation—quite the contrary, it invites a single, univocal reading. The violence of Eakins's "affront to seeing" that manifests itself in *The Gross Clinic* as incision, deformation, and even, in a sense, dismemberment (a violence displaced and contained by being thematized, as Fried notes, in terms of the "necessary" surgery being performed) is matched by the reverse dynamic in Coe. The almost nightmarish, infernal scenes of violence before us *hide nothing,* and for that very reason, the artist, as it were, has no blood on her hands. (*That* is reserved, of course, for the forces of capitalism and Taylorization referenced in the work's semantic content.)

In this light, we can sharpen our sense (if you'll pardon the expression) of the difference between Coe's representationalism and Eakins's by reminding ourselves of the signifying force of the surgeon's scalpel in *The Gross Clinic* as glossed by Fried. If Eakins represents himself allegorically through the figure of Gross, then the scalpel serves to remind us—rather startlingly, even traumatically—that Eakins is "divided or excruciated between competing systems of representation." On the one hand, the scalpel, "being hard and sharp, an instrument for cutting, belongs unmistakably to the system of writing/drawing"; on the other, because the scalpel is marked by an outré, almost three-dimensional drop of blood on its tip, it "refers, by means of an irresistible analogy," to the system of painting—almost as if the drop of blood *were* paint and the surgeon/painter carefully and dramatically deliberates its violent application (88). In this light, we might well say of Coe's *Dead Meat* that the knives and hooks of the slaughterhouse are *never* associated with the brush of the painter and the violence of representation-as-disfiguration. Thus, if Eakins's putative realism in fact harbors a deeper, more unsettling antirealism or, perhaps better, *irrealism*, Coe's melodramatic renderings themselves harbor a more fundamental (and a more fundamentally comforting) representationalism, a signifying regime whose best name might well be "faciality"—even if that faciality extends across species lines to include, even to privilege (as if somehow to redeem their suffering), the nonhuman animals around which the paintings are built.

The opposite of this regime—or more precisely, as Derrida would put it, that which remains heterogeneous to it, not its simple other—might well be figured in the network of asignifying forms and their serial iteration that wends its way throughout the works collected in *Dead Meat*.[14] Chief among these are the chains, hooks, tubes, belts, hoses, ducts, and the like that form (in pieces such as "Horse Slaughterhouse," "McWorld," and "Pecking Order") a kind of ongoing cipher in the paintings, often extending beyond the borders of the pictorial space, suggesting their intrication in some larger insidious network—a logic that is also extended to cover the representation of the masses of animal bodies themselves in pieces such as "Lo Cholesterol Buffalo" or "Feedlot."

From Coe's representationalist point of view, this network is directly associated with the force of capitalism, Taylorization, and the disassembly line they put in place. In the sense I am emphasizing here, however, we might see it as figuring instead a kind of displacement or domestication of the Derridean sense of "iterability" that I discussed in the first half of the book—or, as Fried would have it, a kind of visible repression that traces and scores the otherwise representational logic of the paintings. This logic even extends, I would suggest, to the ubiquitous numbered ear tags that mark the animals as fodder in the larger machine of agribusiness and factory farming, with the sheer abstractness and pure seriality of the numerical system signifying nothing *except* this force. Here the painting "Goat outside Slaughterhouse" is all the more striking in the contrast between the almost sculptural modeling of the animal's head and the abstract numbers of the contrasting ear tag, which

Sue Coe, *Ham Scrubber*, 1988. Copyright 1988 Sue Coe. Courtesy of Galerie St. Etienne, New York.

not only are iterations of the same shape but also in their form recall the network of figures I have just noted in pieces like "Ham Scrubber."

Given the conceptual coordinates of Coe's *Dead Meat* project, we can surmise that this force of abstraction, coding, and seriality would eventually find its most extreme logical extension in genetic engineering and, beyond that, in cloning—an eventuality graphically depicted in Coe's painting "Future Genetics Inc." Here again, however, we can interpret this in a second sense rather at odds with the artist's own. While Coe's painting depicts the perverse extension of Taylorized factory farming to the production of misshapen and deformed animal mutants in a subterranean laboratory, there is another sense in which we may view this logic as endemic to *representation itself.* The clone may be "the image of the perfect servant, the obedient instrument of the master creator's will," as W. J. T. Mitchell puts it, but it also activates "the deepest phobias about mimesis, copying, and the horror of the uncanny double."[15] Or, to put this in Derrida's terms, the dream of pure, Taylorized seriality is repetition *without* difference, but the very meaning of iterability is that repetition—and representation—can take place only in and through the potentially mutating work of difference, the specific material, embodied, pragmatic instance that threatens any dream of purity, always shadowing pure seriality with the uncanny referenced by Mitchell. And this opens up a second ethical register around the question of representation and its logic—one quite different from what Coe has in mind—that harbors real stakes for how we understand the human/animal relation.

As we saw in chapter 2, Derrida has argued that the constitutive fantasy of humanism is that the human separates itself from the rest of the domain of the living by alone escaping subjection to the deconstructive force of iterability and the trace that in fact extends to *all* forms of representation and signification, not just its paradigmatic case, language. And in this second ethical register, the critique of speciesism emerges, in fact, from the critique of representationalism along the lines traced by Derrida in "Eating Well," where he suggests:

> If one reinscribes language in a network of possibilities that do not merely encompass it but mark it irreducibly from the inside, everything changes. I am thinking in particular of the mark in general, of the trace, of iterability, of *différance.* These possibilities or necessities, without which there would be no language, are themselves not only human. . . . And what I am proposing here should allow us to take into account scientific knowledge about the complexity of "animal languages," genetic coding, all forms of marking within which so-called human language, as original as it might be, does not allow us to "cut" once and for all where we would in general like to cut. (116–17)

This may seem to be a very different kind of cut from the ones we witness in *Dead Meat,* but in fact, Derrida suggests, the "sacrificial symbolic economy" of carnophallogocentrism that subordinates woman to man and nonhuman animals to both is directly related to—even motivates—what we witness in Coe's work. "The subject does not want just to master and possess nature actively," Derrida writes. "In our cultures, he accepts sacrifice and eats flesh. . . . In our countries, who would stand any chance of becoming a *chef d'Etat* (a head of State), of thereby acceding 'to the head,' by publicly, and therefore exemplarily, declaring him- or herself to be a vegetarian?" (114).

The More You Look, the Less You See: Eduardo Kac

In October 2001, Eduardo Kac presented his project *The Eighth Day* in a gallery at Arizona State University, on the heels of what is probably his most famous undertaking, *GFP Bunny* (2000). Here again Kac uses transgenic life-forms (in this case, mice, zebra fish, tobacco plants, and a colony of amoebae, instead of a rabbit) modified by introducing into them an enhanced GFP gene (green fluorescent protein, derived from the jellyfish *Aequorea Victoria*) that makes them glow green under certain lighting conditions. As in that earlier work, however, GFP life-forms are only part of the story.[16] In *The Eighth Day*, viewers enter a dark space with a glowing blue-lit Plexiglas semisphere at its center, surrounded by the sounds of waves washing ashore. Inside the terrarium are the life-forms just mentioned, as well as a specially designed "biobot," which contains as its "cerebellum" the GFP amoebae. When the amoebae move toward one of the six legs of the biobot, their movement is tracked by a computer, which makes that particular leg contract. The biobot also serves as an "avatar," as Kac puts it, of Web participants, who can remotely control its "eye" with a pan-and-tilt actuator, so that "the overall perceivable behavior of the biobot is a combination of activity that takes place in the microscopic network of the amoebae and in the macroscopic human network." Meanwhile viewers in the gallery can see the terrarium from both inside and outside the dome, by means of access to a Web interface installed in the gallery space, which includes, in addition to a biobot view, a feed from a bird's-eye-view camera installed above the dome.[17]

When we leave behind the technical and logistical aspects of the piece (which are considerable) to address the work's intellectual, ethical, and social implications, we enter another order of complexity. Arlindo Machado's comments in the collection of essays that accompanied *The Eighth Day* are fairly representative of these discussions:

Eduardo Kac, *The Eighth Day,* 2001 (detail). Transgenic artwork with biological robot (biobot), GFP plants, GFP amoebae, GFP fish, GFP mice, audio, video, Internet. http://sprocket.telab.artic.edu/ekac.

Transgenic forms of life are often stigmatized for being produced in the laboratory, in part because of the economic (and possibly warlike) interests that motivate their creation. It is almost inevitable that non-technical discussions involving biotechnologies take on a conservative bias, recalling scenarios of apocalyptic science fiction or even dogmatic interdictions of religious order. . . . The more experimental and much less conformist sphere of art—with its emphasis on creation, by means of genetic engineering, of works which are simply beautiful, not utilitarian or potentially profit making; along with the relocation of genetically modified products in "cultural" spaces such as museums and art galleries, or in public spaces, or even in homes . . . all this could help to elevate public discussion of genetics and transgenics to a more sophisticated level.[18]

This is essentially the thrust as well of Kac's own manifesto on transgenic art, but the artist takes the additional step there of insisting that "artists can contribute to increase global diversity by inventing new life forms," and he imagines a day in the not too distant future when "the artist literally becomes a genetic programmer who can create life forms by writing or altering a given (genetic) sequence."[19]

This insistence complicates an already complicated situation considerably, because it invites the sorts of trepidations rightly raised by critics such as Steve Baker, who writes that Kac "engages with the animal through techniques that strike many people as meddlesome, invasive, and profoundly unethical."[20] It's not that any of the animals used in his work are harmed (they aren't, and Kac has repeatedly made it clear how seriously he takes his responsibility for the care and well-being of the animals involved) but rather that "Kac seems to overlook the larger picture," as Baker puts it: namely, that his work depends on and in a fundamental sense reproduces an entire set of institutions and practices of scientific research that subject millions of animals a year to distressing, often painful, and usually fatal experimentation, a subjection of nonhuman beings of "unprecedented proportions," as Derrida puts it, in which "traditional forms of treatment of the animal have been turned upside down" and replaced by "an artificial, infernal, virtually interminable survival, in conditions that previous generations would have judged monstrous."[21]

Such concerns are very important, of course, but I don't want to pursue them further here—in part because they have received ample air time in the discussions of Kac's work, but primarily because certain habitual oversimplifications endemic to addressing those concerns have tended to mask crucial aspects of Kac's work, features that have a less obvious and thematic relation to how his projects ethically intervene in our received views of the human/animal relationship and, beyond that, in the question of posthumanism generally. Something of the different direction I want to pursue is evoked by Kac early on in the transgenic art manifesto, where he writes, "More than making visible the invisible, art needs to raise our awareness of what firmly remains beyond our visual reach but, nonetheless, affects us directly. Two of the most prominent technologies operating beyond vision are digital implants and genetic engineering."[22] In a recent essay on art and human genomics, the critic Marek Wieczorek extends the point when he asks, "How do we picture a new age of genetic manipulation . . . a literal synergy between computing and biology?" This is not just a question of *representation* in any straightforward sense, because "the digital code of the genome, emblematic of a new mode of consciousness," is "not a spatial blueprint of life, not a two-dimensional plan of what a heart or liver looks like, but a long string of nucleotides written in endless permutations."[23] What this means, in turn, is that the problem of picturing this immense revolution "may not simply be a matter of new *forms* of visuality" but rather demand "reconciling form with principle."[24]

Here—and this is rather a different understanding from what we find in Fried—Wieczorek finds a precursor to this new work of Kac's that thinks the parallels between art and scientific theory in minimalism, with its "potentially endless sequence of repeated shapes." Just as "digitally encoded information has no intrinsic relationship to the form in which it is decoded"—"it is not tied to a singular, inherently meaningful form"—so in minimalism "repetition replaces singularity." Moreover, in minimalism "art acknowledges the viewer, whose physical interaction with the work produces ever-shifting viewpoints over time, through a kind of feedback loop," which parallels a similar emphasis in systems theory, as we have seen in chapter 1, on the autopoiesis (Humberto Maturana and Francisco Varela) or the self-reference (Niklas Luhmann) of the observing system—a fact we will find Kac's work insisting on again and again, most obviously in his inclusion in the work itself of remote, Internet-based observer-participants. Here, however, the point is not (as Wieczorek puts it) that "reflexivity is regressive," much like the "obsessively pointless variations of LeWitt's incomplete open cubes or Judd's boxes."[25] Rather, it is that reflexivity is *recursive* in the sense discussed in chapter 1; it uses its own outputs as inputs, as Luhmann defines it.[26] It is only on the basis of that recursivity—a dynamic process that takes *time*—that reflexivity becomes *productive* and not an endlessly repeating, proverbial hall of mirrors associated with the most clichéd aspects of postmodernity.

I will explore in greater detail in chapters 8 and 9 the dynamics of recursivity and how they are related to the questions of meaning and form for other kinds of art (poetry, architecture), but for now I want to note that for our current purposes there are two points here, one logical and one biological. As for the first, Wieczorek captures something of how Kac's work thematizes the central fact—a logical and cognitive fact—about recursive self-reference as Luhmann has theorized it: namely, that observation (precisely because it is contingent and self-referential) will always "maintain the world as severed by distinctions, frames, and forms," and this "partiality precludes any possibility of representation of mimesis and any 'holistic' theory." Thus, Luhmann writes, "the world is observable *because* it is unobservable"[27]—a point whose larger resonance and thematics I will explore in chapters 8 and 10.

Of more immediate relevance for Kac's work, however, is the second point, the biological one: that recursive self-reference is crucial to how different kinds of autopoietic beings establish their *difference* from everything else in the world, which is to say their specific ways of *being* in the world—a "being" that is now thoroughly subordinated to an autopoietic *becoming*. For Kac—and here is where Wieczorek is right that it is not simply a matter of new *forms* of visuality—this calls for the kind of recalibration, redistribution, and displacement of the relationship between meaning and the entire sensorium of living beings that I discussed in the previous chapter, in which visuality itself—as the human sensory apparatus par excellence—is now thoroughly decentered and subjected to a rather different kind of logic (a point I return to in some detail in chapter 7).

To put it another way, Kac subverts the centrality of the human and of anthropocentric modes of knowing and experiencing the world by displacing the centrality of its metonymic stand-in, human (and humanist) visuality. He does this in several different ways, some of which are comparatively straightforward, such as *Darker than Night* (1999) and *Rara Avis* (1996). In the former, the viewer is linked in a communicational loop to roughly three hundred fruit bats via a "batbot" implanted in their cave, which enables the viewer to "hear" the converted echolocation sonar signals of the living bats, while the viewer wears a VR headset that converts the batbot's sonar emissions into an abstract visual display.[28] In *Rara Avis,* viewers don a headset linked to a camera in the head of a large robotic bird in an enclosure, surrounded by living birds, which enables the viewer to look out from the robotic bird's point of view. In both works, sounds *(Rara Avis)* and sonar signals *(Darker than Night)* originating from human participants are reintroduced into the animals' environment, allowing them to experience the presence of an absent, human other (162–66).

More interesting still is how Kac's work also exploits what we might call our lust for the visual and its (humanist) centrality by trading on it repeatedly (the glow-in-the-dark creatures, the outré coloring of the bird in *Rara Avis,* or even the playful visual pun on the human eyeball in *Teleporting an Unknown State* [1996], to name a few). This is not just, as one critic puts it, a matter of the "scopic reversal" that is a "recurring theme" in Kac's work (particularly the works on telepresence), nor is it just about a "dialogical interchange" that serves "to multiply

Eduardo Kac, "Teleporting an Unknown State," telepresence work, 1994/96.
http://sprocket.telab.artic.edu/ekac.

the 'points of view' available," as in *The Eighth Day*. Nor is it exactly that "to the extent that something living—particularly a mammal—glows green, we have an index of alterity" (an interpretation resisted by Kac, by the way).[29]

In fact, I would argue that the use of GFP in Kac's work, particularly with the rabbit Alba in *GFP Bunny*, operates as a kind of feint or lure that trades on the very humanist centrality of vision that Kac's work ends up subverting (and in this, it has more than a little in common with Diller + Scofidio's cagey relationship to spectacle in their *Blur* project, as we'll see in chapter 8). On display here, in other words, are the humanist ways in which we produce and mark the other (including the animal other), our carnophallogocentric visual appetite, displayed here in the form of spectacle, which is fed in this instance by GFP. From this vantage, the point is perhaps not so much, as W. J. T. Mitchell puts it in his widely read essay "The Work of Art in the Age of Biocybernetic Reproduction," that "Kac's work dramatizes the difficulty biocybernetic art has in making its object or model visible" because "the object of mimesis here is really the invisibility of the genetic revolution, its inaccessibility to representation."[30] Rather, it is that Kac's work—with its glow-in-the-dark creatures and its black lights, drawn as much from the storehouse of cheesy mass culture as anywhere—makes all of this all too visible by eliciting and manipulating familiar forms and conventions of contemporary visual appetite. In doing so, it may be understood against the backdrop of Mitchell's larger point about the work of art in an age of biocybernetic reproduction: that the "curious twist" of our moment is that "the digital is declared to be triumphant at the very same moment that a frenzy of the image and spectacle is announced" (315).

It is a question, then, of what we might call the "place" of the visual—but, eventually, for that very reason, of everything else too (as we will see in the next chapter). And this involves in Kac's work a circular and indeed recursive procedure, where the artist uses or otherwise appeals to specifically human visual habits and conventions for the purposes of making the point that the visual as we traditionally think of it can precisely no longer be indexed to those conventions and habits at all. In this light, one way to underscore the difference between productive recursivity in Kac's work and a mere hall-of-mirrors reflexivity is to say that the whole point of the glow-in-the-dark rabbit of *GFP Bunny* and how it seizes on certain spectacularizing modes of human visuality is that the harder you look, the less you see. Alba's "meaning," if we want to put it that way, is not to be found in the brute fact of the glow of her coat; in fact, one might well say the meaning of the work is everywhere *but* there.[31]

From this vantage, we might well think of the strategy Kac deploys in the work *Time Capsule* (1997) as framed by this same logic. In that piece, Kac was televised and simultaneously webcast injecting into his leg a microchip with a unique identification number that reveals itself when scanned—a device commonly used for registering and recovering companion animals. As part of the work, Kac registered himself in an Identichip database as both "animal" and "owner." In addition, the work included seven sepia-toned photographs of members of Kac's family from previous generations and a telerobotic Web scanning and x-ray display of the implant in Kac's leg. Here again Kac's deployment of spectacle and the visual generally makes the point, I think, that the significance of the work is everywhere *except* in its elements—vehicles, really—of visuality and spectacle. It begins to dawn on us just how true this is when we understand, as Edward Lucie-Smith points out, that Kac is of Jewish origin, that a number of his family members (some of them pictured in the photographs) were Polish Jews who died in the Nazi Holocaust, and how "the microchip incorporating a number alludes to the numbers tattooed on the arms of those who were herded into concentration camps"—but here, of course, the identifying numbers cannot be read (22). "Herded" is indeed a word to be insisted on here, as this piece also focuses our attention not on livestock animals but the *domestic* animals—mainly cats and dogs—for whom the chip is designed, animals that a vast majority of owners describe as family members. Are they less "animals" than those other living beings we call "meat"? Than the Jews in the eyes of the Nazis who forced them into cattle cars at gunpoint? Moreover, this welter of complicated associations and category crossings can be amplified one last time when we remind ourselves of the questions addressed in chapter 3 around Derrida's characterization of contemporary forms of animal exploitation in biomedical research and factory farming as a "holocaust" (a characterization shared by Coetzee's Elizabeth Costello).

All of this completely changes the understanding of "theatrical-ity" as criticized by Fried. The point is not just, as Fried would have it, that Kac's work is "theater" (which in his terms it would surely be) but that "theater" is not doing the work Fried thinks it does. In Kac, the artwork does indeed "play up" to the viewer, but only, as Derrida would put it, to lead the viewer to the realization that the only place the meaning of the work may be found is no place, not where the viewer irresistibly looks (e.g., at the spectacle of the glow-in-the-dark crea-tures) but rather, as we saw in chapter 5, precisely where the viewer does not see—not "refuses to look," or even "is prevented from see-ing," but rather *cannot* see. If we keep in mind that theatricality de-pends first and foremost on spatial distribution, we can appreciate the resonance of Derrida's comment, invoked in my earlier discussions, for Kac's attempt—and the ethics of that attempt—to *situate* the visual in ways that fundamentally trouble how we have typically indexed the (human) animal sensorium to the human/animal ontological divide: that "space isn't only the visible, and moreover the invisible"—an in-visible that is itself "not simply the opposite of vision."[32] In this light, we can see more clearly—or perhaps I should say more "obliquely"— how Kac's theatricalization of visuality doesn't evade the viewer's "fini-tude" and "humanness" (as Fried would have it) but rather *underscores* it, in the specifically posthumanist sense that the field of meaning and experience is no longer thought to be exhausted by the self-reference of a particularly, even acutely, human visuality.[33]

In the end, then, the contrast between Sue Coe and Eduardo Kac helps us to see, in the realm of art, the difference between two differ-ent kinds of posthumanism that correspond to the distinction drawn at the end of chapter 4: a humanist posthumanism and a posthumanist one. Coe may be viewed as a posthumanist in the obvious and thematic sense that she takes seriously the ethical and even political challenges of the existence of nonhuman animals (this latter, in her cross-mapping of the exploitation of animals and of workers in factory farming within a Marxist frame). But as I demonstrated in some detail in chapters 3 and 4 (and I'll return to the question late in the next chapter), you can well be committed to this posthumanist question in a humanist way— that is to say, in a way that reinstalls a familiar figure of the human at the center of the universe of experience (in animal rights philosophy) or representation (in Coe's work). And it is such a subject who then, on the basis of that sovereignty, extends ethical or artistic consideration outward toward the nonhuman other. In this light, Coe's work is humanist in a crucial sense, indeed, in the only sense that turns out to be fundamental to her work *as art:* it relies on a subject from whom *nothing, in principle, is hidden.* A subject who if blind is blind not constitutively (as I think Kac's work dramatizes in multiple ways) but only because he—and I would insist on the male pronoun in this instance, for reasons that Derrida's analysis of carnophallogocentrism makes clear—has *not yet seen* what Coe's art is calculated to reveal so powerfully, indeed melodramatically. This complicates considerably—one might even say fatefully—Coe's conception of art as a form of "witnessing."[34] For what must be witnessed is not just what we can see but also what we cannot see—indeed, *that* we cannot see. That too must be witnessed. But by whom if not by the other?

7 When You Can't Believe Your Eyes (or Voice)
Dancer in the Dark

GIVEN THE CRITIQUE OF THE HUMANIST SCHEMA OF VISUALITY I have
been developing over the past two chapters, we are now in a better
position to appreciate a cognate assertion with which I want to begin
here: *sound is not voice.* The desire for it to be so seems to lie at the
heart of much compelling art, music, and film. How we feel about this
desire—that to be human at all is to thoroughly take that desire for
granted or, conversely, that to live in post-Enlightenment (much less
posthumanist) culture is to see that desire as romantic in the worst
possible sense—is a question visited on audiences with uncanny and
disconcerting force in Lars von Trier's film *Dancer in the Dark.* When
the film was first released in May 2000, it provoked violently divergent
responses from its audiences; even as it won the Palme d'Or at the
Cannes Film Festival, the audience, as one reviewer reported, "erupted
with an indecipherable storm of cheers and catcalls."[1] Some viewers
walked out of the theater visibly shaken and in tears, while others just
walked out—halfway through the film. This nearly unprecedented polarization carried through to the reviews, which ranged from the awe-
struck to the dismissive and merely nasty. Some praised the film lav-
ishly: "You've never seen anything like *Dancer in the Dark,*" one wrote;
another called it "a work of thrilling originality."[2] At the other end of
the spectrum, a reviewer for the *Nation* complained that the film was
about "seeing how much of the preposterous he [von Trier] can get
you to swallow without gagging"; more pointedly still, another labeled
it "a genuinely infantile work," an "ugly, self-indulgent folly."[3] Even
reviewers who supported the film felt the need to disavow it; while
admitting that "the power of *Dancer in the Dark* is undeniable," David
Ansen, in *Newsweek,* called it "a magnificent sham" riddled with "emotional sadism."[4]

What is going here?

To begin to answer that question, we need to get a fix on how to approach this weird and iconoclastic film, what sorts of generic expectations we may bring to it. That, however, is only the point of entry into the much more complicated question I will take up later: the question of what we might call the film's ethical project and how it might well be the source of its audience's and reviewers' hysterical reactions (a term whose appropriateness will become clear, I hope, in due course). To take up the question of genre first, we have to understand that for *Dancer in the Dark,* any hint of "reality," "character" in the usual sense, verisimilitude, and the like are, for the purposes at hand, the merest—and I do mean the merest—vehicles for the film's deeper concerns. Here it will suffice to simply register the shameless melodrama of the plot: the incredibly innocent Selma (played by the pop phenom Björk, in what nearly everyone agrees is a stunning performance), who is slowly going blind, sacrifices her own life so that her ten-year-old son Gene (Vladica Kostic) may receive an operation that will save his sight from the ravages of the same congenital disease. *Dancer in the Dark,* in other words, is no more satisfactory, fulfilling, or compelling in terms of plausibility and Aristotelian necessity than, say, *The Marriage of Figaro*—and that is precisely the point. In fact, the film's power is in a profound sense *inseparable* from what many viewers will see as its "absurdity" (if one wants to put it that way) precisely in the way that the absurdity of opera (its melodrama, its hyperbole, its staginess—all those qualities that make people either love or hate opera too) is in fact absolutely central to opera's philosophical and ethical project. To put it as bluntly as possible, *Dancer in the Dark,* like opera, isn't about "reality"; it is about what "reality" turns away from, and the "aversion" (to borrow an Emersonian term I will excavate later on) of opera to that turning away. In that, it is (again like opera) more real than reality—but more about that in a moment.

On the question of genre, it needs to be said that although *Dancer in the Dark* invites us to make it legible within the genre of the Hollywood musical, this is ultimately a blind alley. The film is not a musical, at least not in *that* sense. While the musical insists on, as a constitutive feature, the seamless continuity of the world inside and outside the musical numbers themselves—characters engaged in "realistic" dialogue among passersby who (realistically) pay no attention to

them suddenly break into song, and the passersby suddenly join in—
Dancer takes great pains to insist on the radical split between the world
of Selma's fantasy (in which the musical sequences take place) and the
world that the film itself in broader terms constructs and inhabits. Still,
the film certainly does *situate* itself in relation to the Hollywood musical,
its conventions, and what they signify. And in this light, *Dancer* might
be viewed as an intensification of the stakes of the Hollywood musical, taking it more seriously than the musical itself ever did (which
may be in part what so irritates those who despise this film), and, at
the same time, as a deconstruction of the musical's way of imagining
those stakes—a posture that the film achieves by insisting on the clear
distinction between the world of the main character, Selma, and its
own. In these terms, *Dancer in the Dark* would force the question, as it
were, "Would Gene Kelly be willing to *die* to dance with his umbrella
in *Singin' in the Rain*? Fred Astaire put a gun to his head for the sake of
dancing with his mop?" It is as if the problem were not that the musical
as a genre is so preposterous that no one can sit still for it anymore but
that it isn't preposterous *enough*—which is to say that it no longer pur-
sues with enough seriousness and extremity, enough abandonment, its
own claims and project.

   To do so—to be that preposterous and that serious at the same
time—is to move by way of thumbnail definition from the realm of
the musical to the realm of opera, and to realize that on the most basic
level those claims have to do, as Stanley Cavell has suggested, with life
and death, and with sound and vision as modalities for experiencing
the world and the loss of the world—all of which are related to the
question of film as a medium, and how this film relates to the limits of
that medium. From this vantage, we would do better to think of *Dancer
in the Dark* as a kind of postmodern opera rather than a musical. Here
Cavell's work on these questions—spanning by now several books,
from the early study *The World Viewed: Reflections on the Ontology of
Film,* through two books on Hollywood genre films, to the collections
Themes Out of School and the more recent *A Pitch of Philosophy*—can be
of some help. For Cavell, the philosophical and ethical significances of
film and of voice in opera are structured by the larger problematic that
occupies the whole of his work: namely, the problem of philosophical skepticism. I have already touched on the point in chapter 3, and

I will revisit it in much more detail on the terrain of Cavell's reading of Emerson in chapter 9. After Descartes and Kant, skepticism names not just an epistemological problem but a more profound and deeply ethical "loss of the world" that is coterminous with Enlightenment modernity itself, in which the modern condition is to be "homeless" in the world, permanently doomed to "haunt" it rather than inhabit it, as Cavell sometimes puts it. For Cavell, the significance of film and of operatic voice is located at what he calls the "crossing" of the lines of skepticism and romanticism—that is to say, the juncture at which our desire for contact with the world of things and of others, our need to believe that what we know, experience, and love is *of* the world, is crossed by our knowledge that we are profoundly and permanently isolated, locked (as Emerson puts it) in "a prison of glass."

The most famous version of the settlement with skepticism, Cavell argues, is probably Kant's in *The Critique of Pure Reason,* which argues:

> (1) Experience is constituted by appearances. (2) Appearances are of something else, which accordingly cannot itself appear. (3) All and only functions of experience can be known; these are our categories of the understanding. (4) It follows that the something else—that of which appearances are appearances, whose existence we must grant—cannot be known [the famous *Ding an sich,* or "thing in itself"]. In discovering this limitation of reason, reason proves its power to itself, over itself. (5) Moreover, since it is unavoidable for our reason to be drawn to think about this unknowable ground of appearance, reason reveals itself to itself in this necessity also.[5]

The dissatisfaction with Kant's settlement with skepticism is readily imaginable, of course, but what is less clear—and even more important to Cavell—is the "companion satisfaction" that is "expressed in Kant's portrait of the human being as living in two worlds, in one of them determined, in the other free. . . . One romantic use for this idea of two worlds lies in its accounting for the human being's dissatisfaction with, as it were, itself . . . as if the one stance produced the wish for the other, as if the best proof of human existence were its power to yearn, as if for its better, or other, existence. Another romantic use for this idea of our two worlds is its . . . insight that the human being now lives in *neither* world, that we are, as is said, between worlds"—a condition Cavell characterizes as the endemic "worldlessness" or "homelessness" that is of a piece with the modern condition.[6] Philosophical skepticism after the Kantian turn, in other words, names for Cavell a radical form of posthumanism, one that Kant's transcendental turn (cf. items 4 and 5 in the list just cited) attempts to recontain; and romanticism—as we'll see in different permutations in the next three chapters—names the persistence of the humanist desire for holism, unity, and coherence in the face of that knowledge. All of which makes postskeptical, posthumanist philosophy—in a phrase that has obvious resonance not only for the character of Selma in *Dancer in the Dark* but also for the adjacent autism of Temple Grandin—"a philosophy of immigrancy, of the human as a stranger."[7] In this light, Selma's encroaching blindness in the film might be read as a figure for the inevitability of the general human condition of being "in the dark," wandering in a world of shadows and specters, never at home but merely, sometimes, at rest.

Along the same lines, the philosophical import of voice in opera, then, is that it communicates that "we may leap, as it were, from a judgment of the world as unreal, or alien, to an encompassing sense of another realm flush with this one, into which there is no good reason we do not or cannot step, unless opera works out the reasons. Such a view," Cavell continues, "will take singing, I guess above all the aria, to express the sense of being pressed or stretched between worlds—one in which to be seen, the roughly familiar world of the philosophers, and one from which to be heard," a world "to which one releases or abandons one's spirit," a world that "recedes when the breath of the song ends" (144). The resonance of this formulation for the character of Selma is clear enough, and it is only sharpened by Cavell's suggestion that "Kant's vision of the human being as living in two worlds" corresponds roughly to "two general matching interpretations of the expressive capacity of song: ecstasy over the absolute success of its expressiveness in recalling the world, as if bringing it back to life; melancholia over its inability to sustain the world, which may be put as an expression of the absolute inexpressiveness of the voice, of its failure to make itself heard, to become intelligible" (141). This last— abandoning one's spirit to and giving voice to a world that no one will hear—is "evidently a mad state," Cavell adds, and it is one that "seems to be reserved for the women of opera" (140) (and in the case at hand, of course, reserved for Selma). Cavell is here responding to Catherine

Clément's assertion in *Opera, or The Undoing of Women*, that "opera is about the death of women"—that is to say, it is about the "countless forms in which men want and want not to hear the woman's voice . . . to know and not know what she knows about men's desires"[8]—a claim that Cavell will modulate into the rather different (and, shall we say, more strictly philosophical) assertion that a woman's singing "exposes her as thinking, so exposes her to the power of those who do not want her to think" (146), in which case she becomes, for Cavell, a figure for "that philosophical self-torment whose shape is skepticism, in which the philosopher wants and wants not to exempt himself from the closet of privacy, wants and want not to become intelligible, expressive, exposed" (132).

The stakes of this revisionist relationship to Clément's thesis are perhaps apparent enough for a film that ends with Selma's death by hanging. Does she die because she is a woman? Because she thinks? Because she sings from a world that imagines the two might coincide? But the stakes of that revision are complicated by Cavell's surprising suggestion that the "mad state" reserved for women in opera usually takes place "only after their words can treat some difficulty internal to their marrying," as if "skepticism is narratively figured as an assault on marriage" (140–41). What we find in the woman's operatic voice is exposure "to a world of the separation of the self from itself, in which the splitting of the self into speech is expressed as the separation from someone who represents to that self the continuance of the world . . . in whom one's expectation of intelligibility has been placed, and collapses" (151). Moreover, this thematization is redoubled in Hollywood film in the theme of remarriage (Cavell has written a whole book about it, *Pursuits of Happiness: The Hollywood Comedy of Remarriage*), which suggests "that the validity of the bond of marriage is assured . . . by something I call the willingness for remarriage, as a way of continuing to affirm the happiness of one's initial leap. As if the chance of happiness"—the chance of continuing to sing and dance, to hope, in the face of skepticism—"exists only when it seconds itself."[9]

What is pertinent about this aspect of Cavell's thesis is that in *Dancer in the Dark,* what cannot be missed is the matter of Selma's conspicuously absent husband and her equally conspicuous rebuffing of her suitor, Jeff (played by Peter Stormare). And while she permits a certain amount of conversational intimacy with her neighbor and landlord Bill (David Morse) (they talk late into the night about going to musicals when they were kids, and so on), we are to understand that this is possible only *because* Bill is married—as if, in Cavell's terms, Selma's ability to continue to believe in the world that is rapidly receding from sight resides not in the possibility of her (re)marriage (hence her repeated rejections of Jeff's overtures in the film's most important musical number, "I've Seen It All") but in her handing down the gift of (continued) sight to her son. The only way of ensuring the continued existence of the world is not marriage and what it signifies but the rejection of marriage in an act of sacrifice that might be characterized as radically feminine in its rejection of a nuclear heteronormativity that (at the least) lurks in the background of Cavell's speculations on (re)marriage.

The relationship of the two worlds (of vision, associated with epistemology and sense certainty on the one hand, and of voice, associated with the loss of the world under skepticism and the hope of its recovery on the other) is complicated even more by Cavell's contention that the ethical and philosophical project of opera was at a certain point taken over by film—a contention he bases on analogizing "the camera's powers of transfiguration to those of music, each providing settings of words and persons that unpredictably take them into a new medium with laws of its own."[10] Just what those settings are may be clarified by Cavell's adaptation of Heidegger's famous thesis on the broken tool. Film, for Cavell, "is a phenomenon in which a particular mode of sight or awareness is brought into play" by "a disruption of what Heidegger calls the 'work-world,' a disruption of the matters of course running among our tools, and the occupations they extend. It is upon the disruption of such matters of course (of a tool, say by its breaking)" that we find, to use Heidegger's phrase, "the worldhood of the world announcing itself" in all its conspicuousness and obstinacy, its *thereness*.[11] "We have here to do," he continues, "with something about the human capacity for sight"—and here the link with the problem of skepticism becomes clear—"or for sensuous awareness generally, something we might express as our condemnation to project, to inhabit, a world that goes essentially beyond the delivery of our senses." In this light, one may read Buster Keaton in *The General,* for instance, "to exemplify an acceptance of the enormity of this realization of human limitation, denying neither the abyss that at any time may open before our plans, nor the possibility, despite that open possibility, of living honorably" (175). Or, more to the point for our purposes, the same might be said of Fred Astaire's dancing, which, far from being "escapist" (as is usually charged with the Hollywood musical), "is meant as a removal not from life but from death," as "facing the music, as a *response* to the life of inexorable consequences" (23)—a reading that would seem to apply quite poignantly to Selma's musical fantasies in the face of blindness and eventually of death itself.

Keaton's comedy, Astaire's dancing, and Selma's musicals, then, all "face the music" of skepticism in the same way that the aria does in opera, but the difference is that film "democratizes the knowledge, hence at once blesses and curses us with it," by telling us that it is as available to all "as the ability is to hold a camera on a subject, so that a failure so to perceive, to persist in missing the subject, is ascribable only to ourselves." Thus the philosophical and ethical problem of inhabiting "a world that goes essentially beyond the delivery of our senses" is only intensified in film by virtue of its very medium. Our sense of film's specific relation to this problem can be sharpened if we attend to Cavell's distinction between painting and photography (and film, for him, as a mode of photography). After the advent of photography, what painting wanted, he suggests, "was a sense of *presentness*— not exactly a conviction of the world's presence to us, but of our presence to it. At some point the unhinging of our consciousness from the world [as in the "fall" into skepticism after Kant] interposed our subjectivity between us and our presentness to the world. Then our subjectivity became what is present to us, individuality became isolation. The route to conviction in reality was through the acknowledgment of that endless presence of self."[12] In a passage worth comparing with my discussion in chapter 3 of the spectrality of visual media as Derrida describes it, Cavell asserts that photography, on the other hand (and with it film), "overcame subjectivity in a way undreamed of by painting, a way that could not satisfy painting, one which does not so much deflect the act of painting as escape it altogether: by *automatism,* by removing the human agent from the task of reproduction. . . . To maintain conviction in our connection with reality, to maintain our presentness, painting accepts the recession of the world. Photography maintains the presentness of the world by accepting our absence from it. The reality in a photograph is present to me while I am not present to it."[13] We are, to use Derrida's words, "spectralized by the shot."

So it is that film for Cavell has a kind of "magical" ability to meet the threat of skepticism "not by literally presenting us with the world, but by permitting us to view it unseen," "as though the world's projection explains our forms of unknownness and of our inability to know" (40). There is an important reversal here; in fact, two reversals. If music and voice as we find them in opera met the loss of the world under skepticism by an assertion that we nevertheless miraculously exist—in this sense, music and song come to the rescue of language after skepticism, as Cavell sometimes puts it—they did so only at the price of acknowledging that the world of things was always already lost. Gone. In photography and film, on the other hand, the existence of the world is miraculously affirmed via automatism, but the price we pay for the world's recovery is that it no longer exists *for us.* It is radically ahuman, other. We can't know or touch the world precisely because it manifests itself *unbidden,* without our help. Film is thus what the world looks like when we're not there.

What is most interesting here—especially for the purpose of discussing a film such as *Dancer in the Dark,* in which the relationship between the visual, the auditory, and the vocal is so pressing—is Cavell's insistence that while "we don't know how to think of the *connection* between a photograph and what it is a photograph of" ("The image is not a likeness," he rightly insists), "one might wonder that similar questions do not arise about recordings of sound."[14] "Is the difference between auditory and visual transcription," he asks, "a function of the fact that we are fully accustomed to hearing things that are invisible, not present to us, not present with us? We would be in trouble if we weren't so accustomed, because it is the nature of hearing that what is heard comes *from* someplace, whereas what you can see you can look *at.* . . . We are not accustomed to seeing things that are invisible, or not present to us, not present with us. . . . Yet this seems, ontologically, to be what is happening when we look at a photograph" (18). The idea here is that with the visual, the lines of determination run from the intentional subject to the object, to what we "look *at,*" and hence the magic of the photograph and of film is that our role in so making the world manifest is suddenly removed from the equation. With sound, on the other hand, the lines run from the object ("where sound comes *from*") to the subject—it is, as Derrida might put it, a "spatialization" of the subject/object relation—so that a corollary magic would involve our *insertion* into the equation, as if we had to actively listen, just as we actively direct sight, to hear anything at all.

What I want to suggest is that something like this reversal is exactly what happens in *Dancer in the Dark,* with profound implications for how the film stages the relationship between the auditory and the visual and, within that, the relationship of both of these to the project of film as a medium. There are two dynamics at work here, and it is crucial to disarticulate them: on the one hand, Selma's drama and its philosophical and ethical significance and, on the other, what the film, from a quite different vantage, does with that drama. It is here, on the strength of this disarticulation, that we can begin to sense some of the limits of Cavell's work—the extent to which it is, we might say, "Selmacentric." Let us return briefly to Cavell's account of visual versus auditory transcription in *The World Viewed,* specifically his contention "'when I am in the presence of an English horn playing, I still don't literally hear the horn, I hear the sound of the horn. So I don't worry about hearing a horn when the horn is not present, because *what* I hear is exactly the same . . . whether the thing is present or not.' What this rigmarole calls attention to is that sounds can be perfectly copied, and that we have various interests in copying them" (368). It is as if recorded sound has taken the place of Roland Barthes's photograph and its "umbilical cord" to the real critiqued by Derrida in chapter 3. In this light, Cavell's discussion of visual versus auditory transcription would appear to take its place as part of that film theory that "has assured us," as Kaja Silverman puts it, "that there is no difference between recorded and prerecorded sounds—that the apparatus is miraculously capable of capturing and retransmitting the profilmic event in all its auditory plenitude," so that "with each new testimonial to the authenticity of recorded sound, cinema seems once again capable of restoring all phenomenal losses."[15] As Silverman points out, however, it is relatively easy to demonstrate that every acoustic event is inseparable from the space in which it occurs, and that in sound recording (as in image recording), the technological apparatus in question is always highly selective, isolating and intensifying some features and ignoring others. Indeed, as Douglas Kahn has exhaustively shown in his study *Noise Water Meat: A History of Sound in the Arts*, the kinds of qualifications and nuances voiced by Silverman are precisely those that have captivated the huge body of work in sound art in the twentieth century, much of which foregrounds the technological mediation and environmental embeddedness of sound as a medium (think, for instance, of John Cage or Alvin Lucier, to name only two well-known examples).[16] From this vantage, Cavell's remarks on auditory versus visual transcription seem to reintroduce the very kind of phenomenological plenitude that film "automatically" delivers in Cavell's account, but without the attendant (and crucial) clarification that such plenitude is the product of fantasy only.

To linger over this moment in Cavell's work is to realize that there is a crucial and altogether symptomatic aporia—in fact a double aporia—at the heart of his understanding of voice in relation to sound. As for the first, remember that for Cavell sound and voice are in the deepest sense not continuous but *opposed:* voice aligned with the subject (it takes over the function of the Word after language has been subjected to the withering force of skepticism), and sound with the object (as that which comes *from* the world to the subject, as it were unbidden). But it is difficult to see how the difference between sound and voice can be maintained as a constitutive ontological difference, how the interiority of voice as expression can be quarantined from the *exteriority* that is its material medium and condition of possibility in sound. To put it as concisely as possible, voice and sound exist along a continuum, not a divide, which is simply to say, in another register, that one person's voice is another person's noise—a point hardly laid to rest by appeals to the generic norms of opera or any other art form.

More important than this, however, is the second aporia, interior to voice itself. As Cavell explains it, film "reverses the ascension in theater of character over actor"; in theater, the emphasis is that "this character could (will) accept other actors," which thus figures "the fatedness in human existence, the self's finality or typicality." In film, the actor, not the role, is predominant, and this is a vehicle for film's (democratic) emphasis on "the potentiality in human existence, the self's journeying." In opera, however, the relation of actor/singer and role "is unimportant beside the fact of the new conception it introduces of the relation of voice and body," in which "this voice is located in—one might say disembodied within—this figure, this double, this person, this persona, this singer, whose voice is essentially unaffected by the role."[17] What makes Cavell's account here fascinating is its radical ambivalence about the voice as "disembodied within"—but within what? Here the Cavellian voice would seem legible as a variety of what Slavoj Žižek calls "the Cartesian subject in all its abstraction, the empty punctuality we reach after subtracting all its particular contents"; what we might call the "principle" of voice is thus "disembodied within" a subject whose contingent features are unimportant, a subject that is, in Cavell's words, "this figure, this double, this person, this persona"—in short, this *etcetera*.[18] What this suggests, I think, is that voice in Cavell is a figure for *presence,* but a presence that (as in Descartes and Kant) should not be confused with substance and is in fact based on the transcendence of substance as "pathological" contingency and materiality (to use Kant's term). More precisely, then, the apparent opposition of sound and voice in Cavell—the first aporia I touched on—is subtended by a more fundamental commitment to a *presence* that links them: presence of the world to itself captured in the automatism of the photograph and sound recording; and presence of the voice to itself that testifies to the world's loss or passing under skepticism—that knows it and, in voicing that knowledge, sings humanism's last aria.

It is here that the Lacanian schema of the subject I have already invoked by way of Žižek and Silverman, with its interweaving of the two "sides" of voice and sound, Symbolic and Real, and so on, may be of help. Silverman, for example, in her pathbreaking study *The Acoustic Mirror,* insists, following Lacan, that meaning and materiality, subject and object, are always coimplicated and interwoven in a symbolic and psychic economy of *imbalance* constituted by a lack at the center of the subject, who can be subject only insofar as he has acceded to the dictates of a Symbolic order not his own, in what she characterizes as a "pre-Oedipal castration" of "a subject who is structured by lack long before the 'discovery' of sexual difference, a subject whose very coherence and certitude are predicated on division and alienation."[19] This diacritical interweaving, rather than Cavellian opposition, of presence and absence has for her particular and direct implications for reading the engendering and embodying of voice in film. Classical cinema, Silverman writes, "requires the female voice to assume similar responsibilities to those it confers upon the female body," where it operates as a fetish "filling in for and covering over what is unspeakable within male subjectivity. In her vocal as in her corporeal capacity, woman-as-fetish may be asked to represent that phenomenal plenitude which is lost to the male subject with his entry into language," though she is "more frequently obliged to display than to conceal lack—to protect the male subject from knowledge of his own castration by absorbing his losses as well as those that structure female subjectivity" (38–39).

Here we can't help but recall Cavell's contention that opera is about the "countless forms in which men want and want not to hear the woman's voice . . . to know and not know what she knows about men's desires."[20] But it is crucial to remember that in Cavell's account, the idea that "women's singing exposes them to death" is rewritten specifically in terms as "exposes her as thinking, so exposes her to the power of those who do not want her to think" (146)—in which case she becomes for Cavell a figure for "that philosophical self-torment whose shape is skepticism, in which the philosopher wants and wants not to exempt himself from the closet of privacy, wants and want not to become intelligible, expressive, exposed" (132). In making this turn, however, Cavell would seem to take away with one hand what he has given with the other, and that is the specificity and materiality of woman's embodiment in relation to voice—an embodiment that a posthumanist reading would surely insist on. A similar double gesture is at work in Cavell's use of Freud's distinction between orality and vocality (in Freud's essay "Negation") to account for the at once "primitive" (or "bodily") and "sophisticated" (or "performative") power of the voice. Cavell wants to capture the interlacing of "the spectacular vocality of opera in its aspect as orality and in its aspect as exposure or display, sometimes named seductiveness" (145). For Cavell, the power of "voice in opera as a judgment of the world on the basis of, called forth by, pain beyond a concept" is itself rooted in "the oral, primitive basis of judgment," as explained in Freud's theory in "Negation," where introjection and expulsion from the body are the origins of affirmative or negative judgments. As a result, for Cavell, the very drawing and expelling of the breath in singing enacts a kind of ur-dialectic between bringing the world nearer (overcoming skepticism) and then pushing it away in a transcendence that is also a mourning (148).

Here one would simply want to point out, by way of Lacan and his inheritors such as Silverman and Žižek, that the drives (including orality) are always already *denaturalized* because they are accessible only retroactively by means of the Symbolic itself. From this vantage, the fundamental issue with the voice's power is not whether it can be tethered, via the body ("orality"), to the world of the Cavellian ordinary and everyday (thereby ensuring us that the pain of the operatic voice remains real and not, as it were, merely epistemological). Rather, the body itself is already denaturalized and "derailed" (to use Žižek's term) by the Symbolic order, so that the "primitive" basis of voice (the drive), rather than "coming first" as in Cavell, is instead a retroactively determined and "excessive" product of the Symbolic, of desire, in a psychic economy characterized above all by imbalance. It thus *never was* in our power, you might say, to lose the world in the way Cavell imagines, or to lose that loss by means of the voice and its introjection or expulsion. All of which is to say that the suggestive correspondence between the Lacanian theory of the split subject of desire and Cavell's reading of "singing as (dis)embodied within the doubleness of the human" and "the splitting of the self into speech" is and will remain only that—suggestive.[21]

Meanwhile—to clarify the stakes of some of this for the film itself—it is obvious enough that Selma is doubly marked by figures of castration (indeed, by the most canonical such figures there are) in her encroaching blindness and in her death by hanging. But the question—turning now from Cavell's terms to those of psychoanalysis—is the nature of this castration, what it is supposed to signify. Is this, as Silverman might suggest, about killing off the feminine and maternal body in the service of phallic disavowal of pre-Oedipal castration, in which Selma is sacrificed for those losses she is made to bear? Or is something else going on here? In fact, what is most important about Selma's castration is not that it robs her of agency but—quite the reverse—that it makes her the film's maximum *example* of agency. Moreover, the force of her agency would seem to increase in direct proportion to her growing loss of vision, the increasingly melodramatic "absurdity" of her situation, and how she responds to its mounting crisis. This is made clear in any number of ways, not least in her steadfast refusal of the otherwise advantageous romantic overtures by Jeff: her assertion, in the film's most powerful musical number, that "I've seen all I need to see," even as he suggests that if she marries him (and then sees Niagara falls, has grandchildren, and so on), the world will be, in Cavellian terms, restored to her in and through marriage. (Crucial here too is the motif of Selma's absent husband—a point to which I will return in a moment.)

We can clarify the status of castration in relation to the feminine and the Symbolic in the film most readily by recourse to Silverman's fascinating discussion of how in Hollywood "castration is not the only trope through which dominant cinema conflates the female voice with the female body" (63). Here she takes issue quite pointedly with Michel Chion's formulation in *La voix au cinéma* that "in much the same way that the feminine sex is the ultimate point in the *deshabille* (the point after which it is no longer possible to deny the absence of the penis), there is an ultimate point in the embodiment of the voice, and that is the *mouth* from which the voice issues."[22] In Silverman's estimation, Chion here simply reproduces on theoretical terrain Hollywood's conflation of "the female voice with the female body" and so organizes "female sexuality around the image of . . . 'the insatiable organ hole'" that may be figured as either mouth or vagina (63). With this turn, "the interiority which Hollywood imputes to her has nothing whatever to do with transcendence or Cartesian cogitation. On the contrary, that interiority helps to establish the female body as the absolute limit of female subjectivity. . . . Woman's psyche is only a further extension of her body—its other side, or, to be more precise, its inside" (64). What this means for Silverman, however, is that "the yawning chasm of a corporeal interiority" that "is posited as a major port of entry into her subjectivity" is better viewed as "the site at which that subjectivity is introduced into her," with the voice "the preferred point of insertion" (67). In short, the female voice and with it the mouth from which it issues are the point of entry for the phallus, the Law, and the Symbolic into female subjectivity, if classical cinema has its way.

Here, however, valuable as it is for exposing some of the problems with Cavell's work on voice, opera, and film, we glimpse something like the limit of Silverman's thesis for understanding *Dancer in the Dark*—or perhaps we should say that we begin to understand how radically *Dancer* departs from the Hollywood conventions critiqued by Silverman. What is most unmistakable in Selma's drama, of course—and it is crucial to the posthumanist ethical project of the film and how that project is linked to its embodiment—is the unmasking of the Law as a senseless, contingent machine, constructed utterly by factitious self-instantiation. The film makes this clear in any number of ways, from the adjacent drama of Bill, her landlord policeman who betrays Selma and steals her money to pay off bills run up by his free-spending wife, to the almost sadomasochistic courtroom drama and the facile construction of Selma as a murderer, to the fact that "justice" and death by hanging for Selma are determined in the end not by justice but by money. In light of all of this, we might give a rather different interpretation than Silverman's to the altogether unavoidable matter of Björk's performative relationship to the mouth and tongue as site of the female voice; at key moments in the musical numbers, her tongue swells into a kind of fleshy protuberance, a wall blocking entry into the interiority of the female subject as the voice soars and asserts its power. Here the performative use of the mouth and tongue uncannily expresses not the "entry" of the Symbolic and the phallic Law into the feminine subject via the "organ hole" of the mouth and voice—not "the site at which that subjectivity is introduced into her"—but rather, I would argue, its rejection and blockage, which coincides with the raising of the woman's voice itself to its highest registers.[23]

I would like to take this striking performative punctuation of the film by Björk as an index of the fact that there is another, more profound sense of "the feminine" at work in *Dancer in the Dark*—a sense that perhaps accounts for the wild ambivalence and hysteria that greeted the film upon its release. Here Žižek's work on sacrifice, suicide, and "the act as feminine" will help us understand that there are *two* different aspects of the "feminine" at work in the film. The point of agreement between Silverman and Žižek (versus Cavell's reading) would no doubt be their insistence via Lacan that any relationship to the world of the object, the Thing, the body, the drives, and so on is always riven with difference and denaturalized; that is to say, the "human" is thus that fantasmatic object (the "auto-" that the "autobiographical animal" "gives to itself," to use Derrida's phrasing) that constitutes itself by repressing this more fundamental, posthumanist symbolic economy.

Björk in *Dancer in the Dark* (2000, directed by Lars von Trier).

They would disagree, however, on the *ethical ramifications* of this fact vis-à-vis the question of the feminine. Where Silverman would find in the phallic regime of Hollywood film the displacement of pre-Oedipal losses onto the feminine body and voice, Žižek would identify the phallic *itself* with such losses and would therefore locate "the feminine" at the very core, and as the very truth of, the phallic. This is so in Žižek's reading because the phallus in Lacan as the "origin" of desire is not "natural," not given *as such,* but is instead a *signifier*—which is to say that desire and the phallus that constitutes it are socially produced and culturally determined, so that the Real (of the so-called drives, the biological, the body, and, of course, the feminine body in contrast to male *cogito*) becomes accessible only by being retroactively posited as original and natural by the contingent and diacritical system of the Symbolic itself. As Žižek puts it, the phallus-as-signifier thus operates—against the clichéd notion of the phallus as "the siege of male 'natural' penetrative-aggressive potency-power"—as "a kind of 'prosthetic,' 'artificial' supplement; it designates the point at which the big Other [the Symbolic], a decentered agency, supplements the subject's failure," its "lack of co-ordination and unity."[24] The phallus, that is to say, rather than being the very mark and icon of humanism and its law, is, properly understood, always already posthumanist and, in that sense, "feminine."

Žižek explores this theme in any number of registers, including romanticism's commonplace of "madness as the positive foundation of 'normality'" (which "clearly announces the Freudian thesis that the 'pathological' provides the key to the normal"). Given my discussion in chapter 5, most interesting for our purposes, perhaps, is his example of the Enlightenment idea that *blindness* itself provides the key to understanding the logic of vision, in the same way that, in Malebranche, "the 'pathological' case of feeling a hand one does not have" in fact "provides the key to explaining how a 'normal' person feels the hand he actually possesses." In "strict analogy" to Lacan's claim that "a madman is not only a beggar who thinks he is a king, but also a king who thinks he is a king"—because he "directly grounds his symbolic mandate in his immediate natural properties"—Malebranche claims that a madman is not only he who feels his missing hand without having one but also he who feels the hand he really has, "since when I claim to feel my hand directly, I confound two ontologically different registers: the material, bodily hand and the representation of a hand in my mind, which is the only thing I am actually aware of."[25] And this, in turn, is analogous to the status of the phallus itself as prosthetic, since it too is referenced to the "natural" body and yet can only be experienced through mediation by the regime of the signifier and the Symbolic.

There is an important point of contact here, as we know from earlier chapters, between Žižek's account of the Lacanian phallus and the set of terms that cluster in Derrida's work around the prosthesis, the supplement, and so on—a point to which I will return in a moment. For now, however, what needs to be registered for us to understand the status of the feminine in relation to the film's ethical project is that the truth of the phallus is the truth that the subject is always already a *prosthetic* subject, always in need of the supplement provided by precisely that which is castrating in the first place (namely, the Symbolic), thus generating—in contrast to Cavellian skepticism—a constitutively unbalanced psychic economy driven by what Žižek calls "the loop of (symbolic) castration" (135). The fundamental prosthetics of subjectivity are registered and thematized in all sorts of obvious ways in the film. Most obvious of all is the conspicuous fact of Selma's failing eyesight and the various strategies used to supplement it: the crib sheet she uses at her visit to the eye doctor, for example, which she memorizes so that she can pretend to read the eye chart and keep her job; the Coke-bottle eyeglasses that she shares with her son Gene like a prosthetic supplement to the already "natural" and "complete" mother–son bond, which fall to the floor in a cut shot at the moment of her hanging, as if to suggest that only in death does one escape the prosthetics of subjectivity; and the fact that the "natural," originary state of being sighted can be achieved for Gene only by means of surgical intervention—a kind of literalization of the Freudian notion of retroactive causality. Other examples abound. Most fascinating of all, perhaps, is the scene in which Selma and Kathy attend the movies to watch a Hollywood musical. Here, however, "watching the film" takes the following form: Kathy *tells* Selma in a verbal blow-by-blow what is going on on the screen that she cannot see, only to have *that* linear account interrupted by a running argument that erupts with another patron a few rows up who is irritated by her talking. For Selma, "watching" the film consists of seeing nothing and hearing a sound track, overwritten by a verbal account, derailed by a shouting match—all of which, it should be added, she gleefully takes in, as if it's better than seeing the film "normally."

This scene invokes the central prosthetic thematization of the film—how, with failing sight, the realm of sound becomes more and more Selma's way to "bring the world nearer" (to use the Emersonian phrase invoked by Cavell)—a fact painfully evoked in Selma's jail cell on death row as she desperately presses her ear to the ventilation grate in the deafening silence, trying to hold on to one last aural thread of the world around her. At this precise juncture, however, it is crucial to insist on the difference between what the prosthetic relations of vision and sound mean to Selma and what they mean to the *film*, the better to understand the ethical project that drives the film's use of Selma as a character and a vehicle. For what cannot be missed by any viewer, I think, is the striking, even jarring, difference between how the film is shot "inside" and "outside" Selma's fantasy musical scenes, with the inside scenes in vivid color, carefully (in fact, remarkably) choreographed and edited (with footage taken, reportedly, from one hundred digital cameras used to film each sequence), and the outside scenes presented in washed-out sepia tones in the best cinema verité documentary style.

Now the point here is not some untenable distinction between the "cooked" and the "raw," the "artful" and the "authentic," the mediated and the umediated, and so on, but rather the film's startling and

principled insistence on this visual difference. All of which, we must remember, is framed by a question of genre: namely, why the Hollywood
musical as the generic mode of Selma's fantasies? The most succinct
answer, I think, is to say that for Selma the Hollywood musical uses
music, song, and voice to prosthetically assume the functions of "cognitive mapping" (to use Fredric Jameson's well-worn phrase) usually
reserved in the humanistic tradition (as we saw in chapter 5) for the
visual, in which the world presents itself in evidence, as it were, before
the gaze of the "centered" subject around which the world of tables
and chairs (or, in Gene Kelly's case, umbrellas) coalesces. In psychoanalytic terms, in the Hollywood musical it is as if the fantasy structure
of "normal" vision itself is laid bare. For Lacan, on the other hand, "If I
am anything in the picture, it is always in the form of the screen . . . the
stain, the spot"; "in the scopic field," he continues, "the gaze is outside,"
it belongs, as Stephen Melville puts it succinctly, "not to the (small o)
other but to the Other—language, world, the fact of a movement of signification beyond human meaning."[26] In Lacan's analysis, opacity rather
than transparency constitutes the structure of visuality. But is not the
world of the Hollywood musical above all a world that is *not* opaque, a
world of transparency where objects—like Fred Astaire's mop in the famous dance number—are immediately meaningful and obey our every
whim, where the infirmity and foreignness of the body itself are suddenly transcended as we "dance dance dance!" (to borrow the lyrics
from *Dancer*'s musical number "Cvalda")?

As we have seen, it is precisely this willingness to hope against
hope and believe against belief that is invoked by Cavell in viewing the
musical and its dance as "an escape from death," as "facing the music"
of skepticism by reaffirming the hopes of humanism. But what I want
to suggest is that part of the film's genius—and certainly crucial to
its emotional torque—is that it allows Selma's romantic, indeed melodramatic, deployment of this "solution" to her loss of vision as a means
of ensuring the world's consistency while at the same time the *film*
deconstructs that solution—specifically, in how the film "outside" of
Selma's fantasy world is shot. For what the *film* insists on, rigorously
and systematically, is the difference between Selma's "vision" of the
world (and the subject's centered place in it as constituted by fantasy)
and what the world *looks like* when those fantasies and identifications

are suspended—when they are, as it were, subjected to analysis. In so doing, the film uses the "pathological" fact of Selma's blindness and the compensatory strategies it generates to disclose a radically deconstructed notion of the visual, very much along the lines of Žižek's gloss on Malbranche, with the point being, as I put it in chapter 5 with Derrida, not that "*only* those who cannot see can see," but that "*even* those who cannot see cannot see."

The film's most important musical number, "I've Seen It All," would seem to register this theoretical point about fantasy and identification very much in the terms discussed by Žižek in his gloss on MUDs (multiple-user domains) on the Internet: that the point of the Lacanian notion of the split or decentered subject is not that "there are simply *more* Egos/Selves in the same individual" with which one might identify but that this decentering is of "the void of the subject" itself as derailed and constituted by the Symbolic and by the phallus as signifier (its "hollowing out" by the signifier, as Lacanians like to say) in relation to its "content," to "the bundle of imaginary and/or symbolic identifications." Here we might revisit Selma's repeated *rejections* in "I've Seen It All" of the further identifications held out to her by Jeff (of wife, of grandmother, and so on). In her repeated insistence that "I've seen all I need to see," the film registers the fact that "the subject's division is not the division between one Self and another, between two contents, but *the division between something and nothing*, between the feature of identification and the void."[27] In this light, we can understand Selma's rigorous insistence that further identifications ("seeing more" in the song's terms) will change nothing as a kind of unflinching posthumanism—a point punctuated, one might say, as Selma removes her glasses at the beginning of the number and tosses them into the water, then moments later wraps her arms around herself and falls to the ground in a fetal position, dangerously (suicidally?) near the passing train, as a final "answer" to Jeff's repeated calls for further, other identifications with the roles of wife, grandmother, and so on made available to her.

To return, however, to how the film is shot: what makes the film posthumanist is that it mobilizes the investment in a traditional fantasy of vision through its thematization in the story of Selma but at the same time divorces visuality from transcendence, identity, and the ego, around whom visual space might be organized, in its cinema

verité camera work. This apparent realism, however, does not operate to put us in touch with some unmediated relationship with "the
way things are" (that, as we saw with Silverman's critique of aural and
visual transcription, is not in the cards) but instead is calculated to
insist that if we ask, "What does the world look like?" the answer can
only be "It doesn't look 'like' anything at all"—a fact we may index
to the film's conspicuous foregrounding of the apparent contingency
governing the camera work itself. This jarring but crucial contrast is
prepared for in the film's opening moments, in the juxtaposition of
the operatic overture and its painterly affirmation of subject-centered
vision, followed immediately by the mundane local audition for *The
Sound of Music,* filmed in a nearly distracting handheld style. What all
of this suggests is that we are to take the fantasy scenes, with their
vivid coloration and careful choreography (as in the visually stunning "I've Seen It All" or the complexly woven "Cvalda"), in contrast
to the devil-may-care shooting and washed-out color of the everyday
scenes—as *more real* than the "documentary," "real-life" scenes from
which they supposedly depart—*and that this is precisely their problem.*
To put it in psychoanalytic terms, the world paradoxically "comes to
life" only *through* fantasy, but it is the subject's very fantasy itself that
bars her from "what is really going on" in the world itself, which obeys
its own laws and doesn't "look like" the subject's desire (or anybody
else's). This doesn't mean that fantasy is being disavowed, as if one
could escape it, only that it is being carefully situated, and in a way
specific to the medium of film. To modify Cavell's wonderful insight,
we might say that film may be what the world looks like when we're
not there, but it's not what the world looks like when *nobody's* there.
That's why it doesn't look "like" anything at all.

If we want to think of this in deconstructive rather than psychoanalytic terms, the film might be said to enact what Laura Oswald
has called the strategy of "cinema-graphia," which identifies cinema
with "those traces of non-presence" such as the splice, the cut, or the
frame that draw attention to "the endless production/deconstruction
of the meaning and subject of film discourse across the film frame."
In so doing, cinema-graphia "shatters the mirror in which the subject
is held as a unity by defining the image as a trace for another image,"
thus exposing—and here one might readily think of *Dancer's* relation

to the Hollywood musical and its techniques—"mimesis as the endless pursuit of an illusion."[28] Cinema-graphia thus subjects the cinematic field to the deconstructive force of what Derrida called the "spatial." As Derrida characterizes it—in remarks that have obvious resonance with our earlier discussion of Žižek's gloss on Malebranche and the prosthetic—"the painter or the drawer is blind . . . the hand that paints and draws is the hand of a blind person—it is an experience of blindness. Thus the visual arts are also arts of the blind," which is to say that the visual is always subjected to the force the spatial, which is heterogeneous to the space of the centered subject of humanist visuality.[29]

The spatializing effect of cinema-graphia thus operates wholly counter to the cinematic practice of "suture" as popularly theorized in 1980s film theory, in which "the primary identification of the spectator with the film image by means of the look parallels the child's identification with his or her other and the (m)Other in the mirror phase of development," so that "the spectator internalizes the subject-positions of characters in the diegesis." Cinema-graphia, on the other hand, "shatters the mirror in which the subject is held as unity by defining the image as a trace for another image."[30] For this reason, as Peter Brunette and David Wills have put it, what we find in cinema is "the deconstruction of the mimetic operation rather than the confirmation of it, and it is in this sense that the screen can be called a hymen." As Oswald characterizes it, the hymen "corresponds to the elusive trace of the film frame joining/separating elements of the film chain, constructing/deconstructing meaning and subject-address in film discourse" (260).

In this light—or in this space, perhaps we should now say—we might well take issue with Silverman's impatience with Derrida's use of the cognate term "invagination," which, Silverman writes, "has tended to obscure rather than to foreground the ways in which texts engender their readers and viewers" because "it is exploited primarily as rhetorical currency." In the understanding I am pursuing here, nothing would seem to be further from the truth. Indeed, Derrida's rendering of invagination in the essay "Living On: Border Lines" contends that the invaginated structure of all discourse is necessarily repressed by any law, by "the authorities who demand an *author,* an *I* capable of organizing a narrative sequence, of remembering and telling the truth."

"Such is the demand for the story," he continues, "the narrative, the demand that society, the law that governs literary and artistic works, medicine, the police, and so forth, claim to constitute. This demand for truth is itself recounted and swept along in the endless process of invagination."[31] The point Derrida is making here, as I understand it, is that "invagination" is not merely a rhetorical gesture but, quite the contrary, is crucial to understanding the relation of sexual difference to questions of *institution* and law—a point that has obvious relevance for our understanding of a film in which the feminine is subjected to the power of the law in the form of capital punishment. What I want to suggest now, in combining Derrida's rendering of invagination with the psychoanalytic frame of Žižek, is that the castration of Selma by blindness and hanging in the film (which some reviewers have seen as nothing short of a sadistic manipulation of the audience by the film's director) operates not *only* in the service, as Silverman would argue, of a displacement and projection of pre-Oedipal losses onto the feminine by a phallic regime but rather—a much stronger and more complicated ethical project on the film's part—as the rendering of what Žižek calls "*the act* as feminine."

Here again, as with my earlier discussion of the phallus as signifier, we must revisit, according to Žižek, "one of the most notoriously 'antifeminist' theses of the late Lacan": that "woman is a symptom of man."[32] Things look quite different, Žižek argues, if we focus more carefully on just what the term "symptom" means in the late Lacan: "namely as a particular signifying formation which confers on the subject its very ontological consistency, enabling it to structure its basic, constitutive relationship to *enjoyment (jouissance)*." In these terms, the thesis "woman is a symptom of man" "means that *man himself exists only through woman qua his symptom:* all his ontological consistency hangs on, is suspended from, his symptom, is 'externalized' in his symptom. In other words, man literally *ex-sists:* his entire being lies 'out there,' in woman. Woman, on the other hand, does *not* exist, she *insists.*" "In this way," Žižek continues, "the relationship to the death drive is also reversed: 'woman,' taken 'in herself,' outside the relation to man, embodies the death drive, apprehended as a radical, most elementary ethical attitude of uncompromising insistence. . . . Woman is therefore no longer conceived as fundamentally 'passive' in contrast to male activity: the act as such, in its most fundamental dimension, is 'feminine'" (156). This is why, for Lacan, suicide is the epitome of the act considered in this radical ethical dimension; it involves "a kind of temporary eclipse" of the subject in which "I put at stake everything, including myself, my symbolic identity; the act is therefore always a 'crime,' a 'transgression'"—it is "'mad' in the sense of radical *un-accountability*." In this act of annihilation, "we not only don't know what will come out of it, its final outcome is ultimately even insignificant, strictly secondary, in relation to the NO! of the pure act" (44).

We are now better equipped to understand in a more profound way the ethical project of *Dancer in the Dark* and how that project might well be the source of the intense polarization of the film's audience. What is most disturbing about Selma's plight is not that she commits a crime (indeed, this is merely the "motivation of the device," as the Russian formalists used to say, for the film's handling of the relation of the feminine, the act, and the Law). What is far more disturbing, and far more ethically significant, is her *radical passivity* in the face of her condemnation, even as her friends scurry about (in "masculine" activity, as Žižek would say) to gather new information about her situation, contact lawyers, and so on. Selma herself, however, chooses to do *nothing*, and it is this passivity, this "NO!"—which culminates, of course, in her choosing to die—that most forcefully exposes the utter injustice and contingency of the Law, the fact that the Law functions precisely to "actively" and indeed, one might now say, "hysterically" cover over the fact that it is constructed across a void. All of which helps to explain an intuition that nearly all viewers of the film are bound to share, that the most unsatisfactory ending imaginable would be precisely that which is most "reasonable": Selma using the recovered money to hire a lawyer, reopen the case, and win her acquittal, which would only serve to collapse the very abyss between justice and Law that has been opened up in the film by means of the "act as feminine."

From this vantage we can now understand the full significance of the conspicuous fact in the film of Selma's absent husband (curiously unremarked and unexplained), her rejection of Jeff's repeated overtures ("senselessly," as it were), and her reclaiming and renaming of her *own* (name-of-the) father in terms of her own psychic coordinates, pretending that he is named Olrich Novy, a famous comedic song-and-dance man from her homeland (here played by Joel Gray in an altogether unexpected and not entirely successful cameo). Here we might say even more pointedly that the father of Gene is not *just* an *absent* father; he is also *lacking,* and his role has been assumed by Selma, whose embodiment of the act as feminine is the film's supreme example of ethical agency. In these terms, Selma assumes the phallic function par excellence in passing on to her son the gift of vision,[33] but what the ~~father~~ mother passes on to her son is vision without (paternal) Law, vision under the sign of the prosthetic as the very truth of the subject—a fact indexed by the conspicuous, oversized eyeglasses that mother and son share as a kind of visual albatross. Here we find, as David Wills puts it in his wonderful meditation *Prosthesis,* "the body as a whole as metonymic signifier of the phallus" called into question by means of the prosthesis, in which "the relation to the other becomes precisely and necessarily a relation of otherness, the otherness, for example, of artificiality attached to or found within the natural" (a fact neatly indexed here in that Gene's "natural" condition of sight can only exist through prosthetic surgical intervention). "The relation to the other," Wills concludes, is thus "denied the reconfirmation of sameness that freezes its differential effect, rigidifies the oedipal structure, and ultimately represses the feminine, the homosexual, and so on."[34]

What we find here, then, is a subjection of vision to the force of the prosthetic itself in Selma's assumption of the "phallic" function of passing along sight to her son. And this, in turn, must now be mapped in terms of the multiple valences of the film's posthumanist ethical project: of the act as feminine and its exposure of the Law's facticity; of the rescripting of the phallic subject as always already prosthetic; and of the tearing away of the visual as such from its association with the ontological privilege of the subject. Here again we must pay attention to the difference between the film's vantage on this drama and Selma's own. *Selma* may think that the vision she is bequeathing to her son is the ability to see a world that looks the way her fantasies do—a world that is, in a word, beautiful—but the *film* has long since insisted that the world *outside* Selma's fantasy, the world she "merely" inhabits, will not look "like" anything in particular at all. From the film's vantage, she doesn't hand down to her son "her" world, in other words, but simply "a" world—vision without the phallus, and with no guarantees. Indeed, to put it paradoxically, we could say that Selma *hears* in the aural domain the truth of the visual as she frantically listens at the ventilation grate in her cell for any sound at all. Here the signposts for the subject on the way to the void are clear: music, then noise, then silence.

In this light, as Žižek puts it in his writing on David Lynch, the "flatness" of reality that we find in various forms of visual representation (Pre-Raphaelite painting, for instance) "effectively cancels the perspective of infinite openness" that we associate with the Newtonian/Cartesian worldview, and finds its counterpart in a certain ontological or "primordial" concept of noise that is *constitutive of space itself: it is not a noise 'in' space, but a noise that keeps space open as such,*" "the very texture that holds reality together—if this noise were to be eradicated, reality itself would collapse." "This noise is therefore, in a sense," Žižek concludes, "the very 'sound of silence.'"[35] It is this noise, this very texture of reality, that Selma listens for in her jail cell, having now been deprived of music, noise at the moment before it passes over (as it is bound to do for Selma) into music, into a kind of becoming-voice that reassures the subject that she still exists. What I am suggesting, then, is that in the end *Dancer in the Dark* stages the problem of sound and voice in terms that are amenable to Cavell *and* to the rather different analyses of Žižek and Derrida, and it does so by means of a double articulation that insists on the fundamental difference between Selma's psychic drama and the film's larger project. Selma's drama may indeed be read in terms of the *topos* of Cavellian skepticism: the loss of the world (thematized through Selma's blindness) that enables—even necessitates, one might say—the recovery of another world "flush with this one," a world organized around the subject, into which we may step under the guidance or spur, as it were, of the voice. For the *film,* however, this drama is quite clearly reframed as (only) fantasy. For Selma as *character,* sound is always already crossing over into a musicality that is further circumscribed—made all the more melodious, one might say—in terms of the Hollywood musical and its conventions; but for the *film,* music is a kind of post-Cagean phenomenon in which the difference between music and sound is uncertain and unstable, posed anew each moment in the clacking of train tracks, the clamor of the factory floor, and the scratching of the courtroom sketch artist's pencil.

One might note too in this connection the unique vocal style of Björk herself, which seems to have more in common with the film and director, you might say, than with Selma the character. What I am tempted to call the posthumanist voice of Björk's performance ranges rapidly and without warning from the operatic to the flatly verbal to the almost guttural (and all points in between), as if the voice itself were one minute the disembodied transmission of spirit (as Cavell might have it) and the next minute a sampling of various sounds, styles, and mannerisms, not all of them what we usually think of as vocal music at all. What Björk's vocal style seems to emphasize at such moments is not so much that voice floats free of the world and points to another, better one adjacent to this one (as Cavell would have it) but that voice is always already "hollowed out," as Lacan would say, by sound, that "stain" or "thing" that forms the undissolvable residuum of enjoyment that the phallus-as-prosthesis at once generates and attempts to gentrify. It is, as Žižek would put it, the "remainder" of the voice that paradoxically comes *before* the voice. Here we find a concept of voice that is diametrically opposed to what I have called Cavell's "Selmacentric" one. Indeed, from Žižek's perspective, voice as we find it in the operatic aria provides "perhaps the neatest exemplification of what Lacan calls *jouis-sense,* enjoy-meant, the moment at which sheer self-consuming enjoyment of the voice eclipses meaning (the words of the aria)."[36] For Žižek, voice—and this is dramatized in the transition from "silent" film to early talkies—functions "as a strange body which smears the innocent surface of the picture, a ghost-like apparition which can never be pinned to a definite visual object."[37] Here we find an explanation for Charlie Chaplin's well-known aversion to sound, which "is thus not to be dismissed as a simple nostalgic commitment to a silent paradise; it reveals a far deeper than usual knowledge (or at least presentiment) of the disruptive power of the voice, of the fact that the voice functions as a foreign body, as a kind of parasite introducing a radical split."[38]

Here then, on the site of voice, we can not only move toward a provisional summation of the theoretical and ethical stakes involved in *Dancer in the Dark* but also greatly enhance our understanding of one of the most important junctures in postmodern philosophy by using Žižek to triangulate the well-known disagreement between Derrida and Cavell over the question of "ordinary language philosophy," of which the problem of voice may now be seen as but an especially pitched moment. Here we need to recall, however briefly, the most explicit episode of all in this triangulation—namely, Cavell's disagreement with Derrida's reading of Austin in *Limited Inc* and, beyond that, his critique of voice as we find it in Derrida's early book on Husserl. Derrida's critique of voice as exemplary of logocentrism and the metaphysics of presence, from the early work on Husserl, through *Of Grammatology*, and on to his later work, is surely too well-known to need restatement here. What is less known, perhaps, is Cavell's response, which will serve to link him, in an odd and unexpected way (though finally not a decisive one), with Žižek.

Cavell's reading takes place over many pages, chiefly in *A Pitch of Philosophy,* and is often complex and technical, centering on Derrida's understanding of concepts in Austin such as "felicity," "force," "signature," and—the one for which Austin is best known—the "performative." To put it schematically—and I have already explored this divergence in somewhat different terms in chapter 3—the gist of Cavell's objection is that he finds Derrida misreading Austin's philosophical project, even though, for Cavell, both Austin and Derrida seem to be brothers in arms against the metaphysical tradition. As Cavell eloquently puts it:

> Both are philosophers of limitation, both interested in the morality and politics of speech (out of something like a shared sense that concepts, without the most scrupulous attention, impose, and are imposed, upon us), and both take the struggle against metaphysics as a struggle for liberation, for something more than reason, as it were, itself. Most significantly, perhaps, there is an appreciation of the fact Austin's analysis of the performative may be seen to be motivated precisely as an attack on what deconstruction attacks under the name logocentrism.[39]

The question for Cavell is this: why does Derrida not recognize his common cause with Austin and find in him instead an *example* of the metaphysical tradition against which Cavell sees both aligned? For Cavell, the answer is that Derrida is blinded by his too-hasty aversion to voice, although voice for Austin (and for Wittgenstein) means "the voice of the everyday or the ordinary"—and they call it this, according to Cavell, "precisely to *contrast* their appeal with the appeal to metaphysics." More than this—and this, I think, is the nub of the issue for Cavell—"Derrida is every bit as opposed . . . to the metaphysical voice as Austin and Wittgenstein are. But he makes it his business to monitor and to account for its encroachments while seeming . . . to be speaking in it, no one more cheerfully," in a voice that suggests "its final overcoming, that is, that suggests that it will end philosophically" (62).

In the end, then, Cavell finds Derrida's critique of Austin's concept of voice-as-metaphysical to be in fact *exemplary* of the metaphysical voice at work in Derrida himself—the metaphysical explicitly as a flight from the ordinary and its vexations into what one might call "systematic" philosophy. As Cavell puts it in *Philosophical Passages*, "What I think Derrida is objecting to here is something he was already in flight from, the specter of the ordinary," which manifests itself in Derrida's repeated gestures that "of course he is not denying that there are 'effects' of the ordinary"—including, most famously, signatures—which for Cavell furthers "the air of implication that there is something more to do—a further reality to assess, a fullness of certainty to apply—than human beings can compass" (74). And in so doing, Derrida for Cavell exemplifies the philosophical desire to silence the voice of the ordinary and the everyday: exemplifies the desire, in a somewhat different register, to transcend the "human" in the most homely and down-to-earth sense of the term.

My concern at the moment is not to register my agreement or reservations about Cavell's reading of Derrida but to point out that a certain understanding of what we might think of as the unavoidability of the problem of voice links Žižek to this aspect of Cavell, through what one might call a "materialist" gesture, over and against the critique of phonocentrism in Derrida. For both Žižek and Cavell, the voice *insists,* it obtrudes; we cannot free ourselves of it, through critique, or deconstruction, or anything else. More important, however, is how this fact helps sharpen our sense of the difference between Cavell's humanist voice and the rather different understanding made available by Žižek. For both, the presence of the voice may be coterminous with everything that makes us human, but for Žižek that "human" turns out to be inhabited at its core by the *inhuman* Thing that resides at the heart of the humanist subject. To put it telegraphically, for Cavell the fear or danger is over the *loss* of voice, but for Žižek the fear or danger is precisely that the voice *can never be lost*—a point he makes in explicit contrast to Derrida's reading of phonocentrism: "What Derrida remains blind to," Žižek writes, "is the radical ambiguity of the voice. The voice-phenomenon, in its very presence, is simultaneously the Lacanian Real, the non-transparent stain that puts an irreducible obstacle in the way of the subject's self-transparency, a foreign body in its midst. In short, the greatest hindrance to the self-transparency of *Logos* is the voice itself in its inert presence."[40]

But if a certain "materialist" gesture links Cavell and Žižek on the question of the voice over and against what Cavell sees as Derrida's metaphysical bent (what Žižek has called his "quasi-transcendental" side [195]), that is not, I think, the whole story. What is at issue here is also the *disposition* of that materialism, and on those grounds Žižek and Derrida must be paired in sharp contrast with Cavell's humanism. We can bring this difference into focus by heeding Cavell's assertion in *The World Viewed* on silent film that "the world *is* silent to us; the silence is merely forever broken" (150–51). What this silence registers for Cavell, of course, is our distance from the world under skepticism, a silence "merely forever broken" by our words that can never bridge that distance, can never be words *of* the world. How different this is from Žižek's analysis of "primordial" or "ontological" sound in David Lynch, where what is registered is instead that the world is *never* silent and that this "noisiness" (which is also a queasiness) is an index of our *inability* to achieve distance from the world of things and the Real. It is precisely this fact—that the Thing is "in the subject more than the subject itself"—that generates the overarching prosthetic logic of the phallus as master signifier, which then dialectically generates through its failure to "gentrify" the Real the very residuum of the Thing, the stain, and so on that constitutes the Symbolic's raison d'être. Or to put it in Žižekian shorthand: no meaning without enjoyment, and no enjoyment without nauseating remainder.

What becomes clear here, then, is that for Žižek and Derrida, the disposition of this materialism is handled in and through *différance,* through the (Master, the phallus as) signifier, in which subject and object are enfolded (to return to the ethical *topos* of the feminine) in an essentially "invaginated" relationship, whereas in Cavell their difference and distance are, as Derrida might say, too "pure." Indeed, it is that purity of distance that calls forth the voice, as in operatic aria, which registers either ecstasy at overcoming that distance or melancholy at its unsurpassability.[41] But the larger point I wish to make is this: the question here is one not simply of materialism—of counterposing the "ordinary" or the Real to the supposed formalism of deconstruction—but more importantly of the *prosthetic* nature of the ordinary and the everyday itself.[42] To put it another way, "materialism" itself is not a pure category that stands, in its purity, in opposition to formalism or idealism but is instead itself *constituted* by difference, by enfolding, and being enfolded within, that which it is not.[43] And on this point, the decisive difference is between not Žižek and Derrida on one side and Cavell on the other but between Žižek and Derrida themselves.

Žižek has offered in several places what he sees as Lacan's "materialist" answer to Derrida and deconstruction.[44] In *Tarrying with the Negative,* for instance, he writes that "Lacan accepts the 'deconstructionist' motif of radical contingency, but turns this motif against itself, using it to assert his commitment to Truth *as contingent.*"[45] More to the point for our purposes, perhaps, is the series of questions raised in Žižek's "Self-Interview" at the end of *The Metastases of Enjoyment,* where he takes issue with Derrida's "failure to acknowledge fully the ultimate identity of supplement and Master-Signifier." For Derrida, Žižek writes, "the supplement is the undecidable margin that eludes the Master-Signifier," whereas "Lacan . . . locates this undecidability in the very heart of the Master-Signifier. . . . The Master-Signifier proper emerges through the 'neutralization' of the supplement, through the obliteration of its constitutive indecidability," whereas Derrida insists on the "reduction of the Lacanian Symbolic to the balanced economy of exchange"—referenced to the gold standard, as it were, of the phallus—and in so doing fails "to take note of how, in his own theoretical edifice, the notion of gift, of a primordial 'there is' . . . introduces an aspect that is heterogeneous to the standard 'Derridean' problematic of différance-trace-writing," as "presence itself in its ultimate inaccessibility."[46]

To acknowledge as much, however, is to realize instantly that the point cuts both ways. Žižek's reinterpretation of the phallus—and therefore of the ethics of the act as "feminine"—is possible only by virtue of an understanding of the phallus *as signifier,* whose status as such is crucial if Žižek is to avoid the all-too-obvious objection that the Lacanian Real may be characterized, more pointedly than any term we have thus far queried, as positing a form of "metaphysical materialism," to quote Derrida, which posits "an ultimate referent" or "becomes an 'objective reality' absolutely 'anterior' to any work of the mark, the 'semantic' content of a form of presence which guarantees the movement of the text in general from the outside."[47] Žižek may differentiate Lacanian theory from poststructuralism by means of "truth as contingent," but as Judith Butler has repeatedly noted, "By linking this contingency with the real, and interpreting the real as the trauma induced through the threat of castration, the Law of the Father, this 'law' is posited as accountable for the contingency in all ideological determinations, but is never subject to the same logic of contingency that it secures"—in which case "Žižek's theory thus evacuates the 'contingency' of its contingency."[48]

This is a rather different point from the critique we saw Derrida making of Lacan in chapter 2, and it is crucial for assessing Žižek's relationship not only to poststructuralism but also to feminism. As Butler asks, in a rhetorical question if ever there was one: "Is there not a difference between a theory that asserts that, in principle, every discourse operates through exclusion and a theory that attributes to that 'outside' specific social and sexual positions?" (189) (as in Lacanian theory's association of the feminine body with the domain of the Real, the Thing, the stain, and so on). Here, in other words, everything hinges on the deconstructive valence of Žižek's account of the phallus-as-prosthesis; as long as—and *only* as long as—we insist on the phallus *as signifier* and subject the Law to an essentially deconstructive understanding, we are able to move Žižek away from the consequences ferreted out by Butler. Only then can we sustain the ethical transvaluation of the "feminine" for psychoanalytic theory that Žižek wants to pursue[49]—a transvaluation that might make common cause with Butler's own theorization of the "plasticity" of the phallus as directly linked to its status as signifier in a structure that "has to be *reiterated* and, as reiterable, becomes open to variation and plasticity," thus opening sexual difference "as a site of proliferative resignifications" (as in, for example, Butler's own theorization of the "lesbian phallus" [89]). Of course, to arrive at such an understanding of the feminine phallus and its ethical resonance in Žižek requires insisting on the very deconstructive reading of the phallus that he wants to simultaneously criticize and mobilize. All of which would seem willfully perverse, or—we are now in a position to say—necessarily prosthetic.

What Žižek helps us to see, then, is that in *Dancer in the Dark,* we find a powerful posthumanist project that unhinges the humanist coordinates of vision (in relation to spatiality) and voice (in relation to noise) while poignantly staging their fantasy structures (glossed so well by Cavell). And he helps disclose, as Cavell's work does, how those structures are deployed in specific ways by the genres and conventions of film as a medium. More decisively in relation to Cavell's work, he gives us an even sharper sense of how the film undertakes this mobilization and undoing of those visual and vocal modes in terms not so much of the total animal sensorium and its many modes of being in the world that I discussed in chapters 2, 3, and 5, or even (in this last) in questioning the distinction between "disability" and "normality," but rather in drawing out the radical sense of "the feminine" and its ethical force in the film, its assault on the regime of the phallus and the Law, its "perverse" (and devastating) force. But in evacuating "the contingency of its contingency" (to use Butler's phrase), in not fully confronting the consequences of that contingency as necessitating a fundamentally different critical logic that forces us beyond the simple dialectical reversal and elevation of the terms banished by humanism to subservient status (the Real, the Thing, the feminine, and so on), Žižek's work remains within the purview of the very humanism that his radical sense of the feminine wants to eclipse. In doing so, it stops short of the full articulation of the feminine in another, even deeper sense: its "invaginated" relationship with prostheticity that obeys a fundamentally different, posthumanist logic.

8   Lose the Building

Form and System in Contemporary Architecture

The work of art is an ostentatiously improbable occurrence.
—NIKLAS LUHMANN, *Art as a Social System*

Downsview Park: Koolhaas and Mau's *Tree City*

The five remarkable finalists for the much-publicized Toronto Parc Downsview Park competition of 2000—a design for a 320-acre site on a former military base, Canada's first national urban park—are, of course, proposals for works in architecture, landscape architecture (though that difference, as I will suggest later, appears to be of some moment, particularly in the winning entry).[1] They are also remarkable for another reason: as experiments in how to think anew the relationship between nature and culture, or—to use a distinction I borrowed a few years ago from the political scientist Tim Luke—between "green" and "gray" ecologies.[2] (Indeed, one might ask, what else can the seemingly innocuous phrase "urban park" mean at this moment in time other than this very necessity?) Green ecologies: ecologies of the organic, the living, the biomass; and gray ecologies, of the machinic and technological, the electronic. Or to put it in the terms used by Bernard Tschumi's proposal for Downsview, ecologies of the "coyote" and ecologies of the "digital."[3]

In fact, how the Tschumi proposal handles the term "digital" is a good example of what I mean. On the one hand, it refers to electronically mediated mass culture based on binary coding, the sort of thing associated with the large "image screens" that are a central part of his design; on the other hand, the "digital" harkens back etymologically to the digits, the *fingers*. Here it would be tempting—and entirely to the point—to recall Jacques Derrida's reading of the figure of the hand in relation to the nature/culture opposition in Heidegger that was discussed in earlier chapters. In Derrida's *"Geschlecht II:* Heidegger's Hand," for example, the hand stands, as we have seen, as a symptom of Heidegger's all-too-problematic ontological opposition of the world of the human and the world of the animal. For Heidegger, the meaning of the hand, properly understood, is determined not by biological or utilitarian function—"does not let itself be determined as a bodily organ of gripping"[4]—but by its expression of the *geschlecht* or species being of humanity, which, in opposition to the rest of creation, rests on the human possession of speech and thought, which in turn opens an "abyss" between the grasping or "prehension" associated with the "prehensile" organs of the ape,[5] and the hand of man which "is far from these in an infinite way *(unendlich)* through the abyss of its being."[6]

To misunderstand the hand of the human as determined by utility and function is to repeat the sin of "Western conceptualizing as a kind of sublimized violence," as Stanley Cavell has put it, a sort of "clutching" or "grasping" through what we might call "prehensile" conceptualization. This mode of violence is most famously thematized in Heidegger, of course, as the violence "expressed in the world dominion of technology."[7] For the matter at hand (at hand!), we could scarcely do better than to remember Heidegger's aversion to the typewriter and typographic mechanization, which is "asignifying" because it "loses the hand," as Heidegger puts it; in its anonymous standardization and in its spacing of elements, it destroys the unity of thinking, speaking, and writing. And thus, Heidegger laments, "In typewriting, all men resemble one another."[8] For Heidegger, then, the proper subservience of the technological to the human rests on a prior ontological opposition between the natural and the human, the prehensile and the *com*prehensile, we might say, here figured pointedly as the difference between the Man of the Hand and (to return to Tschumi) the Coyote, who is condemned forever to wander between the ontological orders of the stone at one end of the Heideggerian universe and the world "of spirit," of being as such that is proper only to the human, at the other.

Remembering Heidegger on technology helps throw into relief as well the very different and distinctly contemporary reconjugation of the technical and the natural that we find in the Downsview Park proposals. We could call this reconjugation "postmodern," I suppose, to mark its opposition to Heidegger's modernism, but it seems to me that what is going on in the Downsview proposals is something distinct and different from the associations that usually cluster around that term. Here the double take on the digital in Tschumi's proposal is again suggestive for thinking about the proposals as a whole, and it is useful to remember that the etymology of "digit" refers not only to "the terminal divisions of the hand," as the *OED* so sharply puts it, but also to a unit of *measurement* (used, for example, by the Romans). In the Tschumi proposal, the digital refers also to a "perimeter landscape of earthworks" that "interlocks with the interior like the cupped fingers of the left and right hand"—a figure that appears as well in the ravine structure proposed in the Brown and Storey entry. They are "fingers of nature" that "increase the interface between natural artifacts and cultural ones" and "can be compared to the fractal phenomenon of viscous fingering." Indeed, Tschumi and his collaborators argue, "The fractal dimension of all edges and interfaces in the Park is a crucial element of our strategy"—hence the relevance of remembering the digit as a unit of measure—because such fractal phenomena, as John Casti puts it, exhibit *"linear self-similarity,* in the sense that any part of the object is exactly like the whole"; that is to say, "they have exactly the same degree of irregularity at all scales of measurement."[9]

The digital in Tschumi's proposal points, then, in two different directions, and in doing so it provides a dense and compressed instance of a new way of theorizing the relations of nature and culture at work in the Downsview proposals as a whole. "Emergence," "self-organizational unfoldings," "circuit and through-flow ecologies," "sustaining and multiplying complexity over time," "webs" of "strong attractors" and "grammar strings," "open phasing," "function-based circuit systems": there are important differences between these concepts, but what they all have in common is that they thoroughly take for granted the conceptual apparatus of systems theory, which is based on the central innovation of replacing the familiar ontological dualities of the philosophical tradition—chiefly, for our purposes, culture and nature—with the functional distinction between system and environment.

As we know from earlier chapters, systems are self-referential and self-producing—they are autopoietic, to use Maturana and Varela's term—and they secure their autopoiesis by using distinctions based on a self-referential, constitutive code to selectively filter and respond to an environment that is always already infinitely more complex than any given system. But what is important for our purposes at the moment is that there is a reciprocal relationship here of cospecification; the environment is not simply "given" (that would land us back into a thinly disguised concept of nature in the traditional sense) but is in a crucial sense *produced*. It is always the environment *of* the system, the outside or unmarked space produced by the constitutive act of distinction and selection that any system uses to secure its operations. As Niklas Luhmann succinctly puts it, "The environment receives its unity through the system and only in relation to the system. . . . It is different for every system because every system excludes only itself from its environment."[10] In this way, what was previously a rigid, uncrossable ontological boundary between two sides of the distinction—between nature and culture, between the biological and the mechanical, and so on—is now made dynamic and, as it were, *portable* in the sense that the same formal mechanism may now be used to think, and link, across what were in the past discrete ontological domains. (For example, this enables one to compare quite precisely thermo-regulation in biological systems with the self-regulation of thermostatic mechanical systems, or to model the firing of neurons and the behaviors of neuronal nets using digital technologies.)

Now the pragmatic payoffs here would seem obvious enough for the attempts to think through the interlacing of ecological, transportational, and other systems in the Downsview proposals. But what I wish to stress is not just a pragmatic and functional shift but a philosophical one as well, in which the question of the relationship between nature and culture can now be *deontologized* and posed anew, not as questions of *what* but as questions of *how,* not as questions of substance but as questions of *strategy*—which has, of course, profound implications for the design process. It is only in light of such a shift that we can make sense, for example, of Koolhaas and Mau's contention in their winning *Tree City* entry that "instead of restoring Downsview to a previous natural state, Tree City manufactures nature for civic ends. It is a fabricated landscape . . . 100% 'artificial' and 100% 'natural,' . . . unambiguously administrative in ambition AND entirely organic in spirit."

Here, however, we need to recall the important differences I have discussed in earlier chapters between first-order and second-order systems theory. First-order systems theory is more typically concerned with processes of homeostasis, positive feedback, steering, and the like (think here of the work of Gregory Bateson or Norbert Wiener); second-order systems theory is concerned with complexity, contingency, and how they relate to processes that now go by the names of "emergence" and "self-organization." In this light, all the proposals are framed and informed not just by systems theory in some vague sense but specifically by second-order systems theory. Here the rhetoric of the *Emergent Ecologies* proposal of Corner and Allen could scarcely be more representative. "Our approach," they write, "is emergent and dynamic: an organizational matrix for the life of the site to unfold," in which the "landscape of circuits and flows simply guides or steers the always emergent processes [of] matter and information." Similarly, Brown and Storey's *Emergent Landscapes* project proposes "an evolving landscape of stages, phases of order and stability," a "tableau of evolving relationships, momentum and self-organizing structures." Or finally Foreign Office's "new synthetic landscape" grows from the commitment that "faced with complexity, we respond by sustaining and multiplying that complexity over time."

I do not mean to ignore the considerable differences between these proposals and the strategies they employ; I intend simply to highlight the fact that embracing the paradigms of emergence and self-organization creates a new and in fact fundamental problem: a medium associated above all with space now has as its constitutive problem *time* and temporalization—more specifically, how to temporalize design and the constraints and selections built into it. What is threatened here—or promised, depending on how one looks at it—is that the architectural medium is thereby submitted to a kind of dematerialization or decomposition by the problem of time. Here—and this is a question to which I will return in the final chapter—the problem of time cannot be separated from the question of specific media; indeed, what is brought into sharp focus in the relation of time and media is time's own asynchronicity, over and against what Louis Althusser once called an "ideological" concept of time as self-identical, seamless, and continuous across all spaces. Once we pay attention to specific media, the problem of time in relation to design becomes a question of specific speeds and velocities and how to coordinate them; biological and ecological elements and systems have certain rates of development, change, and decay, of course, but so do buildings and other structures, which are subject to quite different speeds.

The Downsview entries confront this problem on a spectrum ranging from Foreign Office and Tschumi at one end—which produce a tight coupling of temporal horizons and possible scenarios with relatively hard-wired structural commitments up front, ones that predispose some temporal horizons and not others—to Corner and Allen and Koolhaas and Mau at the other, in which this relationship is one of relatively loose coupling. This problem of time in relation to specific media, framed of necessity by the embrace of the paradigm of emergence, is registered in an especially pointed way in the Koolhaas/Mau proposal, in which "the landscape will be prioritized over the realm officially known as architecture," and which makes what is humorously called "the ultimate sacrifice" of the construction of "costly new buildings" and devotes those resources instead to the temporalization of the design's meaning through a different medium with a different speed: the "vegetal."

In Tree City, the reduction of "hard" commitments up front is a strategy for engaging in what Luhmann calls the "temporalization of complexity"[11]—of how the complexity of the internal relations of the park's elements can remain responsive over time to changing and unanticipated demands from its surrounding environment. To put it schematically, power over space in the short run, in the form of structures and buildings, is swapped for power over time in the long run, and therefore—to put perhaps too fine a point on it—time, not space, becomes the constitutive medium of the project. In this sense, the "looseness" or "weakness" of the coupling of temporal horizons and structural elements in Koolhaas and Mau is precisely its strength. And from this vantage, the constitutive question for the Downsview project becomes something like "Can you *wait?*" to which Tree City provides what we might think of as the "slowest" answer.

There is, however, a final, less obvious relation between systems theory and the Downsview proposals at work here, and that is the question of their relationship to different observational schema within what Luhmann calls "functionally differentiated" society. To put it sche-

Rem Koolhaas
and Bruce Mau,
final panel art
(no. 3) for *Tree
City*, 2000.

matically, the park is not a thing—certainly not an object—but rather
an accretion of distinctions and selections made from within a particular observational system and its code—a point registered in the
jury report's concluding statement that "Tree City outlines a vision of
future park lands as intriguing as a work of art, but also as malleable
as communities of tomorrow could wish to find." From this vantage,
the aesthetic (or anti-aesthetic) of Koolhaas and Mau may be seen as
a refusal of design, composition, pictorialism, and the like in favor
of a strategy of production and temporalization. On the other hand,

however—and I will explore this question in much more detail when I examine the *Blur* project of Diller + Scofidio—insofar as we are to regard these projects as something like art, then those choices must be seen not only as aesthetic ones but quite exemplary aesthetic ones at that. From one observational schema, then, the park may be viewed as a functional component of the larger urban space for which and in which it provides certain services, in which case the question is not its autonomy but precisely the opposite, how it functions as an element within a larger matrix of social systems of which it is part. On the other hand, it may be viewed as part of the social system of art, in which case the question *is* precisely its autonomy and how that autonomy communicates the larger problem of the autopoiesis of art as a social system in functionally differentiated society.

If we keep in mind these differences—and keep in mind that they are irreducible, that there is no totalizing perspective from which one observation may be subordinated to the other—then "the Park" is quite literally a different entity depending on the observational schema we use, which system we choose (transportation, economic, aesthetic, and so on) as the lens through which to view the park as an agent of that system's autopoiesis. And hence the design decisions about specific media in the proposals—say, the use or refusal of "the realm officially known as architecture"—take on quite different functions and meanings depending on which observation we deploy. It is this irreducible difference between different observational schemas that is addressed most cannily by Koolhaas and Mau, precisely because of what we might think of as *Tree City*'s weakness—its underspecification, its refusal to commit—which makes it *more* available to the autopoiesis of other systems in ways not precluded up front, by choices made *now*. This does not mean that there is no strategy to *Tree City;* indeed, this *is* its strategy.

At the same time, however, that underspecification must be justified on not merely functional but *aesthetic* grounds, and it is here that the proposal of Koolhaas and Mau is cannily anti- or postrepresentationalist in its refusal to try to "do it all," to "include" or "represent" the various elements of the society that surrounds it. From this vantage— the vantage of the Downsview projects seen now as communications within the social system of art—the temporal dimension of the proposals is in a way beside the aesthetic point and might even be seen as simply the alibi for specific design decisions made *right now* as interventions in the contemporary fields of architecture, design, and art. Viewed this way, a major challenge faced by all the entries—and particularly by those that rely on a tight juxtaposition of the "digital" and the "coyote" (to return to Tschumi's terms) or that deploy something like the "dual mode" of Foreign Office—is not so much the problem of composition but rather how *that* problem relates to a second one of thematization, to which Koolhaas and Mau seem especially sensitive.

Once the nature/culture distinction has been replaced by the system/environment distinction—as is certainly the case with all these entries—the problem then becomes how *not* to reproduce the historically founding and framing conundrum of what we might call the "ideology of the park" *within* the park itself. In these terms—because the system/environment distinction is operative at every level and has nothing to do with the apparently cognate distinction nature/culture—the problem is not so much how to escape this conundrum as how to effectively *displace* it. Here the entries that place a premium on the initial outlay of large architectural structures and "gray" ecological spectacles face special challenges, since they would seem to run a much greater risk of reinstating, via thematization, the very distinction between nature and "the social" that—theoretically, at least—they say has already been abandoned. Theoretically speaking, the outside produced by such architectural structures—the unmarked space generated by their constitutive distinctions and selections that make them *this* structure and not some other—need not have anything to do with the question of nature, and in fact the relevance of those distinctions lies, in the terms we are now using, in relation to other architectural structures. As Luhmann puts it, "A spatial position defines itself by providing access to other places. Architecture determines how the context of the edifice is to be seen. A sculpture defines its surrounding space."[12] And in this sense, these projects run a greater risk of inviting the "mistake," we might say, of a thematized reading that they in principle reject.

To put it another way, as Luhmann does in *Art as a Social System*, the question is how a work of art "presents itself to perception in such a way as to be recognizable as art"—or in the case of Downsview Park, how we would know we had wandered not only into a *park* and not some undesigned wasteland in the middle of the city, but a park built now and not a hundred years ago. As we will see later in the chapter, the concept of *form* is crucial here, and in it "two requirements must be fulfilled and inscribed into perception: the form must have a *boundary*, and there must be an 'unmarked space' *excluded by this boundary*" (45). This is obvious enough in works enclosed with a beginning and end (as in narrative fiction), a stage (as in drama), or a framing device. But "sculpture or architecture presents an entirely different case," Luhmann argues.

> Here, the boundary does not draw the viewer's attention inward but instead directs it outward. The work permits no view into its depths, no penetration of its surface, (whatever the surface may betray of the work's mass, volume, or material). The imaginary space is projected outward in the form of distinctions suggested by the work itself. Here, too, space is work-specific space, visible so long as the focus is on the work and disappearing from view when the focus shifts to surrounding objects—to the weeds in the castle garden. (45–46)

It would be tempting at this juncture to invoke the well-known distinction between the "rhizomatic" and "arborescent" in Deleuze and Guattari—a reading suggested by what the jury report calls the "mesh" of connections cast over the surrounding area by Tree City. Indeed, one might very well view the project, with its one thousand paths and what Bob Somol has characterized as its "viral" or "cancerous" infection of the surrounding suburbs, as an attempt to transform the arborescent (Tree) into the rhizomatic (Tree City) in a perversely humorous literalization whose primary message is "Hey, trees are as close to architecture as you're going to get in this project!" Indeed, what is immediately most striking about the Koolhaas and Mau proposal is precisely its negativity, its posture of refusal, its repeated insistence on what it has opted *not* to do as much as what it does—in making "the ultimate sacrifice" of not doing architecture, its refusal to spend money, and so on. And once this fundamental displacement is made, it is as if everything in the proposal must now be read in quotation marks; it is a kind of *antiproposal* or, better still, the kind of *miming* that Derrida associates with dissemination, which is not an achievement of representationalism and mimesis but precisely its displacement and erosion.[13]

This makes *Tree City*, in the end, a quite contemporary intervention, one very different from an earlier moment of the postmodern in architecture, in which "quotation" and the like attempts, as Luhmann puts it, "to copy a differentiated and diverse environment into the artwork," which in turn only raises the further problem of "whether, and in what way, the work can claim unity, and whether it can assert itself against its own (!) 'requisite variety.'"[14] "How," Luhmann asks, "can the art system reflect on its own differentiation, not only in the form of theory, but also in individual works of art?" In this light, we might well view the mode of negativity and refusal, of miming, in the proposal of Koolhaas and Mau as a kind of effort to displace any materialization of a commitment that might temporally constrain and chain their project to a structural representation that ceases to be relevant the moment it comes into being. And in this—to reach back now to Heidegger, with whom we began—the "unhandsomeness" of *Tree City* (to use Stanley Cavell's phrase) is exactly what is most fetching about it; it refuses to grasp and fix the present for us, and in so doing it imagines the future—or at least, let's say a bit more modestly, *a* future.

Diller + Scofidio's *Blur*

The kinds of formal innovations we find in *Tree City*, what and how they signify, how they mobilize an uncanny dematerialization of the architectural medium as part of a radical formal statement, how they engage in an ingenious conceptual displacement of the problem of composition: these form the fundamental concerns as well, in my view, of Ricardo Scofidio and Elizabeth Diller's audacious *Blur* project. The *Blur* building—a manufactured cloud with an embedded viewing deck, hovering over the Lake of Neuchâtel in Switzerland—seems to have enjoyed nearly universal acclaim from the moment it opened to the public in October 2002 as part of Media Expo '02. The reasons for this are not far to seek; they range from what a Swiss newspaper reviewer characterized as the liberating effect of the zany cloud on "the crotchety Swiss"—"What a crazy, idiosyncratic thing! How deliciously without purpose!" he exclaimed—to Diller + Scofidio's knowing deployment of the relationship between public architecture, the history and function of the exposition as a social form, and the manufacture and use of spectacle in relation to both.[15]

Diller Scofidio + Renfro, *Blur*, 2002.

The project went through many different elaborations, enhance-ments, and embellishments between the invitation to Diller + Scofidio to participate in July 1998 and the closing of the expo in October 2002. Almost all of these were, for various reasons, unrealized in the final project. At one point, the cloud was to house an "LED text forest" of vertical LED panels that would scroll text—either from an Internet feed (including live "chat" produced by visitors to the structure) or, in a later version, produced by an artist such as Jenny Holzer (*Blur*, 163, 324). Another idea early on was an adjacent "Hole in the Water" restau-rant made of submerged twin glass cylinders with an aquarium layer in between, in which diners would sit at eye level with the lake and eat sushi (100–111). Another was an open-air "Angel Bar" embedded in the upper part of the cloud, in which patrons could select from an end-less variety of the only beverage served there: water—artesian waters, sparkling waters, waters from both glacial poles, and municipal tap waters from around the world ("tastings can be arranged," we are told) (146–55). Yet another elaborate idea, rather late in the project's evolu-tion, involved the distribution of "smart" raincoats—or "braincoats"—to visitors to the cloud, which would indicate, through both sound and color, affinity or antipathy to other visitors on the basis of a preferences questionnaire filled out upon entry to the cloud (209–51).

As even this brief list suggests, the project went through many permutations. In the end—not least for reasons of money—what we are left with in *Blur* is the manufactured cloud with the Angel Deck (now not a water bar but a viewing deck) nestled at its crest. For reasons I will try to explain by way of contemporary systems theory, the fact that these permutations and sideline enhancements were not realized in the end is not entirely a bad thing, because it rivets our attention not only on what has captivated most viewers from the beginning but also on what makes the project a paradigmatic instance of how contemporary architecture responds to the complexities of its broader social environment in terms of its specific medium—and that is, as Diller + Scofidio put it, "the radicality of an absent building" (15), the remarkable, audacious commitment to a building that was not a building at all but a manufactured cloud: "the making," as they put it, "of nothing." This fundamental commitment was sounded by Diller + Scofidio early and often; at the core of the project, as it were, was no core at all but a commitment to something "featureless, depthless, scaleless, spaceless, massless, surfaceless, and contextless" (162). And this overriding concern was reiterated at the end of the design phase, about a year before the expo opened, in an important communiqué from Diller, in which she writes:

> BLUR is not a building, *BLUR* is pure atmosphere, water particles suspended in mid-air. The fog is a dynamic, phantom mass, which changes form constantly. . . . In contradiction to the tradition of Expo pavilions whose exhibitions entertain and educate, *BLUR* erases information. Expos are usually competition grounds for bigger and better technological spectacles. *BLUR* is a spectacle with nothing to see. Within *BLUR*, vision is put out-of-focus so that our dependence on vision can become the focus of the pavilion.

She adds in boldface type: "The media project must be liberated from all immediate and obvious metaphoric associations such as clouds, god, angels, ascension, dreams, Greek mythology, or any other kitsch relationships. Rather, *BLUR* offers a blank interpretive surface" (325).

Not quite blank, as it turns out. In fact, on the conceptual side of the project, the perceptual experience of the Blur building was thought by the architects at different stages in its development to either meta-phorize or, conversely, throw into relief a larger set of dynamics around electronic media and how we relate to it. Midway through the project, in a presentation to a media sponsor, they characterized it this way:

> To "blur" is to make indistinct, to dim, to shroud, to cloud, to make vague, to obfuscate. Blurred vision is an impairment. A blurry image is the fault of mechanical malfunction in a display or reproduction tech-nology. For our visually obsessed, high-resolution/high-definition cul-ture, blur is equated with loss. . . . Our proposal has little to do with the mechanics of the eye, but rather the immersive potential of blur on an environmental scale. Broadcast and print media feed our insa-tiable desire for the visual with an unending supply of images . . . [but] as an experience, the Blur building offers little to see. It is an immersive environment in which the world is put out of focus so that our visual dependency can be put into focus. (195)

At a different stage—one in which the LED text forest played a central role—the experience of the cloud figures "the unimaginable magni-tude, speed, and reach of telecommunications." As Diller + Scofidio put it, "Unlike entering a building, the experience of entering this hab-itable medium in which orientation is lost and time is suspended is like an immersion in 'ether.' It is a perfect context for the experience of another all-pervading, yet infinitely elastic, massless medium—one for the transmission and propagation of information: the Internet. The project aims to produce a 'technological sublime,' felt in the scaleless and unpredictable mass of fog."[16]

There are some interesting differences here. In the first version, the resonance of the project falls on the iconographic and visually based forms of mass media; in the second, it is the ephemeral yet pervasive presence of electronic, digital forms of telecommunication generally that is in question. In the first, the point of the cloud is that it deprives us of the unproblematic visual clarity, immediacy, and transparency that the mass media attempt to produce in consumers; in the second, the cloud's water vapor metaphorically envelops us in the electronic ether that we inhabit like a medium in contemporary life, but deprives us of the information that usually accompanies it and therefore dis-tracts us from just how immersed in that medium we are. What I am more concerned with here, however, is not the differences between the two accounts but what they have in common: that *this* particular form has been selected by Diller + Scofidio, and selected, moreover, to *represent the unrepresentable*—hence the notion of the "technological sublime" on which both accounts converge.

We ought not, however, take this notion of the sublime (or the term "representation," for that matter) at face value. In fact, resorting to the discourse of the sublime here can only obscure the specificity of the project's formal decisions—*why* it does *what* it does *how* it does—and how those decisions are directly related to the ethical and political point that the project is calculated to make. At its worst, it leads down the sorts of blind alleys we find in the July 2002 issue of *Architecture,* where one reviewer reads the project in terms of the symbolic significance of clouds, and of Switzerland, in romantic literature (Mary Shelley's *Frankenstein,* among others) and painting (J. M. W. Turner, among others), all of which is supposedly mobilized in *Blur's* rewriting of the sublime as a "cautionary tale about the environment."[17] And all of which recycles exactly the sorts of "immediate and obvious metaphoric associations" and "kitsch relationships" that we rightly saw Diller railing against a moment ago.

It might seem more promising, at least at first glance, to pursue more adventurous renderings of the sublime in contemporary theory, most notably in the work of Jean-François Lyotard (though other recent renditions of the concept, such as what we find in Slavoj Žižek's conjugation of Kant and Lacan, might be invoked here as well). In Lyotard—to stay with the best-known example—the locus classicus is a certain reading of Kant. The sublime is rendered as a kind of absolute outside to human existence—one that is, for that very reason, terrifying. At the same time, paradoxically (and this is true of Žižek's rendering as well), that radically other outside emerges as a product of the human subject's conflict with itself, a symptom of the Enlightenment subject running up against its own limits. In Lyotard's famous rendering of the Kantian sublime in *The Postmodern Condition,* it emerges from the conflict between "the faculty to conceive of something and the faculty to 'present' something." "We can conceive the infinitely great, the infinitely powerful," he explains, "but every presentation of an object destined to 'make visible' this absolute greatness or power appears to us painfully inadequate. Those are ideas of which no presentation is possible. Therefore they impart no knowledge about reality (experience)."[18] The entire ethical stake of modern art for Lyotard, then, is "to present the fact that the unpresentable exists. To make visible that there is something which can be conceived and which can neither be seen nor made visible" (78). But how to do this? Here Lyotard follows Kant's invocation of "'formlessness, the absence of form,' as a possible index to the unpresentable," as that which "will enable us to see only by making it impossible to see; it will please only by causing pain" (78). The sublime, then, is a "feeling" that marks the incommensurability of reason (conception) and the singularity or particularity of the world and its objects (presentation). It is an incommensurability that carries ethical force, for it serves as a reminder that the heterogeneity of the world cannot be reduced to a unified rule or reason. And this incompleteness in turn necessitates a permanent openness of any discourse to its other, to what Lyotard elsewhere calls the "differend."[19]

Lyotard's rendering of the Kantian sublime would seem to be useful in approaching *Blur,* and Kant's invocation of "formlessness" as the sublime's index would seem doubly promising. But its limitations may be marked by the fact that Kant's sublime remains tethered to "something on the order of a subject" (to use Foucault's famous phrase)—hence it remains referenced essentially to the language of phenomenology, to the affective states of a subject-supposed-to-know who, in experiencing her nonknowledge, experiences pain and thus changes her relation to herself. What I am suggesting, then, is that in Lyotard's rendering of the sublime—and it would be far afield to argue the point in any more detail here—the price we pay for a certain deconstruction of the subject of humanism (one that will be traced from Kant to Nietzsche in *The Postmodern Condition*)[20] is that the subject remains installed at the center of its universe, only now its failure is understood be a kind of success. Moreover, that this failure *is* ethical—is the hook on which the ethical rehabilitation of the subject hangs in its forcible opening to the world of the object, the differend, and so on—is the surest sign that we have not, for all that, left the universe of Kantian humanism. We must remember that the ethical force of the sublime in (Lyotard's) Kant depends on the addressee of ethics being a member of "the community of reasonable beings" who must be equipped with the familiar humanist repertoire of language, reason, and so on to experience in the ethical imperative not a "determinant synthesis"—not one-size-fits-all rules for the good and the just act—but "an Idea of human society" (which is why Kant argues, for example, that we have no direct duties to non-human animals).[21] This in turn reontologizes the subject/object split that the discourse of the sublime was meant to call into question in the first place.

In contrast to this, Diller + Scofidio insist that their work be understood in "post-moral and post-ethical" terms.[22] What this means, I think, is not that they intend their work to have no ethical or po-litical resonance—that much is already obvious from their foregoing comments on *Blur*—but rather that they understand the relationship between art, the subject, and world in resolutely *post*humanist terms. That is to say, in Diller + Scofidio, the human and the non- or anti- or ahuman do not exist in fundamentally discrete ontological registers but—quite the contrary—inhabit the same postontological space in mutual relations of intrication and instability. This boundary break-down tends to be thematized in their broader body of work in the inter-penetration of the human and the technological (as in, for example, the multimedia theater work *Jet Lag,* the *Virtue/Vice Glasses* series, and the *EJM 2 Inertia* dance piece); but it is also sometimes handled even more broadly in terms of the interweaving of the organic and the inorganic, the "natural" and the "artificial" (think here not only of *Blur* but also of projects like *Slow House* or *The American Lawn*). Sometimes those unstable relations are funny, sometimes they are frightening, but al-most always the signature affect in Diller + Scofidio's work is radical ambivalence—an ambivalence that, in contrast to the sublime, isn't about a clear-cut pain that becomes, in a second, pedagogical moment, pleasure, but rather an ambivalence that is tied to the difficulty of knowing exactly what is being experienced (as in works that intermesh real video surveillance with staged scenes, for example, in the *Facsimile* installation at Moscone Center in San Francisco), or how we should feel about it (think here of *Jump Cuts* or, again, *Blur*)—all of which leads, in turn, to the ultimate question, namely, *Who* is doing the experiencing? Who, in phenomenological and in political terms, are "we," exactly? In this light, Diller + Scofidio (like Lyotard's Kant) show us how ques-tions of ethics are just that, *questions;* but they do so (unlike Lyotard's

Kant) without recontaining the force of that radical undecidability in terms of a humanist subject, an all-too-familiar "we"—a "reasonable being" directed toward an "idea of society"—for whom, and only for whom, those questions *are*.

What this suggests is that a move beyond an essentially humanist ontological theoretical framework is in order if we are to understand the *Blur* project or, indeed, Diller + Scofidio's work as a whole. We need, in other words, to replace "what" questions with "how" questions (to use Niklas Luhmann's shorthand).[23] Here recent work in systems theory—particularly Luhmann's later work—can be of immense help, not least because it gives us a theoretical vocabulary for understanding the sorts of things that Diller + Scofidio have in mind when they suggest that in *Blur* "our objective is to weave together architecture and electronic technologies, yet exchange the properties of each for the other" (*Blur*, 44). The fundamental postulate of systems theory—its replacement of the familiar ontological dichotomies of humanism (culture/nature and its cognates: mind/body, spirit/matter, reason/feeling, and so on) with the functional distinction system/environment—is indispensable in allowing us to better understand the sorts of transcodings that Diller + Scofidio have in mind, because it gives us a theoretical vocabulary that can range across what were, in the humanist tradition, ontologically separate categories. Moreover, systems theory allows us to explain not only how those transcodings are specific to particular systems—how art and architecture, for example, integrate electronic technologies *as art*—but also how, in *being* system specific, they are paradoxically paradigmatic of, and produce, the very situation those systems attempt to respond to.[24] That situation, of course, is hypercomplexity, created by what Luhmann calls the "functional differentiation" of modern society (what other critical vocabularies would call its "specialization" or, more moralistically, "fragmentation"), which only gets accentuated and accelerated under postmodernity.[25]

For Luhmann, the social system of art—like any other autopoietic system, by definition—finds itself in an environment that is always already more complex than itself; and all systems, as we know from our earlier discussions, attempt to adapt to this complexity by filtering it in terms of their own, self-referential codes, which are based on a fundamental distinction by means of which they carry out their operations. The point of the system is to reproduce itself, but no system can deal with everything, or even many things, all at once—hence the need for a code of selectivity. As I noted in my earlier discussions of Luhmann's work, two subsidiary points need to be accented here. First, responding to environmental complexity in terms of their own self-referential codes is how subsystems build up their own internal complexity (one might think here of the various subspecialties of the legal system, say, or the specialization of disciplines in the education system, as I argued earlier in my discussion of disciplinarity); in doing so, systems become more finely grained in their selectivity, and thus they buy time in relation to overwhelming environmental complexity and change. As Luhmann puts it, "The system's inferiority in complexity [compared to that of the environment] must be counter-balanced by strategies of selection."[26] But if the self-reference of the system's code reduces the flow of environmental complexity into the system, it also increases its "irritability" and, in a real sense, its dependence on the environment.

As for this latter point, it is worth noting again the complex and seemingly paradoxical fact that the autopoietic closure of a system—whether social or biological—is precisely what *connects* it to its environment. As Luhmann explains it, "The concept of a self-referentially closed system does not contradict the system's *openness to the environment*. Instead, in the self-referential mode of operation, closure is a form of broadening possible environmental contacts; closure increases, by constituting elements more capable of being determined, the complexity of the environment that is possible for the system" (37). This is why, as Luhmann puts it in *Art as a Social System,*

> autopoiesis and complexity are conceptual coordinates. . . . Assuming that the system's autopoiesis is at work, evolutionary thresholds can catapult the system to a level of higher complexity—in the evolution of living organisms, toward sexual reproduction, independent mobility, a central nervous system. To an external observer, this may resemble an increase in system differentiation or look like a higher degree of independence from environmental conditions. Typically, such evolutionary jumps simultaneously increase a system's sensitivity and irritability; it is more easily disturbed by environmental conditions that, for their part, result from an increase in the system's own complexity. Dependency

and independence, in a simple causal sense, are therefore not invariant magnitudes in that more of one would imply less of the other. Rather, they vary according to a system's given level of complexity. In systems that are successful in evolutionary terms, more independence typically amounts to a greater dependency on the environment.... But all of this can happen only on the basis of the system's operative closure.[27]

The information/filter metaphor invoked above is misleading, however, precisely for the reasons noted at the beginning of the chapter: because systems interface with their environment in terms of, and only in terms of, their own constitutive distinctions and the self-referential codes based on them, the environment is not an ontological category but a functional one; it is not an outside to the system that is given *as such,* from which the system then differentiates itself—it is not, in other words, either nature or society in the traditional sense—but is rather always the outside *of* a specific inside. All of this leads to a paradoxical situation that is central to Luhmann's work, and central to understanding Luhmann's reworking of problems inherited from both Hegel and Husserl: what links the system to the world—what literally makes the world available to the system—is also what hides the world from the system, what makes it unavailable. Given my discussion of the sublime and the problem of "representing the unrepresentable," this should ring a bell—but a different bell, as it turns out (and this is a point I will examine in further detail in the next two chapters). To understand just *how* different, we need to remember a point emphasized from the beginning of this book: that all systems carry out their operations and maintain their autopoiesis by deploying a constitutive distinction, and a code based on it, that in principle could be otherwise. This means that there is a paradoxical identity between the two sides of the system's constitutive distinction, because the distinction between both sides is a product of only one side. In the legal system, for example, the distinction between the two sides legal/illegal is instantiated (or "reentered," to use Luhmann's terminology) on only one side of the distinction, namely, the legal. But no system can acknowledge this paradoxical identity of difference—which is also in another sense simply the contingency—of its own constitutive distinction *and* at the same time use that distinction to carry out its operations. It must remain "blind" to the very paradox of the distinction that links it to its environment.

As we know from our earlier discussions, that does not mean that this "blind spot" cannot be observed from the vantage of *another* system—it can, and that is what we are doing right now—but that second-order observation will itself be based on its *own* blind spot, thus formally reproducing a "blindness" that is (formally) the same but (contingently) not the same as that of the first-order system. And here, as I have suggested elsewhere, we find Luhmann's fruitful reworking of the Hegelian problematic: not the "identity of identity and nonidentity," as in Hegel, but rather the "*non*identity of identity and nonidentity"—and a productive nonidentity at that.[28] As Luhmann explains it in a passage I have cited more than once in these pages: "The conclusion to be drawn from this is that the connection with the reality of the external world is established by the blind spot of the cognitive operation. Reality is what one does not perceive when one perceives it."[29] Or as he puts it in somewhat different terms, the world is now conceived, "along the lines of a Husserlian metaphor, as an unreachable horizon that retreats further with each operation, without ever holding out the prospect of an outside."[30]

The question, then—and this is directly related to the problems raised by the *topos* of the sublime—is "how to observe how the world observes itself, how a marked space emerges [via a constitutive distinction] from the unmarked space, how something becomes invisible when something else becomes visible." Here we might seem far afield from addressing the *Blur* project, but in fact, Luhmann argues, "the generality of these questions allows one to determine more precisely what art can contribute to solving this paradox of the invisibilization that accompanies making something visible" (91). In this way, the problems that the discourse of the sublime attempts to address can be assimilated to the more formally rigorous scheme of the difference between first- and second-order observation. Any observation "renders the world invisible" in relation to its constitutive distinction, and that invisibility must itself remain invisible to the observation that employs that distinction—which in turn can only be disclosed by *another* observation that will also necessarily be doubly blind in the same way (91). "In this twofold sense," Luhmann writes, "the notion of a final unity—of an 'ultimate reality' that cannot assume a form because it has no other side—is displaced into the unobservable. . . . If the concept of the world is retained to indicate reality in its entirety, then it is that which—to a second-order observer—remains invisible in the movements of observation (his own and those of others)" (91; see also 29). This means not only that "art can no longer be understood as an imitation of something that presumably exists along with and outside of art," but more importantly for our purposes, "to the extent that imitation is still possible, it now imitates the world's invisibility, a nature that can no longer be apprehended as a whole" (92). "The paradox unique to art, which art creates and resolves," Luhmann writes, "resides in the observability of the unobservable" (149). And this is a question of form.

It is in these terms—to return now to Diller + Scofidio—that we might best understand the uncanny effect of *Blur's* manufactured cloud hovering over a lake, with the point being not that the cloud is not a cloud but rather that the lake is not a lake, precisely in the sense that art can be said to imitate nature only because nature isn't nature (an insight that is surely at work as well in Diller + Scofidio's *Slow House* project)—which is simply another way of saying that all observations, including those of nature, are contingent *and* of necessity blind to their own contingency. To put it in a Deleuzian rather than Luhmannian register, we might say that *Blur* virtualizes the very nature it imitates, but only, paradoxically, by concretizing that virtualization in its formal decisions—an imitation of nature that formally renders the impossibility of an imitation of nature. As Luhmann puts it, in an analysis that is thematized, as it were, in the blurriness of Diller + Scofidio's project (and in the critical intent they attach to it), "Art makes visible possibilities of order that would otherwise remain invisible. It alters conditions of visibility/invisibility in the world by keeping invisibility constant and making visibility subject to variation" (96). And here I think we can bring into the sharpest possible focus (if the metaphor can be allowed in this context) the brilliance of the project's "refusal" of architecture and its strategy of focusing on "the radicality of an absent building." In this context, one might say that the strength of *Blur's* formal intervention vis-à-vis the medium of architecture is precisely its formlessness, because it is calculated to bring into focus how "the realm officially known as architecture" (to borrow Koolhaas and Mau's phrase) can no longer "keep invisibility constant and make visibility subject to variation." "Official architecture" invisibilizes the invisibility of the world precisely by being *too* visible, too legible. And in so doing, as art, it might as well be *invisible*.

Here we might recall Luhmann's suggestive comments about Christo's wrapping of architectural structures. In an earlier moment of the postmodern in architecture, quotation of historical styles, elements, and the like attempts, as Luhmann puts it in *Art as a Social System,* "to copy a differentiated and diverse environment into the artwork," but this in turn only raises the further formal problem of "whether, and in what way, the work can claim unity, and whether it can assert itself against its own (!) 'requisite variety'" (298–99). "How," Luhmann asks, "can the art system reflect upon its own differentiation, not only in the form of theory, but also in individual works of art?" Christo's response to this problem, he suggests, is "particularly striking: if objects can no longer legitimize their boundaries and distinctions, they must be wrapped" (400n220). From this perspective, we might think of *Blur* as

Christo and Jeanne-Claude, *Wrapped Reichstag, Berlin,* 1971–95. Photograph by Wolfgang Volz. Copyright 1995 Christo.

a wrapped building *with no building inside.* Or better yet, as a wrapped building in which *even the wrapping has too much form* and begins to obsolesce the minute that form is concretized.

But what can it mean to say that an architectural project is concerned primarily with having *little* enough form? Here—and once again the otherwise daunting abstraction of systems theory is indispensable—we need to understand that in no sense are we talking about *objects,* substances, materials, or things when we use the term "form." Nor are we even, for that matter, talking about "shape" when we talk about form in Luhmann's sense.

> The word *formal* here does not refer to the distinction, which at first guided modern art, between form and matter or form and content, but to the characteristics of an indicating operation that observes, as if from the corner of its eye, what happens on the other side of form. In this way, the work of art points the observer toward an observation of form. . . . It consists in *demonstrating the compelling forces of order in the realm of the possible.* Arbitrariness is displaced beyond the boundaries of art into the unmarked space. If . . . one transgresses this boundary and steps from the unmarked into the marked space, things *no longer happen randomly.* (148)

In this way, form stages the question of "whether an observer can observe at all except with reference to an order" (148), which is to say that it stages the inescapability of the fact that the world emerges only through observations employing distinctions, *and* it stages the production of the unobservable (the "blind spot" of observation) that accompanies such observations (149). As Luhmann puts it (rather unexpectedly), "The world displays all the qualities that Nicholas of Cusa ascribed to God: it is neither small nor large, neither unity nor diversity, it neither has a beginning nor is it without beginning—and this is why the world needs forms" (15).

> From this vantage, we can say then that the function of art is to make the world appear within the world—with an eye toward the ambivalent situation that every time something is made available for observation something else withdraws, that, in other words, the activity of distinguishing and indicating that goes on in the world conceals the world. . . . *Yet a work of art is capable of symbolizing the reentry of the world*

into the world because it appears—just like the world—incapable of emenda-
tion. (149; italics mine)

With regard to this "reentry," two related points should be highlighted here to fully appreciate the specificity of *Blur*'s formal innovations. First—and I have already touched on this in my discussion of *Tree City*—form is in a profound sense a *temporal* problem (if for no other reason than because of the contingency of any constitutive distinction). Second, formal decisions operate on two levels, what we might call the internal and external; they operate, that is, in relating the formal decisions of the artwork itself to the larger system of art, but also in relating the artwork as a whole to its larger environment, of which the subsystem of art is only a part.

> What is at stake, operatively speaking, in the production and observation of a work of art is always a temporal unity that is either no longer or not yet observed. In this sense, the artwork is the *result* of intrinsic form decisions and, at the same time, the *metaform* determined by these decisions, which, by virtue of its inner forms, can be distinguished from the unmarked space of everything else—the work as fully elaborated object. (72)

Even more forcefully, one might say that here we are dealing not with objects at all but rather with what systems theory sometimes calls "eigenvalues" or "eigenbehaviors," recursive distinctions that unfold—and can only unfold—over time, even as they can only be experienced in the fleeting moment of the present.[31] From this vantage, "objects appear as repeated indications, which, rather than having a *specific* opposite, are demarcated against 'everything else.'" In fact, Luhmann suggests that we might follow Mead and Whitehead, who "assigned a function to identifiable and recognizable objects, whose primary purpose is to bind time. This function is needed because the reality of experience and actions consists in mere event sequences, that is, in an ongoing self-dissolution."[32]

These terms are remarkably apt for understanding how *Blur*'s significance as a work of art under conditions of (post)modernity goes far beyond the mere thematizations we can readily articulate, which Diller + Scofidio themselves clearly reject. Indeed, in its unstable form, shifting constantly in both shape and density of light and moisture, this building that is not a building could well be described as epitomizing "a temporal unity that is either no longer or not yet observed": a something that is also, to use Diller + Scofidio's words, a nothing. In short, a *blur*! At the same time, paradoxically, as a "metaform," one could hardly imagine a more daring and original formal decision that dramatically distinguishes itself from "the unmarked space of everything else." When we combine this understanding of the artwork as what Luhmann calls a "quasi-object" with attention to the double aspect of its formal decisions outlined earlier, we can zero in on the fact that, paradoxically, the "shapelessness" of the *Blur* building is precisely what constitutes its most decisive and binding formal quality—and not least, of course, with regard to adjacent formal decisions in the realm of architecture. Its "refusal" of architecture and its dematerialization of the architectural medium paradoxically epitomize the question of architectural form from a Luhmannian perspective; that is, the shape-shifting, loosely defined space of *Blur* only dramatizes what is true of *all* architectural forms. As the shifting winds over the Lake of Neuchâtel blow the cloud this way and that, the joke is not on *Blur* but rather on any architectural forms that think they are "solid," real "objects"—that have, one might say, a compositional rather than systematic understanding of the medium. In this light, one is tempted to read those moments when the winds swept nearly all the cloud away to reveal the underlying tensegrity structure—leaving, as one reviewer put it, the view of "an unfinished building awaiting its skin"[33]—as the most instructive all, insofar as THE BUILDING, "official architecture," is revealed to be precisely *not* "the building."

As we have already noted, the effectiveness of these formal decisions is only enhanced by the fact that they are smuggled inside the Trojan horse of the work's savvy play with the "art imitates nature" theme. From a systems theory point of view, we might say that the joke here is not on those who think that art imitates nature but on those who think it *doesn't*—not in the sense of "an imitation of something that presumably exists along with and outside of art" but in the sense that "it now imitates the world's invisibility, a nature that can no longer be apprehended as a whole."[34] Another name for this fact, as we have already noted, is *contingency*—namely, the contingency of the distinctions and indications that make the world available and, because they are contingent, simultaneously make it unavailable. It is against that contingency that the artwork and its formal decisions assert themselves. Luhmann writes: "All forms, especially forms of art, must persist against the challenge that they could be different. They convince by evoking alternative possibilities while neutralizing any preference for forms not chosen" (92). The genius of *Blur* from this vantage is that it submits itself to this contingency in the vagaries and malleability of its shape, its "loose" binding of time (to recall Whitehead and Mead's definition of objects), while simultaneously taking it into account, but as it were preemptively, within its own frame, as "an indicating operation that observes, as if from the corner of its eye, what happens on the other side of form" (148). In doing so, "it employs constraints for the sake of increasing the work's freedom in disposing over other constraints," and this includes those contingencies that, rather than threatening the work with obsolescence, now increase the resonance of the work with its environment (with all that it is not), since those contingencies are now seen to be always already anticipated by the work's *noncontingent* formal decision itself.

Of course, all of this raises the question of what, exactly, *is* art, if the formlessness of the object is being equated with the strength of its formal statement, if the strongest form of "something" turns out to be "nothing." Here, however, we need only remind ourselves that questions of form are not questions of *objects* (indeed, if we follow Whitehead, Mead, and systems theory, even *objects* are not questions of objects). And if that's the case, then perhaps we are better off rephrasing the question along the following lines: What is the relationship between discourse about art and the art object itself? On this point, we would do well, Luhmann rightly suggests, to remember the lessons of Duchamp, Cage, and conceptual art in general.[35] "One can ask how an art object distinguishes itself from other natural or artificial objects, for example, from a urinal or a snow shovel," Luhmann writes. "Marcel Duchamp used *the form of a work of art* to impress this question on his audience and, in a laudable effort, eliminated all sensuously recognizable differences between the two. But can a work of art *at once pose and answer this question?*"[36] The answer, as it turns out, is no, because the meaning of Duchamp's snow shovel—the significance of its first-order formal decisions—depends on (and anticipates and manipulates) a second-order discourse of art criticism and theory in terms of which those first-order decisions are received. The first-order observer need only "identify a work of art as an object in contradistinction to all other objects or processes." But for those who experience the work and want to understand its significance, the situation is quite different. Here the project of Cage and Duchamp is "to confront the observer with the question of how he goes about identifying a work of art as a work of art. The only possible answer is: by observing observations" (71):

> The observer uses a distinction to indicate what he observes. This happens when it happens. But if one wants to observe whether and how this happens, employing a distinction is not enough—one must also indicate the distinction. The concept of form serves this purpose. . . . Whoever observes forms observes other observers in the rigorous sense that he is not interested in the materiality, expectations, or utterances of these observers, but strictly and exclusively in their use of distinctions. (66–67)

Luhmann argues, in fact, that art and art criticism have been struggling with this issue at least since the early modern period. In the convention of the still life, for example, which assumes great importance in Italian and Dutch painting, we are presented with "unworthy" objects that "could acquire meaning only by presenting the art of presentation itself," focusing our attention on "the blatant discrepancy between the banality of the subject matter and its artful presentation" (69)—a process that is only further distilled in Duchamp's snow shovel. Indeed, part of the genius of Duchamp's work is that it reveals how the formula of "disinterested pleasure" fails to clarify what can be meant by artful presentation as "an end in itself," which only begs the question that "there is perhaps a special interest in being disinterested, and can we assume that such an interest also motivates the artist who produces the work, and who can neither preclude nor deny an interest in the interests of others?" (69). For Luhmann, such questions index the situation of art as a social system under functionally differentiated modernity, of art struggling to come to terms with its raison d'être—in systems theory terms, to achieve and justify its operational closure, or "autonomy." "To create a work of art under these sociohistorical conditions," then, "amounts to creating specific forms for an observation of observations. This is the sole purpose for which the work is 'produced.' From this perspective, the artwork accomplishes the structural coupling between first- and second-order observations in the realm of art. . . . The artist accomplishes this by clarifying—via his own observations of the emerging work—how he and others will observe the work" (69).

Such an understanding is well and good, but it would seem to leave wholly to the side the question of the *experience* of art as a perceptual and phenomenological event—something that would appear to be rather spectacularly foregrounded in *Blur,* as Mark Hansen has recently argued, and foregrounded, moreover, quite self-consciously in terms of the function of *spectacle* in the tradition of the international expo as a genre (a matter emphasized in Diller's lectures about the project at Princeton and elsewhere).[37] Indeed, one might well argue that this, and not the coupling of first- and second-order observations by means of form, is what motivates contemporary art, its experimentation with different media, and so on—a rule that is only proved, so the argument would unfold, by the exception of conceptual art. Yet here we find one of the more original and innovative aspects of Luhmann's theory of art as a social system. Luhmann's point is not to deny the phenomenological aspect of the artwork but to point out—which seems rather obvious, upon reflection—that the *meaning* of the artwork cannot be referenced to, much less reduced to, this material and perceptual aspect. Rather, the work of art copresents perception and communication—and does so in a way that turns out to be decisive for what another theoretical vocabulary might call art's "critical" function in relation to society.

To understand how this happens, we need to revisit one of the central points of the opening chapter: that for Luhmann, perception (and beyond that, consciousness) and communication operate in mutually exclusive, operationally closed, autopoietic systems, though they are structurally coupled through media such as language. As Luhmann puts it in a formulation surely calculated to provoke: "Humans cannot communicate; not even their brains can communicate; not even their conscious minds can communicate. Only communication can communicate."[38] "Communication operates with an unspecific reference to the participating state of mind," he continues; "it is especially unspecific as to perception. It cannot copy states of mind, cannot imitate them, cannot represent them."[39] At the same time, however, consciousness and perception are a medium for communication. On the one hand, unperceived communications do not exist (if they did, how would we know?); communication, Luhmann writes, "can hardly come into being without the participation of the mind," and in this sense "the relationship is asymmetrical" (374). On the other hand, "communication uses the mind as a medium precisely because communication does not thematize the mind in question. Metaphorically speaking, the mind in question remains invisible to communication" (378). The mind is (of necessity) its own operationally closed biological system, but because it is also a necessary medium for communication, "we can say that the mind has the privileged position of being able to disturb, stimulate, and irritate communication" (379). It cannot instruct or direct communications—"reports of perceptions are not perceptions themselves"—but it can "stimulate communication without ever becoming communication" (379–80).

For several reasons, the "irreducibility" of perception to communication (and vice versa) and their asymmetrical relationship is crucial to what a different theoretical vocabulary would call art's "critical" function. First, as Dietrich Schwanitz notes, perception and communication operate at different speeds—and this is something that art puts to use. "Compared to communication," Schwanitz writes,

> the dimension of perception displays a considerably higher rate of information processing. The impression of immediacy in perception produces the notion that the things we perceive are directly present. Naturally, this is an illusion, for recent brain research has proven that sensory input is minimal compared with the complexity of neuronal self-perception. . . . Together, cultural and neuronal construction thus constitute a form of mediation that belies the impression of immediacy in perception. That does not, however, alter the fact that perception takes place immediately as compared to communication, the selective process of which is a sequential one.[40]

To put it another way, although both perception and communication operate as autopoietic systems on the basis of difference and distinction, the very different speeds of processing of these systems makes it appear that perception confirms, stabilizes, and makes immediate, while communication (to put it in Derridean terms) differs, defers, and temporalizes. In the work of art, the *difference* between perception and communication is reentered in the services of the work's communication. But because of this asymmetry in speeds, it is reentered in a way that calls attention to the contingency of communication—not of the first-order communication of the artwork, which appears incapable of emendation (it is what it is), but of the second-order observation of the work's meaning and its critical function vis-à-vis the system of art. This can be accomplished, as in *Blur,* by making perception outrun communication, as it were (a process well described by Hansen), the better to provoke a question that the work itself is made to answer. Or, conversely, in a work like On Kawara's *Date Paintings,* it can be accomplished by using the deficit of perceptual depth or complexity in the "paintings" themselves to call attention to the difference between the work's immediate perceptual surface and its larger meaning.[41] Thus the artwork copresents the *difference* between perception and communication, and this difference is what allows art to have something like a privileged relationship to what is commonly invoked as the "ineffable" or the "incommunicable," and it *uses* perception to "irritate" and stimulate communication to respond to the question "what does this perceptual event *mean?*" As Luhmann puts it in a key passage for understanding his theory of art:

> The function of art would then consist in integrating what is in principle incommunicable—namely, perception—into the communication network of society. . . . The art system concedes to the perceiving consciousness its own unique adventure in observing artworks—and yet makes available as communication the formal selection that triggered the adventure. Unlike verbal communication, which all too quickly moves toward a yes/no bifurcation, communication guided by perception relaxes the structural coupling of consciousness and communication (without destroying it, of course). . . . In a manner that is matched neither by thought nor by communication, perception presents *astonishment and recognition in a single instant.* Art uses, enhances, and in a sense exploits the possibilities of perception in such a way that it can present the *unity of this distinction.* . . . The pleasure of astonishment, already described in antiquity, refers to the unity of the difference between astonishment and recognition, to the paradox that both *intensify one another.*[42]

And, Luhmann adds—in an observation directly relevant to *Blur*'s auda-cious formal solution to the "problem" of architecture—"Extravagant forms play an increasingly important role in this process" (141).

This is not, however, simply a matter of "pleasure" or "aesthesis." In fact, it is what gives art something like a privileged critical rela-tionship to society, because art "establishes a reality of its own that differs from ordinary reality." "Despite the work's perceptibility, de-spite its undeniable reality," Luhmann writes, "it simultaneously con-stitutes another reality. . . . Art splits the world into a real world and an imaginary world," and "the function of art concerns the meaning of this split" (142). By virtue of its unique relationship to the difference between perception and communication, art can raise this question in an especially powerful way not available to other social systems. If we think of objects themselves as eigenbehaviors (to seize once again on Heinz von Foerster's term), as stabilizations of various durations made possible by the repeated, recursive application of particular dis-tinctions, then we might observe that "the objects that emerge from the recursive self-application of communication"—versus, say, rocks or trees—"contribute more than any other kinds of norms and sanctions to supplying the social system with necessary redundancies"; they literally fix social space. This is probably even more true, Luhmann observes, of such "quasi-objects" (to use Michel Serres's phrase) "that have been invented for the sake of this specific function, such as kings or soccer balls. Such 'quasi-objects' can be comprehended only in rela-tion to this function"—indeed, it is their sole reason for being. "Works of art," Luhmann continues,

> are quasi-objects in this sense. They individualize themselves by ex-
> cluding the sum total of everything else; not because they are con-
> strued as given but because their significance as objects implies a realm
> of social regulation. One must scrutinize works of art as intensely and
> with as close attention to the object as one does when watching kings
> and soccer balls; in this way—and in the more complex case where one
> observes other observers by focusing on the same object—*the socially
> regulative reveals itself.* (47)

When we remember that for Luhmann this "more complex" case is represented nowhere more clearly than in our experience of the mass media, the relationship between *Blur*'s formal decisions as a work of art and its *critical* agenda of shedding light on "the socially regulative"—on the terrain of an international media expo, no less—comes even more forcefully into view. In these terms, works of art, in calling our attention to the realm of "the socially regulative," cast light on precisely those contingencies, constructions, and norms that the mass media, in their own specific mode of communication, occlude. In the first instance (the artwork), we seem to be dealing with completely ad hoc, constructed objects whose realm of reference is not "the real world" at all but that of the imagination. In the second, we appear to be dealing with the opposite, in which the representations of the mass media are motivated by the objects and facts of "the real world." In fact, however, this thematization in terms of "imaginative" and "real" only obscures the need to rearticulate the relationship in terms of the dynamics of first- and second-order observation of different social systems. As Luhmann points out, "the mass media create the illusion that we are first-order observers whereas in fact this is already second-order observing";[43] or more baldly still, "put in Kantian terms: the mass media generate a transcendental illusion."[44] The mass media's rendering of reality, however—and this is a point that the "postethical" character of Diller + Scofidio's work insists on in a highly specific way—is not to be taken, "as most people would be inclined to think, [as] a *distortion* of reality. It is a *construction* of reality. For from the point of view of a postontological theory of observing systems, there is no distinct reality out there (who, then, would make these distinctions?). . . . There is no transcendental subject. We have to rely on the system of the mass media that construct our reality. . . . If there is no choice in accepting these observations, because there is no equally powerful alternative available, we have at least the possibility to deconstruct the presentations of the mass media, their presentations of the present."[45]

That deconstruction of the mass media in *Blur* proceeds by means of the artwork's second-order observation of the first-order system of the mass media; but that observation, in turn, only happens by art "doing what it does," as *its own* first-order system, with its own code, its own blind spot. That formal symmetry between the two observing systems, however—the fact that the dynamics of communication in autopoietic social systems operate in the same ways in each system (on the basis of paradoxical self-reference, constitutive blindness to the unity of the system's core distinction, and so on)—only throws into critical relief the *difference* in the relationship of communication and perception (and in the case at hand, specifically visual perception) that is specific to each system. And *Blur* will put that difference to critical use under the thematization of "spectacle." We can gain a sharper sense of just how this is the case when we recall that for Luhmann electronic mass media are just the latest in a series of powerful developments in the history of what he calls "media of dissemination," beginning with language and then, crucially, the invention of writing and printing, whose power lies in their ability to make communication independent from a specific perceptual substrate or set of coordinates. "Alphabetized writing made it possible to carry communication beyond the temporally and spatially limited circle of those who were present at any particular time," he writes, and language per se—and even more so writing and printing—"increases the understandability of communication beyond the sphere of perception."[46] Unlike oral speech, which "can compensate for lack of information with persuasion, and can synchronize speaking, hearing, and accepting in a rhythmic and rhapsodic way, leaving literally no time for doubt" (162), writing and printing "enforce an experience of the difference that constitutes communication"—namely, the difference between communication and perception—and "they are, in this precise sense, more communicative forms of communication" (163).

For Luhmann, the electronic mass media represent the culmination of this general line of historical development. Indeed, "for the differentiation of a system of the mass media, the decisive achievement can be said to have been the invention of technologies of dissemination which not only circumvent interaction among those co-present, but effectively render such interaction impossible for the mass media's own communications."[47] This process began with the advent of the printing press, when "the volume of written material multiplied to the extent that oral interaction among *all* participants in communication is effectively and *visibly* rendered impossible" (16). And so it is, Luhmann argues, that

> in the wake of the so-called democratization of politics and its dependence on the media of public opinion . . . those participating in politics—politicians and voters alike—observe one another in the mirror of public opinion. . . . The level of first-order observation is guaranteed by the

continuous reports of the mass media. . . . Second-order observation occurs via the inferences one can draw about oneself or others, if one assumes that those who wish to participate politically encounter one another in the mirror of public opinion, *and that this is sufficient.*[48]

It is just this situation that *Blur* attempts to address, if we believe Diller + Scofidio—namely, by subjecting communication in its mass-mediated mode (as something immediately legible and consumable) to a perceptual *blur,* so that *spectacle* operates here not in the service of immediately meaningful, prefab ideological content (as in the electronic mass media) but rather as the unavoidable provocation to *another* communication whose meaning is far from immediately clear and, in being so, operates directly in the services of art's own communication and autopoiesis (i.e., what does this mean? is this art?). In this way, Diller + Scofidio's project might be understood as bringing into focus (1) how the contingency of communication is managed and manipulated by the "socially regulative" in the electronic mass media and (2) how that dynamic, in turn, is coupled to a certain consumerist schematization of visuality, in which the difference between perception and communication is always already reentered in mass-mediated communication to produce a pre-digested, iconographic visual space readily incorporated by a subject whose (un)ethical relation to the visual might best be summed up as: "CLICK HERE." We might say, then, that *Blur* uses the difference between perception and communication in a way diametrically opposed to what we find in the electronic mass media, and then routes that difference between art and the mass media through the work's formal choices to render them specifically meaningful as art, not just as well-meaning critical platitude. What is remarkable here, of course, is not that *Blur* makes this (somewhat unremarkable) observation about the relationship of perception and communication in electronic mass media, a relationship particularly evident in the realm of visuality. What is remarkable is that *Blur* does so without saying so, by insisting only on itself. This is simply to say that *Blur* communicates this difference *as art*. And if it didn't, we wouldn't pay any attention to it.

9 Emerson's Romanticism, Cavell's Skepticism, Luhmann's Modernity

> If Emerson's "representativeness," his universalizing, is not
> to go unexamined, neither should his habitually condemned
> "individualism." If he is to be taken as an instance of "human-
> ism" . . . then he is at the same time to be taken as some form
> of anti-humanist, working "against ourselves," against what we
> understand as human (under)standing.
> —STANLEY CAVELL, "Emerson's Constitutional
> Amending: Reading 'Fate'"

> Reality is what one does not perceive when one perceives it.
> —NIKLAS LUHMANN, "The Cognitive Program of
> Constructivism and a Reality That Remains Unknown"

AS A MODE OF CULTURAL PRACTICE, Emerson's "romanticism" has often been taken as an especially outlandish—that is to say, an especially incoherent—engagement of the central themes associated with the romantic problematic (the sublime, imagination, etc.) that we have been attempting so far to rescript in these pages, the better to disclose their essential rigor and systematicity, a rigor and systematicity that is achieved because of, not in spite of, the unwillingness to turn away from the paradoxical forms of observation and self-reference that systems theory (but also, in its way, deconstruction) enables us to theorize with some depth and precision. This charge arises against Emerson because of the insistent strangeness, the unremittingly heretical quality, of his writing, in which a signature feature is to take precisely the turn of thought or phrase that seems to undermine at a stroke the entire argument just made, a seemingly relentless drive to pursue thought wherever it may lead, even into paradox and conceptual meltdown. As Emerson's writes in "Self-Reliance," in an altogether characteristic gesture, "Speak what you think now in hard words, and to-morrow speak what to-morrow thinks in hard words again, though it contradict every thing you said to-day."[1] As the philosopher Stanley Cavell has noted, "Along with the gesture of denying philosophy to Emerson goes another, almost as common . . . namely that of describing Emerson's prose as a kind of mist or fog, as if it is generally quite palpable what it is that Emerson is obscurely reaching for words to say and generally quite patent that the ones he finds are more or less arbitrary and conventional . . . as though he cannot mean anew in every word he says."[2]

For Cavell, the power of the Emersonian project begins with the rigor of its confrontation with the inescapability and consequences of philosophical skepticism: the fact, as Cavell puts it, "that the world exists as it were for its own reasons."[3] Emerson both acknowledges—"bears" or "suffers" will be a better term, eventually—and resists what Cavell calls the most famous "settlement" with the problem of skepticism in the philosophical tradition, namely, Kant's in *The Critique of Pure Reason*. As Cavell summarizes it:

> The dissatisfaction with such a settlement as Kant's is relatively easy to state. To settle with skepticism . . . to assure us that we do know the existence of the world, or rather, that what we understand as knowledge is *of* the world, the price Kant asks us to pay is to cede any claim to know the thing in itself, to grant that human knowledge is not of things as they are in themselves. You don't—do you?—have to be a romantic to feel sometimes about that settlement: Thanks for nothing.[4]

The irony of the Kantian settlement with skepticism—and it is an irony that will in no small part structure what Cavell characterizes as nothing less than Emerson's reinvention of philosophy—is that if "reason proves its power to itself, over itself," by discovering the difference between the mere appearances of which it can have knowledge and the *Ding an sich* of which it cannot,[5] then the triumph of philosophy is also, at the same time, its failure (a final failure, as it turns out), because knowledge secures itself only by losing the world, leaving us locked (to borrow Emerson's phrase in "Experience") in "a prison of glass."[6] As Emerson puts it in a famous passage from "Experience" that Cavell returns to time and again, "I take this evanescence and lubricity of all objects, which lets them slip through our fingers then when we clutch hardest, to be the most unhandsome part of our condition" (200).

What this demands from philosophy, then, is a double gesture in the recognition that thinking must henceforward proceed differently. First, Emerson comes to understand—as Cavell brilliantly and even movingly demonstrates—that "philosophy has to do with the perplexed capacity to mourn the passing of the world."[7] In "Experience," that mourning is figured in some of the most shocking and vertiginous lines in all of American literature, where, reflecting on the grief attending the death of his son two years earlier, Emerson writes, "I cannot get it nearer to me," "it does not touch me." Emerson grieves, Cavell suggests, not so much over the death of his son but over the loss of the world, with which even the experience of grief cannot bring him into closer contact: "I grieve that grief can teach me nothing." "Grief too," Emerson writes, "will make us idealists."[8] Second, if the demand for foundational concepts, abstract synthesis, and unity of judgments only drives the world away from us in the very act of trying to grasp and apprehend it, then thinking must be reconceived as what Cavell calls "clutching's opposite."[9] Philosophy, to put it telegraphically, must *get out of hand,* which is exactly what happens in Emerson's reinvention of philosophy as antiphilosophy—hence the demanding wildness of Emerson's writing, which will lead the attentive reader to ask more than once, "Is he serious?"

Emerson thus inaugurates a rethinking of thinking that will eventually lead, as Cavell points out, to Heidegger's assertion that "thinking is a handicraft," but a handicraft carried out in respect of "the derivation of the word thinking from a root for thanking . . . as giving thanks for the gift of thinking."[10] (And eventually—as Cavell does *not* point out—it will lead not only to Derrida's analysis of the gift but also to his critique of Heidegger's humanism in relation to the question of species difference in the essay "*Geschlecht II:* Heidegger's Hand.")[11] There Derrida deconstructs the purity of the distinction between giving and taking that Heidegger's humanism takes (we might even say, holds) for granted—a deconstruction that one might well argue is writ large in Emerson's essay "Fate," where he insists, "See how fate slides into freedom and freedom into fate, observe how far the roots of every creature run, or find, if you can, a point where there is no thread of connection" (273). Thinking with Emerson, then, becomes not active apprehension (prehensile grasping of the world by our concepts, as it were) but an act of *reception,* a reception in which passivity—because it consists of a capacity to be affected by the world in manifold ways that cannot be contained by the choked bottleneck of thought as philosophy has traditionally conceived it—becomes, paradoxically, a maximally *active* passivity. This process is everywhere testified to in Emerson's work from beginning to end, from the "Transparent Eyeball" passage in *Nature,* to the seemingly paradoxical assertion in "Self-Reliance" that "self-reliance is God-reliance," to his assertion in "Experience" that "all I know is reception. I am and I have: but I do not get, and when I fancied I had gotten anything, I found I did not. . . . When I receive a new gift, I do not macerate my body to make the account square, for if I should die I could not make the account square. The benefit overran the merit the first day" (212).

But as crucial as Cavell's work has been for enabling a new and deeply compelling understanding of Emerson and his relationship to Continental philosophy, I want to suggest that a more rigorous and historically compelling understanding of Emerson's work is available to us if we reframe Cavell's account itself within a more comprehensive view of Emerson's romanticism as a response to the condition of *modernity* and its epistemological and ethical fallout—a phenomenon marked in Cavell's reading by the broad brushstroke of skepticism. In this connection, it is surprising, as Paul Jay has pointed out, that Emerson's work as a response specifically to modernity has not received more attention, as debates have instead been preoccupied with arguments in the 1980s and 1990s over whether Emerson is best understood as a transcendentalist or a pragmatist, or, more recently, with the political status of Emerson's work—but "political" understood, it turns out, in a quite ideologically specific way.[12] And even in more recent studies where the context of modernity *does* seem to be cultivated for understanding Emerson's work (for example, in Jay Grossman's *Reconstituting the American Renaissance,* which revisits Emerson in the context of a specifically American version of "the long eighteenth century"), the conjugation remains hampered by a certain American exceptionalism—one replete with a familiar set of assumptions about what politics is, how it is related to questions of ethics and agency, how individuals are related to social institutions, and so on—that has been endemic to American studies and its core theoretical and methodological commitments (as numerous commentators have noted) almost since the inception of the discipline itself.[13]

Those assumptions and commitments, I would argue, are constituted by and reproduce an ideologically specific form of liberal humanism. But as one of its critics, Donald Pease, has recently pointed out, "What Emerson referred to as 'my genius when it calls me' achieved effects that were independent of the processes of identification, interpellation, and internalization associated with liberal institutions," and it thus "also undermined liberalism's conception of the possessive individual as its subject."[14] To put it bluntly, the liberal humanist assumptions taken for granted in most American studies critiques of Emerson are not just tangentially but *directly* under assault in Emerson's work. So it should come as no surprise that we often find the assumption in American studies work on Emerson that to abandon those very ideas about politics, agency, and so on is to be (more or less by default) politically conservative or regressive (which is, after all, the way ideology works through institutions like academia to reproduce itself). Though I cannot pursue the argument in any detail here, I would suggest— particularly in the current geopolitical moment, which can only be called a moment of crisis for liberal democracy and its ideology and institutions—that we would be better off taking seriously Emerson's interrogation of liberalism's assumptions about subjectivity, agency, and politics, even if those queries end (as they often do in Emerson) in anything but a sanguine view of our situation. We should take heed of them for the same reasons that have generated such an upsurge in interest in figures such as Giorgio Agamben and Carl Schmitt. Indeed, what Chantal Mouffe writes about Schmitt could well serve as a paraphrase of Cavell's reading of Emerson's late essay "Fate" and its implications for politics. As Mouffe puts it, "The political cannot be restricted to a certain type of institution, or envisioned as constituting a specific sphere or level of society. It must be conceived as a dimension that is inherent to every human society and that determines our very ontological condition."[15]

We may now return with a somewhat different set of coordinates, and a different sense of their implications, to the question of modernity, whose chief philosophical challenge, as Jay points out, is the well-known process of "secularization." It is this challenge to which romanticism, so the story goes, constitutes a finally flawed and even fanciful response, one whose contours we have already glimpsed in the fundamentally ironic structure of the Kantian transcendentalism and its settlement with skepticism. For Habermas, in *The Philosophical Discourse of Modernity,* secularization means that thought "can and will no longer borrow the criteria by which it takes its orientation from models supplied by another epoch; it has to create its normativity out of itself"; for Foucault—and here we return to Kant once more—it is that thought must put its "own reason to use, without subjecting itself to any authority."[16] If the upside of the philosophical situation of modernity is, as Jay puts it, that "the present represents an exit or a way out of subordination to traditional sources and modes authority" (28), then the downside, already traced in Kantian transcendentalism, is that the ungrounding of reason invites the various forms of idealism that have been attributed to romanticism in the all-too-familiar narratives of secularization, where Mind, Spirit, Imagination, or the equivalent comes to take the place of self-generated knowledge and its authority previously reserved for God.

Now we might imagine any number of responses to this as a standard characterization of Emerson's work. To begin with, one might well argue that such a position too rapidly assimilates Emerson's later work—particularly the second series of essays and *The Conduct of Life*—to the principles articulated in the early essay *Nature.* Cavell, for example, argues that the Emerson of *Nature* and its adjacent early essays is not just superficially different but *fundamentally* different from the later work:

> I am at present among those who find *Nature,* granted the wonderful passages in it, not yet to constitute the Emersonian philosophical voice, but to be the place from which, in the several following years, that voice departs, in "The American Scholar," "The Divinity School Address," and "Self-Reliance." I would characterize the difference by saying that in *Nature* Emerson is taking the issue skepticism as solvable or controllable where thereafter he takes its unsolvability to the heart of his thinking.[17]

It is precisely this unsolvability that generates what Richard Rorty characterizes as an increasingly—and increasingly demanding—*anti-*

representationalist mode of philosophical practice. As Rorty explains it, the problem with philosophical representationalism is the assumption that "'making true' and 'representing' are reciprocal relations," as if "the nonlinguistic item which makes *S* true is the one represented by *S*."[18] For philosophical idealism, that "item" will be something in the changeless character of the subject; for realism, it will be something in the nature of the object that "has a context of its own, a context which is privileged by virtue of being the object's rather than the inquirer's" (96). In either case, what representationalism fails to see is that "'determinacy' is not what is in question—that neither does thought determine reality nor, in the sense intended by the realist, does reality determine thought" (5). Both positions, as Cavell might say, find themselves unduly, even preeningly, "handsome"—hence the strange, insistent movement of Emerson's prose, which takes for granted, as it were, Rorty's contention that "words take their meaning from other words rather than by virtue of their representative character" and their "transparency to the real,"[19] that "'grasping the thing itself' is not something that precedes contextualization."[20]

For these reasons, as Rorty has lucidly explained, leveling the charge of "relativism" at antirepresentationalism is an empty gesture. "Relativism certainly is self-refuting," he writes, "but there is a difference between saying that every community is as good as every other and saying that we have to work out from the networks [where] we are." The idea, he continues, that every tradition or belief or idea or community "is as rational or as moral as every other could be held only by a god. . . . Such a being would have escaped from history and conversation into contemplation and metanarrative. To accuse postmodernism of relativism is to try to put a metanarrative in the postmodernist's mouth" (202). It is precisely this kind of embeddedness, of course, that is everywhere under intense scrutiny in essays of Emerson's such as "Fate." And so—to return now to Cavell—to take the unsolvability of skepticism to heart is not just, at the same stroke, to abandon the representationalist philosophical project; it is also to change our view of the relationship of thinking and language that I have already discussed in some detail in the first half of this book. What Kant confronted as "merely" a problem of thought, Emerson grappled with under the additional rigors of writing and language—of philosophy as a writing practice—so that the "stipulations or terms under which we can say anything at all to one another" will themselves be subjected to endless, and endlessly unfinalized, scrutiny.[21]

As Cavell puts it, in Emerson

> I find the *Critique of Pure Reason* turned upon itself: notions of limitation and of condition are as determining in the essay "Fate" as they are in Kant, but it is as if these terms are themselves subjected to transcendental deduction, as if not just twelve categories but any and every word in our language stands under the necessity of deduction, or say derivation. . . . Emerson is commonly felt to play fast and loose with something like contradiction in his writing; but I am speaking of a sense in which contradiction, the countering of diction, is the genesis of his writing of philosophy. (113)

What this means is that when we come upon such apparently full-bore idealist statements in Emerson as the following, from the essay "Fate"—"Intellect annuls fate. So far as a man thinks, he is free"—"this apparently genteel thought," Cavell writes, "now turns out to mean that . . . our antagonism to fate, to which we are fated, and in which our freedom resides, is as a struggle with the language we emit, of our character with itself."[22]

One striking example of this new philosophical practice that Cavell finds in Emerson—this time in relation not to Kant but to Descartes—occurs in "Self-Reliance," when Emerson writes, "Man is timid and apologetic; he is no longer upright; he dares not say 'I think,' 'I am,' but quotes some saint or sage." If the central feature of the Cartesian subject is, as Cavell writes, that the "discovery that my existence requires, hence permits, proof (you might say authentication) . . . requires that if I am to exist I must name my existence, acknowledge it," then the real rigor of Emerson's confrontation with these "terms" is that it "goes the whole way with Descartes' insight." It insists on the proof of selfhood—including its proof in and through the "terms" of thinking—without providing a fixed, a priori subject on which such a proof could rely and of which it could be, as it were, the representation—"as if there were nothing to rely on," Cavell writes, "but reliance itself."[23] The "beauty" of Emerson's answer to Descartes, Cavell writes, lies in its weakness (you may say in its emptiness)—indeed, in two weaknesses. First, it does not prejudge what the I or self or mind or soul may turn out to be, but only specifies a condition that whatever it is must meet. Second, the proof only works in the moment of its giving, for what I prove is the existence only of a creature who *can* enact its existence, as exemplified in actually giving the proof, not one who at all time does in fact enact it. (87)

The self of Emersonian self-reliance, then, is "not a state of being but a moment of change, say of becoming—a transience of being, a being of transience" (89).

In Cavell—and this marks precisely his difference with Rorty—the paradoxical self-reference of the "proof" of the Emersonian self is crucial to what we might think of as its generative incompleteness. This movement of the Emersonian self—in which the self might be said to be alive only to the extent that it *is* moving—is crucial to what Cavell sees as the political import of Emerson's work, what he calls its "democratic" or "moral" "perfectionism." As Cavell describes it, "I do not read Emerson as saying . . . that there is one unattained/attainable self we repetitively never arrive at, but rather that 'having' 'a' self is a process of moving to, and from, nexts. . . . That the self is always attained, as well as *to be* attained, creates the problem in Emerson's concept of self-reliance . . . that unless you manage the reliance of the attained on the unattained/attainable (that is, unless you side that way), you are left in precisely the negation of the position he calls for, left in conformity."[24] In its "onwardness," the Emersonian self must constantly surpass the selves it has already become, but not to attain an ideal, fixed selfhood. And yet, "since the task for each is his or her own self-transformation," Cavell sensibly observes, "the representativeness implied in that life may seem not to establish a recognition of others in different positions, so as to be disqualified as a moral position altogether." Emerson's remarkable twist on this problem, however, is that his writing "works out the conditions for my recognizing my difference from others as a function of my recognizing my difference from myself";[25] after all, strictly speaking, only you can transform you, and only I can transform me. So "Emerson's turn is to make my partiality itself"—what I am here calling (somewhat at a tangent to Cavell, as will become clear) my "contingency"—"the sign and incentive of my siding with the next or future self, which means siding against my attained perfection (or conformity), sidings which require the recognition of an other—the acknowledgement of a relationship—in which this sign is manifest."[26]

Emersonian perfectionism may thus be conceived as a kind of ongoing act of radical negative capability that provides the foundation (though that is eventually not the word we would want, of course) for democratic relations with others, with those other selves I have not yet been but who also—and this is the engine of Emerson's constant polemical project—need to surpass *themselves,* in an ongoing process of democracy conceived as otherness always yet to be achieved, or *if* already achieved, only achieved in the present by the other and not by me. As difficult as it is to see, Cavell is right that this idea of perfectionism is "projected in contrast to the idea of 'one's own nature'";[27] and all of Emerson's talk—and a considerable amount of talk it is—of "self-recovery" both early and late in his work directs us to not an originary, fixed self-substance but toward a *power* and a *process:* not toward the past but toward the future, or rather toward futurity itself, conceived as a horizon, where, paradoxically, the only "self" to "recover" is a self that one has not yet been, for the self *only* exists in its becoming.[28] Indeed, from this vantage, we might read "recovery" very differently as a "re-covering," as burying and covering over once more the past self, that casualty of what Cavell calls Emerson's "onwardness."

It is in the context and the services of these future selves and against what Emerson calls "conformity" that we are to understand the political involvement of the Emersonian self in the sense insisted on at the end of "Experience," where Emerson writes that "the true romance which the world exists to realize will be the transformation of genius into practical power" (213). As Cavell writes, when Emerson's critics read the line "self-reliance is the aversion of conformity," they "take this to mean roughly that he is disgusted with society and wants no more to do with it."[29] But if we understand the Emersonian self as movement toward futurity and not a being, then instead of *conversion* to a truth we already know and to a being we already are, *aversion* means "that his writing and his society incessantly recoil from, or turn away from one another; but since this is incessant, the picture is at the same time of each incessantly turning *toward* the other."[30] This process is dramatized perhaps nowhere more forcefully than in late essays and addresses like "Fate" and "The Fugitive Slave Law," where Emerson insists time and again on turning away from society and its institutions, toward the domain of justice and ethics, only to turn back to the realization of freedom not in transcendence but in "practical power."[31]

On the one hand, Emerson asserts in "The Fugitive Slave Law," "No forms, neither constitutions, nor laws, nor covenants, nor churches, nor bibles, are of any use in themselves. The Devil nestles comfortably into them all. There is no help but in the head and heart and hamstrings of a man."[32] On the other hand, as Emerson writes in "Fate," "A man must thank his defects, and stand in some terror of his talents. A transcendent talent draws so largely on his forces as to lame him; a defect pays him revenues on the other side" (273), and he reminds us that his "power is hooped in by a necessity which, by many experiments, he touches on every side until he learns its arc" (268). A corollary of this "aversive" movement of the Emersonian self is that the world—and we already know this from the Kantian anatomy of skepticism—always already "vanishes from me," as Cavell puts it, becomes a *horizon* that we can only approach but never reach, one that in a radical sense depends on the terms we use: not to apprehend it but to *receive* or, as Cavell puts it, "acknowledge" it, just as I am impelled toward the other by my "partiality" toward myself, my contingency.

Here we can begin to get a sense of the usefulness of Niklas Luhmann's work for helping us to read the full letter of Emerson's thinking. First of all, Luhmann's theorization of these questions is more analytically precise than Cavell's, which remains largely at the level of a philosophical thematics characterized by what one might call—at least from a Luhmannian point of view—an excessive "literariness." That would be of less moment were it not for the fact identified by Cavell that "literariness" has typically been used as a kind of code for dismissing Emerson's rigor and philosophical seriousness. Second—and this is clearer in light of Rorty—Cavell's reading of Emerson under the master rubric of skepticism remains tied, one might argue, to the representationalism he would otherwise seem to disown, because skepticism holds on to the desire for a representational adequation between concepts and objects even as it knows that desire to be unappeasable (how else are we to understand Cavell's insistence on taking seriously the "mourning" of the loss of the world—and not of the child Waldo, as Sharon Cameron insists in her classic essay "Representing Grief"—in Emerson's "Experience"?).

Third, most important of all, Luhmann puts acute pressure on the relentlessly paradoxical and confounding dynamics of observation that are so central, and so increasingly vexing, in Emerson's work— dynamics that are usually thematized in criticism of romanticism under the rubric of "imagination," and more specifically in Emerson's work, in his well-known theatrics with the trope of vision (as in the famous "Transparent Eyeball" passage in the opening pages of *Nature*, "I am nothing; I see all" [29]). In fact, if we believe Maurice Gonnaud, it is Emerson's movement away from such solutions to the paradoxes of observation in the early 1840s that has made his later work in lectures and essays such as "The Method of Nature" and "Nominalist and Realist" all the more confounding for his critics. After 1840, Gonnaud writes, "If the Romantic was dead, the optimist had survived him and was ready to make a virtue of necessity"—specifically, I will argue in a moment, a necessity called *contingency*.[33] "Although he continued to call himself an idealist," Gonnaud continues, "he had ceased to be one in Kant's sense or even in Coleridge's. The universe gradually comes to resemble that 'old Two-Face, creator-creature, mind-matter, right-wrong' which he was to evoke in 'Nominalist and Realist'" (301).

Emerson's insistence on the contingency, not transcendence, of observation—what Gonnaud calls his effort to "fling out a new bridge—less ethereal, less harmonious perhaps, but tougher—between the One and the Many," purchased by taking it upon himself "to be the champion of the acknowledged facts, honored in their richness and diversity" (299), led to Emerson being even less understood than he had before 1840. Remarking on "The Method of Nature," Gonnaud writes that "his listeners confessed to understanding very little of it; the word 'ecstasy' recurs like a leitmotif, applied now to Nature and now to human beings and thus compounding the confusion" (301), not just for Emerson's contemporaries but even for later critics such as Stephen Whicher, who finds that such work "incorporates two irreconcilable perspectives and suffers from a profound incoherence" (302). What I want to suggest, however—and we will need Luhmann's work to fully explain why—is that it is precisely at these moments that we find Emerson at his most rigorous, systematically extrapolating in his later work the paradoxical dynamics and consequences of observation that were, as both Gonnaud and Cavell rightly observe in their different ways, certainly central to the Emersonian corpus from the beginning but were papered over by the more conventional idealism and romanticism we find in essays such as *Nature*. While Gonnaud regrets in the post-1840 Emerson "the author's centrifugal disposition of mind, which keeps him from transforming the profoundly contradictory impulses within him into dialectical movement," Luhmann's work on observation will help to clarify why Emerson's relentless explorations of these problems cannot and should not resolve themselves into a dialectic. Here again, it is not incoherence or vagueness of thought we find, I would suggest, but rather the genius of what we might call Emerson's undoing of romanticism.

Of the Emerson critics I have read, the one who has come closest to realizing this fact about Emerson's work is Lee Rust Brown in his wonderful book *The Emerson Museum*. As he observes about Emerson's contention in "Compensation" that "the value of the universe contrives to throw itself into every point," such moments "have been cited by readers who attack or applaud Emerson as a cheerful mystic who vaguely sees everything in everything."[34] What we have here instead, Brown suggests, is a more complicated process in which Coleridgean "multeity in unity" is subordinated to the workings of the observers, where "the sense found in natural objects is precisely the viewer's own original *means* for seeing them. . . . By virtue of these means, vision rises to a place of authority over objects, to a kind of perspectival remove sufficient to reveal relations within the whole scope of things" (71, 72). Yet such an observer is not transcendent in the usual idealist sense—indeed, in any sense. Instead, on display here is the more complicated dynamic of Emersonian "transparency"—that ability to perceive the "unity" of the "multeity"—that "is the one fatal condition of moving on intellectually; it is the way we pay for all worthwhile adjustments of attention." It is the only way we achieve what Emerson calls "new prospects"—in Brown's words, "at once the new object and the prospect of its future conversion into transparency" (47). Far from being transcendent, then, "we see one object only at the cost of another" (46), and "transparency, far from signifying a passive state or continuity or unity, testifies to the way the eye manufactures its own discontinuous intervals" (45–46).

At this juncture, Luhmann's work can give us a more fully articulated sense of Emerson's pressure on the problem of observation. It is able to do so in part because observation in Luhmann is *disarticulated* from vision per se, and in part because systems theory takes the additional step of showing how the problem of observation is related to that *other* central *topos* of romanticism invoked by Brown—multeity in unity—which must now be rewritten in systems theory's terms as the problem of *complexity* and how it is handled in system/environment relationships. It is this convergence—the paradoxical dynamics of observation and the related problem of complexity, how observation both reduces *and* produces complexity—that Emerson's writing insists on more and more rigorously as his career unfolds, rendering it in his mature work as literally *unavoidable,* as in, for example, one of his more brazen assertions, in "Circles," that "I am a God in nature; I am a weed by the wall."[35] Such a statement—and there are many of them in Emerson—insists on the radical *identity* of what, in the philosophical tradition, are opposites: namely, on the one hand, the absolute, all-constitutive subject of knowledge familiar to us from various forms of philosophical idealism (the "god" that is secularized as "imagination" in romanticism), and, on the other hand, what Kant called the "pathological" contingency of the object world and the empirical. Luhmann can help us to see how in such apparently outlandish and fanciful paradoxes Emerson precisely registers the epistemological fallout of the very modernity to which his "romanticism" is responding—not as a mystification or "imaginative" solution but as a kind of relentless anatomy. And here we may locate another advantage of Luhmann's work over Cavell's: that it links these philosophical and epistemological complexities to the historical conditions of their emergence. Only by taking this tack can we understand the underlying semantics and systematicity, rather than the incoherence or "fogginess," of the paradox at the core of Emerson's work: his constant movement between asserting, on the one hand, that "thought dissolves the material universe" and, on the other, that "if in the least particular one could derange the order of nature,—who would accept the gift of life?"[36]

Emerson insists, in other words, on the radical contingency and, at the same time, the radical authority of self-referential observation, whose positive existential valence gets figured in the "whim" of "Self-Reliance," while its more vexing effects are registered in the isolation and vertigo of the opening of "Experience" and, finally, in the paradoxical fatedness to freedom of *The Conduct of Life*. Such paradoxes are, from Luhmann's point of view, masked in the theological tradition that Emerson inherits and famously rejects early in his career as a minister. In fact, were we to follow Luhmann's suggestion, the closest thing we could find to Emerson's work in the theological tradition would be not Quakerism or Unitarianism but the line of medieval theology that works its way from Saint Augustine through John Scotus Eriugena to the fifteenth-century theologian Nicolaus Cusanus. "No traditional epistemology," Luhmann writes, "could dare to go this far—obviously because the position from which it would have had to deal with distinctness was occupied by theology."[37] But with the secularization of these questions in romanticism's philosophy of the subject—itself, Luhmann argues, a product of the unavoidable movement from hierarchical to functionally differentiated society under modernity, in which the church no longer has a centering role—they begin to become ever more unavoidable. "With the retreat of the religious world order," Luhmann writes, the "question of how the world can observe itself" becomes more pressing and vexing, and it is typically answered in romanticism and its forerunner, German idealist philosophy, by makeshift such terms as "Spirit," "Idea" and so on.[38] "Inspired by the idea of God as observer," Luhmann writes,

> Theology began to observe this observer, even though it was forced to concede that an observer who creates and sustains the world by virtue of his observation excludes nothing and hence cannot assume an observable form. By externalizing this paradox and by incorporating the notion of observing the unobservable into the idea of God, one sought to shield the conventional notion of the world as *universitas rerum* from infection by logical paradoxes.[39]

The problem with this "solution," of course—as Harro Muller among others has pointed out—is that in an increasingly "acentrically conceived society" (the society of modernity) "it is difficult to preserve the notion of an Archimedean point from which and towards which both world and society might be understood. . . . It is also prohibited from assuming a strictly privileged extramundane observer's perspective. Such a perspective would place collective singulars such as God, Spirit, History, Man, Nature, the subject, the individual or intersubjectivity at the center of a foundational discourse." But these foundational discourses— whether of an ontological, natural, or anthropological nature—"are predominantly a matter of self-attributions or self-simplifications that are functionally in need of explanation."[40] And this is where we need Luhmann.

We need, in other words (to use Luhmann's shorthand), to replace "what" questions with "how" questions.[41] Here the fundamental postulate of systems theory—its replacement of the familiar *ontological* dichotomies of humanism (culture/nature, mind/body, spirit/matter, reason/feeling, and so on) with the *functional* distinction system/ environment—is indispensable in allowing us to better understand how systems respond to modernity's central challenge of "functional differentiation" (what other critical vocabularies would call its "specialization" or, more moralistically or nostalgically, its "fragmentation"). As Muller summarizes it:

> Perspectives are multiplied within functionally differentiated modern society without one's being able to adopt any privileged central perspective or assign a hierarchically superior leading position to any one partial system. . . . No partial system may represent the whole and become active in a representative manner; no partial system may replace another as its functional equivalent. It is precisely functional differentiation, with its internal increase in control in individual partial systems, which increases "disorder" and risk.[42]

As we saw in the opening chapter, for Luhmann, both psychic and social systems respond to this complexity by means of autopoiesis and self-referential closure as a means of self-preservation. Such systems find themselves by definition in an environment that is always already more complex than they are, and all systems attempt to adapt to this complexity by filtering it in terms of their own, self-referential codes. The point of the system is to reproduce itself, but no system can deal with everything, or even many things, all at once. The legal system, for example, responds to changes in its environment in terms of—and only in terms of—the distinction legal/illegal. In litigation, decisions are not based—and it is a good thing too—on whether you are black or white, male or female, whether you went to school at Oxford or Cambridge, and so on.

Two subsidiary points need to be accented here. First, in responding to environmental complexity in terms of their own self-referential codes, subsystems build up their own internal complexity (one might think here of the various subspecialties of the legal system, say, or the specialization of disciplines in the education system discussed in chapter 4). In doing so, systems become ever more finely grained in their selectivity, and thus—in increasing the weblike density of their filters, as it were—they buy *time* in relation to overwhelming environmental complexity. As Luhmann puts it in *Social Systems,* "Systems lack the 'requisite variety' (Ashby's term) that would enable them to react to every state of the environment. . . . There is, in other words, no point-for-point correspondence between system and environment. . . . The system's inferiority in complexity [compared to that of the environment] must be counter-balanced by strategies of selection."[43] Emerson's way of putting this, in "Nominalist and Realist," is that "the world is full. As the ancient said, the world is *plenum* or solid; and if we saw all things that really surround us, we should be imprisoned and unable to move."[44] But if the self-reference of the system's code reduces the flow of environmental complexity into the system, it also increases the system's "irritability" and thus, in a real sense, its *dependence* on the environment.

Here—and this is crucial to understanding the "engine," if you like, of what Cavell calls Emersonian "transience," "onwardness," and "abandonment"—the term "complexity" should be understood not as an aggregation of substance (a big pile of lots of things), or even as an abstract set of *relations,* but more importantly as a set of *temporalized* relations that have the character of the Derridean or Deleuzean "event." Systems use self-reference not just to build up their own internal complexity but also to stabilize themselves in the temporal flow of events and render events meaningful for the system. As Luhmann explains, "We need a concept of meaning . . . as the simultaneous presentation . . . of actuality and possibility."[45] "The totality of the references presented by any meaningfully intended object offers more to hand than can in fact be actualized at any moment. Thus the form of meaning"—the co-presentation of the difference between the actual and possible—"through its referential structure, *forces* the next step, to *selection*."[46] But as we saw in chapter 1, that selection is only momentarily useful and deteriorates immediately under the pressure of the flow of time, which in turn necessitates *another* selection, and so on and so forth. "One could say," Luhmann writes, "that meaning equips an actual experience or action with redundant possibilities"—namely, what *was* selected (the actual) and what could have been (the possible)—and this is crucial for any system's ability to respond to environmental complexity by building up its own complexity via the form of meaning, through which the system uses time even as it is subjected to its pressure. As Luhmann writes in a key passage we focused on in the opening chapter: "The genesis and reproduction of meaning presupposes an infrastructure in reality that constantly changes its states. Meaning then extracts differences (which only as differences have meaning) from this substructure to enable a difference-oriented processing of information. On all meaning, therefore, are imposed a temporalized complexity and the compulsion to a constant shifting of actuality, without meaning itself vibrating in tune with that substructure" (63).

Read against this background, the rigor of moments such as this one in Emerson's "The Method of Nature" becomes, I believe, more apparent:

> The method of nature: who could ever analyze it? That rushing stream will not stop to be observed. We can never surprise nature in a corner; never find the end of a thread. . . . The wholeness we admire in the order of the world, is the result of infinite distribution. . . . Its permanence is a perpetual inchoation. Every natural fact is an emanation, and that from which it emanates is an emanation also, and from every emanation is a new emanation. If anything could stand still, it would be crushed and dissipated by the torrent it resisted, and if it were a mind, would be crazed, as insane persons are those who hold fast to one thought, and do not flow with the course of nature.[47]

Subordinating the problem of self-referential observation to the larger problem of complexity helps clarify why it is misguided at best to charge systems theory in general and the theory of autopoiesis in particular with asserting a kind of solipsistic relationship between the system and its environment. As we have seen throughout the first half of this book, what such a characterization misses is the seemingly paradoxical fact that the autopoietic closure of a system—whether social or psychic—is precisely what *connects* it to its environment. As Luhmann explains it, "The concept of a self-referentially closed system does not contradict the system's *openness to the environment*. Instead, in the self-referential mode of operation, closure is a form of broadening possible environmental contacts; closure increases, by constituting elements more capable of being determined, the complexity of the environment that is possible for the system."[48]

> Autopoiesis and complexity are conceptual coordinates. . . . Dependency and independence, in a simple causal sense, are therefore not invariant magnitudes in that more of one would imply less of the other. Rather, they vary according to a system's given level of complexity. In systems that are successful in evolutionary terms, more independence typically amounts to a greater dependency on the environment. . . . But all of this can happen only on the basis of the system's operative closure.[49]

Or as Luhmann will put it in one of his more Zen-like moments, "Only complexity can reduce complexity."[50]

All of this leads to a paradoxical situation that is central to Luhmann's work, and central (as we saw in the last chapter) to understanding his reworking of problems inherited from Hegel and from romanticism more generally—problems that bear directly on our reading of Emerson: What links the system to the world, what literally makes the world available to the system, is also what hides the world from the system, what makes it unavailable. Given our earlier discussion of the problem of "representing the unrepresentable," this will sound like the familiar *topos* of the romantic sublime but with this crucial difference: if all systems interface with their environments in terms of, and only in terms of, their own constitutive distinctions and self-referential codes, then the "environment" is not an ontological category but a functional one. That is to say, it is not an "outside" to the system that is given *as such* but is rather always the outside *of* a specific inside. Or as Luhmann deftly explains it, the environment is different for every system, because any system excludes only itself from its environment.[51] And "with this turn," Luhmann writes, "the distinction

between self-reference and hetero-reference is relocated within the observed observing system" or, to put it another way, "the distinction
between self- and hetero-reference is nothing other than the re-entry
of the distinction system/environment into the system itself."[52]

As we have seen in greater detail in earlier chapters, however,
this means that there is a paradoxical identity between the two sides of
the system's constitutive distinction, because the "reentered" distinction between both sides (system and environment) is itself a product
of only *one* side (the system). And—a crucial corollary—no system can
acknowledge this paradoxical identity of difference (which is also in
another sense simply the *contingency*) of its own constitutive distinction
and at the same time *use* that distinction to carry out its operations. It
must remain "blind" to the very paradox of the distinction that links it
to its environment. That does not mean that this "blind spot" cannot
be observed from the vantage of *another* observer, *another* system using
another code, but any *second-order* observation will itself be based on
its *own* blind spot—that is to say, it will have the same contingency and
the same formal character.

This is what Emerson is insisting on, I think, when he writes:

> Nature will not be Buddhist: she resents generalizing, and insults the
> philosopher in every moment with a million fresh particulars. It is all
> idle talking: as much as a man is whole, so is he also a part; and it were
> partial not to see it. What you say in your pompous distribution only
> distributes you into your class and section. You have not got rid of parts
> by denying them, but are the more partial. You are one thing, but na-
> ture is *one thing and the other thing,* in the same moment.[53]

Such a passage may be quite precisely unpacked, I think, against the
background of Luhmann's fruitful reworking of the Hegelian problematic that I have already discussed: a *difference* that inheres in the
contingency of self-referential distinction itself ("you are one thing")
or, in another sense, in the difference between first- and second-order
observation ("you have not got rid of parts by denying them, but are
the more partial"). And this is, of course, a *productive* difference; from
the vantage of the problem of overwhelming environmental complexity and a system's need to reduce it, it has no choice but to be.[54]

This is what Emerson is reaching for in "Nominalist and Realist,"

I think, when he writes that "excluded attributes burst in on us with the more brightness, that they have been excluded. 'Your turn now, my turn next,' is the rule of the game. The universality being hindered in its primary form, comes in the secondary form of *all sides:* the points come in succession to the meridian, and by the speed of rotation, a new whole is formed" (142). This might sound, at first blush, Hegelian, but the key difference—contra the invocation of dialectic by Gonnaud—is Emerson's strident insistence on the primacy and paradoxical contingency of the observer, an insistence that reaches its peak in *Essays: Second Series.* As Luhmann, in a passage I have had occasion to cite more than once, explains the relationship between observation and what Emerson calls the "horizon":

> The source of a distinction's guaranteeing reality lies in its own operative unity. It is, however, precisely as this unity that the distinction cannot be observed—except by means of another distinction which then assumes the function of a guarantor of reality. Another way of expressing this is to say the operation emerges simultaneously with the world which as a result remains cognitively unapproachable to the operation.
>
> The conclusion to be drawn from this is that the connection with the reality of the external world is established by the blind spot of the cognitive operation. Reality is what one does not perceive when one perceives it.[55]

The world is now conceived, "along the lines of a Husserlian metaphor, as an unreachable horizon that retreats further with each operation, without ever holding out the prospect of an outside."[56] This is the way Emerson's essay "Circles" begins: "The eye is the first circle; the horizon which it forms is the second; and throughout nature this primary figure is repeated *without end.* . . . Our life is an apprenticeship to the truth that around every circle another can be drawn; that there is no end in nature, but every end is a beginning."[57]

The question, then—and this is directly related to the problems raised by the *topos* of the romantic sublime—is, in Luhmann's words, "how to observe how the world observes itself, how a marked space emerges [via a constitutive distinction] from the unmarked space, how something becomes invisible when something else becomes visible." Any observation "renders the world invisible" in relation to its constitutive distinction, and that invisibility must itself remain invisible to the observation that employs *that* distinction—which in turn can only be disclosed by *another* observation that will also necessarily be doubly blind in the same way.[58] Here is Emerson again, from "Circles": "There is no outside, no inclosing wall, on circumference to us. The man finishes his story,—how good! how final! how it puts a new face on all things! He fills the sky. Lo! on the other side rises also a man and draws a circle around the circle we had just pronounced the outline of the sphere. Then already is our first speaker not man, but only a first speaker. His only redress is forthwith to draw a circle outside his antagonist. And so do men by themselves."[59] "In this twofold sense," as Luhmann puts it—what an observing distinction reveals and what it can be shown to hide—"the notion of a final unity—of an 'ultimate reality' that cannot assume a form because it has no other side—is displaced into the unobservable. . . . If the concept of the world is retained to indicate reality in its entirety, then it is that which—to a second-order observer—remains invisible in the movements of observation (his own and those of others)."[60]

We can return in this light to a rather different understanding of the significance of the Kantian settlement with skepticism, reframed in terms of the signal importance of the formal dynamics of observation. As Luhmann puts it succinctly, if we ask "what new insights the concept of observation (first- and second-order observation) has to offer," the answer is "it traces the problem of unity back to the ultimate form of paradox" (96). In a way, Luhmann writes:

> All this can be handled with the de-reification of the concept of the world introduced already by Kant. World is no longer a totality of things, a *universitas rerum*, but rather the final, and therewith unobservable, condition of possibility of observations, that is, of every sort of use of distinctions. To formulate this another way, the world must be invisibilized so that observations become possible. For every observation requires a "blind spot," or more precisely: it can only indicate one side of the distinction being used, employing it as a starting point for subsequent observations, but not the distinction itself as a unity and above all not the "unmarked space," precisely the world from which every distinction, as soon as it is marked as a distinction, must be delimited.[61]

Even more striking, perhaps, are the *consequences* of this fact, as they are described by Luhmann and recorded with rather bracing astringency in essays like Emerson's "Experience." Luhmann continues:

> This invisibilization of the nevertheless doubtlessly given and presupposed world had dramatic consequences for Kant, Fichte, and above all for the Romantics. Its leads to an overburdening of the individual with expectations regarding the production of meaning and therewith to the collapse of the communication weighed down with such expectations. The individual endowed with reflection now received the title "subject." But the higher and more complex the expectations that subjects direct toward themselves and their others, the greater is the probability of a failure of their communications. (517)

It is precisely this overburdening that haunts Emerson's essay "Experience," where he writes, "We must hold hard to this poverty, however scandalous, and by more vigorous self-recoveries, after the sallies of action, possess our axis more firmly. The life of truth is cold and so far mournful, but it is not the slave of tears, contritions, and perturbations." It is a truth, we are told, "that all the muses and love and religion hate," and they "will find a way to punish the chemist who publishes in the parlor the secrets of the laboratory," not the least of which is the quintessentially Emersonian announcement that "it is very unhappy, but too late to be helped, the discovery we have made that we exist."[62] Such is what Luhmann calls "the toxic quality" of second-order observation,[63] and it is on display not just in Emerson's middle and late phase (in *Essays: Second Series* and *The Conduct of Life*) but even in earlier works as well, such as "The American Scholar," where he writes, "We are lined with eyes; we see with our feet; the time is infected with Hamlet's unhappiness,—'Sicklied o'er with the pale cast of thought.' Is it so bad then? Sight is the last thing to be pitied. Would we be blind?"[64]

Here too we may locate the signal advantage of systems theory's ability to combine epistemological and historical frames in ways that are especially useful for sorting out the relationship between Emerson's thinking and his terminology—ways that open up a rather different understanding of the relationship between Emerson's thinking and writing from what we have already seen in Cavell. What I have been arguing is that a term such as "self-recovery" in the passage just cited should be understood not as recovery of a primordial, preexistent self but as recovery of the onwardness of the self's movement, through which and only in which—as we have already seen in Cavell's analysis of the proof of the self in "Self-Reliance"—the self actually exists at all. As Emerson puts it in "Circles," "The way of life is wonderful. It is by abandonment" (181). Or more flatly still, from "Experience," "Life is a series of surprises, and would not be worth taking or keeping if it were not" (206).

"Self-recovery," then, is paradoxically oriented not toward some originary state but toward *futurity*, toward not being but *becoming*. As Emerson writes in "Circles," "Valor consists in the power of self-recovery, so that a man cannot have his flank turned, cannot be outgeneraled, but put him where you will, he stands. *This can only be by preferring truth to his past apprehension of truth*" (177; italics mine). Paradoxically, as I have been arguing, the only way for the Emersonian self to "stand" is to *not* stand, to not stand still but to move in "abandonment" beyond the self of "apprehension" that one was only a second ago. The only way to "stand," then, is to "*under*-stand," to "stand down," if you like. And the achievement of the self is now to be seen not as an active willing but as a maximally (and paradoxically) active *passivity*. As Emerson puts it in "Experience": "All I know is reception" (212).

This same misdirection could be found in a whole host of terms in Emerson (Intuition, Reason, Law, Spirit, Being, just to name a few) that have encouraged readers for years to understand Emerson's work as a quaintly failed metaphysics. What systems theory enables us to do, however, is to map the residual versus emergent dimensions of Emerson's work (to use Raymond Williams's well-known terms) in ways not reducible to his terminology alone (as Eduardo Cadava has done quite subtly, I think, with Emerson's relationship to the discourse of race), for which we have to attend to the systematicity—and not just the lexicon—of his thought.[65] Once we do so, we find, as Harro Muller puts it, that "self-descriptions must themselves be temporalized. . . . Assumptions of substance or of metahistoric essences, metahistorical anthropologies, metahistorically grounded notions of experience, and so on are all forms of thought that are no longer reconcilable with functional differentiation. From Luhmann's perspective, this is all part of an *old-European* heritage that . . . can at best be correlated with the still existing stratificatory elements in modern society."[66] Which is simply to explain, in so many words, why "Experience"—even as it also uses the term "self-recovery"—is a far more original and forward-looking text than *Nature*.

Moreover, it confronts in a number of emotional and philosophical registers another consequence noted by Luhmann: that "the forcing of subjectivity as the single answer to the problem of world makes intersubjectivity difficult, indeed, if one is conceptually rigorous, actually impossible."[67] As I have suggested elsewhere, it is precisely on the basis of the disclosure of that impossibility that the possibility of democracy is founded—but only, as Cavell would put it, by being "unfounded" or left "foundering."[68] But rather than pursue that argument further here, I will simply end with the last lines of Emerson's essay "Nominalist and Realist," which enigmatically, beautifully, maddeningly gathers together some of the threads I have been tracing, only to throw them to the winds.

> Is it that every man believes every other to be an incurable partialist, and himself an universalist? I talked yesterday with a pair of philosophers: I endeavored to show my good men that I liked everything by turns, and nothing long; that I loved the centre but doated on the superficies; that I loved man, if men seemed to me mice and rats . . . that I was glad of men of every gift and nobility, but would not live in their arms. Could they but once understand, that I loved to know that they existed, and heartily wished them Godspeed, yet, out of my poverty of life and thought, had no word or welcome for them when they came to see me, and could well consent to their living in Oregon, for any claim I felt on them, it would be a great satisfaction.[69]

10 The Idea of Observation at Key West
Systems Theory, Poetry, and Form beyond Formalism

IN THIS CHAPTER, I will revisit on the terrain of literary art generally and poetry specifically some of the questions examined in my earlier discussion of contemporary architecture in light of recent work in systems theory. I also hope to show how my earlier attempts to use systems theory to rethink fundamental questions associated with romanticism can open up a space in which we may describe more precisely the beguiling formal questions that attend the work of romantic modernists such as Wallace Stevens. In extending this line of investigation regarding the theory of art, and more specifically the relations (or disrelations) between literature (and more specifically poetry) and other art forms such as architecture, music, and sculpture, I also hope to intervene in recent conversations driven by a resurgence of interest over the past decade in the question of form in literary and cultural studies. The fundamental contours and stakes of those recent conversations are brought out magisterially and with characteristic even-handedness by Marjorie Levinson in a *PMLA* essay on "the changing profession" titled "What Is New Formalism?" Levinson notes that it is difficult to provide a one-size-fits-all characterization of the concept of form in these recent conversations, whether one is for or against it—and it's no surprise, given the range and sheer heft of material that she surveys, most of it written since 2000.

She does distinguish between what she calls (following Susan Wolfson's introduction to the special issue of *Modern Language Quarterly* in 2000 on the New Formalism) "activist formalism" and "normative formalism." The first complains that "we no longer attend to the processes and structures of mediation through which particular discourses and whole classes of discourses (literary genres, for example, come to represent the real, in the same stroke helping establish that empirical domain *as* the real," over and against the tendency in recent forms of historicism to "treat artworks as 'bundles of historical and cultural content.'" In place of this "simpleminded mimesis," it wants "to restore to today's reductive reinscription of historical reading its original focus on form" of the sort found in the materialist critiques of Adorno, Marx, Althusser, Jameson, and Macherey). As for the second, it attempts to "bring back a sharp demarcation between history and art, discourse and literature, with form (regarded as the condition of aesthetic experience as traced to Kant—i.e., disinterested, autotelic, playful, pleasurable, consensus-generating, and therefore both individually liberating and conducive to affect social cohesion) the prerogative of art."[1]

This last assertion leads us in turn to the first of two important observations by Levinson: first, that for many of these critics, the concept of form "as productive rather than merely reflective" (as one critic cited by her puts it) serves an essentially humanist project of edification—it "takes on a broadly pedagogical, humanizing cast (reviving Schiller's model of aesthetic education)" (563). Second, as Levinson notes, it is curious that in this body of criticism (with only a couple of notable exceptions) we find "no efforts to retheorize art, culture, knowledge, value, or even—and this *is* a surprise—form. The form is either 'the' or 'a' source of pleasure, ethical education, and critical power is a view shared by all the new formalism essays," Levinson contends. "But despite the proliferation in these essays of synonyms for *form* (e.g., *genre, style, reading, literature, significant literature, the aesthetic, coherence, autonomy*), none of the essays puts redefinition front and center" (561).

It is precisely at the conjuncture identified by Levinson that Niklas Luhmann's work intervenes, because it does indeed put front and center a redefinition of form. Moreover, it moves the question of form out of the domain of the strictly literary (though it does attempt to take account of the specificity of literary discourse among the other art forms), and—crucially—it uncouples the question of form from the humanist project of moral edification and ethical education (associated by Levinson with the name of Schiller). It is thus, in this precise sense, posthumanist.

When Luhmann died, he left behind scattered notes on a project titled "Poetry and Social Theory," which were published in 2001 in the special issue of *Theory, Culture, and Society* devoted to his work.[2] Central to Luhmann's understanding of the specificity of poetry is his well-known articulation of the autopoietic closure and difference of psychic systems and social systems, consciousness and communication, which I have discussed in previous chapters. It is within the context of this difference that Luhmann understands the significance to poetry of characteristic themes and problems such as incommunicability, ineffability, silence, and so on. But he understands them specifically within a posthumanist context: that is to say, as expressions not of a psychological or emotional interiority or intentionality that reveals itself in language (even if only to gesture toward language's inadequacy in the face of the "ineffable") but as expressions of a set of differences—most importantly, the difference between communication and perception, which in poetry are "miraculously" made to coincide (as he puts it) when the material form of the signifier seems to duplicate the semantics of communication (in familiar devices such as rhyme, rhythm, and so on). Or we might say even more precisely (in light of W. K. Wimsatt's famous thesis about the differential relations of semantics and acoustics in rhymed English poetry in his classic essay "One Relation of Rhyme to Reason"): in which the material form of the signifier has a *systematic* relation to the semantic content of words, even if that relationship is (systematically, as Wimsatt suggested, in English rhyme) one of difference or contrast.[3]

But this is only part of the story, and what I want to insist on here is that in Luhmann's scattered writings on poetry, we need to separate and indeed disarticulate two main strands that tend to get confused: what we might call the perceptual or the phenomenological on the one hand (which has to do with the familiar prosodic aspects of poetry that I just mentioned) and on the other what we might call poetry's abstract, formal aspect. Take, for example, the following passage from *Art as a Social System:*

> The choice of words as a medium creates a compelling and unusually dense combination of self-reference and hetero-reference running through the entire text. Words carry and "signify" their ordinary meanings, and this is why they refer to something other, not just to themselves. At the same time, however, they also carry and "signify" a special textual meaning, within which they execute and propel the text's recursions. Text-art organizes itself by means of self-referential references that combine elements of sound, rhythm, and meaning. The

unity of self-reference and hetero-reference lies in the sensuous perceptibility of words.[4]

There are, it seems to me, two different claims here: one having to do
with the abstract, recursive dynamics of self-reference in relation to
the form of the artwork as such, and one having specifically to do with
the perceptual, material aspects of words used as a medium, typically
associated with traditional prosodic devices. I want to insist that these
two be kept rigorously separate, for to elide them is to obscure the
most profound and original aspect of Luhmann's work on art, which
is his mobilization of a specific concept of form to make sense of art's
special relationship (special, that is, vis-à-vis the other social systems)
to the paradoxical dynamics of self-reference and observation. What
I want to bring out here is how in Luhmann's analysis the perceptual
and the material are radically subordinated to the problem of form,
and to form's relationship to the paradoxical dynamics of observation. I would even argue more forcefully that the former is even, in
a fundamental sense, superfluous to what makes poetry art at all in
Luhmann's sense—and is superfluous in a way that helps us understand how, paradoxically, poetry that is *least* replete with prosodic features such as stanzaic regularity, rhyme, alliteration, and so on (I have
in mind here the work of a Wallace Stevens, say, or a Marianne Moore,
to name two) can in a sense be regarded, for that very reason, as *most*
poetic in the specific sense developed by Luhmann.

I am going to focus here, however briefly, on the Stevens/
Luhmann pairing, because both have been associated so insistently—
and have often associated themselves—with the core problems of romanticism that make their way from Kant and Hegel through Coleridge
and British romanticism, then detour (importantly for Stevens, if we
believe Harold Bloom) via Emerson in the United States, to more recent
inheritors such as the phenomenology of Husserl.[5] In a classic essay
from about twenty years ago, Albert Gelpi used the Stevens/William
Carlos Williams relationship to tease out the contours of the romantic problematic inherited by Stevens. What Gelpi called the "romantic
modernism" of Stevens and Williams aimed to restore "the primacy
of the imagination" in poetry (versus the historically and anthropologically oriented antiromantic modernism of Pound and Eliot); and it

aimed to do so without falling into the metaphysical conundrums that plagued romanticism, round one. This consisted chiefly in what Gelpi calls the "unstable" "Romantic synthesis" of subject (or imagination) and object (or world), in which "the individual became the inspired locus for an intuitive perception of the spiritual forms and energies that invested the otherwise fragmented phenomenal world with an exalted coherence."[6] Stevens and Williams, Gelpi writes, "considered the chief challenge to the Modernist poet—one of life-or-death urgency—to be the redefinition of the function of the imagination, liberating it from its shaky epistemological premises" (5). But what this ends up meaning—their solution, if you like—is that "the twentieth-century poet became less the recipient than the agent of perception"; or as Williams put it, attempting to finesse the problem further, the poem rejects "plagiarism after nature" and constructs a reality not opposed to nature but "apposed to it." In Gelpi's words, "in its apposition to nature the verbal construct serves to mediate the epistemological schism between subject and object" (6). Really? How so?

What I would like to suggest is that such solutions are simply renamings of the fundamental problem that concerns Gelpi—and concerned Stevens. And so, in Gelpi's essay, we find simply a series of such restatements; for Stevens, for example, "sensation is not just a passively received impression but an actively and accurately achieved response" (7). But what can "accurately" mean here, given everything we've just said? And where we end up, then, is pretty much where we began:

> While Modernism constitutes on one level an overt and programmatic rejection of Romanticism, it constitutes on another level an extension of the epistemological issues that the decadence of Romanticism precipitated. In terms of the subject-object split, Imagism [and for Gelpi, Williams] represents the attempt to render the objects of experience, Symbolism [and for Gelpi, Stevens] the attempt to render subjective psychological and affective states. . . . Faced with the polarity between subject and object, we must try to accommodate both terms; and under that pressure the terms tend to slip in and out of one another. (12)

Gelpi's diagnosis of the problem is also a symptom of the need to find a more precise way of describing it—and describing how what is apparently most paradoxical and self-defeating about it is actually what is most specific and *productive* about it. With the help of systems theory, I think that the core problem here can be stated precisely: it is the paradoxical fact that both self-reference and hetero-reference (or other-reference) are themselves both products of self-reference. "Where do we go from here?" and "why is this not a form of philosophical idealism?" are two questions that the rest of this chapter will attempt to address. In doing so, I hope to also suggest that the problem with understanding Stevens's "romantic modernism" has been more a problem with the criticism itself (his own included, by the way) than with the poetry. In fact, it seems to me that Stevens's poetry navigates the problems outlined by Gelpi with a rigor, subtlety, and keenness for which we have had no adequate critical vocabulary thus far.

What I want to suggest—and I can only gesture toward it here— is that Luhmann's work is especially valuable in helping us to tease out and, if you like, formalize the poetics of the mature Stevens, which for many readers take on an increasingly paradoxical cast and philosophical austerity as his career tends more and more to late poems such as "An Ordinary Evening in New Haven." Or to put this slightly otherwise: Stevens's own description of that poetic project in texts like *The Necessary Angel* and in doctrines (if we can call them that) such as "the supreme fiction" has seemed, for many readers, rather disappointing and insufficiently articulated alongside the rigor and precision of the poetry itself—a rigor that is not logical or conceptual, exactly, but is nevertheless what I would call a "systematic" confrontation with the problems I have already sketched under the rubric of romanticism. In particular, Stevens puts increasingly intense pressure, as few poets have, on the problem of observation: its paradoxical dynamics in relation to "reality" and "imagination," all of which (and this would be another, different kind of chapter) are traced by Luhmann to the fundamental structures of modernity itself (namely, as I have noted in earlier chapters, modernity as functional differentiation).

But to return to the question at hand, to understand why poetry that is least poetic in prosodic terms may be seen as *most* poetic in Luhmann's terms, we have to remember the point emphasized earlier in chapter 8: that in Luhmann's work on art, the difference between perception and communication is paramount. The meaning of a work of art cannot be reduced to its perceptual, material, or phenomenal aspect (this is, we will remember, the lesson for Luhmann of a Duchamp, a Cage, or—as I suggested earlier—Kawara's *Date Paintings*). Instead the work of art copresents the difference between perception and communication and "reenters" that difference on the side of its *own* communication, its own meaning.

To understand how this happens, we need to recall not just that perception (and beyond that, consciousness) and communication operate in mutually exclusive, operationally closed, autopoietic systems (though they are structurally coupled through media such as language); we also need to remember that the relationship between them is asymmetrical.[7] The mind is its own operationally closed (biological) system, but because it is also a necessary medium for communication, "we can say that the mind has the privileged position of being able to disturb, stimulate, and irritate communication" (379). The mind (the psychic system), in other words, constantly produces "noise" (in systems theory parlance) for the communication system (the social system), and the challenge for communication is thus how to secure the (necessary) participation of psychic systems while at the same time ensuring its own continuation through the autopoiesis of its own structures (and not those of the psychic system).[8]

The irreducibility and asymmetry of perception to communication are crucial for several reasons. First, perception and communication operate at different speeds—and this is something art puts to good use. The faster speed of perception and neuronal processing makes it appear that perception stabilizes and makes immediate, while communication, which operates with a sequential selective process, differs and defers.[9] Luhmann observes that "perception (in contrast to thought and communication) can decide *quickly,* whereas art aims to *retard* perception and render it *reflexive*—lingering upon the object in visual art (in striking contrast to everyday perception) and slowing down reading in literature, particularly lyric poetry."[10] In the work of art, this difference between perception and communication is then reentered on the side of the artwork's communication (142)—a communication that "accomplishes this goal or fails to do so by facing the usual, and perhaps even increased, risks involved in all communication. Art communicates by *using perceptions contrary to their primary purpose*" (22). As a reentered element in art's communication, then, perception serves the following role: "What strikes us in an art form—as, in a different way, does the conspicuous character of acoustic and optic signals—engenders a fascination that turns into information by changing the state of the [observer's] system—as a 'difference that makes a difference'" (26).

In fact, as we have already noted, this difference is what allows art to have a special relationship to what is commonly invoked as the "ineffable" or the "incommunicable." (And it is also, as Luhmann shrewdly notes in an observation with some resonance for romanticism, "why the art system must, in principle, distinguish itself—indeed distance itself—from religion." Art achieves that task by its greater mobilization of, and dependence on, perception: hence its emphasis, versus religion, on "innovation" and the like [142]). As Luhmann puts it:

> The function of art would then consist in integrating what is in principle incommunicable—namely, perception—into the communication network of society. . . . The art system concedes to the perceiving consciousness its own unique adventure in observing artworks—and yet makes available as communication the formal selection that triggered the adventure. (141)

With regard to poetry specifically, "the reader might assume that all of this holds exclusively for the so-called visual arts. On the contrary, it holds—much more dramatically because less evidently—for the verbal arts as well, including lyric poetry" (25). It is crucial to understand that, paradoxically, it is all the more true (because more counterintuitive) that for art made of words, "we must focus on types of nonverbal communication that realize the same autopoietic structure as verbal communication . . . but are not bound by the specific features of language and thus extend the realm of communication beyond what can be put into words" (18). Or as Luhmann puts it succinctly: "Art functions as communication although—or precisely because—it cannot be adequately rendered through words (let alone through concepts)" (19); it "permits a circumvention of language" (22).

In poetry, then, "words carry and 'signify' their ordinary meanings. . . . At the same time, they also carry and 'signify' a special textual meaning, within which they execute and propel the text's recursions. Text-art organizes itself by means of self-referential references that combine elements of sound, rhythm, and meaning" (26). But poetry "is not just rhymed prose," he continues:

> If one reads poetry as a sequence of propositions about the world and considers the poetic only as beautification, adornment, or decoration, one does not observe it as a work of art. . . . Only at the level where symbols, sounds, meanings, and rhythms conspire—a level that is difficult to "read"—do poems *refer to themselves* in the process of creating forms. They generate contextual dependencies, ironic references, and paradoxes, all of which refer back to the text that produces these effects. (125; italics mine)

To put it succinctly, the poem begins with a radically contingent distinction and then gradually builds up, through recursive self-reference, its own unique, nonparaphrasable character—its internal necessity, if you like. As Luhmann characterizes it:

> The artwork closes itself off by reusing what is already determined in the work as the other side of further distinctions. The result is a unique, circular accumulation of meaning, which often escapes one's first view (or is grasped only "intuitively"). . . . This creates an overwhelming impression of necessity—the work is what it is, even though it is made, individual, and contingent, rather than necessary in an ontological sense. The work of art, one might say, manages to overcome its own contingency. (120)

But here (and this is my main point), the recursive self-reference of form—and not the materiality of language as medium, the perceptual material per se—is key. And since lyric poetry "communicates not through the propositional content of its utterances, but . . . by virtue of the ornamental structure of mutually limiting references that appear in the form of words" now used as a medium (25), "lyric poetry unites the work of art with its own self-description" (26). The poem aims for a "unity of the description and the described" that is absolutely nonparaphrasable and nongeneric (123). Yet, amazingly enough, it is at the same time absolutely exemplary insofar as it achieves this highly contingent uniqueness. As Luhmann puts it, "in working together, form and medium generate what characterizes successful artworks, namely, *improbable evidence*" (119).

Here we might be tempted to use familiar formulas from the

literature of romanticism such as "unity in multeity," but as Luhmann points out, "It should be clear by now that this analysis precludes comprehending an artwork in terms of the relations between a whole and its parts. Dividing a work and judging the relationship between parts *misses its internal nexus,*" a nexus that is about the recursive and paradoxical self-reference of form that is not limited to the sensuous aspect of words (120; italics mine). "If one wants to isolate parts," he continues, "then one discovers that their contribution to the work consists in what they are *not,* what they make available for further elaboration" (120). This amounts, in a way, to a deconstruction of Coleridge's distinction between "fancy" and "imagination"—in which the workings of fancy (Luhmann's slow, linear processes of "communication") are focused on the aggregative, combinatory buildup of resemblances and variations in a concept or trope in a "mechanic and logical" fashion (as Coleridge put it), while consciousness and imagination are preoccupied with an "intuitive" grasp of the work's form of recursive self-reference on the most abstract level, the larger "organic" or "unifying" power (to use Coleridge's terms) that these "fanciful" combinations serve.

It also helps to clarify the relationship between a systems theoretical analysis of art and the discourse of the romantic sublime, because in this way—as I have already suggested in the discussions of both Emerson's philosophy and contemporary architecture—the problems that the discourse of the sublime attempts to address can be assimilated to the more formally rigorous schema of the difference between first- and second-order observation in systems theory. First-order observations, we recall, use distinctions "as a schema but do not yet create a contingency for the observer himself," as Luhmann puts it. "The distinction is postulated but not designated in the designation"; it thus "does not act in a way that would make it apparent that it could be otherwise."[11] Second-order observations, on the other hand, "provide grounds for including contingency in meaning and perhaps reflecting upon it conceptually," because they are observations *of observations;* they take into account the codes and distinctions used by first-order observers, including what those distinctions leave out or occlude—their "latencies." Or as Luhmann puts it, "Everything becomes contingent whenever *what* is observed depends on *who* is being observed" (48).

Most of all—and here the line of descent from German romanti-

cism through Emerson and on to both Luhmann and Stevens is especially clear—second-order observations take account of the fact that
the two sides of a distinction, which appear in first-order observation
as *opposites,* are in fact, when seen by second-order observation, dependent on a deeper *unity* (what in Hegelian parlance would be called
"the identity of identity and nonidentity"). As I have emphasized in
earlier chapters, it is that paradoxical identity-of-difference to which
the first-order system must remain blind if it is to use that code to
carry out its own operations and observations. But the same is true
for any second-order observations as well. "Observation of the second
order," Luhmann writes, "retains throughout the operative characteristics of all observation. . . . The concept of observation remains invariant for the first and second orders and requires no other language
(metalanguage)" (49).

Thus—and this is the key point for rewriting the problematics
of the romantic sublime—for Luhmann *any* observation "renders the
world invisible" in relation to its constitutive, self-referential distinction in the sense that the very thing that makes the world cognitively
or communicationally available is also the very thing that occludes it
and renders it invisible by its selectivity; and that invisibility must itself remain invisible to the observation that employs that distinction—
which in turn can only be disclosed by *another* observation that will
also necessarily be doubly blind in the same way.[12] "In this twofold
sense," Luhmann writes, "the notion of a final unity—of an 'ultimate
reality' that cannot assume a form because it has no other side—is displaced into the unobservable. . . . If the concept of the world is retained
to indicate reality in its entirety, then it is that which—to a second-
order observer—remains invisible in the movements of observation
(his own and those of others)" (91). So on the one hand, Luhmann
explains, "a work of art must distinguish itself externally from other
objects and events, or it will lose itself in the world"; it "closes itself off
by limiting further possibilities with each of its formal decisions." On
the other hand, "whatever distinction is used at any given time cannot
be indicated as a unity—this condition reproduces itself with every distinction. It merely displaces the blind spot" of observation (29).

As Luhmann summarizes it in a key formulation, "With this
mediation we arrive at a world extant in the difference between the

sameness and otherness of observations (of the first and second order). As so often elsewhere, it is also true here: reducing complexity [by deploying observations] is the means to generate complexity."[13] And this means—as I emphasized earlier in my discussion of Diller + Scofidio's *Blur*—not only that "art can no longer be understood as an imitation of something that presumably exists along with and outside of art" but, more importantly for our purposes, that "to the extent that imitation is still possible, it now imitates the world's invisibility, a nature that can no longer be apprehended as a whole."[14] "The paradox unique to art, which art creates and resolves," Luhmann writes, "resides in the observability of the unobservable" (149). And it is here that *form* finds its function. It is important to note, however, that

> the word *formal* here does not refer to the distinction, which at first guided modern art, between form and matter or form and content, but to the characteristics of an indicating operation that observes, as if from the corner of its eye, what happens on the other side of form. In this way, the work of art points the observer toward an observation of form. . . . It consists in *demonstrating the compelling forces of order in the realm of the possible.* (148)

In this way, form stages the question of "whether an observer can observe at all except with reference to an order" (148), but it also stages the contingency of that order—that is to say, the production of the unobservable (the "blind spot" of observation, the "outside" of the artwork) that unavoidably accompanies such observations (149).

> The function of art is to make the world appear within the world—with an eye toward the ambivalent situation that every time something is made available for observation something else withdraws, that, in other words, the activity of distinguishing and indicating that goes on in the world conceals the world. . . . *Yet a work of art is capable of symbolizing the reentry of the world into the world because it appears—just like the world—incapable of emendation.* (149; italics mine)

The work of art, to put it succinctly, is radically contingent and, at the same time, constituted by internal necessity.

To return to the issue of poetry specifically, what this means for a poet like Wallace Stevens is that the *less* "poetic" Stevens is—the more we find an absence of the traditional prosodic devices (rhyme, alliteration, etc.) that foreground the difference between perception and communication—the *more* poetic he is in the specific sense of formally modeling the very dynamics of the observable-unobservable that Luhmann describes. (This example helps clarify too the difference between Luhmann's recursive self-reference of form and, say, Jakobson's notion of the "projection" of the principle of reduplication from the axis of selection to the axis of combination in poetic discourse.) To put this in an even better way, the paring away of conspicuous "poetic" features in Stevens's work can be seen as functioning in two different ways. First, it serves a communication in which the motivated refusal to indulge traditional prosodic devices is an important element of the poetry's meaning; it communicates its meaning by *not* being present, a calculated formal decision that signifies against its literary-historical background along the lines of Miles Davis's famous pronouncement that what is important is not the notes you play but the notes you *don't* play. Second, that evacuated perceptual substrate makes Stevens's poetry, paradoxically, *more* poetic by directing our attention (without distraction, as it were) to the fundamental formal function of poetry now understood in light of the formal dynamics of observation and invisibility just described. To think otherwise, as Jakobson's theory suggests—that is, to think that the perceptual substrate of an artwork is fundamental to its meaning (in Jakobson's case, the reduplicative features that the poetic function projects from the axis of selection to the axis of combination)—is to have no choice, it would seem, but to call a mediocre rhymed quatrain by Carl Sandburg better poetry than, say, Stevens's "Thirteen Ways of Looking at a Blackbird."

At least a few possibilities suggest themselves here. It would be interesting to think, for example, about the role of onomatopoeia in Stevens's work (most pronounced, as one critic has noted, in Stevens's earlier poetry)—not just the "Mumbled zay, and a-zay, a-zay" of "Ordinary Women" or the "Ohoyaho, / Ohoo / Celebrating the marriage / Of flesh and air" of "Life Is Motion" (both from *Harmonium*) but also their connections to Stevens's penchant for poking fun *and*, alternately, celebrating by means of acoustic repetition (the "Ho-ho" versus "bubbling of bassoons" of "The Man on the Dump").[15] More importantly, I would argue that the general trajectory of Stevens's work—what is often called the increasingly abstract, "philosophical" bent of his poetry—is actually best understood precisely in the terms made available by Luhmann. Stevens's poetics of increasingly rigorous refinement and arid abstraction moves steadily away from a dependence on the perceptual and the prosodic and force us to fix our attention on the fundamental—and fundamentally paradoxical—aspect of poetry, and of art generally, as Luhmann defines it: the crucial determinations between the question of form and the paradoxical relations of the visible and invisible, the observable and unobservable, which have typically been handled in literature and philosophy under the rubrics of the sublime, imagination versus fancy, and so on. For how else are we to account for, much less explain, Stevens's penchant for not just courting but *pressuring* paradox as few poets have, the Stevens whose fundamental mode is to repeatedly insist on *both* "things as they are" ("The Man with the Blue Guitar") *and* "what I saw / Or heard or felt came not but from myself" ("Tea at the Palaz of Hoon")?

But not just Stevens, one might add. I offer here, without further comment, the opening stanza of Laura Riding's remarkable poem "Opening of Eyes":

> Thought looking out on thought
> Makes one an eye.
> One is the mind self-blind,
> The other is thought gone
> To be seen from afar and not known.
> Thus is a universe very soon.[16]

Or the wonderfully realized and only slightly less beguiling "The World and I," here in its entirety:

> This is not exactly what I mean
> Any more than the sun is the sun.
> But how to mean more closely
> If the sun shines but approximately?
> What a world of awkwardness!
> What hostile implements of sense!
> Perhaps this is as close a meaning
> As perhaps becomes such knowing.
> Else I think the world and I
> Must live together as strangers and die—
> A sour love, each doubtful whether

Was ever a thing to love the other.
No, better for both to be nearly sure
Each of each—exactly where
Exactly I and exactly the world
Fail to meet by a moment, and a word. (187)

Those paradoxical dynamics of observation and self-reference are obviously on display as well in a whole host of Stevens poems, and they achieve a pitch and resonance not unlike Riding's at the end of "Esthétique du Mal," where Stevens recurs to the same figural and phenomenological *topos:*

One might have thought of sight, but who could think
Of what it sees, for all the ill it sees?
Speech found the ear, for all the evil sound,
But the dark italics it could not propound.
And out of what one sees and hears and out
Of what one feels, who could have thought to make
So many selves, so many sensuous worlds,
As if the air, the mid-day air, was swarming
With the metaphysical changes that occur,
Merely in living as and where we live.[17]

And it receives what one might call even more technical, topographical treatment in "The Idea of Order at Key West," which is careful to distinguish the observations of "the single artificer" addressed in the poem and the observations of those observations—and their significance—by the speaker and his strange companion, "pale" Ramon Fernandez. Stevens is characteristically assiduous when he writes:

It was her voice that made
The sky acutest at its vanishing.
She measured to the hour its solitude.
She was the single artificer of the world
In which she sang. And when she sang, the sea,
Whatever self it had, became the self
That was her song, for she was the maker. Then we,
As we *beheld* her striding there *alone,*
Knew that there never was a world *for her*
Except the one she sang and, singing, made. (129–30, italics mine)

This does not mean that we are dealing here with "concepts," for as we have already seen, art consists precisely in presenting what cannot be conceptualized but can, nevertheless, be communicated—and communicated, in the case of this poem, by the poem's staging and restaging of, and increasingly recursive responses to, the central question of the poem:

> Whose spirit is this? we said, because we knew
> It was the spirit that we sought and knew
> *That we should ask this often as she sang.* (129; italics mine)

But why not ask "this" just *once*? Because, apparently, it cannot be answered only once—that is, once and for all, a fact the poem recursively builds up through the increasing submission of its key terms (song, sea) to a relentlessly erosive, provisional phalanx of *and*s, *but*s, *if*s, and *yet*s. Or to put it in Luhmann's terms, the "song" of the "single artificer"— her observation that makes "the sky acutest at its vanishing"—discloses a "spirit" and not a substance: not the binaries of mind/nature, subject/ object, imagination/reality, and so on, among which we must choose as either philosophical idealists or realists, but rather a *form*, a *movement* of observation whose engine is *double*, and for that reason irreducible, with no resting place: the paradoxical difference-in-identity of observation's constitutive structure, *and* the difference between first- and second-order observations, a difference that, by definition, of course, takes *time*. Thus not "song" or "sea" but a third term, "spirit." And hence the only answer to the question "Whose spirit is this?" would not be— indeed *could not* be—either "song" or "sea" but might be, oddly enough, "Often."[18]

I put it in this odd way to clarify that we are not dealing here simply with problems of logic. Quite the contrary, for as Luhmann writes, "the problem [of the paradoxical self-reference of any observation] cannot be solved by logical maneuvering but one can only . . . hope to find a less sensitive spot where the problem can be temporarily tolerated," which leads in turn to the realization that "paradoxes can be undertaken more or less skillfully, can have a more or less unblocking effect, can be more or less fruitful."[19] As in art, for example. Indeed, this is perhaps what Stevens meant when he suggested—rather enigmatically, after all—that the function of the poet "is to help people to live their lives." Such is the spirit, I think, of Stevens's suggestion about the poet's function earlier in that same passage that "certainly it is not to lead people out of the confusion in which they find themselves. Nor is it, I think, to comfort them while they follow their readers to and fro."[20]

But it is also not just a problem of logic in a second and more important and compelling sense—a sense that once again depends on our paying attention to the *disarticulation* of consciousness and communication that we have insisted on in these pages. For as Luhmann observes in his "Notes," "The observation of a paradox has a peculiar kind of temporal structure: it makes the present shrink to a point to which no reality any longer corresponds." And yet, because "communication requires more time than experience does"—it is sequential and slower than the movement of consciousness—this very fact "requires a certain period of actuality. Within this time period," he continues, "the paradox can be made to oscillate. . . . The one doing the uttering foresees that at the moment understanding the utterance is already incorrect, and this is exactly what he wants to provoke. . . . He wants to convey the fact that he does not mean what he says, although he does not say anything which he does not mean" (26).

Here we are close to the core dynamic of Stevens's poetry—especially his most resolutely and opaquely "philosophical" poetry—and its signal effect of confirming the otherness and difference of "external" reality precisely by insisting on its inseparability from the mind and imagination. Or to put it in terms of "The Poems of Our Climate," which has been central in these sorts of discussions for a host of critics, "the evilly compounded, vital I"—in Luhmann's terms, the fact that observation is multiple, contingent, and paradoxical in its self-reference—cannot be overcome, and it's a good thing too. It both creates and partakes of a world that is "imperfect," that "lies in flawed words and stubborn sounds," because the world is thus riven by paradoxical difference (the self-reference of any observation *and* the difference between first- and second-order observers) that can never add up to the "simplified" "world of white and snowy scents," of "clear water in a brilliant bowl."[21] Why is the unavailability of the world "as such and in its being" in fact crucial to the ongoing *maintenance* of the world? Because, as Luhmann explains, the phenomenon of paradoxical

self-reference—and the experience of it as an actuality in the disjunc-
tion between consciousness and communication, the experience of
something that, in a way, is impossible and yet "oscillates" before us—
"reveals that the inference from nondescribability to nonexistence is
not logically tenable."[22] And this question opens, in turn, on to another
that I cannot pursue adequately in this book (though it is surely already
on the table in chapter 3): the relations, and disrelations, of philosophy
and literature in the services of that broader thing called "knowledge."
Or as Stevens puts it in "Metaphors of a Magnifico":

> Twenty men crossing a bridge,
> Into a village,
> Are twenty men crossing twenty bridges,
> Into twenty villages,
> Or one man
> Crossing a single bridge into a village.
>
> This is old song
> That will not declare itself.
>
> Twenty men crossing a bridge,
> Into a village,
> Are
> Twenty men crossing a bridge
> Into a village.
>
> That will not declare itself
> Yet is certain as meaning . . . (*Poems,* 19)

A pure paradox, an utter tautology. And yet somehow true. Or, perhaps
we should say, *real.*

11 The Digital, the Analog, and the Spectral
Echographies from *My Life in the Bush of Ghosts*

WHEN BRIAN ENO AND DAVID BYRNE'S RECORD *My Life in the Bush of Ghosts* was rereleased on its twenty-fifth anniversary in 2006, it occasioned much reflection on a piece of music that many listeners felt was far ahead of its time—and many felt, on rerelease, had never gotten its just critical desserts. The record wasn't neglected, by any means, but as Byrne points out in the liner notes for the rerelease, it took some time for legal rights for many of the vocal tracks on the record to clear, and in that interim the third record of the Talking Heads, *Remain in Light* (produced by Eno), was released, which relied on (and thus "scooped," if you will) much of the polyrhythmic, electronic, funk-inflected synthesis that Byrne and Eno forged in the making of the earlier record. Still, what *Ghosts* has that *Remain in Light* doesn't are the "found" recordings that became the vocal tracks. It is one thing to hear the angular, clenched, square, white-guy voice of David Byrne singing "Houses in Motion" on *Remain in Light;* it is quite another to hear in "The Jezebel Spirit" on *My Life in the Bush of Ghosts* the crackling, late-night AM radio voice of an "unidentified exorcist" recorded in New York on a boom box asking an audibly hyperventilating young woman, "Do you hear voices?" over a pulsating rhythm track straight out of the Meters, or to hear the Lebanese mountain singer Dunya Yusin embodying "The Human Voice of Islam" (the source title for her tracks) as that voice, instrument—whatever this sound is—wends its way over a deep groove that recalls Sly Stone or Isaac Hayes.

This element made the record not just cool and fresh but riveting and uncanny. With its vocal elements drawn from what felt like a storehouse of anthropological field recordings—an approach that seemed to render equally strange and foreign (in an ethnographic sense) the contemporary talk radio host, the Lebanese mountain singer of ancient religious hymns, and the evangelical black preacher Paul Morton from

New Orleans (just to name a few)—the record seemed to come from everywhere and nowhere. And with this polyglot glossolalia anchored to a musical fusion of electronica, funk, and Afro-futurism, the record seemed to issue simultaneously from both the past and the future, communicating the portents of ancient and wrathful gods and demons while at the same time constituting a kind of synth-driven laboratory for the music of the future, or what one critic at the time called "avant-funk." A record from a "Fourth World," to borrow Jon Hassell's term, from everywhere and nowhere, past and future.[1] In a word: spectral.

On another level, the uncanniness of the *Bush of Ghosts* project may be understood as a kind of "echography" (to use the phrase of Bernard Stiegler and Jacques Derrida from their conversations collected as *Echographies of Television*) of an electronic medium whose apotheosis (so the story goes) is the digitalization-of-all-media discussed (and sometimes debunked) in texts such as Lev Manovich's *The Language of New Media*.[2] To put it far too telegraphically, my suggestion here will be that the Byrne/Eno record proleptically evokes what will become the seething, hiving "bush" of digital media and then populates it, haunts it, with analog ghosts. Moreover, that echography takes the form of a strategic resistance to a generic, disembodied, abstract "rendering" (and I mean that in a technical sense, as we'll see) of both the voice and the image under digital media whose maximal expression might well be viewed, as Donna Haraway long ago pointed out, as the U.S. military operations theory C³I—command-control-communication-intelligence—and its recent manifestation, for example, in the video images, now widely circulated on the Internet, of various "smart" weapon systems used by the United States in both Gulf Wars.[3] It is worth noting in this connection that the original LP was conceived and recorded on the heels of the year 1979, a year of ominous geopolitical upheaval that included the Iranian hostage crisis and the Soviet invasion of Afghanistan (the connections between the U.S. support of the Mujahideen resistance to the Soviets in Afghanistan and the rise of al-Qaeda are common knowledge at this point); and the anniversary rerelease took place, of course, at the height of the second Gulf War and the occupation of Iraq. In these multiple contexts, the original LP's ample use of vocal materials from Islam and, more pointedly still, the expurgation of the track "Qu'ran" from all but the initial vinyl and CD releases[4] makes the record all the more uncanny—a circumstance made even spookier by the fact that the omission of "Qu'ran" goes unremarked in both the Byrne/Eno and David Toop liner notes accompanying the rerelease. *My Life in the Bush of Ghosts* is itself, you might say, haunted, spooked.[5]

But what it is haunted by, I will argue, is not the "authenticity" of fundamentalism (both inside and outside the United States) that has emerged, in recent discussions, as the radically unassimilable other of modernity and its maximal expression in U.S. globalization (of which the speedy dissemination of digital media to all corners of the globe would be perhaps the most obvious manifestation)[6]—a reading that the manifestly "anthropological," and in some cases explicitly evangelical, nature of the vocal materials on the record more than invites. Indeed, as Simon Reynolds points out, Byrne and Eno were attracted in the vocal materials to "a fervor that felt weirdly alluring against the bland backdrop of anomie and drift that was [Jimmy] Carter's America"; and hence the project "began to coalesce around a central idea, the contrast between the spiritual void of faithless liberalism and the rival (yet weirdly similar) fundamentalisms of East and West."[7] Rather, the line of argument I'd like to pursue runs at a tangent to such a reading and would find, for example, the omission of "Qu'ran"—and the deafening silence around that omission—gesturing toward a kind of radical outside to the bush of digital media from which the record itself seems born as a bona fide product of elaborately produced, state-of-the-art Western (post)modernity: the outside of the analog, that which cannot be expunged by the schemata of the digital. In that light, we might emphasize rather the geo- of the term "geopolitical" to connote a different but related form of political resistance, a site of the antimodern, or more precisely the *amodern*—that is to say, a radical form of exteriority and materiality that constitutes what Derrida calls the *"noncontemporaneity with itself of the living present."*[8]

In these terms, the spectrality of the ghosts here on display (to use Derrida's formulation from *Specters of Marx*) might well be understood as the exteriority and embodiment—what Derrida calls the *"living-on [sur-vie]"*[9]—that resists forms of digital rendering: a rendering that might in turn be linked to the omission of "Qu'ran" insofar, as critics such as Rita Raley have argued, as digitalization is itself indissociable from the globalization of capitalism, and in particular capitalism's tightening of the relationship between information and commodification.[10]

Equally important is the logic of rendering in not just economic but *biopolitical* forms of organization. As Nicole Shukin has argued, "rendering" not only is an expression of what Foucault famously calls "biopower" but also has its roots in the process of rendering animal flesh in the disassembly lines of the Chicago stockyards of the early twentieth century—a process viewed by over a million people during the World's Columbian Exposition of 1893. It also had a profound influence on Henry Ford and thus on the first automobile assembly line processes in the United States (all of which, Shukin reminds us, were contemporary with Eadweard Muybridge's experiments with animal images in his Zoopraxiscope in the 1890s). This fundamental discretization and reorganization of the "assemblage" of knowledges and perceptions in and around the problem of bodies, movement, and time is, Shukin argues, a prolepsis of the "cinematic"; as she puts it, "in the vertical abattoir can be discerned not only the logistical prototype of cars' and films' material production (assembly, suture), but also the mimetic blueprint for a new order of aesthetic experience."[11] But to read the significance of *My Life in the Bush of Ghosts* as *only* an expression of those economic, social, and biopolitical forces would be to engage in another sort of fundamentalism: a fundamentalism calculated to flee precisely those sorts of ghosts that Derrida's work will help us identify and, as it were, reanimate.

Digital media, as Bernard Stiegler puts it, depend above all on a "systematic discretization" and "grammaticalization" of content—itself part of the larger regime of what Derrida calls "calculation," whose philosophical and ethical resonances I have explored in some detail in earlier chapters.[12] Unlike the analog photographic image, for example (and here we will return to some of the questions of visual media that occupied us in chapter 6), in the digital image one has, as Stiegler puts it, "access to the *diacritical* manipulation of the light and of all of the elements *which are differentiated therein*" with "surgical precision" (154). This eventuates in the compilation of lexicons of animated objects in "the movement industries," in the ability of digital technologies to "recognize *automatically* different camera movements, identical objects present in a film, recurrent characters"—all of which was first developed, as he points out, for the colorization of black-and-white films. To this must be added "synthetic libraries of objects and movements, expressions, sounds," of "'morphing,' cloning, embedding, and capture," which are crucial to the computer-generated-image industry and the process of digital rendering (157). For example, as Mary Flanagan points out, research teams working on earlier forms of the digitalization of movement used "custom software to choose areas such as the mouth, eyes, and face of simple 2D photographs and . . . algorithms to mathematically control the 2D image." In this way, one can "create inverse kinematic animation to simulate human movement without parsing stream after stream of real user body data," but the trade-off is that a "former whole" is "segmented, proportioned, and divided."[13]

More recently, such processes have given way to extremely sophisticated kinds of modeling that go far beyond even motion-capture technologies that render movement by means of mathematically plotting data from sensors or markers placed on a moving body. One particularly striking example of this new form of rendering, reported in the *New York Times* on October 15, 2006, is the work being done by Image Metrics Inc. in California, which uses software "to map an actor's performance onto any character, virtual or human, living or dead." While motion capture wires actors with small digital sensors, and a newer technique called Contour "tracks actors' facial and body movements by coating them with phosphorescent powder," Image Metrics "starts with a generic model of the human head and layers onto that a mathematical distillation of an individual's expressions." IM thus solves the main problem with motion capture and standard computer-generated imagery (CGI)—how to convincingly render the eyes, the inner part of the lips, and the tongue. The technique is remarkably convincing, so much so that IM's chairman declares, "I like to call it soul transference. The model has the actress's soul. It shows through."[14]

The *Times* reporter, upon observing a demonstration at Image Metrics, says that the computer-generated avatar appears to possess "something ineffable, something that seems to go beneath the skin," and calls the effect of watching actress and computer model side by side "more than a little bit creepy." But what is creepy here, I would suggest,

For the Emily Project, Image Metrics animated a photorealistic CG face of the actress Emily O'Brien and applied it to the real version of her body. Courtesy of Image Metrics, Ltd.

is the presumption of the image's transparency and exhaustibility, that there is nothing hidden to rendering—not even the soul. Or as Stiegler puts it, "the machine 'sees' planes, detects them automatically, mechanically. Because it neither believes nor knows anything, it isn't afraid of any defect, it isn't haunted by any ghosts."[15] It is the restoration of those ghosts that the Byrne/Eno project engages in, and I mean "project" here in the broadest sense: not just the record *My Life in the Bush of Ghosts* but also the visual art elements associated with it (album covers, etc.) and, beyond that, Brian Eno's own video works.

What is particularly interesting, however—and here we can begin to appreciate the full resonance of the line from *Hamlet* that Derrida seizes on: "The time is out of joint"—is that the Byrne/Eno project engages in that restoration or reanimation *before* the advent of the pervasive digitalization of media. In fact, as has been widely noted, *My Life in the Bush of Ghosts* engages in what would come to

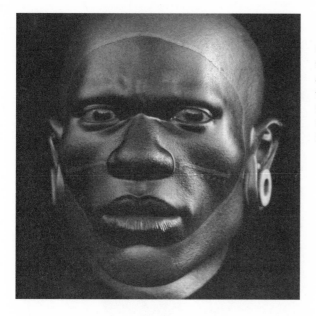

Samburu was the first attempt at photorealistic facial animation by Image Metrics. Courtesy of Image Metrics Ltd.

be known as "sampling" before sampling had really become a wide-spread practice, much less a codified term. As Byrne points out in his *Ghosts* liner notes:

> At that time there were no samplers, so the found vocals were often flown in (this consisted of two tape machines playing simultaneously, one containing the track and the other the vocal) and, if the Gods willed, there would be a serendipity and the vocal and the track would at least seem to feel like they belonged together and it would be a "take." It was all "played" and very seat of your pants—there was none of the incremental tweaking and time correcting that is possible with modern samplers and computers, throwing the vocals against the tracks was in our case almost a performance. Sometimes we'd record radio sermons after-hours on our cassette players that were built in to our late 70's boom boxes.

On the visual side of the project, his account of working through the alternate album covers is also noteworthy:

> Having tried a few different directions for LP cover art, we decided to incorporate the video monitor as a painting tool, as Brian and others were doing here and there. By pointing the camera at the monitor and

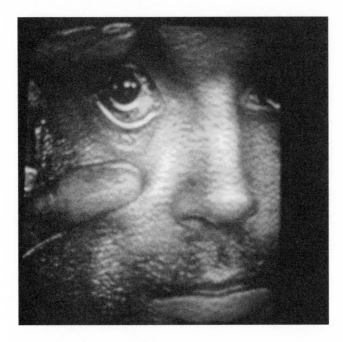

David Byrne,
Polaroid
photograph
from *My Life
in the Bush
of Ghosts*
sessions.

generating video feedback a few little cutout humanoid shapes pasted on the screen would be infinitely multiplied. And by fussing with the color setting on the backs of the TV sets one could saturate and skew the color quite a bit. I also took some pictures of just skewed vortexes and whorls of color, and then we did some images where we skewed the color on pictures that had been taken of ourselves and then took polaroids of the results. Somehow . . . these techniques also seemed analogous to what we were doing on the record.[16]

Indeed, they are analogous for reasons that Eno's descriptions of his own contemporaneous "video paintings" help to bring out. Eno started out working with a Panasonic industrial video camera that he bought from a roadie for the band Foreigner, who were working in an adjacent studio while Eno was producing the Talking Heads' third album, *Fear of Music*. As he recounts it, the camera had no automatic controls, and the manual controls, which were analog, had extremely wide ranges and tolerances. "You could do absolutely mad things with this camera," he recalls; "in fact it was very hard to do anything realistic with it." Moreover, shortly after he bought the camera, he made the mistake of leaving it on and pointing at the sky for four days, which completely fried the tube. But after that, he says, "it produced the most magical results" and "responded to light and colour in a way no other camera" did.[17]

Similarly, the discovery of his signature video format came about by serendipity. After he got the camera, he didn't have a tripod, so he laid it on its side on the window sill with the lens pointed out toward the Manhattan skyline, which meant he also had to turn the TV onto its side to read the image. The result, he recounts, was "an absolute breakthrough," because suddenly the screen looked not like television but like painting. And this was important for two reasons: first, "you lose the reference to theatre and cinema" associated with the television surface and format, and this is important because in the proscenium format you expect narrative, which entails, among other things, an entire formatting (indeed, "calculation," to use Derrida's term) of time and event. And second, as Eno realized years later when he attempted the same thing with digital TVs, the distortion on the television screen

Brian Eno, still from *Mistaken Memories of Medieval Manhattan*, 1980–81.

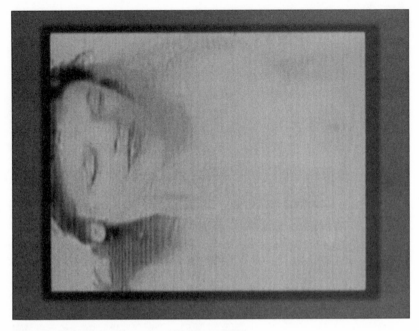

Brian Eno, still from *Thursday Afternoon*, 1984.

created by the horizontal scanlines enabled, with the screen turned on its side, a unique rainfall effect, turning mere analog static into valuable atmosphere, as it were.[18]

Eno's perceptive comments underscore an important fact: what undoes the calculated formatting of narrative and time is the interplay of form (and the cultural expectations elicited and reproduced by it, as in the proscenium or screen format), with what Gregory Bateson calls the "real magnitudes" of analog media; it depends for its effects on the specific, embodied positionality and movement of its components (for example, the proximity of the video camera to the television screen on which it creates feedback and distortion).[19] This means that analog is spooky or spectral for the regime of rendering because, among other things, it depends on the interplay of material forces and bodies, including even things like the weather; it is not wholly subsumable or predictable by programs and schemata, simply because the interplay of real magnitudes in space-time is fundamentally and even inexhaustibly contingent, creating a reservoir of complexity and contingency that is, in principle, bottomless.

That is not to say, however, that the analog is the opposite or the "real" other of the digital that it haunts. Rather, the structure of any "discretization," any diacritical system, is that of a trace in Derrida's sense—the iterability in and through which it can function, and *only* can function, as a medium and archive (hence my earlier emphasis on "interplay"). As Derrida puts it, in a passage I have invoked more than once in this study, "this pure difference, which constitutes the self-presence of the living present, introduces into self-presence from the beginning all the impurity putatively excluded from it." And what this means, in turn, is that "the trace is the intimate relation of the living present to its outside, the opening to exteriority in general."[20] Such is the "corrupting" and "contaminating" work—but also the haunting or spectral character, if you will—of iterability, which thus "entails the necessity of thinking *at once* both the rule and the event, concept and singularity," that "marks the essential and ideal limit of all pure idealization," but not as "the concept of nonideality," as ideality's pure other. In this sense, as Derrida puts, it "remains *heterogeneous*" to, rather than simply opposed to, the order of the ideal and the calculable—that is to say, to the realm of grammaticalization and discretization.[21] The analog, in short, does not exist as a presence, a substance, an "as such" or the "the" of "*the* body."

What this means, as I suggested in chapter 3, is that, in Derrida's words, "tele-technology" (and finally *tekhné* generally) "prohibits us more than ever . . . from opposing presence to its representation, 'real time' to 'deferred time,' effectivity to its simulacrum, the living to the non-living, in short, the living to the living-dead of its ghosts."[22] This unmappable difference impels us, in turn, "beyond present life . . . its empirical or ontological actuality: not toward death but toward a *living-on [sur-vie]*, namely, a trace, of which life and death would themselves be but traces . . . a survival whose possibility in advance comes to disjoin or dis-adjust the identity to itself of the living present."[23] The "living present," in other words, is haunted by the ghosts or specters of what will have been once any kind of archive, analog or digital— or the most fundamental archive of all, language itself (in the broadest sense of a dynamic semiosis that, as we saw in chapters 3 and 4, encompasses language proper and is in no way reducible to it)—is activated. It is "spectral," Derrida holds, "because we know that, once it has been taken, captured, this image will be reproducible in our absence, because we know this *already,* we are already haunted by this future, which brings our death. Our disappearance is already here."[24] "The logic of the specter," he continues, thus "regularly exceeds all the oppositions between visible and invisible, both phenomenal and nonphenomenal: a trace that marks the present with its absence in advance" (117). In short, the analog never manifests itself as a purity, a presence, or an ideality.

Far from being a kind fatalism or necrophilia, however, it is precisely in this fact that futurity itself resides—the fact that the words we record now, the images we make now, will be iterable in our absence, and indeed in the absence of any "empirical being" currently alive in "the living present." We are "spectralized by the shot," as Derrida puts it, "captured or possessed by spectrality in advance" (117), but such is the price of a futurity in which our media, our archives, are to be legible in our absence. And here the logic of spectrality shades over in Derrida's work into the question of the "messianic"—we die so that they, the future ones, may live—but it is, as he puts it, a "messianism without a messiah," since, after all, that future, and the ones who live it to whom we reach out, may not come to pass. It is not guaranteed, in other words, and that is precisely what makes it an ethical act, an act of faith.[25] As Derrida puts it, a messianism without guarantees, without a particular incarnation of the messianic, might elicit despair in some, but "without this latter despair and if one could *count* on what is coming, hope would be but the calculation of a program. . . . Some, and I do not exclude myself, will find this despairing 'messianism' has a curious taste, a taste of death."[26]

All of which provides a context for understanding the inadequacy—in a way, the backwardness—of the often observed and lamented fact about digital media, that, as Raley puts it, "tele-presence absorbs immediate presence and produces distance."[27] But Derrida's point—and it would lead us eventually to the observation that David Wills makes about "the almost Platonic lament" that sometimes characterizes Paul Virilio's discourse[28]—is that the "deadening" or "derealization" typically associated with digital technologies versus the ontological "umbilical cord" of analog is always already in play with *any* form of representation, any semiosis whether of the word or the image. Indeed, the human is itself a prosthetic being, who from day one is constituted *as* human by its coevolution with and coconstitution by external archival technologies of various kinds—including language itself as the first archive and prosthesis. As Wills puts it, we have here in the insights of Derrida and Stiegler

> an investment in forms of exterior memory that will continue all the way to the computer revolution of the end of the twentieth century. The upright hominid stance inscribes a definition of the human that is utterly determined by the idea of exteriorisation, the hand reaching outside the body to enter into a prosthetic relation with a tool, the mouth producing or adopting the prosthetic device that is language. As a result, the archive is born, the human species begins to develop a memory bank, and its relation to time begins to be catalogued by means of the traces of an artificial memory—the artefact, the narrative.[29]

In other words, there is no "immediate presence."

From this vantage, instead of what Wills calls "the Promethean melancholy" that the "deadening" or "distancing" effect of technology often elicits, we might view it instead as a source of creation—and not just from a Derridean point of view. Indeed, it is this distancing that makes possible—makes unavoidable—the recursivity and folding that is key to the emergence of the virtual, the movement that Derrida long ago dubbed the "temporization" and "spacing" endemic to the dynamics of the trace. In this sense, we would certainly agree—to lace together now the ideas of Derrida with those of Deleuze—with Brian Massumi's assertion that "nothing is more destructive for the thinking and imaging of the virtual than equating it with the digital."[30] Or more precisely, the economy of the iterative trace, which, as Derrida puts it, has "to be extended to the entire field of the living, *or rather to the life/ death relation,* beyond the anthropological limits of 'spoken' language,"[31] would itself instance what Massumi imagines as a kind of encompassing of the digital by "analogic process," in which "what is coded is recursivity. . . . The digital processing becomes self-modulating: the running of the code induces qualitative transformation in its own loopy operation." Against this background, we can more fully appreciate

Massumi's observation that "images of the virtual make the virtual appear not in their content or form, but in fleeting, in their sequencing or sampling. The appearance of the virtual is in the twists and folds of formed content, in the movement from one sample to another."[32] In a sense, then, the logic of the virtual is the logic of sampling itself, a sampling that is always *leaving* its source by the time it reaches us, always in the process of vanishing.

This is directly related, I think, to the power of the voice and of the vocal tracks on *My Life in the Bush of Ghosts*. As Stiegler notes, the "grammaticalization" of the visible by the digital image is analogous to

> the grammaticalizaton of speech . . . brought about by the generalization of alphabetic writing. Speech, too, would engender effects of continuity which are largely transformed, in their conditions of analysis and synthesis, with the appearance of writing. . . . We, the literate, *believe we know,* that there is, in all speech, a play of analyzable, diacritical combinatorial elements, which form a sign system, but the "spontaneous" attitude, especially in a society where there is not writing in the everyday sense, is to perceive this as a whole. As a continuity.[33]

In light of my discussion of the voice and Björk's vocal performance in chapter 7, this helps explain the cumulative effect of the vocal tracks on the record, in which the "desemanticizing" aspects of the voice (to use Michael Fried's term from chapter 6) combine with static and the low-fi resonance to override the vocal tracks' denotative dimension. And this is clearly one of the qualities to which Byrne and Eno were drawn in their selection of vocal material. As Eno put it succinctly at the time, "When people speak passionately, they speak in melodies."[34] Or as he elaborated the point in an interview at the beginning of 1980, reprinted in the liner notes to *Ghosts,* after he had become interested in listening to North African vocalists, "Mentally, I'd already given up on the idea of writing songs . . . one of the reasons being that, after hearing those Arabs, I'm less interested in the sound of my own voice. So I started thinking that the dialects are already music, and you could point to that fact by putting them in a musical context."

As we saw in some detail earlier in the discussion of *Dancer in the Dark,* the voice is always already becoming a musicality, instrumentality, and exteriority, a *not-ours,* that points toward the more general condition—and it is in the end for Derrida both an ethical and political condition—described by Roland Barthes in *A Lover's Discourse:* "It is characteristic of the voice to die. What constitutes the voice is what, within it, lacerates me by dint of having to die, as if it were once and never could be anything but a memory. This *phantom being* of the voice is what is dying out, it is that sonorous texture which disintegrates and disappears."[35] In short, what makes the voice the voice is not that it is presence (as the philosophical tradition tropes it according to Derrida) but that it is spectral. One might argue that the fact of the permanence of the recorded voice meets this objection, but as we have already seen, the recorded voice, precisely in its repeatability and iterability, only testifies all the more to the radical absence of "every empirically determinable subject" (to use Derrida's phrase), to the *becoming-ghost* of its origin in a bush of virtuality that its own ability to be sampled feeds and populates.

To put it another way, *My Life in the Bush of Ghosts* abstracts the vocal material from its original anthropological, religious, or political context, but only the better to underscore its strangeness: not an Orientalism or exoticism but a musicality and exteriority that exceeds intention, denotation, and sense, confronting the listener with his or her own nonknowledge in the face of what Byrne called these "transmissions from a desperate planet."[36] Hence the resistance of the voice in *My Life in the Bush of Ghosts* to the regime of rendering, its "grammaticalization" and "discretization," is not provided by any kind of essentialism or clinging to identity or origins. Rather, we would do well to recall Byrne's observation that at the time some people found this use of found vocal material "disturbing" and even "repulsive" because, he wrote, "they would prefer to see music as an 'expression' of emotion, . . . to believe in the artist as someone with something to 'say'"— a "queasiness connected with the idea of authenticity" that, as he notes, "as a contentious issue was resolved years later by electronic and hip-hop artists" and their methods of music sampling, production, and collaboration (19). And we might also remember, as Byrne and Eno point out in the rerelease liner notes, that at the beginning of the project they "fantasized about making a series of recordings based on an imaginary culture." Against the biographical background that Byrne grew up listening to Smithsonian Folkways field recordings and Eno had been immersed in similar work on the French Ocora label, the idea "was to make the record and try to pass it off anonymously as the genuine article." And even though, Byrne writes, they eventually "abandoned the imaginary-cultural-artifact idea. . . . I suspect this fantasy continued to guide us in a subconscious way."[37]

All of that does not mean, however, "nonserious." In fact, the political and ethical dimensions of that "subconscious fantasy" might be teased out by way of Richard Beardsworth's observation that it is the lack of identity and ideality of any "we," of any community whatsoever—the fact that, strictly speaking, "we" are irreducibly and inexhaustibly heterogeneous and different (even to ourselves, of course; what else does the concept of the unconscious name in another theoretical vocabulary?)—that "will have returned from the beginning to haunt any determination of the community." In this sense, the "we"—including the "we" of incipient globalization and its expression in digitalization that animates the Byrne/Eno project and its legion of voice—marks "the excess of time over 'human organization.'"[38] It marks the subjection of any "we" to the alterity and radical otherness of time. This lack of an essential identity is all the more apparent in contemporary society, in which "any country, any locality determines its understanding of time, place and community *in relation* to this process of 'global' spectralization" (146)—a process that itself depends directly on the "teletechnologies" and "digitalization of memory-support systems" (147) that make it possible for such disparate communities to come into (non)knowledge of each other at an ever-accelerating rate: a process in which, as Beardsworth puts it, "the real time of teletechnologies risks reducing the *différance* of time, or the aporia of time, to an experience of time that *forgets* time" (148). And here—to cast a backward glance for a moment—we should remember once more Eno's intense valuation of *slowness* and nonnarratological time in his video work.

As we saw at the end of chapter 3, what this means, as Derrida argues, is that in being "spectralized" by the medium—whose maximum thematization is the alienating and distancing effect attributed to the digital—the other comes "first, always first," as he is fond of putting it: "This is why I am an inheritor: the other comes *before* me."[39] The point here, in other words, is not just that the human is not reducible to its Pixarization via digital mass media, whose aural equivalent would be that everyone would speak in the same synthesized voice. The point is that what transcends that reduction and schematization is not a substance, content, presence, or place—not, in short, an ontological or anthropological authenticity—but rather a "beyond" (as in Byrne's "voices from another planet") that is at the same time radically intimate, a beyond that is not, in Derrida's terms, a place. In short, the *transcendent* must be rethought as the *virtual*.

Such a line of argument would eventually lead us to Derrida's sense of the messianic in relation to the spectral, but therefore to "a messianic without messianism," without content or assurance—in short, to the "living-on" of a futurity "to come," without guarantees.[40] But it also leads us back—or forward—to the odd temporal dislocation, the asynchronicity of the "living present" with itself, remarked on by Eno in his reflections on his video piece *Mistaken Memories of Medieval Manhattan*: "They evoke in me a sense of 'what could have been' and hence generate a nostalgia for a different future. It is as though I am extracting from this reality (the one the camera is pointed at) the seeds of another" (*Video Paintings* liner notes). And—need it be said—one can have "nostalgia for a different future" only if the present is not itself. Only (to borrow the quotation from *Hamlet* with which Derrida begins *Specters of Marx*) if "the time is out of joint."

Notes

Introduction

1. Michel Foucault, *The Order of Things: An Archaeology of the Human Sciences* (New York: Pantheon, 1971), 387.

2. That project was later republished as the more accessible *Observing Complexity: Systems Theory and Postmodernity,* ed. William Rasch and Cary Wolfe (Minneapolis: University of Minnesota Press, 2000).

3. See Neil Badmington, ed., *Posthumanism* (New York: Palgrave, 2000), and his essay "Theorizing Posthumanism," *Cultural Critique* 53 (Winter 2003): 11–27. See also Chris Hables Gray, *Cyborg Citizen: Politics in the Posthuman Age* (New York: Routledge, 2001); and Elaine L. Graham, *Representations of the Post/Human: Monsters, Aliens, and Others in Popular Culture* (Manchester: Manchester University Press, 2002).

4. Neil Badmington, *Alien Chic: Posthumanism and the Other Within* (New York: Routledge, 2004). Haraway's "A Cyborg Manifesto" formed part of her book *Simians, Cyborgs, and Women: The Reinvention of Nature* (New York: Routledge, 1991) but appeared first as "Manifesto for Cyborgs: Science, Technology, and Socialist Feminism in the 1980s," *Socialist Review* 80 (1985): 65–108.

5. Joel Garreau, *Radical Evolution: The Promise and Peril of Enhancing Our Minds, Our Bodies—and What It Means to Be Human* (New York: Random House, 2005), 231–32.

6. Nick Bostrom, "A History of Transhumanist Thought," *Journal of Evolution and Technology* 14, no. 1 (2005): 2.

7. Ibid., 3.

8. Michel Foucault, "What Is Enlightenment?" trans. Catherine Porter, in *The Foucault Reader,* ed. Paul Rabinow (New York: Pantheon, 1984), 43–44.

9. Étienne Balibar, "Racism and Nationalism," trans. Chris Turner, in *Race, Nation, Class: Ambiguous Identities,* by Étienne Balibar and Immanuel Wallerstein (London: Verso, 1991), 56.

10. N. Katherine Hayles, *How We Became Posthuman: Virtual Bodies in Cybernetics, Literature, and Informatics* (Chicago: University of Chicago Press, 1999), 287.

11. See, for example, Bruce Clarke, *Posthuman Metamorphosis: Narrative and Systems* (New York: Fordham University Press, 2008), 5.

12. See in particular Bernard Stiegler, *Technics and Time, 1: The Fault of Epimetheus*, trans. Richard Beardsworth and George Collins (Stanford, Calif.: Stanford University Press, 1999).

13. Foucault, "What Is Enlightenment?" 47.

14. In this connection, see especially *Philosophy in a Time of Terror: Dialogues with Jürgen Habermas and Jacques Derrida*, ed. Giovanna Borradori (Chicago: University of Chicago Press, 2004).

15. R. L. Rutsky, "Mutation, History, and Fantasy in the Posthuman," in "Posthuman Conditions," ed. Neil Badmington, special issue, *Subject Matters: A Journal of Communication and the Self* vol. 3, no. 2–vol. 4, no. 1 (2007): 107.

16. Ibid., 110–11.

17. As James W. Bernauer has pointed out, Foucault directly acknowledges Canguilhem for two of his hallmark ideas. The first "is the suspicion, which Canguilhem himself had derived from Bachelard, of science's account of itself as a story of linear progression, and thus the concomitant disposition to deal with the discontinuities evident in the history of science. . . . The second is the inclination to explore history not in quest of a total dialectical comprehension but in terms of specific problematics within which there was determined for a specific field of study both the object of its reflection and the manner in which that reflection would be carried out. 'We must think problematically rather than question and answer dialectically,'" as Foucault puts it in "Theatrum Philosophicum." James W. Bernauer, *Michel Foucault's Force of Flight: Towards an Ethics for Thought* (Atlantic Highlands, N.J.: Humanities Press, 1990), 97.

18. Clarke, *Posthuman Metamorphosis*, 5.

19. Rutsky, "Mutation," 111.

20. Clarke, *Posthuman Metamorphosis*, 5.

21. Dirk Baecker, "Why Systems?" *Theory, Culture, and Society* 18, no. 1 (2001): 61.

22. Jacques Derrida, "The Animal That Therefore I Am (More to Follow)," trans. David Wills, *Critical Inquiry* 28: 2 (2002): 407.

23. David Wills, "Jaded In America," in *Matchbook: Essays in Deconstruction* (Stanford, Calif.: Stanford University Press, 2005), 13.

24. See, for example, Slavoj Žižek, *Enjoy Your Symptom! Jacques Lacan in Hollywood and Out* (New York: Routledge, 1992), 48–50.

25. Gilles Deleuze and Clair Parnet, *Dialogues*, trans. Hugh Tomlinson and Barbara Habberjam (New York: Columbia University Press, 1987). See the "Preface to the English Language Edition by Gilles Deleuze," vii, and "Translators' Introduction," xii.

26. Bruno Latour, *We Have Never Been Modern*, trans. Catherine Porter (Cambridge: Harvard University Press, 1993), 10–11.

27. See Hans-Georg Moeller's brief outline of Luhmann's relationship to Kant in chapter 9 of *Luhmann Explained: From Souls to Systems* (Chicago: Open Court Press, 2006), 167–71.

28. Niklas Luhmann, *Observations on Modernity,* trans. William Whobrey (Stanford, Calif.: Stanford University Press, 1998), 23.

29. As William Rasch explains it, "if the investigation of reality has also become the investigation of the investigator's construction of reality, then the process of scientific or theoretical observation must include an element of self-observation. . . . In a similar vein, Luhmann notes that it has become a requirement of all theories that claim universality to include themselves as part of what they describe." What this means is that "the process of observation is seen to contribute to the generation of complexity from simplicity. As consequence, complexity can never be fully reduced to an underlying simplicity since simplicity, like complexity, is a construct of observation that could always be other than it is. Contingency, the ability to alter perspectives, acts as a reservoir of complexity within all simplicity." William Rasch, *Niklas Luhmann's Modernity: The Paradoxes of Differentiation* (Stanford, Calif.: Stanford University Press, 2000), 48, 39.

30. For a useful account of the emergence of postmodern science that helps to contextualize this fact against the background of the shift from thermodynamics to the life sciences as models for thinking about organized complexity (which will eventuate, among other things, in the paradigm of autopoiesis that Luhmann will eventually adapt from Maturana and Varela), see Steven Best and Douglas Kellner, "Entropy, Chaos, and Organism in Postmodern Science," chapter 5 in *The Postmodern Turn* (New York: Guilford Press, 1997).

31. Niklas Luhmann, *Social Systems,* trans. John Bednarz Jr. with Dirk Baecker (Stanford, Calif.: Stanford University Press, 1995), 37.

32. Jacques Derrida, "Speech and Phenomena," trans. David B. Allison, in *A Derrida Reader* (New York: Columbia University Press, 1991), 26–27.

33. Jacques Derrida, "Violence against Animals," in *For What Tomorrow . . . : A Dialogue,* by Jacques Derrida and Elisabeth Roudinesco, trans. Jeff Fort (Stanford, Calif.: Stanford University Press, 2004), 63.

34. Humberto Maturana and Francisco Varela, *The Tree of Knowledge: The Biological Roots of Human Understanding,* rev. ed., trans. Roberty Paolucci (Boston: Shambhala Press, 1992), 26.

35. Humberto R. Maturana, "Science and Daily Life: The Ontology of Scientific Explanations," in *Research and Reflexivity,* ed. Frederick Steier (London: Sage Publications, 1991), 34.

36. Quoted in Clarke, *Posthuman Metamorphosis,* 3. In this connection, see

"Data Made Flesh: The Material Poiesis of Informatics," Phillip Thurtle and Robert Mitchell's introduction to their edited collection *Data Made Flesh: Embodying Information* (New York: Routledge, 2004), 1–23. There they offer a useful reconceptualization of the concept of the body and counterpose it to four widespread understandings of the term: the "naturalist body," the "cultural/social determinist" body, the "animal" body, and the "phenomenological" body (3–6). As they put it: "We propose that 'the body' be understood as anything that cannot be divided without changing the fundamental pattern of its dynamics. Thus bodies are made up of organs, tissues, cells, and molecules, but a description of a body cannot be reduced to a description of the parts or their functions. This broad definition brings with it some surprising conclusions. 'Machinic systems,' as popularized by Gilles Deleuze and Felix Guattari, may not be 'sets' but they are bodies. An autopoietic system, in the terms of Varela and Maturana, is most definitely a body. A 'self-referential system,' in the terms outlined by Niklas Luhmann, is a body. A 'network,' as described by Manuel Castells, is a body. An organism bounded by flesh is a body. . . . Moreover, this understanding of the body allows us to distinguish between human and nonhuman bodies without falling into the error diagnosed by Hans-Ulrich Gumbrecht, of employing a 'concept of the human [that] exclud[es] . . . any reference to the human body'" (4–5).

37. For a point of comparison here, see Brian Massumi's rather different, Bergson-inflected sense of this point about the body and virtuality in *Parables for the Virtual: Movement, Affect, Sensation* (Durham, N.C.: Duke University Press, 2002), 30–31. For Massumi, presumably, "first" doesn't mean both "first" and "last"; it just means "first," as it does for any ontologist.

38. Brian Massumi, *A User's Guide to Capitalism and Schizophrenia: Deviations from Deleuze and Guattari* (Cambridge, Mass.: MIT Press, 1992), 70–71.

39. I discuss these matters in detail in *Critical Environments: Postmodern Theory and the Pragmatics of the "Outside"* (Minneapolis: University of Minnesota Press, 1998). See in particular 12–22, 108–28.

40. On this point, see David Wills, *Dorsality: Thinking Back through Technology and Politics* (Minneapolis: University of Minnesota Press, 2008).

41. Niklas Luhmann, *Art as a Social System,* trans. Eva M. Knodt (Stanford, Calif.: Stanford University Press, 2000), 141.

42. Ibid., 149.

43. "The Man with the Blue Guitar" and "Tea at the Palaz of Hoon," in *The Collected Poems of Wallace Stevens* (New York: Random House, 1990), 165, 65.

44. Jacques Derrida, *Specters of Marx,* trans. Peggy Kamuf (New York: Routledge, 1994), xix.

1. Meaning and Event

1. In Donna J. Haraway, *Simians, Cyborgs, and Women: The Reinvention of Nature* (New York: Routledge, 1991), 43–68.

2. My remarks here are a continuation of my attempt to align systems theory and poststructuralist theory more generally in my previous two books. In *Critical Environments: Postmodern Theory and the Pragmatics of the "Outside"* (Minneapolis: University of Minnesota Press, 1998), this took the form not just of separate chapters devoted to Maturana and Varela and Luhmann (on the one hand) and Foucault and Deleuze (on the other) but also of an intensive analysis of Luhmann's and Deleuze's differences as they can be teased out by attention to the theoretical topography of "the fold." In my last book, *Animal Rites: American Culture, the Discourse of Species, and Posthumanist Theory* (Chicago: University of Chicago Press, 2003), the focus was instead not primarily on Luhmann but on Maturana and Varela (and, to a lesser extent, Gregory Bateson) and how their evolutionary theory of the emergence of "linguistic domains" can help us to give some evolutionary content to Derrida's theory of the relationship between signification as a trace structure and the question of nonhuman and posthuman subjectivity.

3. Dirk Baecker, "Why Systems?" *Theory, Culture, and Society* 18, no. 1 (2001): 61.

4. Jacques Derrida, *Of Grammatology*, trans. Gayatri Chakravorty Spivak (Baltimore, Md.: Johns Hopkins University Press, 1976), 9, 84.

5. Francois Jacob, *The Logic of Life: A History of Heredity*, trans. Betty E. Spillmann (New York: Pantheon Books, 1973), 1–2.

6. Derrida, *Of Grammatology*, 9.

7. See the introduction to my edited collection *Zoontologies: The Question of the Animal* (Minneapolis: University of Minnesota Press, 2003), xi.

8. Niklas Luhmann, "Deconstruction as Second-Order Observing," in *Theories of Distinction*, 101.

9. See Gunther Teubner, "Economics of Gift—Positivity of Justice: The Mutual Paranoia of Jacques Derrida and Niklas Luhmann," *Theory, Culture, and Society* 18, no. 1 (2001): 29–47.

10. Jacques Derrida, *Without Alibi*, trans. and ed. Peggy Kamuf (Stanford, Calif.: Stanford University Press, 2002), 210, 72. See also Derrida, *Archive Fever: A Freudian Impression*, trans. Eric Prenowitz (Chicago: University of Chicago Press, 1996).

11. This is probably the point—on withdrawing the thinking of the event from an ontology—to insist once again on the difference between Derrida and Deleuze—or, for that matter and from a certain, more contemporary

vantage, the difference between Luhmann and Varela. For an overview of these questions on the terrain of the Luhmann/Deleuze difference, see my *Critical Environments*, esp. 114–28.

12. Niklas Luhmann, *Social Systems*, trans. John Bednarz Jr. with Dirk Baecker (Stanford, Calif.: Stanford University Press, 1995), 67.

13. Dietrich Schwanitz, "Systems Theory According to Niklas Luhmann— Its Environment and Conceptual Strategies," *Cultural Critique* 30 (Spring 1995): 146.

14. Jacques Derrida, "Signature Event Context," trans. Samuel Weber and Jeffrey Mehlman, in *Limited Inc*, by Jacques Derrida, ed. Gerald Graff (Evanston, Ill.: Northwestern University Press, 1988), 3.

15. Derrida, "Signature Event Context," 7–8.

16. Jacques Derrida, "Différance," trans. Alan Bass, in *A Derrida Reader: Between the Blinds*, ed. Peggy Kamuf (New York: Columbia University Press, 1991), 64.

17. Jacques Derrida, "Speech and Phenomena," trans. David B. Allison, in *A Derrida Reader*, 26–27.

18. "Afterword," trans. Samuel Weber, in Derrida, *Limited Inc*, 119.

19. See Luhmann, *Social Systems*, 139, 145. Luhmann insists on his difference with Derrida's critique of this set of problems, but only by way of a reductive reading of Derrida's approach. I will return to this point, and the stakes involved in it, later.

20. Schwanitz, "Systems Theory," 153.

21. Ibid., 156.

22. See Luhmann, *Social Systems*, 10: "Systems must cope with the difference between identity and difference when they reproduce themselves as self-referential systems; in other words, reproduction is the management of this difference. This is not a primarily theoretical but a thoroughly practical problem, and it is relevant not only for meaning systems."

23. Ibid., 25, 26.

24. "System differentiation," Luhmann writes, "is nothing more than the repetition within systems of the difference between system and environment. Through it, the whole system uses itself as environment in forming its own subsystems and thereby achieves greater improbability on the level of those subsystems by more rigorously filtering an ultimately uncontrollable environment. Accordingly, a differentiated system is no longer simply composed of a certain number of parts and the relations among them; rather, it is composed of a relatively large number of operationally employable system/environment differences, which each, along different cutting lines, reconstruct the whole system as the unity of subsystem and environment" (*Social Systems*, 7).

25. Think here, for example, of the Napster controversy and how changes in technology have forced a renegotiation of the interpenetration of economic and legal systems on the specific subsystemic site of intellectual property law—a classic example of how systems, following Luhmann's analysis of interpenetration, use each other's own complexity to enhance their own for the purposes of controlling (or at least steering) the other.

26. Luhmann, *Social Systems*, 37, 33.

27. Bruce Clarke, *Posthuman Metamorphosis: Narrative and Systems* (New York: Fordham University Press, 2008), 67. The text figure, "The Form of Distinction," was first published in George Spencer-Brown's *Laws of Form* (New York: E. P. Dutton, 1969).

28. As Teubner, a distinguished legal scholar, has pointed out, autopoietic social systems thrive on paradox in the sense that "de-paradoxification means to invent new distinctions which do not deny the paradox but displace it temporarily, and thus relieve it of its paralyzing power," so that, for example, "in European legal history, institutionalized distinctions between natural and positive law or, currently, distinctions between legislation and adjudication, have produced their impressive cultural achievements despite or precisely because of the legal paradox" ("Economics of Gift," 32).

29. Niklas Luhmann, "The Paradox of Observing Systems," in *Theories of Distinction*, 83–84.

30. Luhmann, *Social Systems*, 60.

31. Derrida, "Différance," 65–66.

32. Luhmann, *Social Systems*, 60.

33. On this point, see Luhmann, *Social Systems*, 37: "On this basis," he writes, "one can then distinguish between, on the one hand, organic and neurophysiological systems . . . and, on the other, psychic and social systems, which are constituted by the production and processing of meaning." Luhmann's point is that both types of systems are self-referential, but for the latter, "meaning enables an ongoing reference to the system itself and to a more or less elaborated environment." In a now-obsolete vocabulary, we would say that meaning enables a "representation" of the system/environment relation to the system itself (which is kept from *being* representationalist precisely by the inescapable fact of self-reference of all systems).

34. Luhmann, "How Can the Mind," 169.

35. Luhmann, *Social Systems*, 59.

36. Luhmann, "How Can the Mind," 173; *Social Systems*, 272.

37. Luhmann, *Social Systems*, 272; "How Can the Mind," 173. Although I cannot explore this here in any detail, it is worth noting, as Luhmann argues, that "the relationship of the accommodation of communication to the

mind and the unavoidable internal dynamics and evolution of society is also evident in the fact that changes in the forms in which language becomes comprehensible to the mind, from simple sounds to pictorial scripts to phonetic scripts and finally to print, mark thresholds of societal evolution that, once crossed, trigger immense impulses of complexity in a very short time" ("How Can the Mind," 174).

38. Luhmann, *Social Systems*, 161.

39. Derrida, *Limited Inc*, 148.

40. Luhmann, *Social Systems*, 162.

41. Here, very schematically, one would find Rodolph Gasché's reading of Derrida at one end of the spectrum, and Richard Rorty's at the other. For a useful overview of these different ways of reading Derrida, see Rorty's "Is Derrida a Transcendental Philosopher?" and "Two Meanings of Logocentrism: A Reply to Christopher Norris," in Rorty's collection *Essays on Heidegger and Others: Philosophical Papers*, vol. 2 (Cambridge: Cambridge University Press, 1991).

42. As for the former, see, for example, Luhmann's *Art as a Social System*, trans. Eva M. Knodt (Stanford, Calif.: Stanford University Press, 2000), 98–100, 157–58; for the latter, see, for example, Luhmann's "Deconstruction as Second-Order Observing" and *Social Systems*, 145–47, which seems to endorse Derrida's reading of Husserl in *Speech and Phenomena*, only to assimilate Derrida's work to "a theory of signs (language theory, structuralism)."

43. Jacques Derrida, "'Eating Well' or The Calculation of the Subject," in *Who Comes After the Subject?* ed. Eduardo Cadava, Peter Connor, and Jean-Luc Nancy (New York: Routledge, 1991), 116–17.

44. Jacques Derrida, "And Say the Animal Responded?" trans. David Wills, in *Zoontologies: The Question of the Animal*, ed. Cary Wolfe (Minneapolis: University of Minnesota Press, 2003), 126, 137 (italics mine).

45. "Positions: Interview with Jean-Louis Houdebine and Guy Scarpetta," in *Positions*, trans. Alan Bass (Chicago: University of Chicago Press, 1981), 104–5n32.

46. Teubner, "Economics of Gift," 36.

47. Ibid., 37–38.

48. Niklas Luhmann, "The Cognitive Program of Constructivism and the Reality That Remains Unknown," in *Theories of Distinction*, 134.

49. Niklas Luhmann, *Observations on Modernity*, trans. William Whobrey (Stanford, Calif.: Stanford University Press, 1998), 19.

50. Luhmann, *Social Systems*, 33.

51. Luhmann, *Observations on Modernity*, 48.

52. Luhmann, *Social Systems*, 57.

53. Peggy Kamuf, introduction to *Without Alibi*, 6.

54. Luhmann, *Art as a Social System*, 156.

2. Language, Representation, and Species

1. Terrence W. Deacon, *The Symbolic Species: The Co-evolution of Language and the Brain* (New York: Norton, 1997), 442. Though I cannot make the argument within the confines of this essay, I would suggest that Deacon's work is, if anything, more Cartesian than Dennett's. This becomes clear in the final chapter of the text, which, even as it attempts to argue for a substantial continuity between the mental lives of human and nonhuman animals, reinstates, via the terms "representation" and "experience," the quintessentially Cartesian distinction we will see Dennett run aground on—namely, the distinction between sensations and the *experience* of sensations (possible only for beings who operate with symbolic representations) that anchors Descartes's infamous position on the ethical irrelevance of pain in nonhuman animals. See in particular Deacon, 448–50, where we find question-begging formulations such as the following: "We live most of our concrete lives in the subjective realm that is also shared with other species, but our experience of this world is embedded in the vastly more extensive symbolic world" (450). For a useful critique of the reductionist view, see Alva Noë, *Out of Our Heads* (New York: Hill and Wang, 2009).

2. Rob Stein, "Common Collie or Uberpooch? German Pet's Vocabulary Stuns Scientists," *Washington Post,* June 11, 2004, A1.

3. Tony Czuczka, "Study Shows Dogs Can Remember Words," Associated Press Wire Report, June 10, 2004, http://customwire.ap.org.

4. Daniel C. Dennett, *Kinds of Minds: Toward an Understanding of Consciousness* (New York: Basic Books, 1996), 158.

5. Relevant texts here would be, for example, Jacques Derrida, *Archive Fever,* trans. Eric Prenowitz (Chicago: University of Chicago Press, 1996); Gregory Bateson, *Steps to an Ecology of Mind* (New York: Ballantine Books, 1972); Niklas Luhmann, *Social Systems,* trans. John Bednarz Jr. with Dirk Baecker (Stanford, Calif.: Stanford University Press, 1995); Friedrich Kittler, *Essays: Literature, Media, Information Systems,* ed. John Johnston (Amsterdam: OPA, 1997).

6. Dennett, *Kinds of Minds,* 134–35, 146.

7. "How Can the Mind Participate in Communication?" in *Materialities of Communication,* ed. Hans Ulrich Gumbrecht and K. Ludwig Pfeiffer, trans. William Whobrey (Stanford, Calif.: Stanford University Press, 1994), 381.

8. David Wills, *Matchbook: Essays in Deconstruction* (Stanford, Calif.: Stanford University Press, 2005), 183–84.

9. Dennett, *Kinds of Minds,* 147, 131.

10. Daniel C. Dennett, "Animal Consciousness: What Matters and Why," in *Humans and Other Animals,* ed. Arien Mack (Columbus: Ohio State University Press, 1999), 296.

11. Edelman's position here is somewhat complicated. On the one hand, he argues that "concepts, in our view, precede language, which develops by epigenetic means to further enhance our conceptual and emotional exchanges" (Gerald M. Edelman and Giulio Tononi, *A Universe of Consciousness* [New York: Basic Books, 2000], 217). This means that "even in an animal without language, once its nervous system can carry out perceptual categorization and develop conceptual memory, a huge set of possible actions open up. . . . The dynamic, temporally ongoing, bootstrap between a value-category memory and perceptual categorization reflects an individual history, one illuminated at each moment by a remembered present—primary consciousness, mental life I." On the other hand, "With the emergence of higher order consciousness through language, there is a consciously explicit coupling of feelings and value, yielding emotions with cognitive components that are experienced by a person—a self. . . . A true subjectivity emerges with narrative and metaphorical powers and concepts of self and of past and future" (205). In other words, "while a nonlinguistic animal can have a mental life, that life is necessarily a restricted one because the animal lacks a self concept. Although such an animal has a unique mental history, it is not a subject—a self who is able to be conscious of being conscious" (202). But this distinction depends on the representationalist view of language we have already touched on. In Edelman's words, "such an animal has biological individuality but has no true self, a self aware of itself. Although it has a 'remembered present' . . . it has no concept of the past or future. These concepts emerged only when semantic capabilities—the ability to express feelings and refer to objects and events by symbolic means—appeared in the course of evolution" (194), in which "the appearance of speech allowed reference to inner states and objects or events by means of symbols" (195).

12. For a more detailed discussion of Bateson that situates his work in relation to Maturana and Varela, see my chapter "In the Shadow of Wittgenstein's Lion," in *Zoontologies.*

13. Maturana and Varela, *The Tree of Knowledge,* 212. Further references are in the text.

14. Dennett, "Animal Consciousness," 292.

15. Dennett, *Kinds of Minds,* 119.

16. In *Écrits: A Selection,* trans. Alan Sheridan (New York: Norton, 1977).

17. Jacques Derrida, "And Say the Animal Responded?" trans. David Wills,

in *Zoontologies: The Question of the Animal,* ed. Cary Wolfe (Minneapolis: University of Minnesota Press, 2003), 130.

18. Dennett, *Kinds of Minds,* 159.

19. Donna Haraway, *When Species Meet* (Minneapolis: University of Minnesota Press, 2008), 235, 372–73n44. She is referencing Marc D. Hauser, Noam Chomsky, and W. Tecumseh Fitch, "The Faculty of Language: What Is It, Who Has It, and How Did It Evolve?" *Science* 298 (November 22, 2002): 1574.

20. The paraphrase is of Marc Hauser, *Wild Minds: What Animals Really Think* (Owl Books, 2002), paraphrased in Haraway, *When Species Meet,* 51n47.

21. Jacques Derrida, *Of Spirit: Heidegger and the Question,* trans. Geoffrey Bennington and Rachel Bowlby (Chicago: University of Chicago Press, 1989), 53. Further references are in the text. See also my discussion of these questions in Derrida's work in "In the Shadow of Wittgenstein's Lion: Language, Ethics, and the Question of the Animal" in *Zoontologies,* 1–57.

22. Jacques Derrida, "The Animal That Therefore I Am (More to Follow)," trans. David Wills, *Critical Inquiry* 28, no. 2 (2002): 48–49.

23. Derrida, "And Say," 135–36.

24. It is the "intentional stance" that gives one of Dennett's best-known books its title. See Daniel C. Dennett, *The Intentional Stance* (Cambridge, Mass: MIT Press, 1987), the contours of which are summarized in chapter 2 of *Kind of Minds.*

25. Derrida, *Limited Inc,* 118.

26. Dennett, *Kinds of Minds,* 6.

27. This approach is central, of course, to the argument of animal rights philosophy, whose articulation I take up in detail in *Animal Rites: American Culture, the Discourse of Species, and Posthumanist Theory* (Chicago: University of Chicago Press, 2003). See especially chapter 1 and the conclusion.

28. See Tom Regan's clarification of this point in his discussion of Descartes in *The Case for Animal Rights.* See also in this connection a footnote by Derrida that makes clear the connection of this point in Descartes to the capacity for language, in Derrida's "And Say the Animal Responded?" 143n1.

29. See my discussion of this body of work in *Animal Rites,* chapter 1.

30. See in this connection the self-disintegration of the distinction between "pain" and "suffering" at the end of Dennett's essay "Animal Consciousness," which evinces quite well an understanding of language that hamstrings his every move: "When I step on your toe . . . the pain, though intense, is too brief to matter, and I have done no long-term damage to your foot. The idea that you 'suffer' for a second or two is a risible misapplication of that important notion, and even when we grant that my causing you a few seconds pain may irritate you a few seconds or even minutes—especially if you think I did

it deliberately—the pain itself, as a brief, negatively-signed experience, is of vanishing moral significance" (298).

31. Derrida, "The Animal," 396, 395.

32. Ibid., 396.

33. As in the well-known work with the great apes by Washoe, Kanzi, Koko, and others, but also with birds, as in Irene Pepperberg's research. The literature at this point is extensive, but for an overview, one might consult "Conversations with Apes," in *The Great Ape Project*, ed. Peter Singer and Paola Cavalieri (New York: St. Martin's Press, 1993), 27–79; the essays by Duane Rumbaugh and Colin McGinn in *Humans and Other Animals*, ed. Arien Mack (Columbus: Ohio State University Press, 1999); and "Language" in the collection *Anthropomorphism, Anecdotes, and Animals*, ed. Robert W. Mitchell et al. (Albany: SUNY Press, 1997).

34. Derrida, "The Animal," 416.

3. Flesh and Finitude

1. The phrase belongs to Cora Diamond in her essay "Injustice and Animals," in *Slow Cures and Bad Philosophers: Essays on Wittgenstein, Medicine, and Bioethics*, ed. Carl Elliott (Durham, N.C.: Duke University Press, 2001), 123.

2. Derrida uses this phrase in many places, but the salient context for my purposes is his essay "The Animal That Therefore I Am (More to Follow)," trans. David Wills, *Critical Inquiry* 28 (Winter 2002): 395.

3. Tom L. Beauchamp and LeRoy Walters, eds., *Contemporary Issues in Bioethics*, 5th ed. (Belmont, Calif.: Wadsworth, 1999), v–xi.

4. Derrida, *Limited Inc*, 138.

5. Michel Foucault, "Right of Death and Power over Life," in *The Foucault Reader*, ed. Paul Rabinow (New York: Pantheon, 1984), 259.

6. Michel Foucault, "The Politics of Health in the Eighteenth Century," in *The Foucault Reader*, 277.

7. Ibid., 283.

8. Take, for example, the case of Arthur Caplan, trustee professor and director of the Center for Bioethics at the University of Pennsylvania, and perhaps the country's highest-profile bioethicist, thanks to a media presence as a columnist for MSNBC, frequent appearances in the *Nation*, et cetera. In an interview just after Caplan moved to Penn from the University of Minnesota, when asked why he made the move, he responded (after we are told he shared offices upon arrival with the university's Institute for Human Gene Therapy): "Penn has this emerging gene therapy, testing, and screening interest and was pulling together a group of people to do molecular medicine. So,

intellectually, that was a big draw for me. Also, Minnesota didn't have much of a group doing health economics and policy. But Wharton [Penn's business school] does, and that was another attraction." In addition, Philadelphia "has all these medical schools and hospitals—Fox Chase [Cancer Center], the [American] College of Physicians, and so forth—and it has a lot of pharmaceutical companies. So it looked like a place where one could go and make something happen." Quoted in "Arthur Caplan Discusses Issues Facing the Growing Field of Bioethics," interview by Franklin Hoke and Karen Young Kreeger, *Scientist* 8, no. 20 (October 17, 1994), http://www.the-scientist.com/yr1994/oct/opin, 1.

9. David Shenk, "Biocapitalism: What Price Genetic Revolution?" *Harper's,* December 1997, 44.

10. Carl Elliott, *A Philosophical Disease: Bioethics, Culture, and Identity* (New York: Routledge, 1999), xxii, xxviii.

11. Beauchamp and Walters, *Contemporary Issues in Bioethics,* 18–23.

12. These principles essentially reiterate those first formulated by Beauchamp and James Childress in *Principles of Biomedical Ethics* (New York: Oxford, 1979), which is, according to Elliott, something of a founding tome for the field (xvii).

13. Elliott, *A Philosophical Disease,* 158.

14. Quoted in Carl Elliott, "Introduction: Treating Bioethics," in *Slow Cures and Bad Philosophers,* 12.

15. Elliott, *A Philosophical Disease,* xxxi.

16. Shenk, "Biocapitalism," 44.

17. Ibid.

18. These developments have been widely popularized on cable television venues such as the Animal Planet station and in series such as PBS's *The Animal Mind,* hosted by George Page. But the reader should also consult, among many others, *The Great Ape Project: Equality beyond Humanity,* ed. Paola Cavalieri and Peter Singer (New York: St. Martin's Press, 1993); *Anthropomorphism, Anecdotes, and Animals,* ed. Robert W. Mitchell, Nicholas S. Thompson, and H. Lyn Miles (Albany: SUNY Press, 1997); and especially *Interpretation and Explanation in the Study of Animal Behavior,* ed. Marc Bekoff and Dale Jamieson (Boulder, Colo.: Westview Press, 1990); and Colin Allen and Mark Bekoff, *Species of Mind: The Philosophy and Biology of Cognitive Ethology* (Cambridge, Mass.: MIT Press, 1997).

19. Reliable figures on the exact number of animals used for research in the United States are hard to come by, for one simple reason: mice, rats, and birds account for upward of 80 percent of all animals used, but because they are not covered by the United States Animal Welfare Act, laboratories are

not required to report their numbers. Estimates for total number of animals used range from seventeen to seventy million. See F. Barbara Orlans, "Data on Animal Experimentation in the United States: What They Do and Do Not Show," *Perspectives in Biology and Medicine* 37, no. 2 (Winter 1994). Readers interested in pursuing these questions should consult, among others, Orlans, *In the Name of Science: Issues in Responsible Animal Experimentation* (New York: Oxford University Press, 1993); and Hugh LaFollette and Niall Shanks, *Brute Science: Dilemmas of Animal Experimentation* (New York: Routledge, 1996).

20. In Arthur L. Caplan, *Am I My Brother's Keeper? The Ethical Frontiers of Biomedicine* (Bloomington: Indiana University Press, 1997), 101–14.

21. Ibid., 108.

22. Peter Singer, "Prologue: Ethics and the New Animal Liberation Movement," in *In Defense of Animals,* ed. Peter Singer (New York: Harper and Row, 1985), 9.

23. Paola Cavalieri, *The Animal Question: Why Nonhuman Animals Deserve Human Rights,* trans. Catherine Woollard (New York: Oxford University Press, 2001), 76.

24. Caplan, *Brother's Keeper,* 109.

25. Cavalieri, *The Animal Question,* 28, 29.

26. Caplan, *Brother's Keeper,* 111.

27. Quoted in Cavalieri, *The Animal Question,* 80.

28. Caplan, *Brother's Keeper,* 110.

29. Tom Regan, "The Case for Animal Rights," in Singer, *In Defense of Animals,* 17.

30. Cavalieri, *The Animal Question,* 36.

31. Caplan, *Brother's Keeper,* 107–8.

32. Cavalieri, *The Animal Question,* 60.

33. *An Introduction to the Principles of Morals and Legislation* (New York: Hafner Press, 1948), 4n11; cited in Cavalieri, *The Animal Question,* 61.

34. *Politica,* trans. Benjamin Jowett, book 1, 1253a, in *The Basic Works of Aristotle,* ed. Richard McKeon (New York: Modern Library, 2001), 1129. As Gary Steiner explains in his discussion of Aristotle and the Stoics, Aristotle's "broad conception of logos . . . includes a wide variety of meanings such as articulate speech and logic" (61–62). For Aristotle, while human beings share with animals a few different core faculties (such as "sense perception," "imagination," "appetite," and "spirited desire"), the "possession of rationality enables human beings to form universal concepts, which makes contemplation and practical deliberation possible." Steiner, *Anthropocentrism and Its Discontents: The Moral Status of Animals in the History of Western Philosophy* (Pittsburgh: University of Pittsburgh Press, 2005), 63.

35. Peter Singer, *Animal Liberation* (New York: Avon Books, 1975), 7–8.

36. Tom Regan, *The Case for Animal Rights* (Berkeley: University of California Press, 1983), 203.

37. Martha C. Nussbaum, *Frontiers of Justice: Disability, Nationality, Species Membership* (Cambridge, Mass.: Harvard University Press, 2006), 343.

38. See Regan, *Case for Animal Rights*, 286.

39. As Nussbaum notes, "both because of their commitment to rationality as the ground of dignity and because of their conception of political principles as deriving from a contract among rough equals, they [social contract views] deny that we have obligations of justice to nonhuman animals" (327).

40. Steiner, *Anthropocentrism and Its Discontents*, 57–58.

41. "To be the subject-of-a-life," Regan writes, "involves more than merely being alive and more than merely being conscious." "Individuals are subjects-of-a-life," he continues, "if they have beliefs and desires; perception, memory, and a sense of the future, including their own future; an emotional life together with feelings of pleasure and pain; preference- and welfare-interests; the ability to initiate action in pursuit of their desires and goals; a psychophysical identity over time; and an individual welfare in the sense that their experiential life fares well or ill for them, logically independently of their utility for others and logically independently of their being the object of anyone else's interests" (*Case for Animal Rights*, 243).

42. Nussbaum, *Frontiers of Justice*, 349, 351.

43. To compare with Regan's account, see Nussbaum, *Frontiers of Justice*, 359, 361–62.

44. For example: "A human being can be expected to learn to flourish without homicide and, let us hope, even without most killing of animals. . . . The capability to exercise one's predatory nature, avoiding the pain of frustration, may well have value, if the pain of frustration is considerable" (370). The last two-thirds of Nussbaum's chapter on relations to nonhuman animals—especially beginning on p. 372—is littered with such moments of prevarication, even befuddlement. See, for a particularly clear example, p. 379.

45. Geoffrey Galt Harpham, "The Hunger of Martha Nussbaum," *Representations* 77 (Winter 2002): 68.

46. The list also appears in Nussbaum, *Frontiers of Justice*, 76–78.

47. Harpham, "Hunger of Martha Nussbaum," 73–74.

48. Nussbaum, *Frontiers of Justice*, 356.

49. J. M. Coetzee, *The Lives of Animals*, ed. Amy Gutmann (Princeton, N.J.: Princeton University Press, 1999), 43.

50. J. M. Coetzee, *Disgrace* (New York: Penguin, 1999), 143.

51. Cora Diamond, "The Difficulty of Reality and the Difficulty of Philosophy," in *Philosophy and Animal Life*, ed. Stanley Cavell, Cora Diamond, John McDowell, Ian Hacking, and Cary Wolfe (New York: Columbia University Press, 2008), 45–46.

52. Stanley Cavell, *In Quest of the Ordinary: Lines of Skepticism and Romanticism* (Chicago: University of Chicago Press, 1988), 31.

53. Stanley Cavell, *This New Yet Unapproachable America* (Albuquerque, N.M.: Living Batch Press, 1989), 86.

54. Ibid., 86–87.

55. Stanley Cavell, *Conditions Handsome and Unhandsome: The Constitution of Emersonian Perfectionism* (Chicago: University of Chicago Press, 1990), 39. See, for a more detailed discussion of this point—and also the similarities and important differences between Cavell and Derrida around Heidegger's figure of the hand—my "In the Shadow of Wittgenstein's Lion," in *Zoontologies: The Question of the Animal*, ed. Cary Wolfe (Minneapolis: University of Minnesota Press, 2003), 20–21. As Cavell points out, harbored in Heidegger's famous contention that "thinking is a handicraft" is the "fantasy of the apposable thumb" that separates the human from the animal not just anthropologically but also ontologically. As Heidegger writes, in a moment emphasized by Derrida: "Apes, for example, have organs that can grasp, but they have no hand," for their being is subordinated to utility rather than devoted to thought and the reflection on things "as such" that is possible only for beings who possess language. Jacques Derrida, "Geschlecht II: Heidegger's Hand," trans. John P. Leavey Jr., in *Deconstruction and Philosophy*, ed. John Sallis (Chicago: University of Chicago Press, 1986), 173. Thus the opposite of the "clutching" or "grasping" that will find its apotheosis for Heidegger in the world domination of technology is a thinking that is instead a kind of "reception" or welcoming (Cavell, *Conditions* 39). Or as Derrida puts it, "If there is a thought of the hand or a hand of thought, as Heidegger gives us to think, it is not of the order of conceptual grasping. Rather this thought of the hand belongs to the essence of the *gift*, of a giving that would give, if this is possible, without taking hold of anything" ("*Geschlecht II*" 173). And thus Heidegger's insistence, as Cavell reminds us, on "the derivation of the word thinking from a root for thanking," as if "giving thanks for the gift of thinking" (*Conditions*, 39).

56. Diamond, "The Difficulty of Reality," 44.

57. Diamond, "Injustice and Animals," 123.

58. Diamond, "Losing Your Concepts," *Ethics* 98, no. 2 (January 1998): 276.

59. Cora Diamond, "Experimenting on Animals: A Problem in Ethics," in *The Realistic Spirit: Wittgenstein, Philosophy, and the Mind* (Cambridge, Mass.: MIT Press, 1991), 350.

60. Diamond, "Injustice and Animals," 121.

61. Diamond, "Experimenting on Animals," 353.

62. Ibid., 351.

63. Diamond, "Eating Meat and Eating People," in *The Realistic Spirit*, 333.

64. Ibid., 329.

65. Diamond, "Experimenting with Animals," 351.

66. Diamond, "Injustice and Animals," 141–42.

67. Nussbaum, *Frontiers of Justice*, 349.

68. Harpham, "Hunger of Martha Nussbaum," 59, 58.

69. Nussbaum, *Frontiers of Justice*, 337.

70. On this point, see Paola Cavalieri's discussion in *The Animal Question*, 28.

71. Diamond, "Losing Your Concepts," 263.

72. Jacques Derrida, "The Animal That Therefore I Am (More to Follow)," trans. David Wills, *Critical Inquiry* 28, no. 2 (Winter 2002): 386, 395.

73. Ibid., 396.

74. Diamond, "Injustice and Animals," 131.

75. Derrida, "The Animal," 395.

76. Jacques Derrida, "Force of Law: The 'Mystical Foundation of Authority,'" trans. Mary Quaintance, in *Deconstruction and the Possibility of Justice*, ed. Drucila Cornell, Michal Rosenfeld, and David Gray Carlson (London: Routledge, 1992), 24.

77. Ibid.

78. Diamond, "The Difficulty of Reality," 10.

79. As Derrida has suggested in his reading of Heidegger and the animal in *Of Spirit: Heidegger and the Question*, trans. Geoffrey Bennington and Rachel Bowlby (Chicago: University of Chicago Press, 1989), those "sinister connotations" of "continuism"—which Heidegger's humanist separation of human and animal is dead-set against—include racism, the use of naturalism to countenance xenophobia, and much else besides (56).

80. Derrida, "The Animal," 45–46.

81. Diamond, "Experimenting with Animals," 353.

82. Richard Beardsworth, *Derrida and the Political* (London: Routledge, 1996), 130–31.

83. Derrida, "The Animal," 396 (italics mine).

84. Diamond, "Injustice and Animals," 131.

85. Diamond, "Eating Meat," 333.

86. Ibid., 333–34.

87. Jacques Derrida, *Positions*, trans. and annotated by Alan Bass (Chicago: University of Chicago Press, 1981), 105n32. This will help bring into focus Derrida's differences with Foucault as well. It is certainly of use to locate bioethics

in the context of the rise of biopower and the entire edifice of "health" under modernity, as Foucault has. But from Derrida's vantage, Foucault's historicism, although it focuses on the production of the subject by external agencies, is not sufficiently aware of the production and nontransparency of his *own* discourse. To put it another way—and this has direct relevance for the practice of ethics—what is at stake is not only the entanglement of the subject in the means of her own sociohistorical production but the fact that the process remains for Foucault "accountable" (to use Derrida's phrase), hence leading Derrida to repeat in *Limited Inc* a charge he makes elsewhere: that Foucault's archaeology shares "the metaphysical premises of the Anglo-Saxon—and fundamentally moralistic—theory of the performative, of speech acts or discursive events" (39). See also in this connection Derrida's engagement of Searle's comment in a newspaper article that "Michel Foucault once characterized Derrida's prose style to me as *'obscurantisme terroriste.'*" *Limited Inc*, 158n12.

88. I discuss this problem in detail, and with regard to Rorty specifically, in *Critical Environments: Postmodern Theory and the Pragmatics of the "Outside"* (Minneapolis: University of Minnesota Press, 1998), 20–22, 140–41, 144–45.

89. Jacques Derrida, "'Eating Well,' or The Calculation of the Subject: An Interview with Jacques Derrida," in *Who Comes after the Subject?* ed. Eduardo Cadava, Peter Connor, and Jean-Luc Nancy (New York: Routledge, 1991), 116–17.

90. Diamond, "Injustice and Animals," 134 (italics mine).

91. Jacques Derrida, "Signature, Event, Context," in *Limited Inc*, 15. See also in this connection pp. 128–29.

92. Derrida, *Limited Inc*, 70.

93. "Violence against Animals," in *For What Tomorrow . . . : A Dialogue*, by Jacques Derrida and Elisabeth Roudinesco, trans. Jeff Fort (Stanford, Calif.: Stanford University Press, 2004), 63 (italics mine).

94. Diamond, "The Difficulty of Reality," 10.

95. For a brilliant exploration of the technicity and mechanicity of language in relation to prosthetics and the question of technology, see David Wills's *Dorsality: Thinking Back through Technology and Politics* (Minneapolis: University of Minnesota Press, 2008), and his earlier volume *Prosthesis* (Stanford, Calif.: Stanford University Press, 1995).

96. Roland Barthes, *Camera Lucida: Reflections on Photography*, trans. Richard Howard (New York: Hill and Wang, 1981), 76, 81. Cited in Jacques Derrida and Bernard Stiegler, *Echographies of Television*, trans. Jennifer Bajorek (Cambridge: Polity Press, 2002), 113.

97. Derrida, *Echographies of Television*, 115.

98. Quoted in Diamond, "The Difficulty of Reality," 10.

99. Derrida, *Echographies of Television*, 122.

100. Derrida, *Limited Inc*, 130.

101. Derrida addresses this pointedly in "The Animal That Therefore I Am" when he compares our industrialized and systematized use of animals in factory farming, biomedical research, and much else to "the worst cases of genocide" (394–95).

102. David Wood, *"Comment ne pas manger*—Deconstruction and Humanism," in *Animal Others: On Ethics, Ontology, and Animal Life*, ed. H. Peter Steeves (Albany: SUNY Press, 1999), 33, 18.

103. Diamond, "Injustice and Animals," 142.

104. Derrida, "The Animal," 38–39.

105. Derrida, *Limited Inc*, 138.

4. "Animal Studies," Disciplinarity, and the (Post)Humanities

1. See, for example, Christopher Fynsk, *The Claim of Language: A Case for the Humanities* (Minneapolis: University of Minnesota Press, 2004); and, in a different register, Gayatri Chakravorty Spivak, *Death of a Discipline* (New York: Columbia University Press, 2005). Excellent and wide-ranging briefs are available in Cathy N. Davidson and David Theo Goldberg, "Engaging the Humanities," *Profession* (2004); and "Why We Need the Humanities Now: A Manifesto for the Humanities in a Technological Age," *Chronicle of Higher Education*, February 13, 2004.

2. Two well-known studies here are Bill Readings, *The University In Ruins;* and, even better Gregg Lambert, *Report to the Academy.*

3. Giorgio Agamben, *Homo Sacer: Sovereign Power and Bare Life,* trans. Daniel Heller-Roazen (Stanford, Calif.: Stanford University Press, 1998), 1. In this connection see also Agamben's *The Open: Man and Animal,* trans. Kevin Attell (Stanford, Calif.: Stanford University Press, 2004).

4. Though it should be noted, as Gerald Graff showed long ago in his invaluable study *Professing Literature,* that the coherence of the discipline of literary studies in the United States has always been problematic, and it has only been exacerbated, he argues, by the unwillingness to seriously engage the taken-for-granted organization of the field by national literatures and historical periods.

5. Thomas Pfau, "The Philosophy of Shipwreck: Gnosticism, Skepticism, and Coleridge's Catastrophic Modernity," *MLN: Modern Language Notes* 122, no. 5 (December 2007): 6–7.

6. Ellen Rooney, "Form and Contentment," *MLQ* 61, no. 1 (March 2000): 26.

7. Marjorie Levinson, "What Is New Formalism?" *PMLA* 122, no. 2 (March

2007): 565. Indeed, as Levinson notes, such was the sort of distinction shrewdly made, in so many words, by Alan Liu in his widely read essay from 1989, "The Power of Formalism: The New Historicism," where he observed in New Historicism the tendency to wed "form and content . . . and make them one, and that one is form" (568–69n2).

8. Tilottama Rajan, "In the Wake of Cultural Studies: Globalization, Theory, and the University," *Diacritics* 31, no. 3 (Fall 2001): 69.

9. Note that Rajan's point bears directly on the idea and role of the so-called public intellectual, as Derrida has shrewdly observed in his discussion of the relationship between the idea of the "public" and "publicity" that such a notion takes for granted. See his essay "The University without Condition," in *Without Alibi,* and also, for a closely related discussion, "The Principle of Reason: The University in the Eyes of Its Pupils," in *Eyes of the University: Right to Philosophy 2,* trans. Jan Plug et al. (Stanford, Calif.: Stanford University Press, 2004), 129–55.

10. Rooney, "Form and Contentment," 28 (italics mine).

11. Franco Moretti, "The Slaughterhouse of Literature," *MLQ* 61, no. 1 (March 2000): 207.

12. As Braudel puts it, in terms already touched on by Pfau, "traditional history, with its concern for the short time span, for the individual and the event, has long accustomed us to the headlong, dramatic, breathless rush of its narrative" (cited in Moretti, "The Slaughterhouse of Literature," 224). And it is also—and I can't pursue this point here—to render dubious the kinds of political claims that are often attached to projects of historical "recovery." As Moretti observes incisively, "Right now, Jane Austen is canonical and Amelie Opie is not, because millions of readers keep reading Jane Austen for their own pleasure; but nothing lasts forever, and when readers will no longer enjoy her books (they have seen the movies, anyway), a dozen English professors will suddenly have the power to get rid of *Persuasion* and replace it with *Adeline Mowbray.* Far from being a socially significant act, however, that change in the (academic) canon will prove only that nineteenth-century novels have become irrelevant" (209).

13. Rooney, "Form and Contentment," 34. Susan Wolfson, "Reading for Form," *MLQ* 61, no. 1 (2000): 6.

14. Rajan, "In the Wake of Cultural Studies," 79.

15. John Rajchman, *Michel Foucault: The Freedom of Philosophy* (New York: Columbia University Press, 1985), 51.

16. It should be noted in contrast to Luhmann that, as Rajchman puts it, the ethical and political stakes of Foucault's archaeology become evident when we remember that "for Foucault, freedom lies in our capacity to find alternatives to the particular forms of discourse that define us by reference, among other

things, to universal humanity. Instead of finding enlightenment in universal Reason or Society, he finds it in uncovering the particularity and contingency of our knowledge and our practices" (*Michel Foucault*, 60). What is here called "freedom" Luhmann would simply call "contingency"—and a contingency that, far from being the opposite or hidden subversive element of modernity, is precisely its defining attribute. This does not mean that things cannot be different—indeed, it means that by definition they *will* be—only that "different" does not, as for Foucault, automatically mean "better."

17. James Chandler, "Critical Disciplinarity," *Critical Inquiry* 30 (Winter 2004): 59.

18. Rajchman, *Michel Foucault*, 59.

19. Pfau contends that "the most conspicuous new term to express the accumulative, impersonal, and abstract mode of knowledge production is that of 'system'" (9). Rajan likewise contends (following Baudrillard, but one could also mention Lyotard in *The Postmodern Condition* in this context) that systems theory is a form of an "industrial" or informatic model of differences "in which everything is codified and contained"—that is, rendered transparent. Both Pfau and Rajan, however, are operating with a first-order rather than second-order notion of system (and for that matter, of information). See, for a wide-ranging overview of these questions (and why the difference between first- and second-order systems theory matters, and how), Bruce Clarke and Mark Hansen, eds., *Emergence and Embodiment: New Essays on Second Order Systems Theory* (Durham, N.C.: Duke University Press, 2008).

20. Dirk Baecker, "Why Systems?" *Theory, Culture, and Society* 18, no. 1 (2001): 61.

21. Numerous works by Luhmann could be referenced here, but see, for example, "A Redescription of 'Romantic Art,'" *Modern Language Notes* 111 (1996): 506–22. For a useful overview of these relations, see Hans-Georg Moeller, *Luhmann Explained: From Souls to Systems* (Chicago: Open Court Press, 2006), 167–75, 241–60.

22. "Positions: Interview with Jean-Louis Houdebine and Guy Scarpetta," in *Positions*, trans. Alan Bass (Chicago: University of Chicago Press, 1981), 104–5n32.

23. Moeller, *Luhmann Explained*, 199.

24. Niklas Luhmann, *Social Systems*, trans. John Bednarz Jr. with Dirk Baecker (Stanford, Calif.: Stanford University Press, 1995), 4.

25. Moeller, *Luhmann Explained*, 200.

26. Ibid., 201.

27. Luhmann, *Social Systems*, 16–17.

28. For Luhmann, as is well known, the distinction modern/postmodern is of no moment. "Postmodernism" is simply an intensification or amplification

of fundamental structures and dynamics already present in and as modernity. See, for example, "Why Does Society Describe Itself as Postmodern?" in *Observing Complexity: Systems Theory and Postmodernity*, ed. William Rasch and Cary Wolfe (Minneapolis: University of Minnesota Press, 2000), 35–49.

29. Niklas Luhmann, "The Modernity of Science," in *Theories of Distinction: Redescribing the Descriptions of Modernity*, ed. William Rasch (Stanford, Calif.: Stanford University Press, 2002), 63.

30. Ibid., 64.

31. Humberto R. Maturana, "Science and Daily Life: The Ontology of Scientific Explanations," in *Research and Reflexivity*, ed. Frederick Steier (London: Sage, 1991), 34. I discuss these issues and their relation to scientific accounts of language and subjectivity in nonhuman animals in *Animal Rites: American Culture, the Discourse of Species, and Posthumanist Theory* (Chicago: University of Chicago Press, 2003), 86.

32. Luhmann, *Social Systems*, 71.

33. Immanuel Wallerstein et al., *Open the Social Sciences: Report of the Gulbenkian Commission on the Restructuring of the Social Sciences* (Stanford, Calif.: Stanford University Press, 1996), 48–49.

34. Rajchman, *Michel Foucault*, 55.

35. Dietrich Schwanitz, "Systems Theory According to Niklas Luhmann—Its Environment and Conceptual Strategies," *Cultural Critique* 30 (Spring 1995): 145.

36. The formulation of transdisciplinarity here belongs to Irene Dolling and Sabine Hark in "She Who Speaks Shadow Speaks Truth: Transdisciplinarity in Women's and Gender Studies," *Signs: Journal of Women in Culture and Society* 25, no. 4 (2000): 1195, 1197.

37. See Diamond's essay "The Difficulty of Reality and the Difficulty of Philosophy," in *Philosophy and Animal Life* (New York: Columbia University Press, 2008). The volume also contains responses to Diamond's essay by Stanley Cavell and John McDowell. As for the second example, see my essay "Thinking Otherwise, or Cognitive Science, Deconstruction, and the (Non) Human (Non) Speaking Subject," in "DerridAnimals," ed. Neil Badmington, special issue, *Oxford Literary Review* (2008), reprinted in *Animal Subjects: An Ethical Reader*, ed. Jodey Castricano (Toronto: Wilfred Laurier University Press, 2008).

38. Luhmann, *Observations on Modernity*, 27.

39. Jeffrey M. Peck, "Advanced Literary Study as Cultural Study: A Redefinition of the Discipline," *Profession* 85 (YEAR): 51, cited in Stanley Fish, "Being Interdisciplinary Is So Very Hard to Do," *Profession* 89 (1989): 18.

40. Fish's retort in his insightful (and predictably impish) essay "Being Interdisciplinary Is So Very Hard to Do" to the view represented in the Peck quotation is very close to Luhmann's own position. As Fish puts it, the prob-

lem with the "strategy of self-consciousness" is this: "Can you simultaneously operate within a practice and be self-consciously in touch with the conditions that enable it? The answer could be yes only if you could achieve a reflective distance from those conditions while still engaging in that practice; but once the conditions enabling a practice become the object of analytic attention . . . you are engaging in another practice (the practice of reflecting on the conditions of a practice you are not now practicing)" (20). The advantage of Luhmann's theorization of the problem is that it even more rigorously separates disciplinarity from persons, consciousness from communication, and enables us to take the further step discussed earlier of articulating semantic overburdening and increasing complexity as a motor of disciplinary change—a move that Fish's account of disciplinarity is unable to make. Fish's observations on disciplinarity are extended in his book *Professional Correctness: Literary Studies and Political Change* (Cambridge, Mass.: Harvard University Press, 1999).

41. Luhmann contends that if we "define autopoiesis as a general form of system building using self-referential closure, we would have to admit that there are nonliving autopoietic systems." Indeed, this is the key postulate of his later adaptation of the concept of autopoiesis to *social* systems. "The Autopoiesis of Social Systems," in *Essays on Self-Reference* (New York: Columbia University Press, 1990), 2. Also crucial in this connection is Luhmann's insistence of autopoietic closure and the difference of consciousness and communication, psychic systems and social systems, a detailed discussion of which may be found in my essay "Meaning as Event-Machine, or Systems Theory and 'The Reconstruction of Deconstruction,'" in *Emergence and Embodiment: New Essays on Second-Order Systems Theory,* ed. Bruce Clarke and Mark Hansen (Durham, N.C.: Duke University Press, 2008).

42. N. Katherine Hayles, *How We Became Posthuman* (Chicago: University of Chicago Press, 1999), 2.

43. I discuss these issues in some detail in the section "Disarticulating Language and Species: Maturana and Varela (and Derrida)" in "In the Shadow of Wittgenstein's Lion," in *Zoontologies: The Question of the Animal,* ed. Cary Wolfe (Minneapolis: University of Minnesota Press, 2003), 1–57.

44. A point made similarly by Neil Badmington in "Theorizing Posthumanism," *Cultural Critique* 53 (Winter 2003).

45. Ibid., 21.

46. Hayles, *How We Became Posthuman,* 287.

47. Luhmann, "Modernity of Science," 71.

48. "Once we understand the crisis of modern science as a becoming-visible of its simplifications, its technical character, its functioning without any knowledge of the world," Luhmann writes, "then it is conceivable that this insight could be channeled back into science, to a greater extent that has

hitherto been the case, and become the object of normal research" (71)—as Pierre Bourdieu has attempted to do in the lectures published at the end of his career as *Science of Science and Reflexivity,* trans. Richard Nice (Chicago: University of Chicago Press, 2004).

49. Chandler, "Critical Disciplinarity," 358.

50. See in particular chapter 1 of my *Animal Rites,* "Old Orders for New: Ecology, Animal Rights, and the Poverty of Humanism," 21–43. For a discussion of Nussbaum, see my essay "Flesh and Finitude: Thinking Animals in (Post)Humanist Philosophy," in "The Political Animal," ed. Chris Danta and Dimitris Vardoulakas, special issue, *Substance* (2008).

51. For a more detailed discussion of Rorty and the problem of the liberal *ethnos,* see my *Critical Environments: Postmodern Theory and the Pragmatics of the "Outside"* (Minneapolis: University of Minnesota Press, 2003), esp. 12–22.

52. One could cite any number of texts in this connection, but see, for example, Slavoj Žižek, *Tarrying with the Negative: Kant, Hegel, and the Critique of Ideology* (Durham, N.C.: Duke University Press, 1993), "Introduction" and "The Blind Spot of Liberalism," 211.

53. Žižek, *Tarrying with the Negative,* 4.

54. Hence Žižek undertakes simply an *inversion* of the schema of the humanist subject, rather than a fundamental *rethinking* of the schematics of subjectivity along a nonhierarchical, nondialectical, non-anthropocentric plane. The human for Žižek is not the "subject who knows" but rather, in this inversion, *alone* "the subject who does *not* know"—a non-knowledge, usually explored by Žižek under the thematics of trauma, that never arises as a problem or possibility for animals. For a fuller discussion, see Cary Wolfe and Jonathan Elmer, "Subject to Sacrifice: Ideology, Psychoanalysis, and the Discourse of Species in Jonathan Demme's *The Silence of the Lambs,*" in Wolfe, *Animal Rites,* 97–121. Directly relevant here too is Derrida's discussion of Lacan and the animal in "And Say the Animal Responded?" in Wolfe, *Zoontologies,* 121–46. For a detailed discussion and critique of Žižek's notion of "Truth as contingent," see Judith Butler, Ernesto Laclau, and Slavoj Žižek, *Contingency, Universality, Hegemony: Contemporary Dialogues on the Left* (London: Verso, 2000).

55. See, for example, Slavoj Žižek, *The Sublime Object of Ideology* (London: Verso: 1989), 1–7.

5. Learning from Temple Grandin

1. I refer here and in the chapter's title to the well-known collection of essays *Who Comes After the Subject?* ed. Eduardo Cadava, Peter Connor, and Jean-Luc Nancy (New York: Routledge, 1991), which includes Derrida's semi-

nal discussion "Eating Well," which figures prominently in several chapters of this book.

2. See in particular the concluding chapter of *Animal Rites,* "Postmodern Ethics, the Question of the Animal, and Posthumanist Theory."

3. I am indebted to Richard Nash for pointing out the link between Roberts's case and disability.

4. See Lawrence Scanlan's discussion in his introduction to Monty Roberts, *The Man Who Listens to Horses* (New York: Random House, 1997), xxviii–xxix.

5. Dawn Prince-Hughes, *Songs of the Gorilla Nation: My Journey through Autism* (New York: Harmony Books, 2004), 1.

6. Oliver Sacks, "An Anthropologist on Mars," *New Yorker,* December 27, 1994, 106–25.

7. Oliver Sacks, foreword to *Thinking in Pictures and Other Reports from My Life with Autism,* by Temple Grandin (New York: Random House, 1995), 11.

8. One could cite any number of texts in connection with the so-called linguistic turn in twentieth-century philosophy, but the works of Richard Rorty are especially lucid in describing this transition. For a useful overview, see Richard Rorty, ed., *The Linguistic Turn: Essays in Philosophical Method,* 2nd ed. (Chicago: University of Chicago Press, 1992).

9. Grandin, "My Mind Is a Web Browser," 1, http://www.grandin.com/inc/mind.web.browser.html.

10. As she points out, an even more striking experiment in this regard was one done by NASA involving commercial airplane pilots. During simulated landings, 25 percent of the pilots simply did not register a large commercial airplane parked in the middle of the runway, and literally landed right on top of it. As Grandin observes after seeing photographs of the experiment, "What's interesting is that if you're *not* a pilot, the parked plane is obvious. You can't miss it, and you don't have to be autistic to see it, either. I'd bet the ranch that the only people who could possibly miss that plane would have to be commercial pilots" (*Animals In Translation,* 25).

11. It probably goes without saying that Derrida's point would be that *any* visual space, in being seen, is also and at the same time constituted by blindness, because any seen space is constituted by a semiotic system constituted by *différance,* the interplay of presence and absence, and so on. In other words: seeing that you didn't see the woman in the gorilla suit will in no way "despatialize" the visual field.

12. "The Spatial Arts: An Interview with Jacques Derrida," in *Deconstruction and the Visual Arts,* ed. Peter Brunette and David Wills (Cambridge: Cambridge University Press, 1994), 24. As Derrida points out—amplified by Brunette and Wills in their introduction—this is obviously directly related

to the deployment of the idea of "spacing" in relation to writing as *écriture* in early texts of Derrida's such as *Of Grammatology* and *Writing and Difference*.

13. Jacques Derrida, *Memoirs of the Blind: The Self Portrait and Other Ruins*, trans. Pascale-Anne Brault and Michael Naas (Chicago: University of Chicago Press, 1993), 51–52.

14. "The Principle of Reason: The University in the Eyes of Its Pupils," in *Eyes of the University: Right to Philosophy 2*, trans. Jan Plug et al. (Stanford, Calif.: Stanford University Press, 2004), 130–31.

15. Derrida, "The Principle of Reason," 139.

16. Jacques Derrida, "Others Are Secret Because They Are Other," in *Paper Machine*, trans. Rachel Bowlby (Stanford, Calif.: Stanford University Press, 2005), 156. See in this connection Derrida's fascinating discussion of Aristotle in "The Principle of Reason": "Opening the eyes to know, closing them—or at least listening—in order to know how to learn and to learn how to know: here we have a first sketch of the rational animal. . . . I shall run the risk of extending my figuration a little farther, in Aristotle's company. In his *De Anima* (421b) he distinguishes between man and those animals that have hard, dry eyes, the animals lacking eyelids, that sort of sheath or tegumental membrane that serves to protect the eye and permits it, at regular intervals, to close itself off in the darkness of inward thought or sleep. What is terrifying about an animal with hard eyes and a dry glance is that it always sees. Man can lower the sheath, adjust the diaphragm, narrow his sight, the better to hear, remember, and learn" (132). Over and against this, he reminds us, it is thus "not a matter of distinguishing here between sight and nonsight, but rather between two ways of thinking sight and light, as well as between two conceptions of listening and voice. But it is true that a caricature of representational man . . . would readily endow him with hard eyes permanently open to a nature that he is to dominate, to rape if necessary, by fixing it in front of himself, or by swooping down on it like a bird of prey. The principle of reason installs its empire only to the extent that the abyssal question of the being that is hiding within it remains hidden" (139).

17. Grandin, *My Life in Pictures*, 144.

18. For example, its echo, if only between the lines, of the ancient religious rites of animal sacrifice (which one might well gloss in light not only of Derrida's "Eating Well" but also of Bataille's *The Theory of Religion*); the rhetorical decision to designate the slaughtered animal with the generic pronoun "he"; the obvious ethical issues that present themselves around the unnecessary killing of animals, however comfortably or compassionately carried out, for human consumption, the mechanization of that process as part of the larger regime of factory farming and agribusiness, and so on—something we would surely want to explore in another context.

19. For example, Rosemarie Garland-Thomson, a leading disability scholar, notes that in the artistic careers of Claude Monet and Chuck Close, disability was not an impediment but rather "enabled what we think of as artistic evolution" toward their most important work; "they were great artists not in spite of disability but because of disability." "Disability and Representation," *PMLA* 120, no. 2 (March 2005): 524.

20. Luc Ferry, *The New Ecological Order,* trans. Carol Volk (Chicago: University of Chicago Press, 1995), 27. Regarding the politics of recognition, see, for example, Nancy Fraser and Axel Honneth, *Redistribution or Recognition? A Political-Philosophical Exchange* (London: Verso, 2003).

21. Richard Rorty, "Postmodernist Bourgeois Liberalism," *Journal of Philosophy* 80 (October 1983): 585.

22. "Violence against Animals," in *For What Tomorrow: A Dialogue,* by Jacques Derrida and Elisabeth Roudinesco, trans. Jeff Fort (Stanford, Calif.: Stanford University Press, 2004), 63, 74–75.

23. Paola Cavalieri, *The Animal Question: Why Nonhuman Animals Deserve Human Rights,* trans. Catherine Woollard (New York: Oxford University Press, 2001), 29. It goes without saying that Derrida would object to the formulation of the problem that frames Cavalieri's book, and in fact, Cavalieri's work is the subject of discussion (more by Roudinesco than by Derrida) in the dialogue mentioned in note 22.

24. Cora Kaplan, "Afterword: Liberalism, Feminism, and Defect," in *"Defects": Engendering the Modern Body,* ed. Helen Deutsch and Felicity Nussbaum (Ann Arbor: University of Michigan Press, 2000), 303, 304.

25. Michael Davidson and Tobin Siebers, "Introduction," *PMLA* 120, no. 2 (March 2005): 498–99.

26. Simi Linton, "What Is Disability Studies?" *PMLA* 120, no. 2 (March 2005): 520.

27. Lennard Davis, "Disability: The Next Wave or Twilight of the Gods?" *PMLA* 120, no. 2 (March 2005): 529.

28. Derrida, "Violence against Animals," 66.

29. Jacques Derrida, "The Animal That Therefore I Am (More to Follow)," trans. David Wills, *Critical Inquiry* 28, no. 2 (Winter 2002): 395–96.

30. Garland-Thomson, "Disability and Representation," 524.

31. Derrida, "The Animal That Therefore I Am," 402, 416.

32. Garland-Thomson, "Disability and Representation," 524.

33. On the complex, temporally dynamic relations of communication, interdependency, and trust involved in human/canid training relationships, see especially Donna J. Haraway, *When Species Meet* (Minneapolis: University of Minnesota Press, 2008), in particular chapter 8, "Training in the Contact Zone: Power, Play, and Invention in the Sport of Agility."

34. Mairian Corker and Tom Shakespeare, "Mapping the Terrain," in *Dis-ability/Postmodernity: Embodying Disability Theory*, ed. Mairian Corker and Tom Shakespeare (London: Continuum, 2002), 14.

35. Zygmunt Bauman, *Postmodern Ethics*, cited in Wolfe, *Animal Rites*, 195–96. I discuss these issues in much more detail in the concluding chapter of that book, where I also point out that a fundamental problem with Bauman's position is that, in the end (and like Levinas), it limits *who can be* the subject of such a heteronomic ethical relation to a fairly familiar (and Kantian) figure of the human-as-rational-agent alone. This begs the question of the very analogy insisted on by animal rights philosophers such as Tom Regan: between so-called marginal cases of severely disabled humans (toward whom ethical consideration is extended) and cognitively advanced forms of nonhuman life (such as great apes) who enjoy no such ethical consideration though they possess demonstrably equal or superior mental capacities that are thought to warrant ethical recognition.

6. From Dead Meat to Glow-in-the-Dark Bunnies

1. Jacques Derrida, "The Animal That Therefore I Am (More to Follow)," trans. David Wills, *Critical Inquiry* 28, no. 2 (2002): 369–418. For the most thorough overview we have of animals in contemporary art, see Steve Baker, *The Postmodern Animal* (London: Reaktion, 2000).

2. Slavoj Žižek, *The Metastases of Enjoyment: Six Essays on Woman and Causality* (London: Verso, 1994), 202.

3. Sue Coe, *Dead Meat*, with an introduction by Alexander Cockburn, foreword by Tom Regan (New York: Four Walls Eight Windows, 1995), v.

4. Jacques Derrida, "'Eating Well,' or The Calculation of the Subject," in *Who Comes After the Subject?* ed. Eduardo Cadava, Peter Connor, and Jean-Luc Nancy (New York: Routledge, 1991), 112–13. I discuss the difference between Derrida and Levinas on this point in my essay "In the Shadow of Wittgenstein's Lion: Language, Ethics, and the Question of the Animal," in *Zoontologies: The Question of the Animal*, ed. Cary Wolfe (Minneapolis: University of Minnesota Press, 2003), 1–57, esp. 17–18, 23–28.

5. Derrida, "The Animal That Therefore I Am," 380.

6. Gilles Deleuze and Félix Guattari, *A Thousand Plateaus: Capitalism and Schizophrenia*, trans. Brian Massumi (Minneapolis: University of Minnesota Press, 1987), 167–91. See also my *Animal Rites*, 227–28n1; and Alphonso Lingis, "Animal Body, Inhuman Face," in *Zoontologies*, 165–82.

7. Michael Fried, *Realism, Writing, Disfiguration: On Thomas Eakins and Stephen Crane* (Chicago: University of Chicago Press, 1987).

8. Ibid., 114.

9. Derrida, "Eating Well," 113. For a by-now-classic analysis of this process of production and renaming, which is also concerned with its phallocentrism, see Carol J. Adams, *The Sexual Politics of Meat* (New York: Continuum, 1990).

10. Fried, *Realism*, 163n1, 185n28.

11. Ibid., 59. I use the term "melodrama" in the sense that has some centrality to Fried's body of criticism and its fundamental contrast of "theatricality" (or "literalism") and "opticality" (or "absorption"), about which I will say more later.

12. See Fried's discussion in "An Introduction to My Art Criticism," in *Art and Objecthood: Essays and Reviews* (Chicago: University of Chicago Press, 1998), 40.

13. Fried, *Realism*, 59.

14. Jacques Derrida, "Afterword," in *Limited Inc*, ed. Gerald Graff (Chicago: Northwestern University Press), 116.

15. W. J. T. Mitchell, *What Do Pictures Want? The Lives and Loves of Images* (Chicago: University of Chicago Press, 2005), 25.

16. Eduardo Kac, *Telepresence and Bio Art: Networking Humans, Rabbits, and Robots,* with a foreword by James Elkins (Ann Arbor: University of Michigan Press, 2005), 66.

17. Ibid., 291–92.

18. Arlindo Machado, "Towards a Transgenic Art," in *The Eighth Day: The Transgenic Art of Eduardo Kac,* ed. Sheilah Britton and Dan Collins (Tempe: Institute for Studies in the Arts, Arizona State University, 2003), 94–95.

19. Kac, *Telepresence and Bio Art*, 237, 243.

20. Steve Baker, "Philosophy in the Wild?" in *The Eighth Day*, 29.

21. Derrida, cited in Baker, "Philosophy in the Wild?" 34–35.

22. Kac, *Telepresence and Bio Art*, 236.

23. Marek Wieczorek, "Playing with Life: Art and Human Genomics," *Art Journal* 59, no. 3 (Fall 2000): 59.

24. Ibid., 60. A misrecognition of which by artist Thomas Grunfeld has led several critics—rightly, to my mind—to find his well-known taxidermy "hybrids" of body parts from different animals to be a radically unsatisfactory way of addressing this question. See Wieczorek, "Playing with Life," 60; or Edward Lucie-Smith's criticism in "Eduardo Kac and Transgenic Art," in *The Eighth Day*, 20–26, esp. 23.

25. Wieczorek, "Playing with Life," 59–60.

26. Niklas Luhmann, "The Cognitive Program of Constructivism and a Reality That Remains Unknown," in *Selforganization: Portrait of a Scientific Revolution,* ed. Wolfgang Krohn et al. (Dordrecht: Kluwer, 1990), 72.

27. Niklas Luhmann, "The Paradoxy of Observing Systems," *Cultural Critique* 31 (Fall 1995): 44, 46.

28. Kac, *Telepresence and Bio Art*, 202–3.

29. Dan Collins, "Tracking Chimeras," in *The Eighth Day*, 99. For Kac's resistance, see the section "Alternatives to Alterity" in his essay "GFP Bunny," in *Telepresence and Bio Art*, 273–75.

30. W. J. T. Mitchell, "The Work of Art in the Age of Biocybernetic Reproduction," in *What Do Pictures Want?* 328.

31. This is directly related not only to the general point that Kac's work is to be viewed against the background that immediately precedes it (namely, conceptual art), as Mitchell notes (*What Do Pictures Want*, 328), but also to Luhmann's insistence that the meaning of any work of art cannot be referenced, much less reduced, to its phenomenological or perceptual substrate.

32. Peter Brunette and David Wills, "The Spatial Arts: An Interview with Jacques Derrida," trans. Lauri Volpe, in *Deconstruction and the Visual Arts*, ed. Peter Brunette and David Wills (Cambridge: Cambridge University Press, 1994), 24.

33. Fried, *Art and Objecthood*, 42.

34. Coe, *Dead Meat*, 72.

7. When You Can't Believe Your Eyes (or Voice)

1. Brian D. Johnson, "Singin' in the Brain: Björk Hits an Ethereal Note as a Day-Dreaming Martyr," *Maclean's*, October 16, 2000, 74.

2. Peter Travers, *Rolling Stone*, October 12, 2000, 99; Johnson, "Singin' in the Brain," 74.

3. Stuart Klawans, "A One and a Two," *Nation*, October 5, 2000, 34; Jonathan Romney, *New Statesman*, September 18, 2000, 44.

4. David Ansen, "Light and Dark," *Newsweek*, September 25, 2000, 66.

5. Stanley Cavell, *In Quest of the Ordinary* (Chicago: University of Chicago Press, 1988), 30.

6. Ibid., 31–32.

7. Stanley Cavell, *A Pitch of Philosophy: Autobiographical Exercises* (Cambridge, Mass.: Harvard University Press, 1994), xv.

8. Ibid., 132.

9. Stanley Cavell, "The Thoughts of Movies," in *Themes Out of School: Effects and Causes* (San Francisco: North Point Press, 1984), 13.

10. Cavell, *A Pitch of Philosophy*, 136, 137.

11. Cavell, *Themes Out of School*, 174.

12. Stanley Cavell, *The World Viewed: Reflections on the Ontology of Film*, enlarged ed. (Cambridge, Mass.: Harvard University Press, 1979), 22.

13. Cavell, *The World Viewed*, 23.

14. Ibid., 18

15. Kaja Silverman, *The Acoustic Mirror: The Female Voice in Psychoanalysis and Cinema* (Bloomington: Indiana University Press, 1988), 42.

16. Douglas Kahn, *Noise, Water, Meat: A History of Sound in the Arts* (Cambridge, Mass.: MIT Press, 1999). Kahn's chapter, "Drawing the Line: Music, Noise, and Phonography" is particularly instructive in this connection.

17. Cavell, *A Pitch of Philosophy*, 137.

18. Slavoj Žižek, *Looking Awry: An Introduction to Jacques Lacan through Popular Culture* (Cambridge, Mass.: MIT Press, 1991), 163. Cavell himself makes the connection, in his way, in his analysis of Emerson's rewriting of Descartes's proof of the self in *In Quest of the Ordinary* (Chicago: University of Chicago Press, 1988), 109. Emerson, of course, is Cavell's preeminent philosopher of the democratic promise. See also Cavell's contention, immediately after the passage just cited, that "a Cartesian intuition of the absolute metaphysical difference between mind and body . . . appears to describe conditions of the possibility of opera"—a contention that, unfortunately, Cavell leaves telegraphic at best (*A Pitch of Philosophy*, 138).

19. Silverman, *The Acoustic Mirror*, 16.

20. Cavell, *A Pitch of Philosophy*, 132.

21. Ibid., 151. Though I cannot pursue the matter here, it should be pointed out that this is taken up rather explicitly by Cavell on pp. 145–51, where he discusses Clément's debt to (and waning interest in) Lacan and—even more importantly—attempts to use the Freudian distinction between "primitive" orality and "sophisticated" vocality.

22. Cited in Silverman, *The Acoustic Mirror*, 50.

23. Ibid., 67. As I suggest near the end of this study, Judith Butler's theorization of "the lesbian phallus" in *Bodies That Matter* would be very much to the point here, in light of which Björk's tongue performatively signifies the "phallic" rejection of the Symbolic, of marriage and the need of a husband, et cetera—all that is thematized by Selma's assertion that "I've seen all I need to see."

24. Slavoj Žižek, *The Plague of Fantasies* (London: Verso, 1997), 135–36.

25. Ibid., 142–43.

26. Lacan is quoted in Stephen Melville, "In the Light of the Other," *Whitewalls* 23 (Fall 1989): 18–20.

27. Žižek, *The Plague of Fantasies*, 141.

28. Laura R. Oswald, "Cinema-Graphia: Eisenstein, Derrida, and the Sign of Cinema," in *Deconstruction and the Visual Arts: Art, Media, Architecture*, ed. Peter Brunette and David Wills (Cambridge: Cambridge University Press, 1994), 261.

29. Peter Brunette and David Wills, "The Spatial Arts: An Interview with Jacques Derrida," in *Deconstruction and the Visual Arts*, 24. All of which might be said to find its theme song in the film's penultimate musical scene, "107 Steps," where the abyssal endlessness of space, here figured as the unnavigable walk to the gallows (a journey of 107 steps), can be fathomed by Selma only by *counting* her footsteps, an organization and regularization of space that is immediately countered by what can only be called an aria to sheer seriality, as the only lyrics contained in the song are randomly selected numbers, her voice rising to the crescendo of "seventy-*nine!*, eighty-two, eighty-*six!*"

30. Oswald, "Cinema-Graphia," 261.

31. *A Derrida Reader: Between the Blinds*, ed. Peggy Kamuf (New York: Columbia University Press, 1991), 265.

32. Slavoj Žižek, *Enjoy Your Symptom! Jacques Lacan in Hollywood and Out* (New York: Routledge, 1992), 154. Žižek's most detailed and "scandalous" explanation of this thesis takes place in the chapter "Otto Weininger, or Woman Doesn't Exist," in *The Metastases of Enjoyment* (London: Verso, 1994), 137–64.

33. And "gift" here should be taken precisely in the radically ethical sense invoked by Derrida, as that which, like the act as feminine and the feminine as the truth of the phallus, is "unaccountable," which undermines any closed symbolic economy. See Žižek's discussion of this moment in Derrida in *The Metastases of Enjoyment*, 194–95.

34. David Wills, *Prosthesis* (Stanford, Calif.: Stanford University Press, 1995), 43, 44.

35. Žižek, *The Metastases of Enjoyment*, 115.

36. Ibid., 156.

37. Žižek, *Enjoy Your Symptom*, 1.

38. Ibid., 2. See also in this connection Žižek's discussion of "A Voice That Skins the Body" in David Lynch's films (*The Metastases of Enjoyment*, 116).

39. Cavell, *A Pitch of Philosophy*, 79.

40. Žižek, *The Metastases of Enjoyment*, 195–96.

41. One might well turn aside here to explore the more strictly theoretical question of whether this relationship is essentially dialectical (as in Žižek) or not. Suffice it to say that the very idea of "invagination" would constitute a resounding "no," as would Deleuze's related concept of the fold.

42. Here an interesting point of contact between Žižek and Derrida with regard to the prosthetic nature of the "ordinary" emerges in their shared antipathy toward John Searle. Derrida's polemic against Searle in *Limited Inc* is well-known, of course, but of similar interest are Žižek's remarks in *The Plague of Fantasies* on Searle's polemics against artificial intelligence, in which his famous Chinese Room experiment "proves" that machines cannot

think, "so, since there is the ontological-philosophical guarantee that the machine does not pose a threat to human uniqueness, I can calmly accept the machine and play with it," a form of "disavowal" that allows the threatening technical prosthesis to be "'gentrified' and integrated into the user's everyday attitude" (137).

43. A point that has been pursued with some density in contemporary theory, whether in Deleuze's work on the fold and double articulation, in Luhmann's adaptation of the theory of autopoiesis to questions of complexity and meaning, and so on. See, for a fuller account, my *Critical Environments: Postmodern Theory and the Pragmatics of the "Outside"* (Minneapolis: University of Minnesota Press, 1998), esp. 117–28.

44. See, for example, *Tarrying with the Negative: Kant, Hegel, and the Critique of Ideology* (Durham, N.C.: Duke University Press, 1993). There Žižek argues that what makes Lacan so important is that he *resists* "the 'anti-essentialist' refusal of universal Foundation, the dissolving of 'truth' into an effect of plural language-games," and so on (4). See also pp. 202, 216.

45. Žižek, *Tarrying with the Negative*, 4, 202.

46. Žižek, *The Metastases of Enjoyment*, 196, 195.

47. Jacques Derrida, *Positions*, trans. and annotated by Alan Bass (Chicago: University of Chicago Press, 1981), 65.

48. Judith Butler, *Bodies That Matter: On the Discursive Limits of "Sex"* (New York: Routledge, 1993), 195–96.

49. For Žižek's response to this line of argument and to Butler, see *The Metastases of Enjoyment*, 201–3.

8. Lose the Building

1. The finalists were "Tree City" by Rem Koolhaas, Office for Metropolitan Architecture (Rotterdam), Bruce Mau Design (Toronto), Oleson Worland Architect (Toronto), and Inside/Outside (Amsterdam) (winner); "Emergent Landscapes" by Brown and Storey Architects (Toronto); "Emergent Ecologies" by James Corner/Field Operations (Philadelphia) and Stan Allen, Stan Allen Architect (New York); "A New Synthetic Landscape" by Foreign Office Architects (Tokyo), Kuwabara Payne McKenna Blumberg Architects (Toronto), and Tom Leader and James Haig Streeter of PWP Landscape Architects (Berkeley); "The Digital and the Coyote" by Bernard Tschumi Architects (New York), Dereck Revington Studio (Toronto), and Sterling Finlayson Architects (Toronto).

2. Specifically, in the special *Critical Ecologies* issue of *EBR: Electronic Book Review* that I coedited with Joe Tabbi, to which Luke contributed, http://www.electronicbookreview.com/thread/criticalecologies.

3. All quotations from the architectural teams are taken from the original submissions for the Downsview Park competition, Toronto, 1999. For a useful overview of the competition and each finalist project, see Marco Polo, "Environment as Process," *Canadian Architect,* October 2000, 14–19.

4. Jacques Derrida, "*Geschlecht II:* Heidegger's Hand," in *Between the Blinds: A Derrida Reader,* ed. and Peggy Kamuf (New York: Columbia University Press, 1991), 172.

5. Jacques Derrida, *Of Spirit: Heidegger and the Question,* trans. Geoffrey Bennington and Rachel Bowlby (Chicago: University of Chicago Press, 1989), 11.

6. Derrida, "*Geschlecht II,*" 172.

7. Stanley Cavell, *Conditions Handsome and Unhandsome: The Constitution of Emersonian Perfectionism* (Chicago: University of Chicago Press, 1991), 38, 41.

8. Derrida, "*Geschlecht II,*" 178–79. In opposition to all of which Cavell finds Heidegger's emphasis on thought as "reception," as a kind of welcoming, elaborated by Heidegger in passages that insist on "the derivation of the word thinking from a root for thanking and interprets this particularly as giving thanks for the gift of thinking" (*Conditions Handsome,* 38–39). On the point of technology and the typewriter, as Derrida notes, "The protest against the typewriter also belongs—this is a matter of course—to an interpretation of technology [*technique*], to an interpretation of politics starting from technology," but also and more importantly to a "devaluation of writing in general" as "the increasing destruction of the word or of speech" in which "the typewriter is only a modern aggravation of the evil" ("*Geschlecht II,*" 180).

9. John Casti, *Complexification: Explaining a Paradoxical World through the Science of Surprise* (New York: Harper Collins, 1994), 237, 232.

10. Niklas Luhmann, *Social Systems,* trans. John Bednarz (Stanford, Calif.: Stanford University Press, 1999), 17.

11. Ibid., 46.

12. Luhmann, *Art as a Social System,* 114.

13. As Derrida notes, with the mime, "the plays of facial expressions and the gestural tracings are not present in themselves since they always refer, perpetually allude or represent. But they don't represent anything that has ever been or can ever become present" ("The Double Session," in *A Derrida Reader,* 184). In this sense, "The act always plays out a difference without reference, or rather without a referent. . . . The mime mimes reference. He is not an imitator; he mimes imitation" (188).

14. Luhmann, *Art as a Social System,* 298–99.

15. For both references, see the book that documents the project from beginning to end, *Blur: The Making of Nothing* (New York: Abrams, 2002). The

comments from the Swiss newspaper article on *Die Wunder-Wolke* (the "wonder cloud"), appear on p. 372; Diller's comments regarding spectacle and expositions—in her seminar at Princeton, where she teaches, and in presentations by the team in Switzerland—may be found on pp. 92, 162. Further references to this immensely useful and aesthetically breathtaking book will be given in the text.

16. Quoted in an essay from the catalog produced for the retrospective of Diller + Scofidio's work at the Whitney Museum of American Art from March 1 to May 25, 2003, *Scanning: The Aberrant Architectures of Diller + Scofidio* (New York: Abrams, 2003): Edward Dimendberg, "Blurring Genres," 79.

17. Ned Cramer, "All Natural," *Architecture* 91, no. 7 (July 2002): 53.

18. Jean-François Lyotard, *The Postmodern Condition: A Report on Knowledge,* trans. Geoff Bennington and Brian Massumi (Minneapolis: University of Minnesota Press, 77–78.

19. In Jean-François Lyotard, *The Differend: Phrases in Dispute,* trans. George Van Den Abbeele (Minneapolis: University of Minnesota Press, 1988).

20. See specifically p. 77 of *The Postmodern Condition.*

21. See my discussion of Lyotard's rendering of Kant and ethics in *Animal Rites: American Culture, the Discourse of Species, and Posthumanist Theory* (Chicago: University of Chicago Press, 2002), 54–62.

22. *Scanning: The Aberrant Architectures of Diller + Scofidio,* 79.

23. Luhmann, *Art as a Social System,* 89.

24. As is abundantly clear in the Whitney catalog, *Scanning* (among other places), the distinction between art and architecture is of comparatively little moment for Diller + Scofidio. Indeed, their body of work is calculated toward their intrication. The same is true for Luhmann, who treats architecture as a subspecies of art, even while addressing here and there its differences from, say, painting.

25. It should be noted that the term "postmodern" is one for which Luhmann has no use. For him, the postmodern is merely an intensification of features already fully present in modernity. On this point, see, for example, Niklas Luhmann, "Why Does Society Describe Itself as Postmodern?" in *Observing Complexity: Systems Theory and Postmodernity,* ed. William Rasch and Cary Wolfe (Minneapolis: University of Minnesota Press, 2000), 35–49.

26. Luhmann, *Social Systems,* 25.

27. Luhmann, *Art as a Social System,* 158.

28. See my *Critical Environments: Postmodern Theory and the Pragmatics of the "Outside"* (Minneapolis: University of Minnesota Press, 1998), 67–68.

29. Niklas Luhmann, "The Cognitive Program of Constructivism and a Reality That Remains Unknown," in *Selforganization: Portrait of a Scientific*

Revolution, ed. Wolfgang Krohn et al. (Dordrecht: Kluwer Academic Publishers, 1990), 76.

30. Luhmann, *Art as a Social System,* 92.

31. "Objects are therefore nothing but the *eigenbehaviors* of observing systems that result from using and reusing their previous distinctions." Luhmann, "Deconstruction as Second-Order Observing," *New Literary History* 24 (1993): 768.

32. Luhmann, *Art as a Social System,* 46.

33. Ashley Schafer, "Designing Inefficiencies," in *Scanning: The Aberrant Architectures of Diller + Scofidio,* 93.

34. Luhmann, *Art as a Social System,* 92.

35. In this connection, I would note, with Roselee Goldberg, how influential conceptual art was for Diller + Scofidio's early career. See her essay "Dancing About Architecture" in *Scanning: The Aberrant Architectures of Diller + Scofidio,* 46.

36. Luhmann, *Art as a Social System,* 34.

37. See Hansen's essay "Wearable Space," *Configurations* 10 (2002): 321–70. For Diller's remarks, see *Blur,* 92–94.

38. Niklas Luhmann, "How Can the Mind Participate in Communication?" in *Materialities of Communication,* ed. Hans Ulrich Gumbrecht and K. Ludwig Pfeiffer (Stanford, Calif.: Stanford University Press, 1994), 371.

39. Ibid., 381.

40. Dietrich Schwanitz, "Systems Theory and the Difference between Communication and Consciousness: An Introduction to a Problem and Its Context," *MLN* 111, no. 3 (1996): 494.

41. Kawara's *Date Paintings* consist of a date (the date the painting was executed) in simple white letters painted on a monochromatic field in one of eight predetermined shapes of horizontal orientation. Each painting is stored in its own cardboard box alongside a news item taken on the date of the painting from the newspaper in the city in which the painting was executed. He has created date paintings in more than 112 cities and says he will continue the project until his death. For a useful brief overview of the project and related works, see Lynne Cooke's essay "On Kawara" at the Dia Beacon Web site, http://www.diabeacon.org/exhibs_b/kawara/essay.html.

42. Luhmann, *Art as a Social System,* 141.

43. Luhmann, "Deconstruction as Second-Order Observing," 775.

44. Niklas Luhmann, *The Reality of the Mass Media,* trans. Kathleen Cross (Stanford, Calif.: Stanford University Press, 2000), 4.

45. Luhmann, "Deconstruction as Second-Order Observing," 776.

46. Luhmann, *Social Systems,* 161.

47. Luhmann, *Reality of the Mass Media,* 15–16.

48. Luhmann, *Art as a Social System,* 64–65.

9. Emerson's Romanticism, Cavell's Skepticism, Luhmann's Modernity

1. *Emerson's Prose and Poetry,* selected and edited by Joel Porte and Saundra Morris (New York: Norton, 2001), 125.

2. Stanley Cavell, "Finding as Founding: Taking Steps in Emerson's 'Experience,'" in *Emerson's Transcendental Etudes,* ed. David Justin Hodge (Stanford, Calif.: Stanford University Press, 2003), 111.

3. Ibid., 79.

4. Cavell, "Emerson, Coleridge, Kant," in *Emerson's Transcendental Etudes,* 63.

5. Ibid., 62.

6. Emerson, *Prose and Poetry,* 201.

7. Cavell, "Finding as Founding," 115.

8. Emerson, "Experience," in *Prose and Poetry,* 200.

9. Cavell, "Finding as Founding," in *Emerson's Transcendental Etudes,* 117.

10. Cavell, "Aversive Thinking: Emersonian Representations in Heidegger and Nietzsche," in *Emerson's Transcendental Etudes,* 147.

11. See my discussion of this cluster of texts in *Animal Rites: American Culture, the Discourse of Species, and Posthumanist Theory* (Chicago: University of Chicago Press, 2003), 63–64.

12. Paul Jay, *Contingency Blues: The Search for Foundations in American Criticism* (Madison: University of Wisconsin Press, 1997), 21.

13. Jay Grossman, *Reconstituting the American Renaissance: Emerson, Whitman, and the Politics of Representation* (Durham, N.C.: Duke University Press, 2003). One should no doubt applaud Grossman's "opposition to the standard model derived from Matthiessen in which the abundance of the Renaissance springs, Athena-like, out of the head of an Emerson-Zeus," which he attempts to move beyond by "looking backward to the nation's founding for a renewed understanding of the intersections between the political and the literary" (hence the pun, "representation," that anchors the volume) (6–7). The problem is that in "specifying the discursive contexts out of which the period known as the Renaissance emerges," Grossman's study does not go far enough in this direction. By simply attacking the periodizing break between the eighteenth and nineteenth centuries that has been taken for granted in American studies, and insisting instead that "debates over representation that catalyzed the Revolution . . . continued to swirl at the time of Constitution" (4), forming the key discursive context in which the writing of Emerson and Whitman "resonate anew with echoes that have their origins in facets of the

Constitutional settlement" (15), Grossman simply extends, rather than disposes of, exceptionalism. What is crucial here is not the chronological terrain reaching backward to the Revolution but the *ideological and methodological* commitment to liberal humanism and to liberal democracy that accompanies it. If it is true, as Grossman rightly points out, that "representing" and "constituting" inescapably depend on the "originary relations between the political and the literary " (6), and that "finding a beginning within this history opens out a pattern of potentially infinite regress" (7), then the exceptionalist decision that frames Grossman's book can only be justified on pragmatic or ideological grounds (especially in light of his salutary critique of work that takes for granted the unproblematic distinction between the "literary" and the "empirical" [18]). That is to say, it can only be understood in terms of a strategic decision to limit the full implications of these questions within a prior commitment to the context of liberal democracy itself and its core assumptions about what politics and agency are (a fact made even more evident, ironically enough, by reading Grossman's study alongside the book that is key to its framing and formation, Brian Seitz's *The Trace of Political Representation* [Albany: SUNY Press, 1995]). But Emerson, I am suggesting, respected no such limit and thus took those questions—and their implications for politics, agency, and much else—more seriously than Grossman understands. To put it another way, if Emerson is antidemocratic in places, it is in the services of a more fundamental commitment to being anti-*ideological*.

14. Donald E. Pease, "'Experience,' Anti-slavery, and the Crisis of Emersonianism," *Boundary 2* 34, no. 2 (Summer 2007): 75.

15. Chantal Mouffe, *The Return of the Political* (London: Verso, 1993), 3.

16. Quoted in Jay, *Contingency Blues*, 26, 29.

17. Cavell, "Finding as Founding," in *Emerson's Transcendental Etudes*, 111–12.

18. Richard Rorty, *Objectivity, Relativism, and Truth: Philosophical Papers*, vol. 1 (Cambridge: Cambridge University Press, 1991), 4.

19. Richard Rorty, *Philosophy and the Mirror of Nature* (Princeton, N.J.: Princeton University Press, 1979), 368.

20. Rorty, *Objectivity*, 100.

21. Cavell, "Finding as Founding," in *Emerson's Transcendental Etudes*, 113.

22. Cavell, "Emerson, Coleridge, Kant," in *Emerson's Transcendental Etudes*, 72.

23. Cavell, "Being Odd, Getting Even (Descartes, Emerson, Poe)," in *Emerson's Transcendental Etudes*, 84, 87. Cavell reminds us that most readers will "remember or assume the cogito always to be expressed in words that translate as 'I think, *therefore* I am.' But in Descartes's Second Meditation, where I suppose it is most often actually encountered, the insight is expressed: '*I am, I exist,* is necessarily true every time that I pronounce or conceive it in

my mind.' Emerson's emphasis on the *saying* of 'I' is precisely faithful to this expression of Descartes's insight" (85).

24. Cavell, "Introduction: Staying the Course," in *Conditions Handsome and Unhandsome: The Constitution of Emersonian Perfectionism* (Chicago: University of Chicago Press, 1990), 12.

25. Cavell, "Aversive Thinking," in *Emerson's Transcendental Etudes*, 160.

26. Cavell, "Introduction," in *Conditions Handsome and Unhandsome*, 31.

27. Cavell, "Aversive Thinking," in *Emerson's Transcendental Etudes*, 160.

28. Emerson, "Nature," in *Prose and Poetry*, 51; "Experience," in *Prose and Poetry*, 211.

29. Cavell, "Hope against Hope," in *Emerson's Transcendental Etudes*, 181.

30. Cavell, "Emerson's Constitutional Amending," in *Emerson's Transcendental Etudes*, 193.

31. Emerson, "Experience," in *Prose and Poetry*, 213.

32. Emerson, "The Fugitive Slave Law," in *The Portable Emerson*, new ed., ed. Carl Bode and Malcolm Cowley (New York: Penguin, 1981), 551.

33. Maurice Gonnaud, *An Uneasy Solitude: Individual and Society in the Work of Ralph Waldo Emerson*, trans. Lawrence Rosenwald (Princeton, N.J.: Princeton University Press, 1987), 299.

34. Lee Rust Brown, *The Emerson Museum: Practical Romanticism and the Pursuit of the Whole* (Cambridge, Mass.: Harvard University Press, 1997), 73.

35. Emerson, "Circles," in *Prose and Poetry*, 176.

36. Emerson, "Fate," in *Prose and Poetry*, 270, 278.

37. Niklas Luhmann, "Cognition as Construction," trans. Hans-Georg Moeller, appendix B in *Luhmann Explained: From Souls to Systems*, by Hans-Georg Moeller (Chicago: Open Court Press, 2006), 250. As Luhmann summarizes the point, if "God is beyond all distinctions, even beyond the distinction between distinctness and indistinctness" (250), then the problem becomes how can that which is transcendent insofar as it transcends distinctions be observed to be compatible with Christian dogma ("identifiable as a person and as the trinity," and so on) (251). "One had, in God, to save the possibilities of observation and thus on the one hand to be careful not to ascribe to God the impossibility of self-observation, and, on the other hand, to avoid to come close to the devil who was the boldest observer of God. . . . The escape route came fatally close to the assumption that God needed creation and the damnation of the devil in order to be able to observe himself, and it led to writings that Nicolaus believed unprepared minds with their weak eyes had better not read" (251).

38. Niklas Luhmann, *Art as a Social System*, trans. Eva M. Knodt (Stanford, Calif.: Stanford University Press, 2000), 90.

39. Ibid., 92.

40. Harro Muller, "Luhmann's Systems Theory as a Theory of Modernity," *New German Critique* 61 (Winter 1994): 40.

41. Luhmann, *Art as a Social System*, 89.

42. Muller, "Luhmann's Systems Theory," 45.

43. Niklas Luhmann, *Social Systems*, trans. John Bednarz Jr. with Dirk Baecker (Stanford, Calif.: Stanford University Press, 1995), 25.

44. *The Collected Works of Ralph Waldo Emerson*, vol. 3, *Essays: Second Series*, ed. Alfred R. Ferguson and Jean Ferguson Carr (Cambridge, Mass.: Harvard University Press, 1983), 142.

45. Luhmann, "The Paradoxy of Observing Systems," *Cultural Critique* 31 (Fall 1995): 41–42.

46. Luhmann, *Social Systems*, 60.

47. Emerson, *Prose and Poetry*, 84.

48. Luhmann, *Social Systems*, 37.

49. Luhmann, *Art as a Social System*, 158.

50. Luhmann, *Social Systems*, 26.

51. Ibid., 51.

52. Luhmann, "A Redescription of 'Romantic Art,'" *MLN* 111, no. 3 (1996): 508, 511.

53. Emerson, "Nominalist and Realist," in *Collected Works*, 3:139.

54. But see here the discussion in chapter 1 of the difference between "meaning" and "information" in Luhmann's sense.

55. Niklas Luhmann, "The Cognitive Program of Constructivism and a Reality That Remains Unknown," in *Selforganization: Portrait of a Scientific Revolution*, ed. Wolfgang Krohn et al. (Dordrecht: Kluwer Academic Publishers, 1990), 76.

56. Luhmann, *Art as a Social System*, 92.

57. Emerson, *Prose and Poetry*, 174 (italics mine).

58. Luhmann, *Art as a Social System*, 91.

59. Emerson, "Circles," in *Prose and Poetry*, 175.

60. Luhmann, *Art as a Social System*, 91.

61. Luhmann, "A Redescription of 'Romantic Art,'" 517.

62. Emerson, "Experience," in *Prose and Poetry*, 211, 209.

63. Luhmann, *Art as a Social System*, 95.

64. Emerson, *Prose and Poetry*, 66.

65. See Cadava's *Emerson and the Climates of History* (Stanford, Calif.: Stanford University Press, 1997), esp. chap. 1.

66. Muller, "Luhmann's Systems Theory," 47.

67. Luhmann, "A Redescription of 'Romantic Art,'" 516.

68. Specifically, in the conclusion to my *Critical Environments*.

69. Emerson, *Collected Works*, 3:145.

10. The Idea of Observation at Key West

1. Marjorie Levinson, "What Is New Formalism?" *PMLA* 122, no. 2 (March 2007): 561, 559.

2. Niklas Luhmann, "Notes on the Project 'Poetry and Social Theory,'" trans. Kathleen Cross, *Theory, Culture, and Society* 18, no. 1 (2001): 15–27.

3. Wimsatt argues that the fundamental dynamic of rhyme in English poetry is one that yokes acoustic similarity and semantic contrast, and that, canonically, the more extreme the contrast the better, as in the classic rhyme "king/thing." His essay is part of *The Verbal Icon: Studies in the Meaning of Poetry* (Lexington: University Press of Kentucky, 1954).

4. Niklas Luhmann, *Art as a Social System*, trans. Eva M. Knodt (Stanford, Calif.: Stanford University Press, 2000), 26.

5. The literature on this point is at this juncture quite extensive, but see, in connection with Stevens, texts such as Harold Bloom's *Wallace Stevens: The Poems of Our Climate* (Ithaca, N.Y.: Cornell University Press, 1977); and Simon Critchley's *Things Merely Are: Philosophy in the Poetry of Wallace Stevens* (London: Routledge, 2005). A useful short overview is provided by Bart Eeckhout in "Stevens and Philosophy," in *The Cambridge Companion to Wallace Stevens*, ed. John N. Serio (Cambridge: Cambridge University Press, 2007), 103–17. As for Luhmann, his relationship to romanticism is everywhere present in his later work, but *Art as a Social System* is an especially important text in this regard. See, for an important and concise explanation of key points of convergence (and divergence) between the problematics of romanticism and Luhmann's work, his essay "A Redescription of 'Romantic Art,'" *MLN* 111, no. 3 (1996): 506–22.

6. Albert Gelpi, "Stevens and Williams: The Epistemology of Modernism," in *Wallace Stevens: The Poetics of Modernism*, ed. Albert Gelpi (Cambridge: Cambridge University Press, 1990), 5.

7. Niklas Luhmann, "How Can the Mind Participate in Communication?" in *Materialities of Communication*, ed. Hans Ulrich Gumbrecht and K. Ludwig Pfeiffer, trans. William Whobrey (Stanford, Calif.: Stanford University Press, 1994), 372, 374.

8. Luhmann, *Art as a Social System*, 374.

9. Dietrich Schwanitz, "Systems Theory and the Difference between Communication and Consciousness: An Introduction to a Problem and Its Context," *MLN* 111, no. 3 (1996): 494. See also Luhmann, *Art as a Social System*, 8–9.

10. Luhmann, *Art as a Social System*, 14.

11. Niklas Luhmann, *Observations on Modernity*, trans. William Whobrey (Stanford, Calif.: Stanford University Press, 1998), 47.

12. Luhmann, *Art as a Social System*, 91.

13. Luhmann, *Observations on Modernity*, 48.

14. Luhmann, *Art as a Social System*, 92.

15. See Beverly Maeder, "Stevens and Linguistic Structure," in *The Cambridge Companion to Wallace Stevens*, ed. John N. Serio (Cambridge: Cambridge University Press, 2007), 149–63. As Maeder observes of Stevens's conspicuous acoustics, "Word choice in these cases means less the search for the right word or *le mot juste* than the experimental combination of surprising signifiers, whose strangeness of sound, tone, register, and connotation combine to draw attention to, and stimulate pleasure in, the poem's constructedness or artifice" (154).

16. Laura Riding (Jackson), *The Poems of Laura Riding*, new ed. (1938; New York: Persea, 1980), 95. This is not to suggest that this is what Riding (Jackson) *thought* she was doing, as her unusual and iconoclastic notion of the relationship between poetry and "truth" makes quite clear. See, for example, her 1980 introduction in this reprint edition of her 1938 *Poems*.

17. *Collected Poems of Wallace Stevens* (New York: Random House, 1982), 326.

18. On why this is not a Hegelian schema but quite the contrary, see my *Critical Environments: Postmodern Theory and the Pragmatics of the "Outside"* (Minneapolis: University of Minnesota Press, 2003), 68. Briefly: because recognizing "the identity of identity and nonidentity" in any observation's paradoxical self-reference is itself dependent on the *difference* between first- and second-order observation (that is, on different distinctions): hence the "*non*-identity of identity and nonidentity."

19. Niklas Luhmann, "Sthenography," trans. Bernd Widdig, *Stanford Literature Review* 7 (1990): 135.

20. Wallace Stevens, "The Noble Rider and the Sound of Words," in *The Necessary Angel: Essays on Reality and the Imagination* (New York: Random House, 1951), 29. Such is the drift too, I think, of one recent critic's observation that Stevens's function in this regard is not so much philosophical as "pragmatic": "Stevens can speak to the lawyer or legal theorist as a kind of therapist for the habitual and institutional rigidities of binary thought." Thomas C. Grey, *The Wallace Stevens Case: Law and the Practice of Poetry* (Cambridge: Harvard University Press, 1991), 6–7, cited in Eeckhout, "Stevens and Philosophy," 114. Grey's observation is especially appropriate in this context, given the common habit of misreading Luhmann as a rigidly binary thinker, rather than one who precisely deontologizes binaries by making them mo-

mentary, functional distinctions that systems use to reduce overwhelming environmental complexity by virtualizing and temporalizing it. For a more detailed articulation of this claim, see chapter 1.

21. Stevens, *Poems*, 193–94.

22. Luhmann, "Sthenography," 135.

11. The Digital, the Analog, and the Spectral

1. As Simon Reynolds reports, Hassell was originally to have collaborated on the project, and the concept of the "Fourth World" that he coined denotes "the merger of high-tech Western music and archaic ethnic music from all corners of the globe." Simon Reynolds, *Rip It Up and Start Again: Postpunk, 1978–1984* (New York: Penguin, 2005), 165.

2. See, for example, Manovich, "The Myth of the Digital," in *The Language of New Media* (Cambridge, Mass.: MIT Press, 2001), 52–55.

3. See Donna J. Haraway, "A Cyborg Manifesto: Science, Technology, and Socialist-Feminism in the Late Twentieth Century," in *Simians, Cyborgs, and Women: The Reinvention of Nature* (New York: Routledge, 1991), 150, 164.

4. For the original vinyl release, "Qu'ran" appeared as track 6, and the track that replaced it on all but the first CD release, "Very, Very Hungry," does not appear at all. The January 1981 CD release by Sire records contains both tracks; subsequent CD releases replace "Qu'ran" with "Very, Very Hungry." The rerelease follows the latter track list, not that of the original vinyl and CD.

5. Such political speculations might seem at first glance far-fetched, but here I would reference Derrida's discussion of Francis Fukuyama in *Specters of Marx,* where he draws attention to Fukuyama's continual slippage (intentional, of course) between "fact and ideal essence" in his discussion of liberal democracy (64). *"On the one hand,"* Derrida writes, "the gospel of politico-economic liberalism needs the event of the good news that consists in what has putatively *actually* happened" (the "fall of the Wall," the failure of Soviet communism, etc., that Fukuyama regularly invokes). "It cannot do without the recourse to the event; however since, *on the other hand,* actual history and so many other realities that have an empirical appearance contradict this advent of the perfect liberal democracy"—and these include now, conspicuously, not just the "economic war" between the United States, the European Community, and Japan that plays out in events like the GATT treaty, and not just "all the contradictions at work within the trade between the wealthy countries and the rest of the world, the phenomena of pauperization and ferocity of the 'foreign debt'" (63), but also most pointedly the use of preemptive war,

imprisonment, and torture by the United States—"one must at the same time pose this perfection as simply a regulating and trans-historical ideal." This means that in neoliberal discourse such as Fukuyama's, "the event is now the realization, now the heralding of the realization," of liberal democracy. And this is why "a thinking of the event is no doubt what is most lacking from such a discourse" (63). All of which leads directly to Derrida's discussion of the spectral and of the messianic, which I investigate in more detail hereafter.

6. See, for example, *Philosophy in a Time of Terror: Dialogues with Jurgen Habermas and Jacques Derrida*, ed. Giovanna Borradori (Chicago: University of Chicago Press, 2004).

7. Reynolds, *Rip It Up*, 166.

8. Jacques Derrida, *Specters of Marx*, trans. Peggy Kamuf (New York: Routledge, 1994), xix.

9. Ibid., xx.

10. See, for example, Raley's essay "eEMPIRES," *Cultural Critique* 57 (Spring 2004): 111–50. Raley contends that "the Electronic Empire" and "the automatism of the network [are] instead paradigmatic for our period, the speculative stage of finance capital" (120). See also in this connection, but from a more logistical and less economistic perspective, Alexander R. Galloway and Eugene Thacker, *The Exploit: A Theory of Networks* (Minneapolis: University of Minnesota Press, 2007).

11. Nicole Shukin, *Animal Capital: Rendering Life in Biopolitical Times* (Minneapolis: University of Minnesota Press, 2009), chap. 2.

12. Bernard Stiegler, "The Discrete Image," in *Echographies of Television*, by Jacques Derrida and Bernard Stiegler, trans. Jennifer Bajorek (Cambridge: Polity Press, 2002), 148–49.

13. Mary Flanagan, "The Bride Stripped Bare to Her Data: Information Flow + Digibodies," in *Data Made Flesh*, ed. Robert Mitchell and Phillip Thurtle (New York: Routledge, 2004), 169.

14. Sharon Waxman, "Cyberface," *New York Times*, October 15, 2006.

15. Stiegler, "The Discrete Image," 156.

16. *Ghosts*, liner notes. The various permutations and versions of the album covers and Polaroid photographs referred to here, for both the original and the rerelease, may be viewed at the rerelease Web site, http://bushofghosts.wmg.com/home.php.

17. Brian Eno, *14 Video Paintings*, DVD (Hannibal Studios, 2005), liner notes, 2.

18. Ibid., 3–4.

19. Gregory Bateson, *Steps to an Ecology of Mind* (New York: Ballantine Books, 1972), 373.

20. Jacques Derrida, "Speech and Phenomena," trans. David B. Allison, in *A Derrida Reader*, 26–27.

21. Jacques Derrida, "Afterword," trans. Samuel Weber, in *Limited Inc* (Evanston, Ill.: Northwestern University Press, 1988), 119, 116.

22. Derrida, *Specters of Marx*, 169.

23. Ibid., xx.

24. Derrida, *Echographies of Television*, 117.

25. Derrida, *Specters of Marx*, 27–28, 65.

26. Ibid., 169.

27. Rita Raley, "Statistical Material: Globalization and the Digital Art of John Klima," *CR: The New Centennial Review* 3, no. 2 (Summer 2003): 83.

28. David Wills, "Technēology, or the Discourse of Speed," in *The Prosthetic Impulse: From a Posthuman Present to a Biocultural Future*, ed. Marquard Smith and Joanne Morra (Cambridge, Mass.: MIT Press, 2006), 246.

29. Ibid., 241.

30. Brian Massumi, "On the Superiority of the Analog," in *Parables for the Virtual: Movement, Affect, Sensation* (Durham, N.C.: Duke University Press, 2002), 137.

31. "Violence against Animals," in *For What Tomorrow. . . . A Dialogue*, by Jacques Derrida and Elisabeth Roudinesco, trans. Jeff Fort (Stanford, Calif.: Stanford University Press, 2004), 63 (italics mine).

32. Massumi, *Superiority*, 142, 133.

33. Stiegler, "The Discrete Image," 160 (italics in original).

34. Reynolds, *Rip It Up*, 165.

35. Barthes, quoted in Flanagan, "Bride Stripped Bare," 165 (italics mine).

36. *Ghosts*, liner notes, 15.

37. Ibid., 11–12.

38. Richard Beardsworth, *Derrida and the Political* (London: Routledge, 1996), 147.

39. Derrida, *Echographies of Television*, 122.

40. Derrida, *Specters of Marx*, 65.

Publication History

A version of chapter 1 was published as "Meaning as Event-Machine, or Systems Theory and the 'Reconstruction of Deconstruction,'" in *Emergence and Embodiment: New Essays in Second-Order Systems Theory,* ed. Bruce Clarke and Mark Hansen (Durham, N.C.: Duke University Press, 2009).

A version of chapter 2 was published as "Cognitive Science, Deconstruction, and the (Post)Humanist (Non)Humans," in "DerridAnimals," ed. Neil Badmington, special issue, *Oxford Literary Review* 29 (2007): 103–25; reprinted as "Thinking Other-Wise: Cognitive Science, Deconstruction, and the (Non) Speaking (Non)Human Animal Subject," in *Animal Subjects: An Ethical Reader,* ed. Jodey Castricano (Toronto: Wilfrid Laurier University Press, 2008), 125–44. Reprinted with permission from Edinburgh University Press.

Portions of chapter 3 appeared as "Exposures," in *Philosophy and Animal Life,* ed. Cora Diamond, Stanley Cavell, John McDowell, Ian Hacking, and Cary Wolfe (New York: Columbia University Press, 2008), 1–41; as "Bioethics and the Posthumanist Imperative," in *Signs of Life: Bio Art and Beyond,* ed. Eduardo Kac (Cambridge, Mass.: MIT Press, 2007), 95–114; and as "Flesh and Finitude: Thinking Animals in (Post)Humanist Philosophy," in "The Political Animal," ed. Chris Danta and Dimitris Vardoulakas, special issue, *Substance* 117, no. 33 (2008): 8–36; copyright 2008 by the Board of Regents of the University of Wisconsin System; reprinted courtesy of the University of Wisconsin Press.

A shorter version of chapter 4 appeared as "The Changing Profession: 'Animal Studies,' Disciplinarity, and the Posthumanities," *PMLA* 124, no. 2 (March 2009): 564–75.

A version of chapter 5 was published as "Animal Studies and Disability Studies; or, Learning from Temple Grandin," in "Earthographies: Ecocriticism and Culture," ed. Wendy Wheeler and Hugh Dunkerley, special issue, *New Formations* 64 (2008): 110–23.

Chapter 6 was published as "From *Dead Meat* to Glow in the Dark Bunnies: Seeing 'The Animal Question' in Contemporary Art," in "Animal Beings," ed. Tom Tyler, special issue, *Parallax* 38 (January–March 2006): 95–109; reprinted in *Ecosee: Image, Rhetoric, Nature,* ed. Sid Dobrin and Sean Morey, 129–51 (Albany: SUNY Press, 2009).

A version of chapter 7 appeared in *Electronic Book Review,* http://www .electronicbookreview.com; original post on September 1, 2001. Chapter 7 was also published as "When You Can't Believe Your Eyes: The Prosthetics of Subjectivity and the Ethical Force of the Feminine in *Dancer in the Dark,*" in "Posthuman Conditions," ed. Neil Badmington, special double issue, *Subject Matters* 4, no. 1 (Fall 2007): 113–44.

Portions of chapter 8 were published in "Shifting Ground: The Downsview Park Competition," in *Beyond Form: Architecture and Art in the Space of Media,* ed. Peter Dorsey, Christine Calderon, and Omar Calderon (New York: Lusitania Press, 2004), 82–92; and "Lose the Building: Systems Theory, Architecture, and Diller + Scofidio's *Blur,*" *Postmodern Culture* 16, no. 3 (May 2006), http:// muse.jhu.edu/journals/postmodern_culture/toc/pmc16.3.html.

Chapter 10 was previously published as "The Idea of Observation at Key West: Systems Theory, Poetry, and Form beyond Formalism," *New Literary History* 39, no. 2 (Spring 2008): 259–76.

Chapter 11 was published as "The Digital, the Analogue, and the Spectral: Echographies from *My Life in the Bush of Ghosts,*" *Angelaki: Journal of the Theoretical Humanities* 13, no. 1 (2008): 85–94.

Index

Cary Wolfe holds the Bruce and Elizabeth Dunlevie Chair in English at Rice University. His previous books include *Critical Environments: Postmodern Theory and the Pragmatics of the "Outside," Observing Complexity: Systems Theory and Postmodernity,* and *Zoontologies: The Question of the Animal,* all published by the University of Minnesota Press.